The Next Arms Race

Attention Authors

The Next Arms Race

Henry D Sokolski
Editor

Manas Publications
(We Convert Fighters into Writers)
New Delhi-110002 (INDIA)

MANAS PUBLICATIONS
(We Convert Fighters into Writers)
(Publishers, Library Suppliers, Importers & Exporters)
4402/5-A, Ansari Road (Opp. HDFC Bank)
Darya Ganj, New Delhi-110 002 (India)
Off. ☎ 23260783, 23265523, Res. ☎ 23842660
Fax: 011-23272766
E-mail: manaspublications@gmail.com
manaspub6@gmail.com
Website: www.manaspublications.in

ISBN 978-81-7049-455-3
₹ 995/-

Maps included in the book are not to scale

Designed at
Manas Publications

Printed in India at
RK Offsets, Delhi
and published by Mrs Suman Lata for
Manas Publications, 4402/5-A,
Ansari Road, (Opp HDFC Bank),
Darya Ganj, New Delhi-110 002 (INDIA)

Contents

Foreword

This volume is the 15th in a series of edited volumes of contracted research the Non-proliferation Policy Education Center (NPEC) has published in cooperation with the Strategic Studies Institute (SSI) of the US Army War College. The volume showcases studies that were done over the past 3 years on what the next set of strategic nuclear competitions might look like. Funding for this project came from the Carnegie Corporation of New York and the US Department of Defense. Much of the work to format the book was done by NPEC's research associate, Kate Harrison. Without her help and that of Dr James Pierce and Rita Rummel of SSI, this book would not have been possible. Finally, thanks are due to the project's authors and reviewers who contributed their time and ideas.

Henry D Sokolski

Executive Director
The Non-proliferation
Policy Education Center

Chapter 1

Overview

Henry D Sokolski

With most of the world's advanced economies now stuck in recession; Western support for defense cuts and nuclear disarmament increasing; and a major emerging Asian power at odds with its neighbors and the United States; it is tempting to think our times are about to rhyme with a decade of similar woes—the disorderly 1930s.[1]

Might we again be drifting toward some new form of mortal national combat? Or, will our future more likely ape the near-half-century that defined the Cold War—a period in which tensions between competing states ebbed and flowed but peace mostly prevailed by dint of nuclear mutual fear and loathing?

The short answer is, nobody knows. This much, however, is clear: The strategic military competitions of the next 2 decades will be unlike any the world has yet seen. Assuming US, Chinese, Russian, Israeli, Indian, French, British, and Pakistani strategic forces continue to be modernized and America and Russia continue to reduce their strategic nuclear deployments, the next arms race will be run by a much larger number of contestants—with highly destructive strategic capabilities far more closely matched and capable of being quickly enlarged than in any other previous period in history.

Looking Backward

To grasp the dimensions of this brave new world, one need only compare how capable states were of destroying strategic targets instantaneously a half-century ago, with what damage they could inflict today. In 1961, Washington and Moscow engaged in the last and most significant Cold War confrontation over the status of Berlin. At the time, the United States had over 24,000 operationally deployed nuclear weapons. Russia had nearly 2,500. The other nuclear powers—Great Britain and France—had an aggregate of no more than 50 (with France lacking any deployed nuclear weapons).[2] The difference in nuclear weapons deployment numbers between the top and bottom nuclear powers—a figure equal to at least three orders of magnitude—was massive. America, moreover, was clearly dominant.

In contrast, today, the United States has no more than 1,980 deployed nuclear weapons, and Russia has between 4,537 and 6,537.[3] India, Pakistan, the United Kingdom (UK), France, and Israel have 1 to 400 each, and China may have anywhere from between 200 to more than 1,000.[4] Putting aside North Korea's nascent nuclear force (cf. France's force of 1961), the difference in the numbers of nuclear deployments between the top and bottom nuclear powers, then, has fallen at least two full orders of magnitude and is projected to decline even further. (see Figure 1-1.)

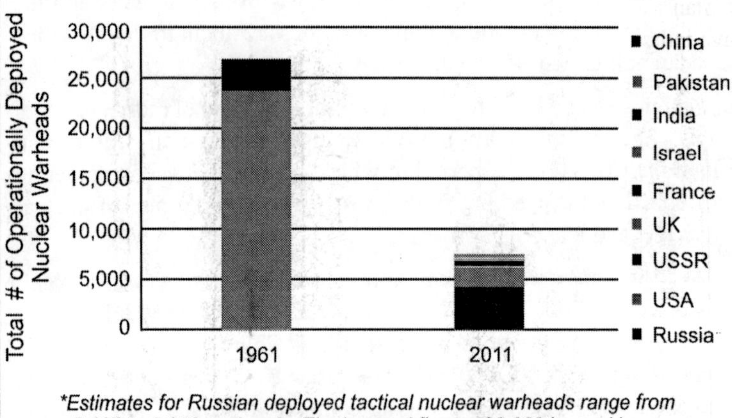

**Estimates for Russian deployed tactical nuclear warheads range from 3,000 to 5,000 warheads. The low-end figure of 3,000 is used here.*

Figure 1-1. From US Strategic Dominance to a Compressed Nuclear Crowd.[5]

As tight as the nuclear deployments between the world's nuclear-armed states has become, the potential for this nuclear balance to shift quickly and dramatically is far greater still than was the case a half-century ago. In 1961, the United States, Russia, the UK, and France had militarized nearly all of the nuclear weapons materials they had—they held little or nothing back in reserve. Nor could any of them militarize civilian stockpiles of separated plutonium or highly enriched uranium, as none were then available.

Today, matters are quite different (see Figures 1-2 and 1-3). First, the United States and Russia alone could reconfigure reserve fissile materials and start redeploying over tens of thousands of additional nuclear weapons that they have in reserve. Second, officials in Japan have publicly allowed that they have the technical capacity to militarize nearly 2,500 bombs' worth of "civilian" plutonium they have stored domestically.[6]

India, meanwhile, has roughly 1,300 bombs' worth of separated reactor-grade plutonium on tap, is planning on expanding its capacity to produce more of this material significantly over the next 3 to 10 years, and has claimed to have tested a nuclear device using this material.[7] Third, China has tons of nuclear material that it either could or already has militarized and is still planning on building a "civilian" plutonium reprocessing plant adjacent to one of its major military nuclear production plants that could produce as many as 1,000 bombs' worth of plutonium annually.[8] Also, not only these states, but Pakistan, Germany, the Netherlands, Brazil, Iran, Argentina, and North Korea, either make or plan to produce such nuclear fuels soon, while several other states have indicated a desire to do likewise.

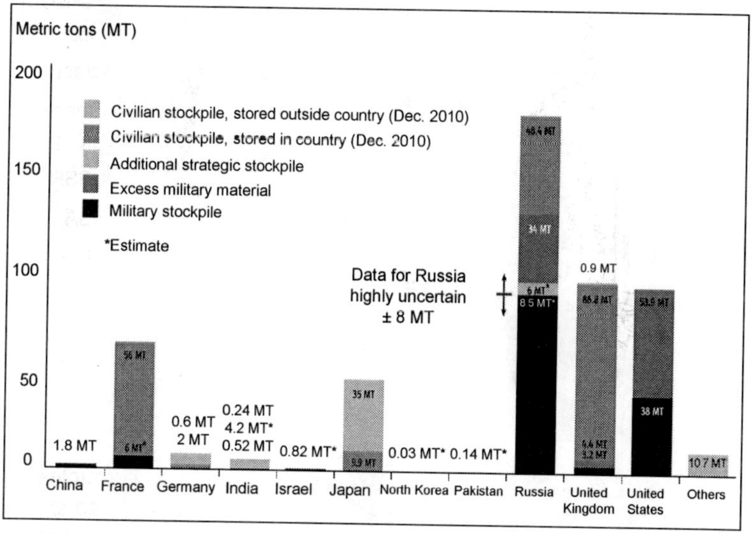

Source: International Panel on Fissile Materials, ***Global Fissile Material Report 2011*****, p. 17, available from** ***fissilematerials.org/publications/2012/01/global_fissile_material_report.html*****.**

Figure 1-2. National Stockpiles of Separated Plutonium, 2011.

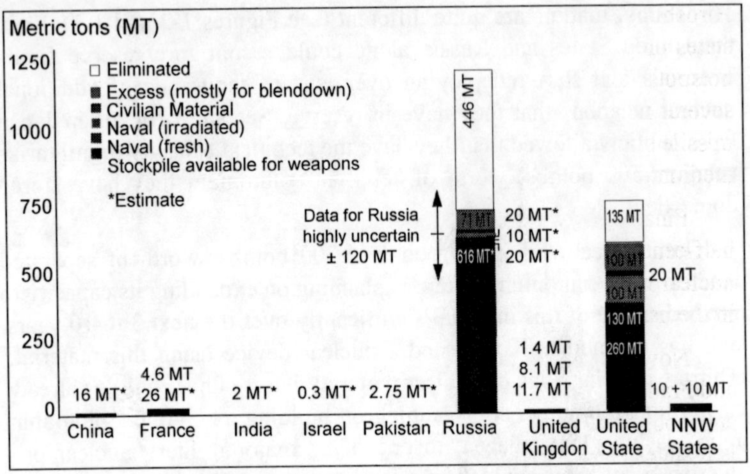

Source: International Panel on Fissile Materials, *Global Fissile Material Report 2011,* **p. 9, available from** *fissilematerials.org/publications/2012/01/global_fissile_material_report.html.*

Figure 1-3. National Stockpiles of Highly Enriched Uranium, 2011.

Then, there is the matter of missile delivery. In 1961, only the United States and the Soviet Union had missiles capable of delivering a

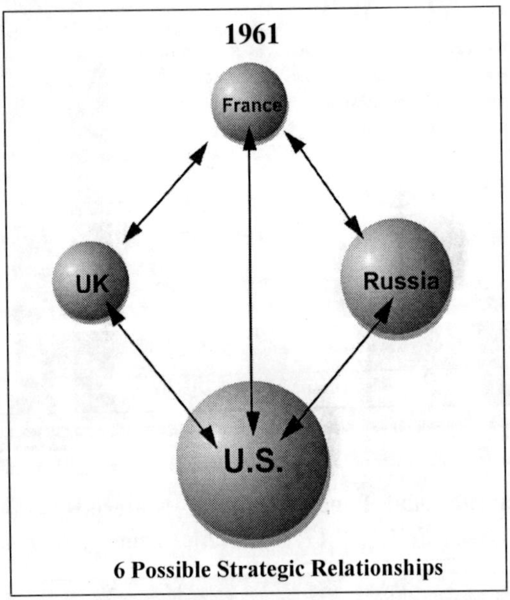

Figure 1-4. Four Nuclear Weapons States in 1961.

Hiroshima-sized bomb. Today, 27 states do.[9] To be sure, many of these states only have theater-range missiles. But most of these states are in hotspots like the Middle East, where such missiles are sufficient to target several neighbors. Meanwhile, the rest of the world's nuclear-capable missile states are able to target this same region with intercontinental or medium-range systems.

Finally, the total number of nuclear-armed states has increased. A half-century ago, only the United States, Russia, the UK, and France had nuclear weapons, and an overwhelming numbers of these weapons were in the hand of the United States (see Figure 1-4).

Now, there are nine nuclear-armed states. Two of these states—the UK and France—are within the North Atlantic Treaty Organization (NATO) and coordinate their nuclear plans closely. North Korea, meanwhile, is a state that the major powers hope will only be nuclear armed for a temporary period, i.e., that it will give up its few nuclear arms in ongoing negotiations. In this world, the United States likes to think that most of the currently nuclear-armed states are allies or strategic partners of the United States (see Figure 1-5). This world, however, may not last long. Certainly, Tehran is waiting in the wings, and Turkey, Saudi Arabia, Algeria, South Korea, Syria, and Japan are all poised as possible mid-term nuclear-weapons-options states. Unlike France, China, Russia, and

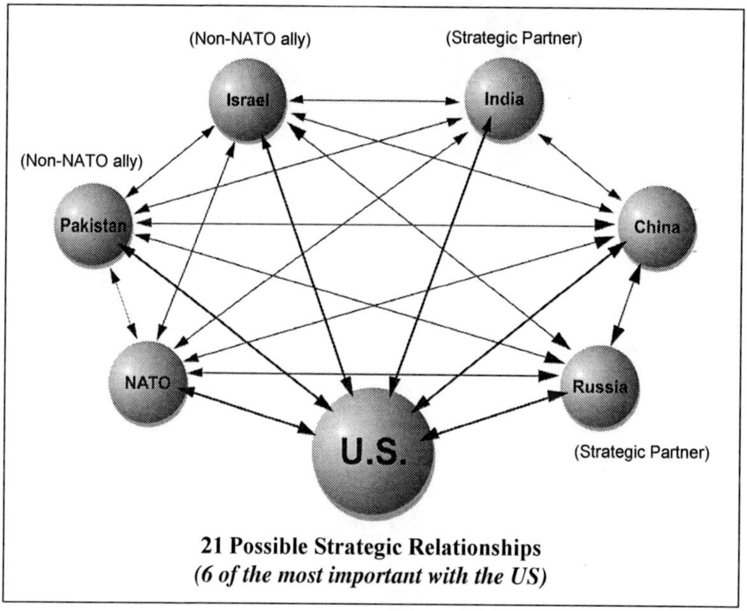

Figure 1-5. Nuclear Weapons States Today.[8]

the UK, though, these Post-Cold War nuclear-weapons aspirants may not afford the world the courtesy of testing before deploying their first bomb. Instead, initially, they are likely to develop "peaceful" nuclear energy programs, as Iran, India, Iraq, and North Korea did, and then move toward nuclear weapons only when they conclude it is useful to do so. Whether or not "safety" and nuclear stability in this new world will be "the sturdy child of [mutual] terror" (Churchill's description of Cold War stability), remains to be seen. Certainly, the stool of nuclear deterrence will have many more legs that could give way in many more surprising ways than were possible a half century ago. (see Figure 1-6.)

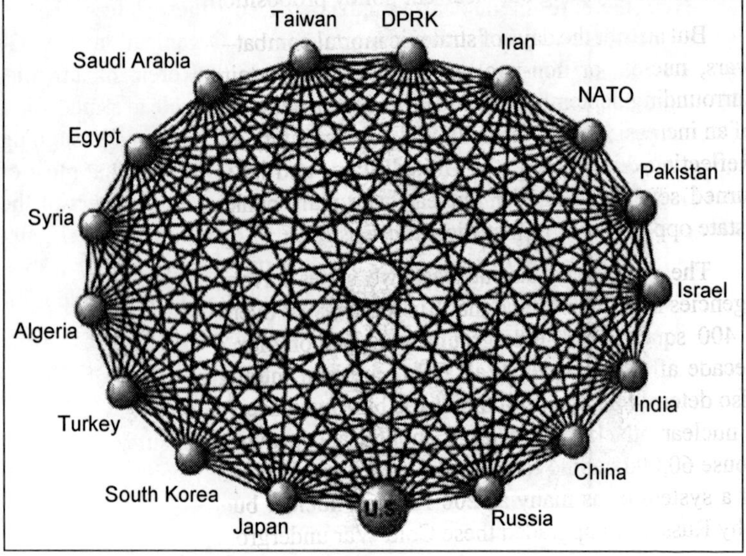

(136 chances for strategic miscalculations)

Today Plus

Iran	***DPRK***	***Taiwan***	***Saudi Arabia***	***Egypt***
Syria	***Algeria***	***Turkey***	***South Korea***	***Japan***

Figure 1-6. Possible Nuclear States in the Future.

Why Worry

An increasingly fashionable rejoinder to such broodings is to maintain an optimistic brand of nuclear realism. Any intelligent state, it can be argued, knows that using nuclear weapons is militarily self-defeating and that these weapons' only legitimate mission is to deter military threats. Fretting about nuclear use and nuclear proliferation (vertical or horizontal), as such, is mistaken or overwrought.[10]

But is it? Can states deter military threats with nuclear weapons if their actual use is self-defeating? Which states, if any, actually believe they are militarily useless? The Russians and Pakistanis clearly do not. Just the opposite: They have gone out of their way to develop battlefield nuclear weapons and plan to use them first to defeat opposing advanced conventional forces. As for the United States, France, and the UK, all have studiously and repeatedly refused to renounce first use. Israel, meanwhile, insists that while it will not be first to introduce nuclear weapons in the Middle East, it also will not be second. This leaves North Korea—a wild card—and India and China, whose declared no first-use policies are anything but clear-cut policy propositions.

But are not the days of strategic mortal combat—of all-out industrial wars, nuclear or non-nuclear—behind us? Certainly, with the events surrounding September 11, 2001 (9/11), this view has gained the backing of an increasing number of US and allied military analysts and pundits.[11] Reflecting this outlook, the United States and its European allies have turned several Cold War nuclear "survival" bunkers into private real estate opportunities or historical tourist sites.[12]

The problem is that at least two states have not. US intelligence agencies have determined that Russia invested over $6 billion to expand a 400 square mile underground nuclear complex at Yamantau a full decade after the Berlin Wall fell. American intelligence officials have also determined that this complex is burrowed deep enough to withstand a nuclear attack, and is large enough and provisioned sufficiently to house 60,000 people for months (see Figure 1-7). They believe it is one of a system of as many as 200 Russian nuclear bunkers.[13] It is unclear why Russia has upgraded these Cold War underground centers.

Figure 1-7. Russian Underground Nuclear Complex at Yamantau.

China's nuclear passive-defense activities are no less perplexing. In 2009, China's strategic missile command, the 2nd Artillery Brigade, revealed that it had completed 3,000 miles of dispersed, deep, underground tunnels for the deployment of its nuclear-capable cruise and ballistic missile forces (see Figure 1-8). China spent enormous sums to build this system and is still expanding the complex. This system appears to be designed and provisioned to house thousands of military staff during a protracted nuclear exchange.[14]

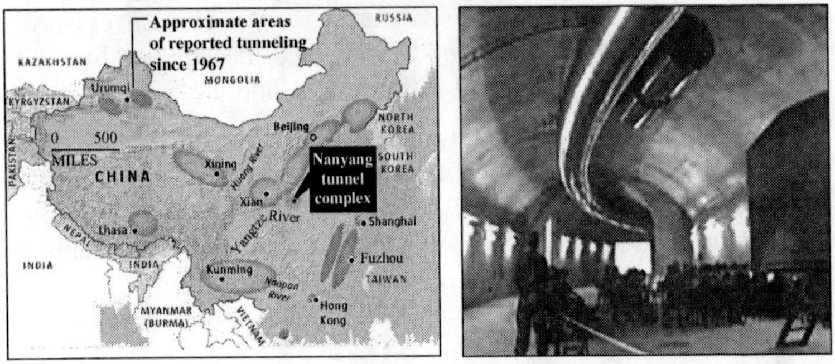

Figure 1-8. Chinese Underground Tunnels.

North Korea also has gone to extensive lengths to protect its strategic assets. Almost all of its nuclear and long-range military systems have underground tunneled bases or host areas. US intelligence agencies estimate that North Korea has in excess of 10,000 major tunnels to protect its key military and civilian assets.

Going Ballistic

All of this suggests that several nuclear-armed states still believe they may have to endure or engage in major wars involving nuclear arms. Fortifying this suspicion is the increasing capacity states have to deliver both nuclear and non-nuclear payloads quickly against one another. Back in 1961, only the United States and Russia had nuclear-capable missile systems—i.e., cruise or ballistic missile systems capable of delivering a first-generation nuclear bomb at least 500 kilograms, 300 kilometers, or further. Now, 27 countries have perfected or acquired such systems, and no fewer than nine can launch a satellite into orbit—i.e., have what is prerequisite to develop intercontinental ballistic missiles (ICBMs) (see Figure 1-9).[15] In addition, the United States, China, Iran, South Korea, Israel, and key NATO states are all working on precision missiles capable of achieving major results using only conventional munitions—i.e., of knocking out large military bases and major naval surface combatants.[16] More nuclear-capable missile states are likely to emerge.

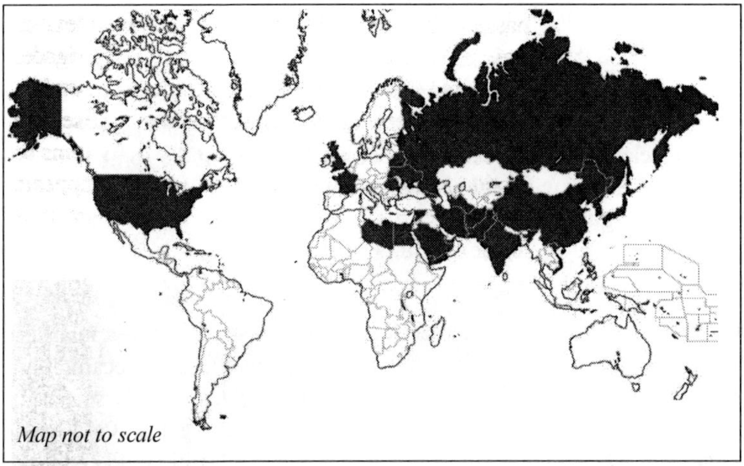

Figure 1-9. 27 Nuclear Capable Missile Countries in 2011.

The strategic importance of these missile trends is difficult to exaggerate. First, they cannot help but increase the chances for war. One way to measure a state's diplomatic shadow or potential to influence others is simply to map out the range arcs of its deployed missiles. Today, increasingly, these range arcs overlap. Consider Iran. The reach of its missiles now intersects with that of missiles based in Israel, Egypt, the United Arab Emirates (UAE), Syria, Russia, Pakistan, France, Saudi Arabia, China, the UK, and the United States.

This is a very different world than that of a half-century ago. In 1961, when alliance loyalties within the Communist and Free World Blocs were at their height, only Russia and America's missiles were aimed at each other. Now, there is no Communist Bloc, what remains of the Free World alliance system (e.g., NATO, Australia-New Zealand-US Treaty [ANZUS], etc.) is relatively weak, and nuclear-capable missiles in hotspots like the Persian Gulf could be fired from any number of states—both near and far. For nuclear-armed states, this situation places a premium on securing nuclear weapons assets against surprise attack. It also raises first-order questions about nuclear escalation, which brings us to the second reason more missiles in more hands is a major worry: These missiles can act as conventional catalysts for nuclear war.

Increasingly, with precision guidance and submunitions technologies, it is possible to destroy targets that once required nuclear weapons—e.g., large air strips and air fields, command centers, naval ports, and moving surface ships—with a handful of conventionally armed missiles instead. This has raised the prospect of states being able to knock out a significant portion of an opponent's key military forces without having to use nuclear weapons.[17]

The good news is that this scenario makes the initial use of nuclear weapons far less likely. The bad news is that with enough precision guidance capabilities, a state might be tempted to initiate combat in the expectation of winning without ever having to go nuclear and end up miscalculating fatally.

War Scenarios

A real-world case, now taken seriously by Pakistani security analysts, is the mid-term prospect of an Indian conventional missile decapitation strike against Pakistani strategic assets. The Indians, in this scenario, would use precise, offensive, long-range missiles against Pakistan's nuclear forces and command centers. Then, New Delhi could fend off any Pakistani retaliatory nuclear strike with India's much larger nuclear forces and with Indian non-nuclear missile defenses. Finally, India would be able to prevail against Pakistani armor and artillery, with superior Indian military conventional forces.[18]

To hedge against this prospect, Pakistan has already ramped up its nuclear weapons production and is now toying with deploying its nuclear weapons in ways designed to further complicate Indian opportunities to knock them out (e.g., delegation of launch authority under certain circumstances, forward deployment, dispersal, mobility, etc.).[19] All of these methods only increase the prospects for nuclear use and have goaded India to develop nuclear ramp-up options of its own.

Beyond this, advanced conventional weapons might ignite a nuclear conflict directly. Again, consider India and Pakistan. After being hit by so many Pakistani-backed terrorist attacks, the Indian government has toyed with a conventional counterstrategy known as "Cold Start." Under this approach, India would respond to Pakistan-backed terrorist attacks by quickly seizing a limited amount of Pakistani territory, with Indian forces deployed to march on command immediately (i.e., from a "Cold Start").

The idea here would be to threaten to take enough away from Pakistan that it holds dear (including Islamabad's desire to defend all of Pakistan), but not enough to prompt Pakistan to threaten India with its nuclear weapons. Unfortunately, India's Cold Start plan has had nearly the reverse effect. Shortly after New Delhi broached its strategy, Pakistani military officials announced their intent to use tactical nuclear weapons against any invading Indian force and deployed new, short-range nuclear-armed tactical missiles along the Pakistani-Indian border precisely for this purpose.[20]

Unfortunately, Pakistan's inclination to rely on nuclear weapons to counter conventional threats is not unique. Moscow, faced with advanced Chinese and NATO conventional forces, has chosen to increase its reliance on tactical nuclear weapons. For Russia, employing these weapons to counterbalance China and NATO's conventional forces is far less stressful economically and is militarily pragmatic, given Russia's shrinking cohort of eligible military servicemen. China, in response, may, according to some experts, be toying with deploying nuclear artillery systems of its own.[21]

China and the Arms Race Ahead

All of these trends are challenging in their own right. They also suggest what the next strategic arms race might look like. First, as the United States and Russia try to reduce or contain their nuclear weapons deployments, at least one nuclear-weapons state may be tempted to close the gap. Of course, in the short-and even mid-term, Pakistan, Israel, and India could not attempt to play catch up. For these states, getting ahead of the superpowers would take great effort and at least 1 to 3 decades of continuous, flat-out military nuclear production. It is quite clear, moreover, that none of these states have yet set out to meet or beat the United States or Russia as a national goal.

China, however, is a different matter. It clearly sees the United States as a key military competitor in the Western Pacific and in Northeast Asia. China also has had border disputes with India and historically has been at odds militarily with both it and Russia. It is not surprising, then, that China has actively been modernizing its nuclear-capable missiles to target key US and Indian military air and sea bases with advanced conventional munitions, and is developing similar missiles to threaten US carrier task forces on the open seas. In support of such operations, China is also modernizing its military space assets, which include military communications, command, surveillance, and imagery satellites and an emerging anti-satellite capability.[22]

Then there is China's nuclear arsenal. For nearly 30 years, most respected security analysts have estimated the number of deployed Chinese nuclear warheads to be between 150 and 400. Yet, by any account, China has produced enough weapons-usable plutonium and uranium to make four or more times this number of weapons. Why, then, have Chinese nuclear deployments been judged to be so low?

First, there is China's declared nuclear weapons strategy. In its official military white papers since 2006 and in other forums, Chinese officials insist that Beijing would never be the first state to use nuclear weapons and would never threaten to use them against any non-nuclear-weapons state. China also supports a doctrine that calls for a nuclear retaliatory response that is no more than what is "minimally" required and to use nuclear weapons only for its defense.[23] Most Western Chinese security experts have interpreted these statements to mean Beijing is interested in holding only a handful of opponents' cities at risk; this, in turn, has encouraged interpreting uncertainties regarding Chinese nuclear warhead deployments toward the low end.

What China's actual nuclear use policies might be, though, is open to debate. As one analyst recently quipped, with America's first use of nuclear weapons against Japan in 1945, it is literally impossible for any country other than the United States to be first in using these weapons. More important, Chinese officials have emphasized that Taiwan is not an independent state and that under certain circumstances, it may be necessary to use nuclear weapons against this island "province." Finally, there are the not-so-veiled nuclear threats that senior Chinese generals have made against the United States if it should use conventional weapons against China in response to a Chinese attack against Taiwan (including the observation that the United States would not being willing to risk Los Angeles to save Taipei).[24]

The second cause for conservatism in assessing China's arsenal is the extent to which estimates of the number of Chinese warheads have been tied to the observed number of Chinese nuclear weapons missile launchers and, so far, the number of these systems that actually have been seen has been low. Moreover, few, if any, missile reloads are assumed for each of these missile launchers, and it is presumed that none of China's missiles have multiple warheads. The numbers of battlefield nuclear weapons, such as nuclear artillery, are also presumed to be low or nonexistent.

All of this may be right, but there are reasons to wonder. The Chinese, after all, claim that they have built 3,000 miles of tunnels to hide China's missile forces and related warheads and that China continues to build such tunnels.[25] Employing missile reloads for mobile missile systems has been standard practice for Russia and the United States. It would be odd if it was not also a Chinese practice, particularly for the country's growing number of solid fueled rocket and cruise missile systems. There is also evidence that China may soon have multiple warhead dispensers for some of its rockets. Finally, several experts believe China may be fielding battlefield artillery for the delivery of tactical nuclear shells.[26]

Precisely how large is China's nuclear arsenal, then? The answer is unclear. What is not is the relevance of the answer. Several Chinese sources suggest China may have deployed roughly nine times the 150 to 400 nuclear weapons most analysts currently estimate the country has. If this is so, China would have as many or more deployed warheads as the United States and nearly as many as Russia.[27]

The first issue this possibility raises is how sound are current US and Russian nuclear modernization and missile defense plans. It hardly would be in Washington or Moscow's interest to let Beijing believe it could operate more freely with Chinese conventional forces against Taiwanese, Japanese, American, Indian, or Russian interests in the belief that China's nuclear capabilities could deter Russia or the United States from responding. (see Figure 1-10.)

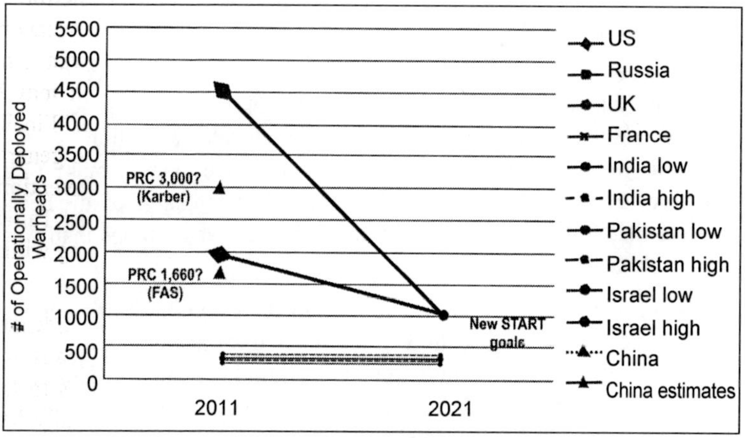

Figure 1-10. The Next Decade, Nuclear Uncertainties, and Competitions.[28]

Yet another question a much larger Chinese nuclear strategic force would raise is how it might impact Washington and Moscow's current strategic arms negotiations. Would the United States and Russia be eager to make much deeper nuclear weapons cuts if they thought China might, as a result, end up possessing more deployed weapons than either Washington or Moscow? At this point, would they not have to factor China into their arms control calculations? And if so, how?

Interested Parties

Japan would be another interested party. It already has nearly 2,500 weapons' worth of separated plutonium on its soil that it was supposed to use to fuel its light-water reactors and its fast reactors. Now, however, Japan has decided not to build more nuclear power reactors domestically. It also is reviewing the merits of continuing its fast reactor efforts, a program that is technically premised on Japan expanding its current domestic fleet of light-water reactors.

A related and immediate operational question is whether or not Japan will bring a $20-billion civilian nuclear spent fuel reprocessing plant capable of producing 1,000 bombs' worth of plutonium a year at Rokkasho online as planned in late 2012. This plant and Japan's plutonium recycling program have been controversial, since they were decisions made under Prime Minister Nakasone and can be tied to internal Japanese considerations for developing a plutonium nuclear weapons option. Although this plant is not necessary for the management of Japan's spent fuel, the forward costs of operating it could run as high as $100 billion over its lifetime.[29]

In light of the questionable technical and economic benefits of operating Rokkasho, it would be difficult for Tokyo to justify proceeding with this plant's operation unless it wanted to develop an option to build a nuclear weapons arsenal. What, then, would one have to make of a Japanese decision to open Rokkasho, if this decision came on the heels of news that China actually had many more nuclear weapons than was previously believed?

South Korea, which has attempted to get its own nuclear weapons at least once and is asking the United States to back Seoul's efforts to separate "peaceful" plutonium from US-origin spent fuel in Korea, is sure to be watching what Japan decides. After North Korea's sinking of the Cheonan and the bombardment of Yeonpyeong Island, South Korean parliamentarians called for a possible redeployment of US tactical nuclear weapons. Washington, however, rejected this request.[30] This raises the worry that Seoul might again consider developing a nuclear-weapons option of its own. South Korea already has its own nuclear-capable rockets and cruise missiles. How North Korea might react to South Korea developing a nuclear weapons option is anyone's guess.

In addition to Japan and South Korea possibly reacting negatively to news of a Chinese nuclear ramp up, there is India. It already has hedged its nuclear bets with plans to build five unsafeguarded plutonium-producing breeder reactors by 2020, and by laying the foundations of an enrichment plant that may double its production of weapons-grade uranium.[31] India, too, has roughly 1,000 bombs' worth of separated plutonium it claims it can convert into nuclear weapons. It also has pushed the development of a nuclear submarine, submarine ballistic missiles, missile defenses, and long-range cruise missiles. Late in 2011, India announced it was working with Russia to develop a terminally guided ICBM in order to off-balance Chinese medium-range ballistic missile deployments near India's borders.[32] India has never tried to compete with China weapon-for-weapon, but if Chinese nuclear warhead numbers were to rise substantially, India might have no other choice but to try.

Pakistan, of course, will do its best to keep up with India. Since Islamabad is already producing as much plutonium and highly enriched uranium as it can, it would likely seek further technical assistance from China and financial help from its close ally, Saudi Arabia. Islamabad may do this to hedge against India, whether China or India build their nuclear arms up or not. There is also good reason to believe that Saudi Arabia might want to cooperate on nuclear weapons-related activities with Pakistan to help Saudi Arabia hedge against Iran's growing nuclear weapons capabilities.

Not-So-Peaceful Energy and Arms Control

In this regard, Saudi Arabia has made it known that it intends to buildup its "peaceful" nuclear energy capabilities. It recently announced (after the Fukushima nuclear accident) that it would spend over $100 billion to build 16 large-power reactors in the kingdom before 2030. This would constitute one of the most lucrative, best financed near- and mid-term nuclear power markets in the world. The reactors also could serve as the basis for development of a major nuclear weapons option. As Saudi Arabia's former head of intelligence recently told NATO ministers, the kingdom would have to get nuclear weapons if Iran did. Other news reports claim the kingdom is eager to work with Pakistan to secure such an option.[33]

In this regard, Saudi Arabia is not alone. Turkey also announced an ambitious "peaceful" nuclear power program shortly after Iran's nuclear enrichment efforts were revealed in 2002; Turkey expressed an interest in 2008 in enriching its own uranium.[34] Given Turkish qualms about Iran acquiring nuclear weapons, the possibility of Ankara developing a nuclear weapons option (as it previously toyed with in the late 1970s) must be taken seriously.[35] In addition, Algeria and Egypt (political rivals) and Syria (a historical ally of Iran) all have either attempted to develop nuclear weapons options or refuse to forswear making nuclear fuel, a process that can bring them within weeks of acquiring a bomb.[36] Israel, meanwhile, continues to make nuclear weapons materials at Dimona, and all of these states have nuclear-capable missile systems of some sort. (see Figure 1-11.)

Note: States in light grey already have established nuclear power programs.

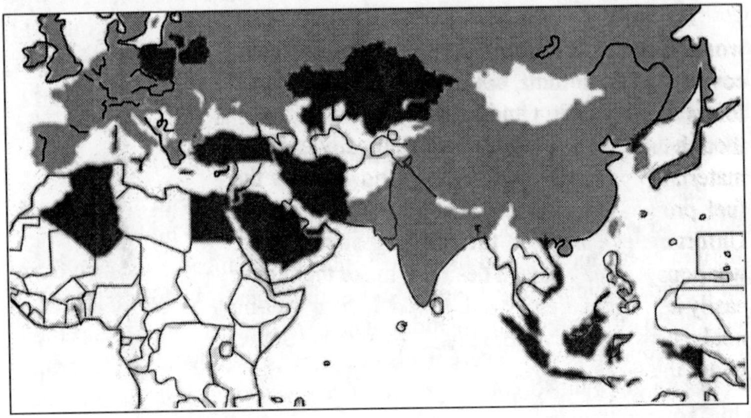

Figure 1-11. States Planning to Have Their First Nuclear Power Reactor by or before 2031.

Clearly, these trends, if continued, could spell trouble. How bad they might get, though, depends largely on what the United States, Russia, China, and other key states choose to do. The United States is focused on negotiating nuclear weapons reductions with Russia. The New Strategic Arms Reduction Treaty (New START) is supposed to be followed by an agreement that will cover both strategic and theater nuclear arms in Europe. Washington arms control planners are reported to be toying with reducing nuclear weapons deployments to levels as low as 300 warheads.[37] Given Russian concerns about US and NATO missile defense efforts and advanced NATO conventional forces, though, it is unclear how soon a follow-on agreement to START might be reached.

Meanwhile, the Obama administration is doing all it can to secure an international agreement to end the military production of fissile material for nuclear weapons. The prospects for finalizing such an agreement, though, are poor. Iran, Pakistan, North Korea, and Egypt all must consent to ratify it. But they are unlikely to do so until Israel, India, the United States, and South Korea take dramatic disarming steps.

Worse, the treaty's promotion risks complicating the establishment of effective fissile controls in nuclear fuel-producing states that lack nuclear weapons. Under the proposed treaty, no controls would be placed over production of nuclear weapons-usable fuels if they were committed to civilian purposes; the treaty would ban only military fissile production. Also, under the treaty, nuclear weapons states would be permitted to keep the weapons they already have along with any nuclear weapons-usable materials they might have acquired.

The good news is that the states most constrained under the treaty would have little incentive to make more nuclear weapons materials covertly. This, in turn, could allow the treaty to have relatively relaxed forms of verification and be relatively effective. This would be so even though there is no reliable way technically to account fully for past fissile material production or to detect and prevent the diversion of nuclear fuel production to military purposes in a reliable and timely manner. Unfortunately, nuclear fuel-making states that currently lack nuclear weapons but may have a desire to make them covertly (e.g., Iran), could easily argue that their own declared nuclear fuel-making activities should not be inspected any more tightly than those of the nuclear weapon states under the proposed treaty. This could set a bad precedent.[38]

The United States and allied governments are also trying to bring the Comprehensive Test Ban Treaty (CTBT) into force. In the United States, it is unclear if the White House can muster the votes needed in the US Senate to permit ratification. What is clear, though, is that bringing the treaty into force would also require ratification by India, Pakistan, China, Egypt, and North Korea, and this is unlikely to happen soon.

Supporters of the CTBT claim that the United States has a general obligation under the Nuclear Non-proliferation Treaty (NPT) to ratify the CTBT. Yet, with AQ Khan's circulation of a proven, Chinese missile-deliverable warhead design to Libya, Iran, and Pakistan and the International Atomic Energy Agency's (IAEA) public validation and sharing of a workable bomb design by Saddam, it is unlikely that banning nuclear testing will prevent nonweapons states from developing workable first-generation nuclear weapons. A ban will, however, make it more difficult for complying nuclear weapons states to upgrade their existing arsenals. This may be desirable, but it has only an indirect connection, if any, to preventing the further proliferation of nuclear weapons to new states.

Finally, the United States has tried to secure civilian and military facilities and stores of nuclear weapons-usable materials against theft or sabotage and has tried to persuade nonweapons states not to make their own nuclear fuels. There has been some progress in getting several states to surrender the highly enriched uranium they use to fuel their research reactors and to exchange it for less dangerous, low-enriched uranium.

Getting other states to forgo making nuclear fuel, however, has been difficult. The UAE has agreed to do so, but Egypt, Turkey, Saudi

Arabia, Vietnam, and Jordan have all held back from making such a commitment. Iran, Brazil, Argentina, South Korea, and South Africa have all either begun to make their own nuclear fuel or are committed to doing so in the next few years. Quiet US efforts to create an international fuel bank in Mongolia, meanwhile, were rebuffed recently by the Mongolian government.[39]

What To Do

The United States need not abandon its current nuclear control agenda. But it is clear that more will be needed to constrain what lies ahead. What else would help? These three things at least.

1. Take more concerted action alone, with our allies and friends, and with Russia to clarify and constrain China's offensive strategic military capabilities. In the first instance, this means clarifying precisely what strategic forces China has deployed and is building. Beijing's recent revelations that it has built 3,000 miles of deep tunnels to protect and hide its dual-capable missiles and related nuclear warhead systems more than suggest the desirability of reviewing our current estimates of Chinese nuclear-capable missile and nuclear weapons holdings. Are China's revelations about its tunnels disinformation meant simply to intimidate; is it hiding more military assets than we currently assess it to have? It would be useful to get the answers.

It also would be useful to know what China is planning to do. How much military fissile material does China currently have on hand? How likely is it that it has or will militarize or expand these holdings? How many different types of nuclear weapons does China have or intend to deploy? How much fissile material does each type require? How many missile reloads does China currently have; how many is it planning to acquire? Have the Chinese developed or will they develop multiple warheads for the country's missiles? If so, for which missile types, and in what numbers?

How many nuclear and advanced conventional warheads is China deploying on its missiles, bombers, submarines, and artillery? What are its plans for using these forces? How might these plans relate to China's emerging space, missile defense, and anti-satellite capabilities? All of these questions, and more, deserve review within the US Government, with America's allies and, to the extent possible, in cooperation with the Chinese.

As this review is underway, it also would be helpful to game alternative war and military crisis scenarios relating to China's possible use of these forces at a senior political level in the US and allied governments.

Such gaming would likely impact allied arms control and US and allied military planning. With regard to the latter, a key focus would have to be how one might defend, deter, and limit the damage Chinese nuclear and non-nuclear missile systems would otherwise inflict against the United States, its bases in the Western Pacific, America's friends, and Russia. This could entail not only the further development and deployment of active missile defenses, but of better passive defenses (e.g., base hardening and improving the capacity to restore operations at bases after attacks) and possibly new offensive forces—more capable, long-range conventional strike systems to help neutralize possible offensive Chinese operations.

Such gaming also should prompt a review of our current arms control agenda. In specific, it should encourage discussion of the merits of initiating talks with China and Russia and other states about limiting ground-based, dual-capable ballistic and cruise missiles. Unlike air and sea-based missiles, these ground-launched systems can be fired instantaneously and are easiest to command and control in protracted nuclear exchanges—ideal properties for employment in a first strike. These dual-capable missiles also can inflict strategic harm against major bases and naval operations conventionally.

Ronald Reagan referred to these weapons as "nuclear missiles," and looked forward to their eventual elimination. Toward this end, he concluded the Intermediate Nuclear Forces (INF) Treaty agreement, which eliminated an entire class of ground-based nuclear-capable missiles, and negotiated the Missile Technology Control Regime (MTCR), which was designed to block the further proliferation of nuclear-capable systems (i.e., missiles capable of lifting 500 kilograms or more at least 300 kilometers). With the promotion of space-based missile defenses, Reagan hoped to eliminate all such ground-based missiles.

What states have an incentive to eliminate these missiles? The United States has no intermediate ground-launched missiles, which it eliminated under the INF Treaty. Most of its shorter-range missiles are either air-launched or below MTCR range-payload limits. As for its ground-based ICBMs, they are all based in fixed silos, and as such are all nuclear sitting ducks. Russia, on the other hand, has a large, road-mobile ICBM force. Yet, it too is worried about growing Chinese precision missile strike capabilities that it cannot defend against.[40]

India and Pakistan have ground-launched ballistic missiles, but some of their most seasoned military experts have recently called for the elimination of short-range missiles, since these can only serve to escalate border disputes. As for China, it has much to gain by deploying more ground-launched missiles, unless, of course, it causes India, Russia, and the United States to react. The United States has been developing hypersonic boost glide systems that could provide it with prompt global strike options. It also has hundreds of silo-based ICBMs that it could affordably convert to deliver conventional warheads precisely. None of this would be in China's interest. Talks about reducing such nuclear-capable ground-based systems should be explored.[41]

Finally, although it may not be possible to conclude a fissile material cutoff treaty anytime soon, all of the other nuclear weapons-state members of the United Nations Security Council should press China to follow their lead in unilaterally forswearing making fissile material for weapons. It also would be helpful to call for a limited moratorium on commercial reprocessing with China and as many other states as possible. The US Blue Ribbon Panel on nuclear energy recently determined that it would not be in America's interest to pursue commercial reprocessing in the near- or midterm. Japan, meanwhile, is reviewing its own commercial reprocessing and fast reactor program, given its decision to move away from nuclear power. South Korea wants to recycle plutonium but is having difficulty persuading the United States to grant it permission to do so, with the many tons of US-origin spent fuel located in South Korea.[42]

China is committed to having AREVA build it a commercial reprocessing plant that is nearly identical to the one Japan is now reconsidering opening late next year at Rokkasho. China wants to site its plant adjacent to a major nuclear military production facility at Jiayuguan. As already noted, these "peaceful," commercial reprocessing plants produce at least 1,000 bombs' worth of nuclear weapons-usable plutonium annually. Still, they are not technically necessary for the operation of nuclear power and are uneconomical, compared with using fresh fuel and not recycling it. Promoting a limited plutonium recycling moratorium, in short, would be useful and could garner some support for a fissile material cutoff treaty.

2. Encourage nuclear supplier states to condition the further export of civilian nuclear plants upon the recipient forswearing the making of nuclear fuel and the opening of their nuclear facilities to the latest, most intrusive, international nuclear inspection procedures. Besides moderating increased pressures on more states to develop nuclear weapons options of their own or to increase their existing nuclear arsenals, the United States and other nuclear supplier states need to do

more to reduce the further spread of nuclear weapons in the Middle East. Here the worry is that Iran's pursuit of "peaceful" nuclear energy will serve as a model of sorts for Saudi Arabia (who wants to build 16 large-power reactors before 2030), Turkey (20), Egypt (1), Algeria (3), and Syria (1). When asked, none of these countries has been willing to forgo making nuclear fuel. Nor have any of them. So far, only Turkey and the UAE have ratified the IAEA's tough nuclear inspection regime under the Additional Protocol.

All of this is a worry, since the IAEA cannot find covert enrichment or reprocessing facilities or reactor plants with much confidence (cf. recent history regarding nuclear plants in Iran, Iraq, North Korea, and Syria). Also, once a large reactor is operating in a country, fresh enriched uranium is on tap that could be seized for possible further enrichment to weapons grade in a covert enrichment plant. Finally, plutonium-laden spent fuel is available that could be reprocessed to produce many bombs' worth of plutonium. Admittedly, without the authority to inspect anywhere at any time without notice, one may not be able to verify the pledge of states not to make nuclear fuel with high confidence. Still, securing such a legal pledge is valuable: It at least would put a violating country on the wrong side of international law and so make such action sanctionable.

Other than the United States, though, no nuclear supplier state (i.e., Russia, France, Japan, China, or South Korea) has yet to ask any of their prospective customers if they might agree to commit not to make nuclear fuel and to ratify the Additional Protocol. Worse, the United States itself is backing away from insisting on these conditions.

Some in the US Congress want to change this situation by making it more difficult to finalize any future US nuclear cooperative agreements with nonnuclear weapons states like Saudi Arabia, Jordan, or Vietnam, unless they agree to the UAE nuclear cooperative conditions.[43] These congressmen know that the United States is paying France billions to supply the US Department of Energy with a mixed-oxide fuel fabrication plant. The United States has also made billions more in taxpayer-backed federal energy loan guarantees available to French government-owned nuclear firms to build commercial nuclear plants in the United States. Russia, meanwhile, would likely ask for such loan guarantees for an enrichment plant it says it wants to build in the United States. The United States affords defense security guarantees to South Korea and Japan and is extending civilian nuclear assistance to the Russians. All of this affords reasonable leverage to encourage these other nuclear suppliers to follow America's lead.[44]

Certainly, it would be useful to get as many of the key nuclear suppliers to agree to condition their nuclear exports along the same lines as the UAE agreement stipulations as possible. This could be done either through the US leveraging its influence or by making the case before the Nuclear Supplier Group. Neither approach is mutually exclusive. Finally, clarifying what kinds of military diversions the IAEA can reliably detect and what kinds of diversions the agency is unlikely to detect in a timely fashion would be helpful.[45]

3. Do more to reduce the access of states to the surplus nuclear weapons and fissile material stockpiles that they could convert into bombs. As already noted, the United States and Russia maintain surplus nuclear weapons and nuclear weapons materials stockpiles, and India, Israel, Pakistan, the People's Republic of China (PRC), Japan, France, and the UK hold significant amounts of nuclear weapons-usable plutonium and uranium. This fissile material overhang increases security uncertainties regarding what each nuclear weapons country may have or could deploy relatively quickly. Given the verification difficulties with the proposed fissile material cutoff treaty and the improbabilities of such a treaty being brought into force, it would be useful to consider alternative approaches.

One idea detailed by several analysts at different times is a voluntary initiative now known as the fissile material control initiative (FMCI). It would call on nuclear weapons-usable material producing states to set aside whatever fissile materials they have produced in excess of their immediate military or civilian requirements for either final disposition or internationally verified safekeeping.[46] Russia and the United States have already agreed to dispose of 34 tons of weapons-grade plutonium, and Moscow has blended down 500 tons of weapons-grade uranium for resale as power reactor fuel. Much more can be done both between the United States and Russia and among the other fissile-producing states listed above. Encouraging as many states as possible to forgo recycling spent reactor fuel to produce plutonium-based reactor fuel also could be useful. Given that Germany, the UK, and the United States have essentially already made this decision for both the near- and mid-term, and Japan could easily justify doing likewise, much of a de facto, international recycling moratorium is already in place. The United States and other like-minded nations might do more to formalize this reality.

Conclusion: A Future Unlike Our Past

It is easy to romanticize how stable the balance of nuclear terror between Russia and the United States was a half-century ago. That balance nearly tipped into nuclear war in the case of Berlin and the Cuban Missile Crisis. On the other hand, it is just as easy to overplay the political, military, diplomatic, and economic problems we are currently experiencing. However, 2012 is not 1937. In the late 1930s, war was increasingly seen as an economic imperative. Today, just the opposite is the case. Mutual deterrence, never all that strong or reliable during the height of the Cold War, will be less certain to prevail in places like Southwest Asia or the Middle East. Still, long-term industrial wars between the United States, Russia, or China seem difficult to imagine.

Unfortunately, wars between Pakistan and India; China and Taiwan; Israel and Iran; and India and Vietnam are possible. Increased diplomatic, political, economic, and military competition among China, Russia, India, the United States, or Japan also seems likely. Equally worrisome is the further spread of nuclear weapons capabilities to the Middle East, North Africa, and Turkey and the further proliferation of nuclear-capable missiles.

In this more voluble world, the United States will need to pay more attention to competing and negotiating with China on strategic military matters. Washington and its friends will also have to do more to stabilize relations between Pakistan, India, and China, and to firm up security alliance relations with Korea, Japan, and other key states in the Pacific.

While the hope of eliminating nuclear weapons may continue, the United States and other like-minded states will need to do more to reduce the numbers and types of ground-launched nuclear-capable missiles and the production of, and access to, nuclear weapons-usable materials. Finally, far more will need to be done to restrict and condition the further spread of "peaceful" nuclear energy programs to new states, lest the Middle and Far East be peppered with more Irans and North Koreas.

What will happen if we fail to take on these new, additional challenges? At a minimum, nuclear weapons and first-strike missiles will spread, and so increase the prospect of use. In the worst case, there will be wars that may well go nuclear. In this case, the 1930s and 1960s could end up looking quite benign.

Endnotes

1. Cf., Matthew Continetti, "A World in Crisis: What the Thirties Tell Us about Today," *The Weekly Standard,* January 3, 2011, available from *www.weeklystandard.com/articles/world-crisis_524865.html*; and "Briefing—Lessons of the 1930s: There Could Be Trouble Ahead," *The Economist,* December 10, 2011, pp. 76-78.

2. See Natural Resources Defense Council, "Table of Global Nuclear Weapons Stockpiles, 1945-2002," last revised November 26, 2002, available from *www.nrdc.org/nuclear/nudb/datab19.asp*.

3. The total number of deployed US warheads includes 1,800 strategic warheads, and 180 tactical ones. The official number of deployed strategic warheads in the Russian Federation is 1,537. Estimates for the number of Russian deployed tactical warheads ranges from 3,000 to 5,000. For the strategic warhead figures, see US Department of State, "New START Treaty Aggregate Numbers of Strategic Offensive Arms," Fact Sheet, June 1, 2011, available from *www.state.gov/t/avc/rls/164722.htm*. Information on the estimates of deployed tactical warheads for the United States and Russia is drawn from Hans M. Kristensen, "Tac Nuke Numbers Confirmed?" FAS Strategic Security Blog, *Federation of American Scientists*, December 7, 2010, available from *www.fas.org/blog/ssp/2010/12/tacnukes.php*.

4. See "New START Treaty Aggregate Numbers" Fact Sheet; Robert S. Norris and Hans M. Kristensen, "US Tactical Nuclear Weapons in Europe, 2011," *The Bulletin of Atomic Scientists* Vol. 67, No. 1, January/February 2011, pp. 64-73, available from *bos.sagepub.com/content/67/1/64.full*; Zia Mian, A. H. Mayyar, R. Rajaraman, and M. V. Ramana, "Fissile Materials in South Asia and the Implications of the US-India Nuclear Deal," in Henry D.Sokolski, ed., *Pakistan's Nuclear Future: Worries Beyond War,* Carlisle, PA: Strategic Studies Institute, 2008, pp. 167-218; Shannon N. Kile, Vitaly Fedchenko, Bharath Gopalaswamy, and Hans M. Kristensen, "World Nuclear Forces," *SIPRI Yearbook 2011*, available from *www.sipri.org/yearbook/2011/07*; "Nuclear Weapons: Who Has What at a Glance," *Arms Control Association*, available from *www.armscontrol.org/factsheets/Nuclearweaponswhohaswhat*; "Statusof World Nuclear Forces," *Federation of American Scientists*, available from *www.fas.org/programs/ssp/nukes/nuclearweapons/nukestatus.html*; Alexander Glaser and Zia Mian, "Fissile Material Stockpiles and Production, 2008," *Science and Global Security*, Vol. 16, Issue 3, 2008, pp. 55-73, available from *www.tandfonline.com/doi/abs/10.1080/08929880802565131*; Warner D. Farr, "The Third Temple's Holy of Holies: Israel's Nuclear Weapons," *USAF Counterproliferation Center*, Counterproliferation Paper No. 2, September 1999, available from *www.au.af.mil/au/awc/awcgate/cpc-pubs/farr.htm*; and Kenneth S. Brower, "A Propensity for Conflict: Potential Scenarios and Outcomes of War in the Middle East," *Jane's Intelligence Review*, Special Report No. 14, February 1997, pp. 14-15.

5. The information used to generate this graph was drawn from the sources in Endnote 4. Also see Robert S. Norris and Hans M. Kristensen, "US Nuclear Forces, 2011," *Bulletin of the Atomic Scientists* Vol.

67, No. 2, March/April 2011, pp. 66-76, available from *bos.sagepub.com/content/67/2/66.full*; Robert S. Norris and Hans M. Kristensen, "Russian Nuclear Forces, 2011," *Bulletin of the Atomic Scientists* Vol. 67, No. 3, May/June 2011, pp. 67-74; and Robert S. Norris and Hans M. Kristensen, "Global Nuclear Weapons Inventories, 1945-2010," *Bulletin of the Atomic Scientists*, Vol. 66, No. 4, July 2010, pp. 77-83.

6. See Frank Von Hippel, "Plutonium, Proliferation and Radioactive-Waste Politics in East Asia," analysis published on the Nonproliferation Policy Education Center website on January 3, 2011, available from *www.npolicy.org/article.php?aid=44&rid=2*; and Takuya Suzuki, "Nuclear Leverage: Long an Advocate of Nuclear Energy, Nakasone Now Says Japan Should Go Solar," *Asahi.com*, July 7, 2011, available from *www.asahi.com/english/TKY201107210339.html.*

7. Zia Mian, *et al*., "Fissile Materials in South Asia," pp. 193-95.

8. See "China's Nuclear Fuel Cycle," *World Nuclear Association*, updated December 2011, available from *www.world-nuclear.org/info/inf63b_china_nuclearfuelcycle.html*; and International Panel on Fissile Materials, *Global Fissile Material Report 2011*, p. 17, available from *fissilematerials.org/publications/2012/01/global_fissile_material_report.html.*

9. See "World-wide Ballistic Missile Inventories," *Arms Control Association*, available from *www.armscontrol.org/factsheets/missiles.*

10. For example, see John Mueller, *Atomic Obsession: Nuclear Alarmism from Hiroshima to Al-Qaeda,* New York: Oxford University Press, 2010, pp.129-42; John Mueller, *Overblown: How Politicians and the Terrorism Industry Inflate National Security Threats and Why We Believe Them,* New York: Free Press, 2006; and Steve Kidd, "Nuclear Proliferation Risk—Is It Vastly Overrated?" *Nuclear Engineering International,* July 22, 2010, available from *www.neimagazine.com/story.asp?storyCode=2056931.*

11. Cf. Robert Taber, *The War of the Flea,* Washington, DC: Brassey's Inc., 2002; and George and Meredith Friedman, *The Future of War,* New York: Crown Publishers, 1996.

12. See Sharon Weinberg, "How To: Visit A Secret Nuclear Bunker," *Wired*, June 11, 2008, available from *www.wired.com/dangerroom/2008/06/how-to-visit-a/*; 20th Century Castles LLC, which sells decommissioned US missile bases including bases for Atlas, Titan, and Nike missiles, available from *www.missilebases.com/properties*; Smartbunker, which uses NATO bunkers to secure and host computer servers, available from *www.smartbunker.com/infrastructure*; Siegfried Wittenburg, "East German Nuclear Bunker Opens to Tourists," *Spiegel Online International*, August 26, 2011; Burlington Bunker in Corsham,

Wiltshire, UK, was formally a Cold War NATO nuclear bunker and is now a tourist sight, available from *www.burlingtonbunker.co.uk/*; and guided tours of a missile launch facility and silo are offered by the National Park Service at the Minuteman Missile National Historic Site in South Dakota, available from *www.nps.gov/mimi/index.htm*.

13. See "Yamantau," *GlobalSecuirty.org,* available from *www.globalsecurity.org/wmd/world/russia/yamantau.htm*; and "What's Going on in the Yamantau Mountain Complex?" *Viewzone*, available from *viewzone.com/yamantau.html*.

14. James R. Holmes, "China's Underground Great Wall, *The Diplomat*, August 20, 2011, available from *the-diplomat.com/flashpoints-blog/2011/08/20/chinas-underground-great-wall/*; and Bret Stephens, "How Many Nukes Does China Have?" *The Wall Street Journal,* October 24, 2011, available from *online.wsj.com/article/SB10001424052970204346104576639502894496030.html.*

15. See Endnote 9.

16. See, e.g., Ian Easton and Mark Stokes, "China and the Emerging Strategic Competition in Aerospace Power," in this volume.

17. See, e.g., Steven Lukasik, "To What Extent Can Precision Conventional Technologies Substitute for Nuclear Weapons?" in this volume.

18. Dr. Subhash Kapila, "India's New 'Cold Start' War Doctrine Strategically Reviewed," Paper No. 991, South Asia Analysis Group, April 5, 2004, available from *www.southasiaanalysis.org/%5Cpapers10%5Cpaper991.html*; and Commander Muhammad Azam Khan, "India's Cold Start Is Too Hot," *US Naval Institute Proceedings*, March 2011, available from *www.usni.org/magazines/proceedings/2011-03/indias-cold-start-too-hot*.

19. See Rodney Jones, "War Games: Pakistan's Answer to Cold Start?" *The Friday Times,* May 13, 2011, available from *www.thefridaytimes.com/13052011/page7.shtml*.

20. See Mike Mazza, "Pakistan's Strategic Myopia: Its Decision to Field Tactical Nuclear Weapons Will Only Make the Subcontinent More Unstable," *The Wall Street Journal*, April 2011, available from *online.wsj.com/article/SB10001424052748704099704576288763180683774.html?mod=googlenews_wsj*.

21. See, e.g., Jacob Kipp, "Asian Drivers of Russian Nuclear Force Posture," in this volume; and Dr. Mark B. Schneider, "The Nuclear Forces and Doctrine of the Russian Federation and the People's Republic of China," testimony given October 12, 2011, before the House Armed Services Subcommittee on Strategic Forces, available from *www.worldaffairscouncils.org/2011/images/insert/Majority%20Statement%20and%20Testimony.pdf*.

22. See Ian Easton, "The Asia-Pacific's Emerging Missile Defense and Military Space Competition," January 3, 2001, available from *www.npolicy.org/article_file/The_Asia-Pacifics_Emerging_Missile_Defense_and_Military_Space_Competition_280111_1143.pdf.*

23. On China's no first use policies, see China's 2008 White Paper, "China's National Defense in 2008," available from *www.fas.org/programs/ssp/nukes/2008DefenseWhitePaper_Jan2009.pdf*; also see analysis of this paper by Hans M. Kristensen, "China Defense White Paper Describes Nuclear Escalation," *FAS Strategic Security Blog*, January 23, 2009, available from *www.fas.org/blog/ssp/2009/01/chinapaper.php*; and M. Taylor Fravel and Evan S. Medeiros, "China's Search for Assured Retaliation: The Evolution of Chinese Nuclear Strategy and Force Structure," *International Security*, Fall 2010, available from *belfercenter.ksg.harvard.edu/files/Chinas_Search_for_Assured_Retaliation.pdf.*

24. See Jonathan Watts, "Chinese General Warns of Nuclear Risk to US," *The Guardian*, July 15, 2005, available from *www.guardian.co.uk/world/2005/jul/16/china.jonathanwatts*; and Mark Schneider, "The Nuclear Doctrine and Forces of the People's Republic of China," *Comparative Strategy*, Spring 2009, available from *www.tandfonline.com/doi/abs/10.1080/01495930903025276#preview*. Also see an earlier version, dated 2007, available from *www.nipp.org/Publication/Downloads/Publication%20Archive%20PDF/China%20nuclear%20final%20pub.pdf.*

25. See Endnote 13.

26. See Endnote 22. Also see "China, Russia: PRC Navy Status, Development Prospects Detailed," Moscow, Russia, *Morskoy Sbornik (Nautical Collection),* August 17, 2003, Translated in Open Source Center, Doc. ID: CPP20031120000002; and David Shambaugh, *Modernizing China's Military: Progress, Problems, and Prospects*, Berkeley, CA: University of California Press, 2002, p. 91.

27. As to how many nuclear weapons China has, no one knows. A sharp critic of an estimate that China might have as many as 3,000 nuclear weapons, though, was hardly reassuring regarding the actual total. He emphasized that China could *only* "theoretically" have as many as 1,660 nuclear weapons. For more on this controversy, see Hans Kristensen, "No, China Does Not Have 3,000 Nuclear Weapons," *FAS Strategic Security Blog,* December 3, 2011, available from *www.fas.org/blog/ssp/2011/12/chinanukes.php#more-5086.*

28. The numbers used to generate this chart came from the sources cited in Endnote 5, plus William Wan, "Georgetown Students Shed Light on China's Underground Missile System for Nuclear Weapons," *The Washington Post*, November 29, 2011; Hans Kristensen, "No, China

Does Not Have 3,000 Nuclear Weapons"; and Robert Burns, "US Weighing Steep Nuclear Arms Cuts," *Associated Press*, February 14, 2012, available from *www.boston.com/news/nation/washington/articles/2012/02/14/ap_newsbreak_us_weighing_steep_nuclear_arms_cuts/*.

29. On these points, see Von Hippel, "Plutonium, Proliferation and Radioactive-Waste Politics"; Henry Sokolski, "The Post-Fukushima Arms Race?" *Foreign Policy Online*, July 29, 2011, available from *www.foreignpolicy.com/articles/2011/07/29/the_post_fukushima_arms_race*; and Takuya Suzuki, "Nuclear Leverage: Long an Advocate of Nuclear Energy, Nakasone Now Says Japan Should Go Solar," *The Asahi Shimbun*, July 22, 2011, available from *www.asahi.com/english/TKY201107210339.html*.

30. See Julian Borger, "South Korea Considers Return of US Tactical Nuclear Weapons," *The Guardian*, November 22, 2010, available from *www.guardian.co.uk/world/2010/nov/22/south-korea-us-tactical-weapons-nuclear*; and David Dombey and Christian Oliver, "US Rules Out Nuclear Redeployment in South Korea, *Financial Times*, March 1, 2011, available from *www.ft.com/cms/s/0/e8a2d456-43b0-11e0-b117-00144feabdc0.html#axzz1oCEG4jBm*.

31. See "India to Commission Breeder Reactor in 2013," *Express Buzz,* February 20, 2012, available from *expressbuzz.com/nation/india-to-commission-breeder-reactor-in-2013/365268.html*; and Paul Brannan, "Further Construction Progress of Possible New Military Uranium Enrichment Facility India," *ISIS REPORTS*, October 5, 2011, available from *isis-online.org/isis-reports/detail/further-construction-progress-of-possible-new-military-uranium-enrichment-f/7*.

32. See "Russia to Provide 'Seeker' Tech for Agni-V ICBM," *Pakistan Defense*, October 26, 2011, available from *www.asian-defence.net/2011/10/russia-to-provide-seeker-tech-for.html;* Air Marshal (Ret.) B. K. Pandey, "Agni-V to Be Launched By March End," *SP's Aviation.net,* available from *spsaviation.net/story_issue.asp?Article=900*; "Why Is This DRDO Official in Moscow?" *TRISHUL,* October 5, 2011, available from *trishul-trident.blogspot.com/2011/10/why-is-this-drdo-official-in-moscow.html.*

33. See "Report: Saudis to Buy Nukes if Iran Tests A-bomb," *MSNBC,* February 10, 2012, available from *worldnews.msnbc.msn.com/_news/2012/02/10/10369793-report-saudi-arabia-to-buy-nukes-if-iran-tests-a-bomb*; Andrew Dean and Nicholas A. Heras, "Iranian Crisis Spurs Saudi Reconsideration of Nuclear Weapons," *Terrorism Monitor,* Vol. 10, Issue 4, February 23, 2012, available from *www.jamestown.org/programs/gta/single/?tx_ttnews%5Btt_news%5D=39048&tx_ttnews%5BbackPid%5D=26&cHash=9aecde0ac8f6849d8877289c07a*

49ad7; and Mustafa Alani, "How Iran Nuclear Standoff Looks from Saudi Arabia," *Bloomberg,* February 15, 2012, available from *www.bloomberg.com/news/2012-02-16/how-iran-nuclear-standoff-looks-from-saudi-arabia-mustafa-alani.html*.

34. See RIA Novosti, "Turkey Considers Uranium Enrichment for Own Nuclear Power Plants," January 1, 2009, available from *www.gab-ibn.com/IMG/pdf/Tr1-_Turkey_considers_uranium_enrichment_for_own_nuclear_power_plants.pdf*.

35. Turkish nuclear engineers in the late 1970s investigated how plutonium from spent light-water reactor fuel might be used to make nuclear explosives. They determined that it was quite feasible. See US Department of Energy, Office of Nonproliferation and International Security, *International Safeguards: Challenges and Opportunities for the 21st Century*, Washington, DC: National Nuclear Security Administration, NA-24, October 2007, pp. 93-94.

36. See Bruno Tertrais, "Alternative Proliferation Futures for North Africa," in this volume.

37. Burns, "US Weighing Steep Nuclear Arms Cuts."

38. On these points, consider Christopher A. Ford, "Five Plus Three: How to Have a Meaningful and Helpful Fissile Material Cutoff Treaty," *Arms Control Today*, March 2009, available from *www.armscontrol.org/act/2009_03/Ford*.

39. Badrakh, "Mongolia Abandons Nuclear Waste Storage Plans, Informs Japan of Decision," *Business-Mongolia.com*, October 17, 2011, available from *www.business-mongolia.com/mongolia/2011/10/17/mongolia-abandons-nuclear-waste-storage-plans-informs-japan-of-decision/*.

40. See Jacob Kipp, Endnote 21.

41. For a fuller discussion, see the "Missiles for Peace" Chapter by Henry D. Sokolski in this volume. Also listen to the audio of a panel discussion, "Missiles for Peace," held at the Carnegie Endowment for International Peace in Washington, DC, September 13, 2010, available from *d2tjk9wifu2pr3.cloudfront.net/2010-09-13-Sokolski.mp3*.

42. See "U.S Unlikely to Allow S. Korea to Reprocess Nuclear Fuel: Diplomat," *Yonhap News Agency*, March 3, 2012, available from *english.yonhapnews.co.kr/northkorea/2012/03/08/23/0401000000AEN20120308007100315F.HTML*; and Frank Von Hippel in Endnote 6 above.

43. See H.R. 1280, "A Bill to Amend the Atomic Energy Act of 1954 to Require Congressional Approval of Agreements for Peaceful Nuclear Cooperation with Foreign Countries and Other Purposes," reported out of the House Committee on Foreign Affairs during the first session of the 112th Congress, available from *thomas.loc.gov/cgi-bin/query/z?c112:H.R.1280*; and "Chairman Ros-Lehtinen Opening Statement: HR1280, The Atomic Energy Act of 1954," April 20, 2011, available at *www.youtube.com/watch?v=Qrvz2_gzik8*.

44. See Henry Sokolski, "What Nuclear Power's Revival Will Now Require: Tightening the Rules," testimony given before a hearing of the House Committee on Foreign Affairs, March 17, 2011, available from *www.npolicy.org/article.php?aid=629&rtid=8*; and "Obama's Nuclear Mistake: The President Converts Bush's Anti-Proliferation 'Gold Standard' into Lead," *National Review Online,* February 7, 2012, available from *www.npolicy.org/article.php?aid=1149&rtid=5*.

45. See "In Pursuit of the Undoable: Troubling Flaws in the World's Nuclear Safeguards," *The Economist*, August 23, 2007, available from *www.economist.com/node/9687869?story_id=9687869;* and *World At Risk: The Report of the Commis-sion on the Prevention of WMD Proliferation and Terrorism*, December 2, 2008, pp. 49-50, available from *www.cfr.org/terrorism/world-risk-report-commission-prevention-wmd-proliferation-terrorism/p17910*.

46. For the original presentation of the Fissile Material Control Initiative, see Robert J. Einhorn, "Controlling Fissile Materials and Ending Nuclear Testing," presented at an international conference on nuclear disarmament, "Achieving the Vision of a World Free of Nuclear Weapons," held in Oslo, Norway, February 26-27, 2008, available from *www.ctbto.org/fileadmin/user_upload/pdf/External_Reports/paper-einhorn.pdf*. Mr. Einhorn currently serves as the US Secretary of State's Special Advisor for Nonproliferation and Arms Control.

Part 1

Asia

Chapter 2

Asian Drivers of Russia's Nuclear Force Posture

Jacob W Kipp

Overview

This chapter takes issue with the Euro-centric view of Russian nuclear posture based upon Cold War assumptions, which stressed strategic nuclear systems, bipolarity, and Euro-centric military confrontation between the North Atlantic Treaty Organization (NATO) and the Soviet-led Warsaw Treaty Organization. Russia's nuclear arsenal was never so narrowly focused, even during the Cold War. But in the post-Cold War era, it is even less so. Beginning in the mid-1990s, Russia's national security elite began to speak of Russia as a Eurasian power with specific national security interests in the "near abroad." The Russian elite has, since the late 1990s, spoken of NATO and the United States as threats and challenges, depending on the immediate character of US-NATO and Russian relations. The key drivers have been NATO's expansion into Eastern Europe and former Soviet territories, and NATO's out-of-area operations when seen as threatening Russian national interests. However, even this picture misses a key dimension of Russian nuclear policy (i.e., the threats posed to Russian interests in the Caucasus, Central Asia, and the Far East).

This chapter addresses one of those areas in detail: the Russian Far East and Siberia. The Russian government has sought, by political means, to reduce antagonisms, but finds itself an object in a dynamic Asian-Pacific world, where Russian weakness is evident and where other powers are jockeying for position and advantage. Silence on Asian threats in Moscow's political discourse should not be taken as the final word on the Asian dimensions of Russian nuclear policy—in which demographic crisis, economic weakness, and limited conventional military capabilities create both vulnerability and the incentives to rely on nuclear weapons to de-escalate a potential military conflict. In these calculations, Russia's relative isolation in the region and its inability to control other areas of conflict could draw the Russian Far East into that conflict. Looming large in these calculations is the emergence of the People's Republic of China (PRC) as a major economic power with enhanced conventional military capabilities. This Asian dimension will make bilateral attempts at arms control agreements on nonstrategic nuclear weapons problematic, in the absence of any means to address Russia's Asian threats and challenges, which are only partially military.

Russia's Nuclear Weapons, its New Look, and China

While the signing of the New Strategic Arms Reduction Treaty (New START) by Presidents Barack Obama and Dmitry Medvedev in Prague, Czech Republic, in April 2010, kept the nuclear focus on the Cold War issue of reducing the nuclear strategic forces of the United States and Russia, the profound shift in the nuclear equation over the past 2 decades made this agreement more the harbinger of the end of an era than a vision of things to come for both powers. The language of the treaty stresses measures to ensure strategic stability between the two signatories, even as the global security environment has moved from bipolar, through unipolar, to an emerging multipolar system. In the case of the United States, which still sees itself as the leading global actor, the Obama administration has an ambitious program to curtail global nuclear proliferation and to seek peace and security in a world without nuclear weapons. This agenda, with its global context, does not provide a regional context to nuclear weapons, which shape Russia's position in Eurasia.

Indeed, US policy has generally framed its approach to Russia in the post-Cold War era in terms of a European security dialogue focused primarily on NATO expansion and NATO-Russian cooperation or conflict, depending upon operational circumstances defined by NATO out-of-area operations in the Balkans and Afghanistan. While new NATO members in Eastern Europe have focused on Russian threats to their territorial integrity and sovereignty in keeping with the notion of collective defense that was the heart of the alliance during the Cold War, NATO, under US leadership, has moved toward collective security with a global focus that treats Russia as another regional actor and not the core threat to international stability. Obama's reset of US-Russian relations seeks mutually advantageous cooperation in support of international stability.[1] In seeking cooperation with other regional actors, the new US National Security Strategy does not take into account the extent to which regional tensions may bring the issue of Russia's nuclear arsenal into play in local crises, which are not necessarily defined by US-Russian relations. The case of Georgia in 2008 should have highlighted the difficulties associated with stability outside of the main European framework, which became even more complex within Russia's Asian frontiers. Nor does it address the military-technical dynamic associated with advanced conventional weapons, informatization, and network-centric warfare, which is complicating the role of nuclear weapons as an instrument of theater deterrence.

In this context, Russia's nuclear arsenal remains, however, a key variable in Eurasian security. At present, that arsenal is estimated to be significantly smaller than that of the 40,000 at the end of the Cold War, but is certainly in excess of 14,000 weapons (including 3,113 strategic warheads and 2,079 nonstrategic warheads deployed and another 8,000 in storage or waiting dismantling as of 2008.)[2] A significant portion of these are stored east of the Urals and form a major component of Russia's geo-strategic posture in the non-European strategic axes that include the Caucasus, Central Asia, Siberia, the Russian Far East, and the Arctic.[3] With regard to Asian security, the nuclear weapons deployed and stored in the Siberian Federal Okrug and the Far Eastern Federal Okrug form the basis of Russia's theater nuclear forces. These forces include the nuclear weapons of the Russian Pacific Fleet, Air Force, Strategic Rocket Forces, and Army deployed there.[4] The theater role of such forces in case of armed conflict with the PRC has been candidly described by Aleksandr Khramchikhin.[5]

At present, the Russian Ministry of Defense and the General Staff are in the process of redefining those strategic axes and of reducing the number of military districts from six to four and creating operational-strategic commands in each. They include: the Western, covering Europe with its headquarters in St. Petersburg; the Southern, covering the Black Sea; the Caucasus and Caspian, with its headquarters in Rostov-on-Don; the Central, covering Central Asia, with its headquarters in Yekaterinburg; and the Eastern, covering the Far East and Pacific Ocean, with its headquarters in Khabarovsk. This concept is to be tested in conjunction with "Vostok-2010," a major exercise in Siberia and the Russian Far East scheduled for execution in late June and early July.[6] Since 1999, Russia has conducted operational-strategic exercises dealing with its Western strategic direction on a regular basis. Those exercises have included the first use of nuclear weapons to de-escalate and bring about conflict termination in a scenario involving a conventional attack upon Russia from the West by coalition forces enjoying tactical-technical qualitative superiority over Russian conventional forces. The limited nuclear strikes seemed to have been designed to disrupt command, control, communications, computers, and intelligence surveillance and reconnaissance (C4ISR) and precision strike capabilities of the aggressor forces in order to halt the attack.[7] Vostok-2010 is the first to address the Eastern strategic direction and has been associated with the implementation of the "New Look" championed by Minister of Defense Anatoly Serdiukov and Chief of the General Staff General Nikolai Makarov, as part of the transformation of the Russian military into a brigade-centric force capable of conducting advanced conventional operations and network-centric warfare.[8] As one of the Russian reformers described the "New Look," it was a gamble on the nature of the future war the Russian Army would face.[9]

The driver behind this shift in direction is not military-technological development in the West, but a deep reappraisal of the security situation in Russian Siberia and the Far East. In an article devoted to Russia's "Eastern Vector," General Makhmut Gareev pointed to the emergence of NATO as a global security organization, with a footprint in Central Asia as a result of the Afghan War and predicted rising tensions between a US-led NATO and the PRC. While he focused on NATO's nonmilitary means of exerting influence, particularly on the model of the "color revolutions" in Ukraine and Georgia that had brought regimes hostile to Russia to power, Gareev's primary focus was on the unleashing of armed conflict in regions where Russia was lacking in combat potential and especially combat readiness.[10] Gareev returned to this theme of combat readiness in a follow-on article about lessons learned from the Great Patriotic War. In addition to citing the surprise attack of Nazi Germany in 1941, Gareev pointed to the outbreak of local fighting between the Soviet Union and the PRC along the Amur River in 1969, which forced the mobilization of an entire military district. He also noted the risks involved when national political leadership did not appreciate the military-political situation they were addressing when they ordered the use of force. Gareev here drew attention to the decision to intervene militarily in Afghanistan in 1979 and the decision to intervene in Chechnya in 1994. In both Afghanistan and Chechnya, the governments blundered into wars they did not want because they failed to understand the implied tasks that followed from the initial order and failed in their political guidance to take into account the real situation on the ground. The relevance of these lessons from all four conflicts is the nature of the true connection between politics and strategy.

The final and decisive word belongs to the political leadership, but in the working out of the most important military-political decisions, military professionals and other specialists must take part; otherwise, policy will not apply to real life. The main point is that politicians and diplomats are obliged to create favorable conditions for the actions of the Armed Forces.[11]

On the issue of the "New Look," Gareev endorsed its content (i.e., the creation of its own precision strike weapons and the necessary technological base to support the conduct of network-centric warfare). At the same time, he called for the working out and implementation of more active and decisive strategies, operational art, and tactics to impose upon the enemy those actions, including contact warfare, which he most seeks to avoid.[12]

Combat readiness becomes in this regard one of the primary concerns of military professionals, since combat potential, when not linked to actual combat readiness, can create a false appreciation of the military power available. Here the nation's capacity to mobilize additional military power defines its ability to manage the escalation of a local conflict toward a decision in keeping with national interests.[13]

This is supposed to be the exact focus of Vostok-2010.[14] The "New Look" military—which the Ministry of Defense has set out to create via a brigade-base ground force capable of launching precision strikes and conducting network-centric warfare—faces a particular challenge in Siberia and the Far East, where Chinese military modernization has moved the People's Liberation Army (PLA) from a mass industrial army built to fight the people's war to a force seeking to rearm as an advanced conventional force and conduct its own version of network-centric warfare. A year ago, informed Russian defense journalists still spoke of the PLA as a mass industrial army seeking niche advanced conventional capabilities. Looking at the threat environment that was assumed to exist under Zapad 2009, defense journalist Dmitri Litovkin spoke of Russian forces confronting three distinct types of military threats:

1. An opponent armed to NATO standards in the Georgian-Russian confrontation over South Ossetia last year.

2. In the Eastern strategic direction, Russian forces would likely face a multi-million-man army with a traditional approach to the conduct of combat: linear deployments with large concentrations of manpower and firepower on a different axis.

3. In the Southern strategic direction, Russian forces expect to confront irregular forces and sabotage groups fighting a partisan war against "the organs of Federal authority" (i.e., Internal troops, the border patrol, and the Federal Security Service [FSB].)[15]

By spring of this year, a number of those involved in bringing about the "New Look" were speaking of a PLA that was moving rapidly toward a high-tech conventional force with its own understanding of network-centric warfare.[16] Moreover, the PLA conducted a major exercise, "Stride-2009," which looked like a rehearsal for military intervention against Central Asia and/or Russia to some Russian observers. PLA units engaged in strategic-operational redeployments of units from the Shenyang, Lanzhou, Jinan, and Guangzhou military commands by air and rail movement.[17] Aleksandr Khramchikhin warned in the fall of 2009 that China and its military were well on the way to becoming a real military superpower, combining numbers and advanced technology. The PLA no longer needed to go hat-in-hand to Russian defense industries for advanced weapons, but was set upon building its own in partnership with other powers. Looking at the geo-strategic situation in the Far East and Central Asia, Kramchikhin warned:

> In conclusion, I repeat once more: it is possible to assert that the leadership of the PRC and the PLA high-command are seriously considering the possibility of conducting in the foreseeable future offensive actions against Russia and the states of Central Asia. To some degree precisely such a scenario of war is considered the most probable. At the same time operations for the forceful seizure of Taiwan have been removed from the order of the day.[18]

Speaking of the deployment of two newly organized brigades along the Russian-Chinese border on the Irkutsk-Chita Axis, Lieutenant-General Vladimir Valentinovich Chirkin, the recently appointed commander of the Siberian Military District, stated that the brigades were deployed there to counter the presence of five PLA combined-arms armies across the border. From 2003 to 2007, Chirkin commanded an army in the Siberian military district. On the rationale for the deployment, Chirkin stated: "We are obligated to keep troops there because on the other side of the order are five Chinese armies and we cannot ignore that operational direction." He added that the Ministry of Defense intended to develop an army headquarters for command and control of the brigades.[19] In a related report, Chirkin described the PLA forces across the border as composed of three divisions and 10 tank, mechanized, and infantry brigades—which he described as not little but also "not a strike force." As to the role of the new brigades, Chirkin put them as part of a deterrent force aimed as a friendly reminder to the PRC: ". . . despite the friendly relations with China our army command understands that friendship is possible only with strong countries, that is whose (sic) who can quiet a friend down with a conventional or nuclear club."[20]

The gamble on the nature of future war described by Kondrat'ev in supporting the development of network-centric warfare capabilities comes down to the issue of Russia's capacity to arm, create, train, deploy, and keep combat-ready forces capable of conducting advanced conventional warfare. In the absence of such forces, the deterrence equation is reduced to the credibility of the nuclear option in deterring conventional attacks. Given the economic and demographic realities of Siberia and the Russian Far East, Russia seeks, by nonmilitary means, to preclude the emergence of a Chinese military threat. However, Russian observers also are aware of the fact that an imminent military threat from Beijing can emerge out of regional instability, which is beyond Russia's unilateral means to control. As the most recent Russian Military Doctrine of 2010 states, nuclear weapons remain the primary instrument of deterrence against both nuclear and conventional attacks upon Russia and in defense of Russian interests, territorial integrity, and sovereignty.[21] The doctrine does not explicitly state that Russia will use nuclear weapons in preemptive attacks against such threats, as had been discussed by senior members of the Security Council in the Fall of 2009, but leaves the decision to use such weapons in the hands of the President of the Russian Federation. The context of use, however, is defined by the nature of the challenges and threats that Russia faces across Eurasia.

A second classified document, "The Foundations of State Policy in the Area of Nuclear Deterrence to 2020," issued at the same time as the Military Doctrine, has had portions leaked to the mass media. These describe two types of threats that could lead to the use of nuclear weapons: 1) attacks upon vital economic and political structures, early warning systems, national command and control, and nuclear weapons systems, which fit a US-led NATO threat involving conventional forces capable of conducting global strikes against such targets; and 2) during an invasion by an enemy's ground units onto its territory if Russia's Armed Forces do not manage to stop their progress deep into the country through conventional means of making war, which fits more closely with an assault by the PLA against the Russian Far East.[22]

The first concept resembles one popularized by General-Major Vladimir Slipchenko in his discussions of sixth-generation warfare and no-contact warfare on the model of NATO's campaign against Kosovo but applied on a global scale.[23] The second concept, which was not contained in the 2000 version of Russian military doctrine, is quite new and reflects what the Russian military recognizes is an emerging threat from the PRC. Relying upon nuclear deterrence in such a conflict with China is not considered by some Russian military observers to be a viable course of action. Khramchikhin has engaged in a debate with Aleksei Arbatov, one of Russia's most respected commentators on nuclear issues and a strong believer in the continued utility of nuclear deterrence—even in the face of the spread of advanced conventional capabilities.

Khramchikhin's answer has been to call nuclear deterrence an illusion. The illusion arises from Russia's general weakness in conventional forces, its limited mobility to support forces in distant frontiers, and the inapplicability of nuclear strikes to resolve limited conflicts over border issues. Advanced conventional capabilities will soon make possible global conventional strikes with the effects of nuclear weapons. In the case of China, Khramchikhin argues that there is a great need to protect Siberia and the Far East as key sources of critical raw materials and energy for the future development of the country, but demographic weakness, obsolete infrastructure, and weak conventional forces make that task nearly impossible, and nuclear deterrence in this context is a shallow hope. Khramchikhin leaves one with the impression that the situation confronting Russia in the Far East is not too different from that confronting Pakistan in the case of India's development of advanced conventional capabilities to strike toward Islamabad. In neither case does nuclear retaliation become a solution for slowly mobilizing conventional forces in the hands of a more developed and more populous opponent.[24]

Facing West and East

For Russia, which inherited the Soviet nuclear arsenal but has faced a serious change in its international position, the nuclear equation is, in fact, shaped by Russia's status as a regional power in a complex Eurasian security environment. The nuclear issues in that environment are not defined exclusively by the US-Russian strategic nuclear equation but by security dynamics involving interactions with Russia's immediate periphery. On the one hand, Russia's security responses have been shaped by a post-Soviet decade of sharp internal political crises, economic transformation, social instability, demographic decline, and the collapse of conventional military power. The impact of these developments has been uneven across Russia, leading to very distinct security environments that have demanded regional responses. The initial focus of security concerns for both the Soviet Union and the Russian Federation was primarily upon European security. This was the primary focus of the US-Soviet strategic competition and the place where its militarization was most evident.

The end of the Cold War began with the attempt to reform the Soviet system under Mikhail Gorbachev by means of Perestroika and Glasnost; this effort embraced the idea of getting time and space for reform by removing the ideological roots of East-West confrontation from Europe. As presented by Aleksandr Yakovlev, one of Gorbachev's key advisors, the policy involved the removal of the primary driver of the East-West conflict—the military confrontation between NATO and the Warsaw Treaty Organization.[25] Demilitarization of the Cold War in Europe and Soviet military disengagement from international conflicts, especially Afghanistan, were part of an effort to save a system that had lost the capacity to innovate and survived on the basis of bureaucratic inertia and coercion. Reform risked both domestic and international complications.[26] In Europe, the first real indicator of successful demilitarization was the Intermediate Range Nuclear Forces (INF) Treaty of 1987, which abolished entire classes of intermediate-range nuclear forces with operational-strategic impact on the European theater. This treaty was followed by moves under the Organization for Security and Cooperation in Europe (OSCE) toward greater military transparency, and consummated by the Conventional Forces in Europe Treaty of 1990—setting limits on forward-deployed conventional forces in Central Europe and on its flanks from the Atlantic to the Urals.[27]

Political developments, however, made this security regime obsolete when the Velvet Revolutions of 1989 replaced governments allied with the Soviet Union and led to the abolition of the Warsaw Treaty Organization in December 1991. In the meantime, political discontent and rising nationalism within the Union of Soviet Socialist Republics (USSR) undermined Gorbachev's program of gradual reform, and led to a confrontation between hardliners opposed to further reform and nationalists calling for both the abolition of Soviet power and the end of the Soviet Union. Boris Yeltsin, elected President of the Russian Soviet Federative Socialist Republic (RSFSR) in June 1991, became the spokesman for national democratic opposition to the existing Soviet order. The attempted coup by hardliners in August 1991 failed, and Yeltsin emerged as leader of a Russian Federation that was willing to see the Soviet Union abolished, which occurred on December 31, 1991. In a matter of months, the Cold War's bilateral international system had shifted to a unipolar order dominated by a US-led Atlantic-European community. The Russian Federation found itself dealing with the dismemberment of the Soviet Union. It also had to deal with the regathering of the Soviet nuclear arsenal under its control and the prevention of the proliferation of nuclear weapons, fissionable materials, and nuclear weapons expertise—a policy supported by the George Bush and Bill Clinton administrations. Hope of a strategic partnership, which flourished in Washington and Moscow in the early 1990s, was cooling by the second half of the decade.

On the other hand, the emergence of the United States as the sole superpower brought about a distinct complication in Russia's responses to these regional issues and led to efforts to cultivate the creation of a multipolar counterbalance to US influence. As framed by Foreign Minister Evgenii Primakov, the new order was supposed to rest on cooperation among Moscow, Beijing, and New Delhi to balance Washington's global influence. Neither New Delhi nor Beijing endorsed a policy of trilateral balancing, but Moscow and Beijing did move toward a de facto security system with the signing of the five-power Treaty on Deepening Military Trust in Border Regions in 1996. The agreement, a part of the relaxation of tensions associated with the end of the Cold War, was seen in Moscow as the foundation for balancing in a relatively benign environment in Central Asia and the Far East. Russia embraced arms sales to the PRC as a desperate measure to keep its own military-industrial complex from complete collapse. In the absence of domestic orders, foreign sales kept design bureaus and production facilities operational. A case in point was the 1992 sale of Su-27M fighters to the PRC, which kept the design bureau in Moscow and the production plant at Komsomosk-na-Amure open.[28] Russia did not see the PRC as an immediate military threat, was interested in reducing its own forces deployed in the Far East, and was most concerned with averting the total collapse of its defense industry. Primakov's vision of a trilateral balancing mechanism among Moscow, Beijing, and New Delhi did not depend upon arms sales but provided geopolitical justification for such sales to China and India. His vision had assumed relatively stable and benign relations among all three actors.[29]

The Vladimir Putin decade of recovery, which began in 1999 and still continues under the Medvedev-Putin Tandem, was marked by a significant economic recovery, internal stability, state recentralization, and, until very recently, only marginal improvements in conventional military power. For much of the decade, favorable oil and gas prices allowed Russia to practice Putin's own brand of energy diplomacy across Eurasia by cultivating supplier-consumer relations with major powers, while exercising energy discipline on states on its own periphery.[30] The decade began with a fundamental shift in the content of the Russian security relationship in Asia. The point of departure was the disillusionment with Euro-Atlantic engagement after NATO expansion and the NATO-conducted air campaign against Yugoslavia that occurred in the face of Russia's vigorous objections to military actions undertaken without a mandate from the UN Security Council. At the same time, deteriorating security in the Caucasus and Central Asia invoked the need to create a new security regime to cover Asiatic Russia.[31] On the one hand, renewed war in Chechnya raised the prospect of increased involvement by radical Islamic elements there and across the Caucasus. In Central Asia, the spread of Islamic radicalism by the Taliban out of Afghanistan had called into question the existing security structures provided by the Commonwealth of Independent States. Russia, which had intervened in the Tajik civil war of 1992-97 and helped the United States to broker a peace settlement there, now found itself faced by a more general regional Islamic threat that had actually helped to drive the opposing Tajik factions into cooperation.

That threat was the spread of jihad from Afghanistan into Central Asia. The PRC, which faced its own Islamic separatist threat among the Uyghur population that made up plurality of the population in Xinjiang—China's frontier region with Central Asia—had its own reasons to support collective security arrangements in the late 1990s. In this context, in 2001, Russia joined with four other Central Asian states (Kazakhstan, Kyrgyzstan, Tajikistan, and Uzbekistan) and China to form the Shanghai Cooperation Organization (SCO), with an expressed mandate to cooperate against "terrorism, separatism and extremism."[32] In addition to this regional security function, the SCO also became a vehicle for Moscow and Beijing to express their concerns over US hegemony in the international system and to create a counterweight to NATO—as the Alliance moved more actively into out-of-area operations affecting Central Asia, especially after its intervention into Afghanistan and the US development of bases in the region, especially Uzbekistan and Kyrgyzstan. The tensions became particularly acute after the US intervention in Iraq, when it appeared that the United States was planning for a long-term presence in both Iraq and Afghanistan. The acquisitions of nuclear weapons by India and Pakistan in 1998 had intensified the India-Pakistan conflict and brought with it the possibility of a new "great game" in Central and South Asia, played by nuclear-armed states and increasing tensions among Moscow, Beijing, and New Delhi—with the United States and NATO directly engaged in Afghanistan.[33]

For most of the decade, Russian official literature on foreign policy, national security strategy, and military doctrine focused upon the United States and NATO as the chief sources of challenges and threats to Russian national security, with secondary attention given to internal sources of instability (extremism and separatism) and to international terrorism. This official position masked what were developing concerns regarding the security of Russia's own Eastern Siberian and Far Eastern domains. Those security concerns are rooted in Russia's historical experience with this distant and relatively isolated territory.

Russian Cossacks pushed across Siberia and into the Far East by the mid-17th century and planted a network of settlements spread across the vast region's tundra and taiga. These remote lands were weakly governed into the early-19th century, because the distance from Moscow and St. Petersburg by land and sea was so vast. It fell to the Russian Navy to maintain a nominal presence in the Far East and Alaska (Little Russia) to enforce Russian territorial claims.[34] Imperial retrenchment after the Crimean War led to the sale of Alaska, as Russia pressed its claims on the Asian mainland at the expense of China and Japan.[35] The integration of these regions into Imperial Russia took a quantum leap in the last decade of the 19th century, with the construction of the Trans-Siberian railroad under the leadership of Minister of Finance Sergei Witte. Witte saw the railroad as the key to the Russian development of Siberia and to access to the China market. However, before those benefits could be reaped, Russia found itself drawn into imperial rivalries over Manchuria and Korea, leading to war with Japan and defeat. During the war, the railroad became the chief means of Russian strategic mobility and underscored the need for the development of more infrastructures in Eastern Siberia and the Far East. But the tsarist regime collapsed in the course of another war, and foreign powers (the United States and Japan) found it easy to intervene there during the Russian civil war, which followed the Bolshevik seizure of power and the decision to make peace with the Central Powers. Bolshevik power was slow to consolidate its control in the Far East, which did not come until 1922—when the Japanese military withdrew, and the Far Eastern Republic, which had served as a buffer between Soviet territory and the Japanese zone of occupation, was abolished. Under Joseph Stalin, there was a major effort at developing the Soviet Far East, which included mobilization of Komsomol (young communist) cadre to set up new settlements and the creation of vast mining and forestry projects under the People's Commissariat of Internal Affairs (NKVD) and composing islands in the Gulag archipelago.[36]

After the Japanese occupation of Manchuria in 1931, intensive efforts were made to strengthen the defenses of the Soviet Far East and the Mongolian People's Republic, an ally of the Soviet Union from its establishment in 1924. Soviet forces fought two limited border engagements with the Japanese Kwantung Army: in 1938, at Lake Khasan, near Vladivostok, and at Khalkhin-Gol in the Manchukou-Mongolian border, in 1939. During World War II, the Soviet Far East was the arrival point for Lend-Lease materials from the United States shipped on Soviet-flagged ships. It served as the staging area for the Soviet offensive of August 1945, which announced the Soviet entry into the war against Japan and led to the Soviet occupation of Manchuria and North Korea and the seizure from Japan of southern Sakhalin and the

Kurile Islands. In both Manchuria and North Korea, the Soviet military presence facilitated the establishment of local communist regimes. In the postwar period, the Soviet Far East continued to be a major part of the Gulag until Stalin's death and the dismantling of the camp system. During the Cold War, the Soviet Far East was the staging area for support to North Korean and Chinese Communist forces engaged in the Korean War. With the emergence of the Sino-Soviet conflict, and especially after the border incidents with China in 1969, the Far East became a military bastion, which it remained until the collapse of the USSR.[37]

By the 1980s, Siberia and the Far East suffered from some of the worst environmental pollution in the world. W. Bruce Lincoln described it in the following terms:

> Everywhere, Siberia's Soviet masters had transformed the fragile ecology of tundra and taiga that for tens of thousands of years boasted some of the planet's purest water, air and soil into some of the most noxious surroundings on earth.[38]

In the decade that followed the collapse of the USSR, Siberia and the Russian Far East experienced ecological crisis, demographic decline, and economic collapse, from which it began a slow recovery. The region has faced a persistent energy crisis, and rising criminality and corruption. Tensions between Moscow and the Far East grew sharp, with the global economic downturn and the decline in world energy prices in 2008. Moscow sought to impose a tariff on imported automobiles to increase purchases of domestic products and threatened automobile imports, which had become a thriving business in Vladivostok and the other Far Eastern port cities. In December 2008, local protestors took to the streets under the slogan: "Authorities: Raise the Standard of Living, not the Tariff." They were met by Russian Ministry of Internal Affairs (MVD) riot police sent from Moscow to restore order by applying their batons to the demonstrators' bodies.[39]

Many of these problems were a legacy of the collapse of the Soviet system, which had treated those regions as colonies for extractive industries and as forward bastions of its security. This had been the case throughout the Stalin era, during the Cold War, and during the decades of Sino-Soviet conflict, especially after the border incidents of 1969 and the deterioration of relations with the PRC. Moscow had invested heavily in maintaining a military presence and infrastructure in the region by intensive investment, including the Baikal-Amur Magistral (Mainline), which was to provide a deeper transportation infrastructure away from the Chinese border to give the region strategic depth for defense but was never completed. With the collapse of the Soviet Union, that military infrastructure was allowed to decay, since Moscow had no resources to fund it and saw conciliation with Beijing to be to its advantage.

In the absence of continuing investment credits, Moscow granted the regions local self-government and looked to economic transformation on the basis of international trade to revive the area. There was much hope expressed in Moscow that Japanese capital, Chinese workers, and Russian raw materials would make the Russian Far East into a part of the dynamic Asia-Pacific economy. Instead, the Far East saw a radical decline in population (7.9 million in 1989) and economic activity, leading to a total population in the Far East of 6.7 million by the 2002 census and making the region one of the most underpopulated regions in the world in terms of persons per square mile. In fact, however, most of the population in the Russian Far East is concentrated in a 90-mile belt of settlement—from Chita in the West to Vladivostok on the Pacific with the Trans-Siberian Railroad providing the single corridor for transregional transportation through it. Russia did move to resolve border disputes with the PRC under President Yeltsin, which led to a general settlement in 1995 but left the settlement of conflicting claims over certain strategic islands in the areas of Chita and Khabarovsk unresolved. In 2005, these issues were resolved, with the transfer of about half the disputed territory to China. In spite of the fact that the islands near Khabarovsk were directly across from this major Russian city and defense center, military authorities downplayed any military threat to the city, although the Border Guards did express concern about possible illegal immigration.[40] In the general climate of improved Sino-Russian relations no military threat seemed to exist, and when security concerns did emerge in the last few years, they were not spoken about officially.

There were, of course, all sorts of concerns about illegal Chinese settlers coming into the Far East. Viktor Ishaev, the Governor of Khabarovsk Krai from 1991 to 2009, repeatedly raised the issue of Chinese migration into the region as part of a plan for the "peaceful capture" of the Russian Far East.[41] But, unlike under Yeltsin, a stronger central government was able to keep local problems and perceptions from impacting the conduct of bilateral relations. Likewise, on nuclear issues, if the great concern had been regionalism and the actions of local officials with regard to supporting and protecting the existing nuclear infrastructure from decay, criminal penetration, and incompetent management in the 1990s when the center was weak, under Putin the center re-established control and co-opted local political leaders to its interests—reducing the risks of crisis between the center and the Far Eastern periphery.[42]

Putin's strategy, which has continued under President Medvedev, was to seek to bring about the economic integration of Russia into the global economic processes that have turned Asia into an engine of globalization. Russia has formally engaged with regional organizations such as the Asia-Pacific Economic Council (APEC), which it joined in 1998, and fostered a partnership relationship with the Association of Southeast Asian Nations (ASEAN). In the Far East, Russia's primary gamble was on the prospect of good relations with China. Up to 2009, China was consistently described as Russia's strategic partner and the primary engine of Asia's economic transformation and growing global influence. Russia was to serve as a source of advanced military technology and raw materials and provide China with a stable rear supporting its international position.[43] No mention of China as a strategic threat came from official sources, although commentators might worry about a "yellow peril" of Chinese settlers into the Far East or complain of Chinese goods driving out domestic products in local markets. Konstantin Pulikovsky, a former general and President Putin's envoy to the Far Eastern Federal Okrug from 2000 to 2009, spoke of Chinese investment as vital to the future of the region.[44] In 2009, the Russian military still published articles that addressed China's economic progress as a "savior to Russia."[45] This changed shortly thereafter. China's rise as a major military power set off alarms among civilian commentators, who now spoke of Russia's "nearest neighbor" as an emerging military super power.[46]

Russia's residual influence in North Korea had declined rapidly after the collapse of the Soviet Union, as the issue of North Korean nuclear weapons development emerged. In 2000, President Putin invited Kim Jong Il to visit Russia, which he did in the summer of 2000. Pulikovsky, who accompanied Kim on his rail trip to Moscow, became the Russian official with the closest ties to Kim Jong Il and appreciated both the importance of North Korea to Russia's own security interests and China's strongest influence in Pyongyang.[47] After Kim Jong Il's visit to Russia in 2000, some spoke of the personal ties between Kim and President Putin as redefining Russian-North Korean relations, but developments over the rest of the decade confirmed China's greater access and influence during the Six Party Talks over North Korea's nuclear program. Russia's approach to that ongoing crisis has been to support its legitimate security interests in Northeast Asia via preserving peace and stability on the Korean Peninsula.[48] In this capacity, Russia has engaged in the Six Party Talks. Russia could and did develop economic ties with South Korea over the last 2 decades while it kept its limited influence in North Korea.

This balance has been evident in Moscow's approach to the crisis set off by the sinking of the South Korean patrol corvette, the Cheonan, by an acoustic torpedo—which an international investigation, carried out by US and Australian experts, concluded was fired by North Korean forces.[49] Moscow most wants to avoid a regional crisis becoming (or escalating into) an armed conflict and inviting the intervention of other powers, especially the United States and the PRC, in support of South and North Korea. What concerns Russian observers is the real cause for the current war scare between North and South Korea. They see the situation as driven by the increasingly desperate situation in the North and its leadership's inclination to use "threats"—including ones that risk creating real casus belli by the unprovoked sinking of another nation's warship, even if a de facto state of war has existed for decades between the two states. North Korea depends on the Republic of Korea to feed its own population, and in its isolation strikes out, conveying to the outside world its own inability to deal with its internal crisis. The logic of war exists, but it will not serve the political ends of any power.[50]

Over the last 2 decades, Russia has looked to Japanese investment, even in the face of the lack of progress in resolving the territorial dispute over the Kurile Islands, which had kept Japanese-Soviet and now Japanese-Russian relations frozen; the Soviet Union and then Russia offered a two-of-four split of the island chain—with Russia retaining the northern and Japan getting the southern half. Japan demanded the return of all four islands, which Russia refused. Russian energy diplomacy under Putin favored Chinese interests over Japanese ones. Realists in Moscow saw no major movement in Tokyo's security regime with Washington and simply gave a lower priority to the improvement of bilateral political relations, even though Moscow continued to court Japanese investors in the Russian Far East. Border incidents and disputes over fishing rights led to periodic flare-ups but no major crisis, so Moscow was willing to keep its policy toward Japan in line with that of Beijing. Moscow supported the Six Party talks, but with the clear understanding that Beijing had the best leverage with Pyongyang. Moscow supported counterproliferation initiatives, but has worried that US impatience and/or North Korea provocations could lead to war and greater instability in Northeast Asia and even risk a Sino-American confrontation. The Russian concern about Sino-American conflict rises in conjunction with the two major points of contention between the two powers: Taiwan and the Korean Peninsula. The concerns have become greater as the conduct of the North Korean regime has become more erratic.

This historical digression, like Leo Tolstoy's comments on the laws of war in War and Peace, may try the patience of those readers who see nuclear weapons in isolation from the tensions and contradictions that could lead to their employment. In the case of the Russian Far East, the historical narrative makes manifest the relative isolation of the region from European Russia, and its relative weakness in the context of a dynamic Asia that is in the process of becoming a global economic and political center of gravity. Russia cannot and has not ignored this development. Post-Cold War development of Russian grand strategy has moved from Euro-centric to Eurasian-centric, with a distinct emphasis upon its "near abroad." This has brought about a distinct set of adjustments in the nuclear weapons within that strategy.

Russia's Ambiguous Asian Nuclear Future

Strategic nuclear weapons loomed very large in the Yeltsin era, when the strategic arsenal was expected to play a major political role in ensuring Russia a strategic partnership with the United States and a major say in the emerging post-Cold War order in Europe. Since 1999, Russia has emphasized the deterrent function of its strategic nuclear forces but has focused its posture on conflict management to discourage military intervention on Russia's periphery. The Russian military has for 2 decades placed the likelihood of nuclear war at a very low level and even seen the possibility of a general, coalition war at a low probability. That said, the Russian government has also recognized that its immediate periphery is quite unstable, fraught with local conflicts that can turn into local wars and lead to foreign military interventions against the national interests, territorial integrity, and sovereignty of Russia. The question of the "near abroad"—a euphemism for the independent states that emerged on Russia's periphery with the breakup of the USSR—has been closely tied to Russian national interests, a Russian sphere of influence, and the protection of Russian minorities living in the successor states. Russian intervention in ethnic conflicts in this region has been seen in the West as one of the central areas of conflict with Russia, especially in the aftermath of the Russo-Georgian War in August 2008.[51] For Russian leaders, the Russo-Georgian conflict revealed a number of problems associated with command and control of modern conventional forces, especially the integration of air-land combat, which became a driver for the Ministry of Defense's "New Look."[52] At the same time, however, Chinese military modernization made the gamble on strategic partnership less inviting, if China was intent upon developing large-scale theater warfare capabilities embracing advanced conventional weapons and network-centric operations. The default military gamble of nonstrategic nuclear forces to deter a remote Chinese threat became less appealing.

Thus, in June and July, the Russian Military Defense and General Staff will conduct Vostok-2010—with the intent of assessing Russia's capacity to mobilize and deploy its "New Look" conventional forces to defeat a military intervention against the Russian Far East—and will test both the combat capabilities and combat readiness of these forces to deal with that threat.[53] The outcome of that exercise will be a major test for the "New Look" and will define the role of theater nuclear forces in the Far East—whether they will remain the response of necessity or become a true second-order response, giving Moscow the capacity to manage such a conflict to a political solution that does not put into risk the territorial integrity of Russia or its survival as a sovereign state.

Much will depend upon Russia's capacity to rearm its forces with advanced conventional capabilities—which will depend on the adaptability of its military-industrial complex and on its capacity to escape its relative geo-strategic isolation in the Far East if relations with China should deteriorate. In recent articles, Aleksandr Khramchikhin raised two issues that make this problem particularly difficult. First, he did a strategic assessment of the threats faced by Russia on all strategic axes and then examined the military capabilities available to deal with them. He noted conventional military deficiencies in the West, the South, and the North, but said that Russia's defenses in the East were clearly the weakest of all. In this, he included the defenses covering Sakhalin and the Kuril Islands, but focused on the Sino-Russian border in Siberia and the Far East. There, Khramchikhin described Russia as effectively defenseless against Chinese aggression. Against a massive array of PLA conventional ground and air forces, the Siberian and Far Eastern military districts contain only one tank; eight motorized rifles; two air-assault, three missile, four artillery, two rocket-artillery, one covering, and four air-defense brigades; and about 300 combat aircraft, with their bases located close to the border. China has a much greater capacity to reinforce its units in the theater by rail movement, while Russia must face the fact that the Trans-Siberian railroad is vulnerable to air interdiction in Siberia and direct attack in the Far East.[54] The second point is concerned with the conduct of Russian policy in the context of military weakness, in which Russia invites confrontations with the United States even as it faces threats on other axes—on which its very weakness provokes the emergence of new threats.[55]

The new tenor of relations between Moscow and Beijing was evident at the recent SCO Summit in Tashkent, where Moscow and Beijing discretely jockeyed for position. Moscow has put greater emphasis on security in Central Asia and has revived military cooperation with Kazakhstan, Kyrgyzstan, Tajikistan, and Uzbekistan under the Cooperative Security Treaty Organization, just as joint military exercises under the SCO have declined since 2007. China has emphasized economic penetration via investment and follows a coherent long-range policy of regional integration with China's economy. James Nixey of Chatham House commented on the recent summit, saying that between the lines Russia now recognizes China as a major security concern but is unwilling to say so openly.[56] Moreover, the threat is not just to Central Asia. Tensions between Russia and China have mounted over the Russian Far East. Press reports, citing sources in the Russian Border Guards, speak of Chinese efforts to dredge the Ussuri near Khabarovsk and change the navigational challenge to China's advantage in order to get additional territory ceded to China.[57]

Such incidents are not the real challenge to Russian sovereignty over its Far Eastern territories. The real challenge is to be found in the very contradictory claims about the Far East coming out of Moscow, where some see the region as the economic engine and source of raw materials to pull Russia into the 21st century, while others see a region as already lost to the country as a de facto part of the Chinese economy. Dr. Viktor Larin, Director of the Institute of History, Archeology, and Ethnography of the Peoples of the Far East, took these conflicting opinions as the point of departure for a major analytical report on "The Asia-Pacific Region in the Early 21st Century: Challenges, Threats, and Chances of Pacific-Ocean Russia." Colleagues saw this piece as an intellectual provocation and an invitation for reflection on the current situation. Larin is skeptical about Russian government declarations regarding investment in the region and questions its willingness to sustain such investments in the region's oil, gas, and transportation infrastructure. He notes that there is nothing inevitable about a Russian presence in the Far East. Other European colonial powers have failed to keep their Asian empires. Why should Russia be any different? Over the last 2 decades, government programs and foreign investments have not led to improvements in the lives of local population—Larin cites oil and gas development in Sakhalin as an example. Russia is still really on the margins of the emerging Asia-Pacific economy. Larin says that the center talks about investment in the Far East because it fears that it will lose the region. Moscow is motivated by external threats, but the real problem is that the remaining population in the region has no stake in its future with Russia. Looking back 15 years, Russians spoke of a "yellow peril" from Chinese immigration, but that is not the case today. The real Chinese presence today is in the pervasive economic presence across the markets for consumer goods and food stuffs. Russia missed the train to European economic integration and is likely to miss the Asian train as well. If Moscow does not stop thinking of the Far East as a colony to be milked and start thinking about it as a fully integrated part of the Russian and Asian-Pacific economies, it will, at some time in the not-too-distant future, face the real threat of separatism. The Soviet answer of treating the Far East as a military bastion has no prospect of success.[58]

These developments may fundamentally shift the geo-strategic context of President Obama's global zero initiative on nuclear weapons. For the last 2 decades, Russia's nuclear arsenal in Asia was seen internationally as a problem of management and control as it declined in size and operational readiness. Operationally, even in its reduced capacity, this arsenal was for Russia the only military option open in case of attack in a region effectively denuded of conventional military power. China's relative military inferiority made that prospect remote. Both Moscow and Beijing could look to strategic partnership without the prospect of an emerging military threat. Chinese military modernization has in the last year changed that perception in Moscow. Now, with the emergence of a potential conventional threat from its former strategic partner, Russia is in the process of evaluating whether its reformed conventional forces might achieve a viable deterrence in case of attack from a modernized Chinese military. In the absence of such a capability, Russia will be forced to gamble even more on theater nuclear forces and be even less willing to consider reductions in its nonstrategic nuclear forces. In the context of an increasing military confrontation on the Korean peninsula and periodic tensions between Washington and Beijing over Taiwan, Russia's increased fears of China's growing power and its military response add one further complication to Eurasian security for all parties and make Asian nuclear force reductions an even more complex problem for Washington to manage.

Endnotes

1. *The National Security Strategy of the United States*, Washington, DC: The White House, May 27, 2010, p. 44, available from *www.whitehouse.gov/sites/default/files/rss_viewer/national_security_strategy.pdf.*

2. Robert S. Norris and Hans S. Kristensen, "Russian Nuclear Forces, 2008," *Bulletin of the Atomic Scientists*, Vol. 64, No. 2, May-June 2008, pp. 54-57, 62.

3. Iurii Mikhailov, "Sistema ugroz bezopasnosti Rossiiskoi Federatsii in ee obespechenie" ("System Security Threats to the Russian Federation and its Software"), *Orientir* (*Landmark*), No. 5, May 2010, pp. 49-52.

4. On the facilities in these two okrugs, see the two chapters by Christina Chuen and Dmitry Kovchegin in James Clay Moltz, Vladimir A. Orlov, and Adam M. Stulberg, eds., *Preventing Nuclear Meltdown: Managing Decentralization of Russia's Nuclear Complex,* Aldershot, United Kingdom (UK), and Burlington, VT: Ashgate, 2004, pp. 105-134, 184-210.

5. Aleksandr Khramchikhin, "Neadekvatnyi vostok" ("Inadequate East"), *Nezavisimoe voennoe obozrenie (Independent Military Review),* July 27, 2010.

6. "The Quantity of Military Districts in Russia Will Be Reduced from Six to Four by December 1 and Operational Strategic Commands Will Be Formed," *Defense & Security Analysis,* May 31, 2010.

7. Jacob W. Kipp, "Russian Non-strategic Nuclear Weapons," *Military Review*, Vol. 81, No. 3, May-June 2001, pp. 27-38.

8. Aleksei Nikolsky, "Assessment of the East," *Vedomosti* (*Knowledge),* March 9, 2010, p. 2. On the "New Look" as a gamble on advanced technology and network-centric warfare, see Aleksandr Kondrat'ev, "Stavka na 'voiny budushchego" ("Bet on the War of the Future"), *Nezvasimoe voennoe obozrenie* (*Independent Military Review),* June 27, 2008.

9. *Ibid.*

10. Gennadii Miranovich, "Vostochnyi vektor" ("Eastern Vector"), *Krasnaia zvezda (Red Star),* March 3, 2010.

11. Makhmut Gareev, "Opyt pobeditelei v Velikoi voine ne mozhet ustaret" ("The Experience of the Winners of the Great War Cannot Be Obsolete"), *Nezavisimoe voennoe obozrenie (Independent Military Review),* March 9, 2010.

12. *Ibid.*

13. *Ibid.*

14. Alesksei Nikolsky, "Otsenku dast 'Vostok'" ("Assessment of the East"), *Vedomosti* (*Knowledge),* March 9, 2010.

15. Dmitri Litovkin, "Ucheniia popali v seti" ("The Teachings Come from the Network"), *Izvestiia* (*News*), September 28, 2009.

16. A. Kondrat'ev, "Nekotorye osobennosti realizatsii kontseptsii 'setetsentricheskaia voina' v vooruzhennykh silakh KNR" ("Some Features of the Concept of 'Network-centric Warefare'—in the Armed Forces of China"), *Zarubezhnoe voennoe obozrenie (Foreign Military Review),* No. 3, March 2010, pp. 11-17.

17. "Ucheniya" (Exercises), *Zarubezhnoe voennoe obozrenie (Foreign Military Review)*, No. 8, July 31, 2009; and Aleksandr Khram-

chikhin, "Starye osnovy novoi doktriny" ("The Old Foundations of a New Doctrine"), *Voyenno-Promyshlennyy Kuryer (Military-Industrial Courier),* Bo. 6, February 17, 2010, p. 5.

18. Aleksandr Khramchikhin, "Milliony soldat plius sovremennoe vooruzhenie" ("Millions of Soldiers, plus Modern Weapons"), *Nezavisimoe voennoe obozrenie (Independent Military Review)*, October 9, 2009.

19. "Novosti" ("News"), *VPK-Voennopromyshlennyi kurer* (*Military Industrial Courier*), Vol. 3, March 3, 2010.

20. "Russia Strengthens the Border with China," *Argumenty nedeli (Arguments of the Week),* March 4-10, 2010.

21. Prezident Rossii, *Voennaia doktrina Rossiiskoi Federatsi (Military Doctrine of the Russian Federation)*, February 5, 2010.

22. Vladimir Mokhov, "Osnovy natsional'noi bezopashosti" ("Fundamentals of National Security"), *Kasnaia zvezda (Red Star)*, February 6, 2010.

23. V. I. Slipchnko, *Voina budushchego (The War of the Future)*, Moscow, Russia: Izdetl'skii sentr nauchnykh i uchebnykh programm (Publishing Center of Scientific and Educational Programs), 1999; and V. I. Slipchenko, *Beskontaktnye voiny (Contactless War),* Moscow, Russia: Gran-Press, 2001. On the debate between Slipchenko and Makhmut Gareev over the prospects of "no-contact war" vs. mass mobilization advanced conventional war with ground forces, see Makhut Gareev and Vladimir Slipchenko, *Future War,* Ft. Leavenworth, KS: Foreign Military Studies Office, 2007.

24. Aleksandr Khramchikhin, "Illiuziia iadernogo sderzhivaniia" ("Illusion of Nuclear Deterrence"), *VPK Voenno-promyshlennyi kur'er (VPK Military-Industrial Courier)*, Vol. 24, March 24, 2010.

25. Christopher Shulgan, *The Soviet Ambassador: The Making of the Radical Behind Perestroika*, London, UK: McClelland and Stewart, 2008.

26. Jacob W. Kipp. "Perestroyka and Poryadok [Order]: Alternative Futures and Their Impact on the Soviet Military," *Military Review*, No. 12, December 1989, pp. 2-16.

27. George L. Rueckert, *Global Double Zero: The INF Treaty From Its Origins to Implementation*, Westport, CT: Greenwood Press, 1993; John Borawski, *From the Atlantic to the Urals: Negotiating Arms Control at the Stockholm Conference,* Washington, DC: Pergamon-Brassey International Defense Publishers, 1988; Ivo H. Daalder, *The CFE Treaty: An Overview and an Assessment,* Washington, DC: The Johns Hopkins Foreign Policy Institute, 1991; and Michael R. Beschloss and Strobe Talbott, *At the Highest Levels: The Inside Story of the End of the Cold War,* Boston, MA: Little, Brown, and Company, 1993.

28. V. Usol'tsev, "'Golubye molnii' i Rosssiiskie letchiki edut v Kitai"("'Blue Lightning' and Russian Pilots go to China"), *Krasnaia zvezda (Red Star)*, April 11, 1992.

29. R. Weitz, "The Shanghai Cooperation Organization: The Primakov Vision and Central Asian Realities," *Fletcher Forum of World Affairs,* Vol. 31, No. 1, 2007, pp. 103-118.

30. Marshall I. Goldman, *Petrostate: Putin, Power and the New Russia,* New York: Oxford University Press, 2008.

31. Roy Allison and Lena Jonson, eds., *Central Asian Security,* London, UK: Royal Institute of International Affairs, 2001.

32. "Shanghai Cooperation Organization Charter," *China Daily*, June 12, 2006, available from *www.chinadaily.com.cn/china/2006-06/12/content_614628.htm*.

33. Feroz Hassan Khan, "The New Great Game in Central Asia/South Asia: Continuity and Change," in Charles Hawkins and Robert L. Love, eds., *The New Great Game: Chinese Views on Central Asia,* Ft. Leavenworth, KS: Foreign Military Studies Office, 2006, pp. 1-16.

34. W. Bruce Lincoln, *The Conquest of a Continent: Siberia and the Russians,* Ithaca, NY: Cornell University Press, 2007, pp. 33-154.

35. Jacob W. Kipp, "Russian Naval Reformers and Imperial Expansion, 1856-1863,"*Soviet Armed Forces Review Annual*, Vol. I, 1977, pp. 118-139.

36. Lincoln, *The Conquest of a Continent*, pp. 155-366.

37. *Ibid*., pp. 367-399.

38. *Ibid*., p. 400.

39. G. A. Ziuganov, "Rasprava vo Vladivostoke ne dolzhena ostat'sia beznakazannoi" ("The Massacre in Vladivostok Must Not Go Unpunished"), *Pravda,* December 15, 2008.

40. Sergei Blagov, "Russia Hails Border Deal with China Despite Criticism," *Eurasian Daily Monitor*, Vol. 2, No. 102, May 25, 2005, available from *www.jamestown.org/single/?no_cache=1&tx_ttnews%5Btt_news%5D=30445*.

41. Jeanne L. Wilson, *Strategic Partners: Russian-Chinese Relations in the Post-Soviet Era*, Armonk, NY: M. E. Sharpe, 2004, pp. 126-127.

42. This process has been addressed in the work of Christina Chuan, "Nuclear Issues in the Far Eastern Federal Okrug," in James Clay Molts, Vladimir A. Olav, and Adam M. Stolberg, eds., *Preventing Nuclear Meltdown: Managing Decentralization of Russia's Nuclear Complex,* Aldershot, UK, and Burlington, VT: Ashgate, 2004, pp. 105-134.

43. Vladimir Pylaev, "Spasitel'nyi Kitai?" ("Saving China"), *Orientir (Landmark)*, No. 3, March 2009, pp. 8-11.

44. "Far East Looks to China for Investment," *The Russian Journal*, October 10, 2003, available from *www.russiajournal.com/node/16455*.

45. Pylaev, pp. 8-11.

46. Aleksandr Khramchikhin, "Blizhaishii sosed—budushchaia voennaia sverkhderzhava" ("Next door Neighbor—A Future Military Superpower"), *Nezavisimoe voennoe obozrenie (Independent Military Review)*, March 27, 2009.

47. Konstantin Preobrazhensky, "Through Russia With Kim Jong Il," *North Korean Review*, Vol. 1, No. 1, February 29, 2004, available from *www.jamestown.org/single/?no_cache=1&tx_ttnews%5Btt_news%5D=26321*.

48. Alexander Vorontsov, "Current Russia-North Korea Relations: Challenges and Achievements," Washington, DC: The Brookings Institution, February 2007, available from *www.brookings.edu/papers/2007/02northkorea_vorontsov.aspx*.

49. "Russian Specialists Arrive in S. Korea to Probe Warship Sinking," *RIA Novosti*, May 31, 2010; "Russia, N. Korea to Continue Consultations to Settle Inter-Korean Conflict, *RIA Novosti*, May 28, 2010; and "Russia, South Korea to Discuss Cheonan Issue Thursday," *RIA Novosti*, June 2, 2010.

50. Aleksandr Khramchikhin, "Podopleka Koreisko-Koreiskogo konflikta" ("Background of the Korea Conflict"), *VPK Voenno-promyshlennyi kur'e (VPK Military-Industrial Courier)*, June 9, 2010.

51. Ronald D. Asmus, *A Little War that Shook the World: Georgia, Russia, and the Future of the West*, New York: Palgrave Macmillan, 2010.

52. Mikhail Barabanov, Anton Lavrov, and Viacheslav Tseluiko, *Tanki augusta: Sbornik state (Tanks Augusta: Collected Articles)*, Moscow, Russia: Tsentr Analiza Strategii i tekhnologii (Center for Analysis of Strategies and Technologies), 2009.

53. Valerii Shcheblanin, "Voennaia bezopasnost' na vostok Rossii budet obespechena" ("Military Security to the East of Russia Will Be Provided"), *Buriatiia*, February 20, 2010.

54. Aleksandr Khramchikhin, "Chetyre vektora Rossiiskoi oborony" ("Four Vectors of the Russian Defense"), *Nezavisimoe voennoe obozrenie (Independent Military Review)*, May 21, 2010.

55. Aleksandr Khramchikhin, "Slabost' provotziruet sil'nee, chem moshch'" ("Weakness Provokes More Strongly than Power"), *Nezavisimoe voennoe obozrenie (Independent Military Review)*, March 19, 2010.

56. Bruce Pannier, "Unspoken Russian-Chinese Rivalry Is Subtext of SCO Summit," *RFE/RL*, June 10, 2010.

57. "Kitaisky odvigaiut granitsu s Rossiei"("The Chinese Move the Border with Russia"), *Vremia i den'gi (Time and Money)*, June 8, 2010.

58. Natal'ia Ostrovskaia. "Zachem Rossii Dal'nyi Vostok?" ("Why Does Russia Need the Far East?"), *Komsomol'skaia Pravda* (*Komsomol Truth*), May 28, 2010.

Chapter 3

China's Strategic Forces in the 21st Century:

The People's Liberation Army's Changing Nuclear Doctrine and Force Posture

Michael Mazza
Dan Blumenthal

Introduction

When it comes to its development and deployment of nuclear weapons—China first tested a weapon in 1964—China maintains a narrative in which it holds the moral high ground. According to the Chinese Communist Party line, China detests nuclear weapons, which are inhumane. But because the United States and the Soviet Union were both building large nuclear arsenals during the Cold War and because (China thought) they used those weapons to coerce non-nuclear states, China had no choice but to pursue those weapons itself. China, the narrative goes, would prefer to see nuclear weapons abolished rather than maintain its own arsenal, but reality requires that China arm itself.

Whatever legitimacy this narrative may have once had, it has become less credible. Given China's complicity in the Pakistani and Iranian nuclear programs—for example, China delivered fissile material to A. Q. Khan—it appears that China sees a use for these weapons other than simple self-defense. Though China appears to have halted its proliferation activities, those programs suggest a more casual attitude toward nuclear weapons than one of abhorrence. Indeed, actions speak louder than words. That Beijing proliferated nuclear technology, materials, and know-how—and to relatively unstable regimes that may be less cautious about using nuclear weapons—is worrying.

Considered in this context, China's movement toward an increased reliance on nuclear weapons and shifts in its nuclear doctrine are both unsurprising and of potentially great concern. While China has been growing its nuclear arsenal and fielding new ballistic missiles and ballistic missile submarines, Chinese strategists have been engaged in doctrinal debates over how those weapons should be used. As a younger generation of military thinkers has come to the fore, the long-held tenets of China's nuclear doctrine as originally set forth under Mao—namely, the "no first use" policy and minimum deterrence—are increasingly coming under scrutiny. Indeed, some strategists argue that the People's Republic of China (PRC) should cast these policies aside and adopt a new nuclear doctrine that will grant strategic forces a more prominent role in the country's defense.

External and internal factors are driving changes in China's nuclear policy and force structure and will continue to do so in the future. Concerns over what the Chinese see as a US threat have led some to call for a greater reliance on nuclear weapons for deterring Washington. Should South Korea or Japan ever "go nuclear"—and there are growing worries that they might—that would similarly impact China's nuclear force posture and doctrine. Internally, economic and demographic challenges will make it more difficult for China to maintain a large standing army in the coming decades and may very well lead Beijing to rely increasingly on nuclear forces for its national defense.

Still, the extent of Beijing's reliance on nuclear weapons in the future is difficult to predict. Old thinking dies hard, and the People's Liberation Army (PLA) would likely prefer to rely on conventional means to defend China. Yet, even conventional deterrence can complicate nuclear deterrence relationships. To wit, China's growing medium-range ballistic missile threat to America's Pacific bases will force the United States to rely on long-range assets for conventional deterrence. Beijing will find this destabilizing, and may rely on its nuclear arsenal to deter America's use of long-range weaponry.

In short, changes in China's nuclear weapons force planning, posture, and doctrine are likely to complicate both the Sino-American deterrence relationship and the US military's ability to operate in the Asia-Pacific region. American military and political leaders must watch these developments closely as they consider changes to America's own strategic force posture in the years ahead.

China's Strategic Weapons Modernization in Brief

The PLA's strategic weapons modernization program has been aimed at ensuring China's second-strike capability. While China has not designed a new warhead since the early 1990s, it has slowly grown its warhead arsenal and has modernized its ballistic missile force. In short, China has been replacing liquid-fueled, silo-based missiles with solid-fueled, road-mobile DF-31s and DF-31As.

Moreover, China has built two new nuclear-powered ballistic missile submarines (SSBNs)—operational status unknown—and has at least two more on the way. These Type 094 Jin-class submarines will be armed with JL-2 submarine-launched ballistic missiles (SLBMs), a sea-based variant of the DF-31 that is still in development. SSBNs serve to deter a nuclear attack on the mainland, to deter foreign intervention in a "regional war," and to ensure a second-strike capability. Some analysts estimate that China will be able to keep one SSBN on patrol at all times in the 2010-2015 timeframe.[1] If the PLA Navy (PLAN) develops longer-range SLBMs in the future (the JL-2's range is projected to be 8,000 kilometers (km), its SSBNs will be able to operate from littoral bastions, where they may be safer from anti-submarine warfare operations.

Nuclear Doctrine for the 21st Century

Having established itself as a nuclear power in the mid-1960s, China adopted a "no first use" policy—strategic weapons would only be used in retaliatory counterattacks. China also promised never to use nuclear weapons against non-nuclear states. In addition, Beijing has long maintained a doctrine of minimum deterrence. This posture required that China maintain a small force of intercontinental ballistic missiles (ICBMs), only a few of which needed to survive a nuclear attack. Following such an attack, surviving ICBMs would be launched at countervalue targets in the attacking nation. For minimum deterrence to be effective, Beijing needed to ensure a survivable second-strike capability, which would permit China to strike and do unacceptable damage to just a handful of enemy cities. All that was needed was a small, survivable arsenal, which is essentially what China has maintained.

Though officially China appears to adhere to a doctrine of minimum deterrence, there is evidence to suggest that in recent decades China has moved or is moving to a limited deterrence nuclear doctrine. In 1995, Alastair Iain Johnston argued that in post-Cold War China there had been "more comprehensive and consistent doctrinal arguments in favor of developing a limited flexible response capability."[2]

In the late 1980s and early 1990s, the PLA launched a series of research programs aimed at strengthening the intellectual underpinnings of its nuclear doctrine. According to Johnston, these programs arrived at a consensus on "limited deterrence." In limited deterrence, nuclear weapons play a critical role in the deterrence of both conventional and nuclear wars, as well as in escalation control (intrawar deterrence) if deterrence fails. In other words, nuclear weapons have a wider utility than proponents of minimum deterrence would suggest.[3]

Johnston's analysis portends a significant change for two reasons. First, in order to use nuclear weapons to deter a conventional attack, one must be prepared to use nuclear weapons in response to a conventional attack—in other words, "no first use" goes out the window.

There are strategists within the Chinese military community who are thinking along these lines. General Zhang Wannian, former chief of the PLA General Staff Department, thinks it is important to deter both nuclear and conventional attacks. Writing for the US Army War College, Larry Wortzel paraphrased Zhang's argument:

> The conduct of 'bloody actual combat' (during conventional war), in itself, is a deterrent measure, and the more destructive the actual combat in which a nation engages, the greater the likelihood of effective deterrence.[4]

In other words, for example, in order to deter the United States from intervening in a Taiwan Strait conflict, Beijing must convince Washington that it will sustain unbearably high casualties. Zhang does not explicitly argue that nuclear weapons could serve this purpose. But a younger generation of strategists, which is rethinking China's nuclear weapons policy, may very well contend that Zhang's logic should be followed to its logical end.

Second, if one is to use nuclear weapons for intra-war deterrence—or escalation control—one must foresee an operational use for those weapons. If China has adopted a doctrine of limited deterrence, this implies that China uses its nuclear weapons not only to deter nuclear attack on itself but, if necessary, to fight and win a nuclear war—or, if not win, at least deny victory to an adversary.

In this regard, Major General Yang Huan—former Deputy Commander of the Second Artillery—refers to using nuclear weapons in "actual fighting" (my emphasis).[5] Similarly, Major General Wu Jianguo, formerly of China's Antichemical Warfare Academy, argues that if deterrence fails, a country will "strive to win a victory through actual combat" (my emphasis). According to Wu, "The immense effect of nuclear weaponry is that it can serve as a deterrent force and, at the same time, as a means of actual combat."[6]

Again, the idea that nuclear weapons would be used for "actual combat" suggests something other than a role as a minimum deterrent. Indeed, Johnston argues that many Chinese strategists have rejected the anti-Clausewitzian nature of nuclear weapons. They are not only useful as a deterrent, but can actually be used to achieve political ends in wartime. The horrifying nature of nuclear weapons, these strategists argue, does not mean that their use negates Clausewitz's central tenet—namely, that war is simply politics by other means. As Clausewitz himself wrote, "War is an act of force, and there is no logical limit to the application of that force."[7]

In trying to get a handle on China's nuclear doctrine, it is also important to look at the PLA's nuclear arsenal and weapons deployment. Consider the Second Artillery's nuclear-capable medium-range ballistic missiles (MRBMs). Some of these are located in southern and central China, within striking range of India (and Southeast Asia). Others, however, are deployed to east and northeast China, within range of South Korea and Japan, both non-nuclear states. Of course, these countries are home to large US military bases, which would likely play a role in any Sino-American conflict. If China is prepared to launch nuclear-tipped missiles at these targets, this would suggest something other than a minimum deterrence posture, which relies on countervalue rather than counterforce targeting.

Even more telling would be the existence of tactical nuclear weapons. Whether or not such weapons exist has been fiercely debated. Though China has conducted a couple of low-yield nuclear tests and has conducted military exercises in which a tactical nuclear weapon was "used," this is not proof-positive that the PLA fields such weapons. The US intelligence community has at times asserted that China does have tactical weapons, and at other times suggested that the opposite is true. In 1989, two PLA officers in the General Staff Department chemical defense department wrote:

> At present, although we have not yet equipped ourselves with theater and tactical nuclear weapons, this is not the same as saying in the future we will not arm ourselves. Moreover, our air force's nuclear bombs and the Second Artillery's nuclear missiles can also be used against the rear of the enemy's theater.[8]

Whether China has tactical weapons in its arsenal is an open question. But if we learn that China does, or if China has considered the tactical use of strategic assets (as suggested in the quote above), this would also suggest a shift toward limited deterrence.

No First Use

Concurrent to this possible shift to "limited deterrence" are increasing calls for the abandonment of the PRC's "no first use" policy. No first use is still state policy, though official statements attesting to that fact have grown increasingly ambiguous. The following is from China's 2006 Defense White Paper:

> China remains firmly committed to the policy of no first use of nuclear weapons at any time and under any circumstances. It unconditionally undertakes not to use or threaten to use nuclear weapons against non-nuclear-weapon states or nuclear-weapon-free zones. . . .

It is no mistake that China is only "firmly committed" to no first use—while it "unconditionally" promises not to use or threaten to use nuclear weapons against non-nuclear states. The difference is subtle, but it is there nonetheless.[9]

The 2008 Defense White Paper is even more ambiguous: "The Second Artillery Force sticks to China's policy of no first use of nuclear weapons. . . ."[10] This is not particularly reassuring, and may indicate a relaxation of China's commitment to no first use.

It is not only official statements that bring the no first use policy into question, but also writings and speeches by current and former Chinese military officers. There is an ongoing debate about how to respond to a conventional attack on strategic assets and how to respond to a warning of imminent strategic attack. In either of these situations, retired General Pan Zhenqiang writes:

> China will feel [itself] in a dilemma to make the decision to use its nuclear retaliatory force to counter-attack. For one thing, from an operational point of view, China's no-first-use pledge seems to have greatly bound its hands to maintain flexibility in seeking the optimum options. For another, China will find lack of multiple means to differentiate its responses to different scenarios.[11]

In the case that China receives warning of an imminent attack on its strategic forces, is it really in Beijing's interests to wait to launch its own missiles?

General Pan here is also commenting on minimum deterrence. Imagine that the United States was to use tactical nuclear weapons in a conflict over Taiwan. As it currently stands, China would respond by launching strategic attacks on US cities, which would force the United States to retaliate. In this case, deterrence failed in the first instance, and China had no recourse to attempt escalation control. According to Pan and others, increasing numbers of Chinese thinkers be lieve this problem requires a change in China's nuclear doctrine.

A shift in China's warfighting doctrine also calls into question China's continued commitment to no first use and minimum deterrence. For the first few decades of the PRC's existence, the PLA maintained a doctrine of "People's War." The PLA would make use of China's greatest resources—its large population and strategic depth—to defeat a superior enemy on Chinese territory. The PLA now plans to fight "localized wars under conditions of informatization" instead. China will fight short, high-tech wars on its periphery. The PLA no longer expects or is prepared to fight wars deep in Chinese territory, and given Chinese government assertions that its nuclear capability "is solely for self-defense with a view to maintaining independence, sovereignty and territorial integrity,"[12] it is quite possible that China would be tempted to use nuclear weapons to prevent an adversary from controlling territory on the Chinese mainland.

In PLA doctrine, "active defense" is an old idea, but one with an evolving meaning—some Chinese thinkers believe it provides a rationale for preemption. According to the PLA's Science of Campaigns, "The essence of [active defense] is to take the initiative and to annihilate the enemy."[13] According to China's 2008 Defense White Paper, "Strategically, [the PLA] adheres to the principle of . . . striking and getting the better of the enemy only after the enemy has started an attack." "Attack," however, seems to be defined broadly by the PLA. See, for example, The Science of Military Strategy, an authoritative text used by the PLA's Academy of Military Science:

> Striking only after the enemy has struck does not mean waiting for the enemy's strike passively. . . . It doesn't mean to give up the 'advantageous chances' in campaign or tactical operations, for the 'first shot' on the plane of politics must be differentiated from the 'first shot on that of tactics' . . . . If any country or organization violates the other country's sovereignty and territorial integrity, the other side will have the right to 'fire the first shot' on the plane of tactics.[14]

Indeed, China has a history of defining military offensives as strategic defenses. This is not to say that China can be expected to engage in preemptive attacks—whether conventional or nuclear. Rather, it is to point out that the intellectual framework exists upon which to make the argument that using nuclear weapons first in a conflict can be justifiable. Apparently, increasing numbers of Chinese military thinkers are making that argument.

Primary Determinates of China's Nuclear Force Posture and Policy

There are a number of items driving China's nuclear modernization. Perhaps first and foremost among these is the United States. From China's point of view, the United States is the number one threat. There is a perception that the United States wants to contain China and keep it from becoming a great power. The United States, moreover, is the only country that can challenge all of Beijing's three core interests: regime survival, sovereignty and territorial integrity, and continued economic growth.

How so? With regard to regime survival, it is no secret that the United States would like to see political liberalization in China. Indeed, this has long been used as a justification for trading with the PRC—economic liberalization would one day lead to democracy. Having watched America "effect" regime change in Afghanistan and Iraq and support democratization in the former Soviet Union and in Eastern Europe, China is suspicious of any US attempt to "interfere" with its internal affairs.

Similarly, Beijing is concerned with any perceived impingement of its sovereignty and territorial integrity. There are historical reasons for this concern, as the Central Intelligence Agency (CIA) supported separatists in Tibet during the Cold War. In the present day, the United States provides a home for Rebiya Kadeer, Xinjiang's leading activist, and awards medals to the Dalai Lama. Most worrisome for China, the United States is the only country with a Taiwan Relations Act and thus the only country that is obligated to ensure that Taiwan can defend itself. Many Chinese believe the United States would intervene in any conflict over Taiwan's ultimate disposition, and that, to Beijing, is a serious threat.

Finally, Washington can threaten China's continued economic prosperity as well. The United States is China's largest trading partner, and the United States dominates the sea lines of communication. Should Sino-US tensions spike or conflict break out, the United States is able to not only cut off its own trade with Beijing, but also to impede the flow of oil and other natural resources to China.

A number of US military and nuclear policy developments in particular have driven PLA discussions on China's own nuclear force. First among these was the Bush administration's decision to exit the anti-ballistic missile treaty and develop ballistic missile defenses (BMD). China fears that an effective American BMD system will undermine its deterrent. This leads to greater urgency in China's nuclear development program—strategists believe that more penetrative weapons are needed, and in greater numbers. And some thinkers, again, question the no first use policy. They wonder if it is in China's best interests to maintain a policy in which it will absorb an American strategic attack, and then launch whatever weapons remain against an effective missile defense system. If a conflict is to go nuclear, these people would argue, China should launch its weapons first in the hope of oversaturating America's missile defenses.

China's leaders were also worried by an apparent shift in US nuclear policy, as evidenced in the 2002 Nuclear Posture Review (NPR). The NPR named China as a target for US nuclear weapons and listed a Taiwan Strait Crisis as an example of a conflict that could go nuclear.[15] Though this was not new policy for the United States, its public airing was ill received by the Chinese.

Perhaps more worrisome for China, though, were some specific policy recommendations within the NPR. The inclusion in a "New Triad" of "offensive strike systems (both nuclear and non-nuclear)" once again raised the question in the PLA of how it should respond to a conventional attack upon its strategic assets. The NPR's proposal that the United States develop "improved earth penetrating weapons (EPWs)," (or nuclear bunker busters), "warheads that reduce collateral damage," and enhanced satellite constellations "to locate successfully and maintain track on mobile targets" raised fears: (1) that the United States was more likely to use nuclear weapons; and, (2) that China's second-strike capability would be threatened and thus, its deterrent capabilities undermined.[16]

General Pan Zhenqiang asks readers to put themselves in China's shoes:

> Imagine the military pressure from the US that Beijing may well be confronted with: A numerically reduced but upgraded precision-guided offensive nuclear capability; a robust missile defense system; some offensive capability in space . . . and a more aggressive preemptive nuclear doctrine. All these are backed up by powerful conventional capabilities and the potential resurging capabilities of a nuclear infrastructure that had been rebuilt even after drastic reductions to the size of the arsenal.[17]

Whether this all comes to pass remains to be seen. But from the vantage point of a Chinese war planner, there is every reason to continue modernizing the PLA's nuclear arsenal and debating China's future nuclear doctrine—perhaps with much greater urgency.

Regional Deterrence

If China develops adequate strategic forces to respond to the US strategic threat, it will also have sufficient forces to deal with Russian and South Asian contingencies. Even so, China is not nearly as worried about Russia as it once was. China no longer views Russia as a serious threat and no longer fears a Russian invasion into Manchuria. The most likely source of conflict between China and Russia is resource competition. China depends on pipelines from Kazakhstan and Tajikistan, countries traditionally within Russia's sphere of influence. There are also abundant resources in eastern Siberia (along with a relatively large and growing Chinese population), which Beijing might want to control some day. Still, Russia and China have developed closer relations since the Cold War's end, often cooperating on the United Nations (UN) Security Council and together providing leadership and direction for the Shanghai Cooperation Organization (SCO). These developments, supplemented by each country's deterrent force, are likely to ensure that any conflict that arises remains bloodless, at least in the foreseeable future.

The Sino-Indian nuclear relationship is, however, much more complicated. India is China's 10th largest trading partner, and China is India's largest. From an economic perspective, it would appear that Asia's two giants have an interest in maintaining friendly, peaceful relations. Still, Beijing and Delhi have a long history of distrust and incompatible strategic interests. The most obvious areas of tension are the ongoing border disputes and China's close military relations with Pakistan—Beijing has provided assistance to Islamabad in its nuclear weapons and ballistic missile programs. Additionally, with its "Look East" policy, Delhi aims to increase its reach into an area considered by China to be its own sphere of influence; the reverse is true for China's "String of Pearls" strategy, through which it is increasing its presence in the Indian Ocean and leaving India feeling encircled.

Perhaps more than any other region in the Asia-Pacific, South Asia has great potential for an arms race and for explosive conflict. India has shown remarkable restraint in response to terror attacks emanating from Pakistan in recent years, though things could spiral downhill very quickly. Even though India has strategic weapons, that has not kept China from provoking Delhi, especially in recent years. References to China's victory in the 1962 War have appeared much more frequently in official Chinese statements; some Chinese officials have laid claim to sovereignty over all of Arunachal Pradesh—or "Southern Tibet"—and PLA forces have crossed the line of actual control and destroyed Indian military bunkers and outposts.[18]

Tibet—now reportedly home to nuclear weapons targeted on India[19]—is also a flashpoint. India is home to the Dalai Lama and the Tibetan government-in-exile, and to this day recognizes only Chinese suzerainty (rather than sovereignty) over Tibet. Some of Tibet's holiest sites are in Indian territory, and the Chinese fear the Dalai Lama may name a successor somewhere outside of China. According to India scholar Dan Twining:

Some Indian strategists fear that China may act to preempt, or respond to, an announcement of the Dalai Lama's chosen successor in India . . . by deploying the People's Liberation Army to occupy contested territory along the Sino-Indian border.[20]

Chinese officials often list Tibetan separatism as one of China's top three threats, so Beijing may have an itchy trigger finger (on its conventional forces) when it comes to ensuring security on the Tibetan plateau.

Though China certainly does not want a war with India at this time, it seems like Beijing does not necessarily fear one either—and that is a frightening thought, given the nuclear component of the relationship. Although both countries at the moment maintain no first use pledges and have relatively small arsenals, these arsenals are likely to grow. As China modernizes its nuclear force and potentially changes its nuclear doctrine to meet the needs of deterring America, India will need to respond to China's buildup, which will have a domino effect on Pakistan's nuclear forces as well. Similar logic applies to conventional buildups.

While China must now consider its economic relationship with India when providing (conventional) arms to Pakistan, Beijing's strategic logic has not changed all that much since the days of the Cold War—India presents a threat to China's sovereignty and territorial integrity (and economy, given that it sits astride key shipping lanes). Arming Pakistan complicates India's strategic environment and forces Delhi to divide its attention.

As China modernizes its conventional and strategic arsenals and develops its own missile defense system, it will pose a greater and more varied threat to India. In turn, India may believe it necessary to adjust its own nuclear doctrine. Moreover, given the apparent change in India's strategic thinking as it prepares for a potential two-front war against both Pakistan and China, Delhi may in the future rely more heavily on its strategic weapons if it fails to develop conventional forces sufficient to deal with both foes at once. All of this is to say that the nuclear balance in South Asia may soon enter a period of flux—with potentially destabilizing consequences for the region.

China also has concerns about Japan and South Korea. Since the end of World War II, China has had a constant fear of Japanese rearmament, conventional or otherwise. For Beijing, the thought of a nuclear-armed Japan is a terrifying prospect. While Japan is not now on the nuclear precipice, there are a number of trends that are beginning to make nuclear weapons an attractive option for Tokyo. Perhaps first among these is the emergence of a nuclear-armed and increasingly aggressive (see discussion below) North Korea, with no solution in sight for returning to a nuclear-free Korean peninsula. Pyongyang's unceasing belligerence directed at Tokyo—to include missile launches over the Japanese islands and the kidnapping of Japanese citizens—means that Tokyo must take the North Korean nuclear threat seriously. Any loss of confidence in the US nuclear umbrella—as might result from significant cuts in the US nuclear arsenal—could push Japan over the edge.

Another trend that may impact Japanese thinking on nuclear weapons is the rise of China. As China's military continues to grow, Japan will find it increasingly difficult to defend itself with conventional forces, especially if the United States draws down its own forces in the region. At the same time, suggestions that China may be increasing its reliance on nuclear weapons cannot be well received in Tokyo. A China that is prepared to use nuclear weapons against US forces in Japan (as discussed above) or a China that poses an overwhelming conventional threat to the islands will make nuclear forces a much more attractive option in Tokyo. Japan, whose citizens have so vehemently opposed the presence of nuclear weapons on their soil, may need to acquire such weapons to ensure it does not once again come under nuclear attack. Ironically, then, China's military modernization and changing nuclear doctrine may very well induce the very development Beijing so wishes to avoid.

China is concerned about South Korea as well. Though Seoul, at present, remains committed to a nuclear-free peninsula, it faces an existential threat from the North even more dire than the threat Pyongyang poses to Japan. North Korea's possession of nuclear weapons, moreover, seems to have emboldened Kim Jong Il—a series of aggressive actions beginning in 2009 culminated in North Korea's March 2010 sinking of South Korean naval vessel, the Cheonan, and the November 2010 shelling of Yeonpyeong Island. Seoul may eventually conclude it needs its own nuclear weapons to reset the balance on the peninsula. As in Tokyo, any loss of confidence in US extended deterrence may also encourage South Korea to develop such weapons. Moreover, historical enmities have resulted in a Seoul-Tokyo trust deficit; any move toward nuclearization by either would likely encourage the other to follow suit.

Over the longer term, there is a real, if distant, prospect of wider nuclear proliferation in East Asia. The resulting web of deterrence relationships would be complex and significantly different from those of the Cold War. As such, it is difficult to say how China might alter its nuclear forces or strategic weapons doctrine to confront such a new reality. The building of a PLA arsenal consisting of a variety of delivery systems, from tactical to theater-range missiles, and including greater numbers of SSBNs and bombers, would be a logical response to such a development.

Demographics and the PLA

It is not only external factors that are driving China's nuclear modernization but internal factors as well. Demographics in particular may be having a significant impact. A number of demographic trends are interacting to create an unfavorable environment for the PLA. The population of people aged 65 and over is growing rapidly, both absolutely and relative to younger age brackets. Yet, as of 2003, the pension system covered only 16 percent of retirees.[21] The labor force (aged 15-64) will top out around 2015 and then begin to shrink; meanwhile, the populations of people aged 0-14 and 15-24 are already shrinking.[22]

These trends will have a number of consequences for the Chinese military. First, the 4-2-1 population structure (four grandparents, two parents, one child), in combination with the underfunded pension system, will make PLA volunteers harder to come by and retention more difficult, as only children will feel pressure to care adequately for their elders. Moreover, having been doted upon for their entire lives, only children may be less willing to engage in risky training, less likely to bond with their units, and more likely to claim illnesses—in short, it may be difficult to make good soldiers out of spoiled children.

Additionally, the underfunded pension system, along with the lack of children to care for their parents and grandparents, will likely increase budgetary pressure and force more difficult "guns versus butter" decisions. In 2050, 23 percent of the Chinese population will be elderly, at which point the official dependency ratio (the number of elders per 100 individuals 15-64 years of age) will be 38.[23] Considering, however, China's real retirement age (not 65, but 45 for women and 55 for men), the World Bank estimates that the dependence ratio is already 26 and will reach 79 by 2050.[24] Estimates of the current pension system debt obligations range from two to seven trillion yuan, or 25-85 percent of the gross domestic product (GDP); these obligations will only rise as the population ages, and will become more onerous as the labor force shrinks relative to the elderly population.[25] In order to ensure continued domestic stability, the government may need to siphon resources from the military in favor of social spending programs.

Finally, the shrinking populations of people aged 0-14 and 15-24 means that the PLA's recruitment pool is shrinking as well. While future high unemployment or underemployment may make the PLA an attractive option for some job seekers, they are unlikely to be ideal conscripts and volunteers. Indeed, educated and skilled workers—which the PLA will increasingly value as it moves to a modern, high-tech force[26]—will prefer civilian sector employment.

What are the implications of these trends for China's nuclear weapons policy? First, China may respond to its demographic crunch much in the way Russia has. Faced with a shrinking population, Russia in 1993 abandoned its no first use policy and in 1999 adopted a new nuclear doctrine, which stated that nuclear weapons would be used to deter limited conventional wars.[27] In other words, Russia increased its reliance on nuclear weapons for self-defense at least in part to compensate for a demographic environment nonconducive to the maintenance of a large standing military.

Second, China may come to rely more heavily on its nuclear arsenal in order to deal with the increasing budgetary pressures. With a coming pension crisis, which is likely to cost billions of dollars—not to mention the fact that increasing numbers of economists are forecasting a near-term end to China's high economic growth rates—the PRC may have to make some difficult "guns versus butter" decisions. Over the long term, China might find it cheaper (much as Dwight D. Eisenhower did in the 1950s[28]) to field a robust nuclear force rather than to man a large, modern military.

China's Missile Buildup And Arms Control

Technological developments in China and abroad may have an impact on China's future nuclear policy. China, for example, aims to develop a global precision strike capability. Its much-discussed anti-ship ballistic missile (ASBM) program is, in fact, just one step in its precision-guided munitions development program. According to Mark Stokes, the PLA has set the following timeline for achieving prompt global strike:

- 2010: 1,500-2,000 km range ASBM
- 2015: 3,000 km range ASBM

- 2020: 8,000 km range precision strike capability
- 2025: global precision strike capability.[29]

Such a program will not only allow China to hold US carrier strike groups out of a Taiwan conflict, for example, but will eventually enable the PLA to hold American military assets in the United States at risk with conventional weapons. While perhaps not a pleasing prospect for US forces, this capability might lessen China's dependence on strategic nuclear forces and lead the Second Artillery to abandon countervalue targeting.

China's buildup of short- and medium-range ballistic and cruise missiles may also, inadvertently, impact its nuclear doctrine. These missiles threaten US air bases in South Korea, Japan, and Guam, as well as carriers at sea. While the PLA has understandably sought to bring nearby US fighters into its crosshairs, it is forcing the United States to lessen its reliance on tactical aircraft for deterrence and warfighting.

China has been able to engage in a buildup of short- and medium-range missiles because it is not a party to the Intermediate-Range Nuclear Forces Treaty (INF). The INF Treaty, signed by the United States and the Soviet Union in 1987, eliminated all ground-launched ballistic and cruise missiles with ranges between 500 km and 5,500 km; the United States and Russia are constrained where China is not. The INF Treaty prevents the United States from relying on ground-launched missiles in the Asia-Pacific within 5,500 km of Chinese targets.

Instead of relying on tactical aircraft and short- and medium-range missiles for deterrence and warfighting, the United States will increasingly rely on standoff conventional strike weaponry (to eventually include a prompt global strike capability), which China finds destabilizing; it will be difficult, Beijing argues, for a Chinese soldier to determine whether an incoming missile is nuclear-tipped or conventionally armed or what kind of munitions a long-range bomber is carrying. In effect, China has created a dilemma for itself. In most imaginable scenarios, the delivery of munitions on Chinese targets by US tactical aircraft would be much less escalatory than the delivery of munitions by long-range missiles or bombers. Yet China's own buildup of short- and medium-range missiles is forcing the United States to rely on long-range assets. American strategists must assume that as they move toward greater reliance on long-range standoff weapons, the Chinese nuclear threshold will decrease.

In order to avoid further destabilization, China should be invited to accede to the INF Treaty or to sign a new INF treaty, not only with the United States, but with regional states such as Japan, South Korea, and Taiwan as well. If China refuses, the United States should abrogate the INF Treaty and begin an energetic buildup of short- and medium-range missiles on the Intermediate-Range Nuclear Forces Treaty (INF). The INF Treaty, signed by the United States and the Soviet Union in 1987, eliminated all ground-launched ballistic and cruise missiles with ranges between 500 km and 5,500 km; the United States and Russia are constrained where China is not. The INF Treaty prevents the United States from relying on ground-launched missiles in the Asia-Pacific within 5,500 km of Chinese targets.

Instead of relying on tactical aircraft and short- and medium-range missiles for deterrence and warfighting, the United States will increasingly rely on standoff conventional strike weaponry (to eventually include a prompt global strike capability), which China finds destabilizing; it will be difficult, Beijing argues, for a Chinese soldier to determine whether an incoming missile is nuclear-tipped or conventionally armed or what kind of munitions a long-range bomber is carrying. In effect, China has created a dilemma for itself. In most imaginable scenarios, the delivery of munitions on Chinese targets by US tactical aircraft would be much less escalatory than the delivery of munitions by long-range missiles or bombers. Yet China's own buildup of short- and medium-range missiles is forcing the United States to rely on long-range assets. American strategists must assume that as they move toward greater reliance on long-range standoff weapons, the Chinese nuclear threshold will decrease.

In order to avoid further destabilization, China should be invited to accede to the INF Treaty or to sign a new INF treaty, not only with the United States, but with regional states such as Japan, South Korea, and Taiwan as well. If China refuses, the United States should abrogate the INF Treaty and begin an energetic buildup of short- and medium-range missiles on Guam, in Japan, and in South Korea. Having done so, the United States will be in position to barter away weapons it does not truly need when China determines that a missile race in Asia is counterproductive and destabilizing.

A new INF treaty would allow the United States and China to rely on tactical aircraft for deterrence and warfighting and would decrease their need for long-range bombers and a prompt global strike capability. This would ease regional tensions, lessen the possibility of miscalculation, and raise nuclear thresholds. The elimination of the missile threat to South Korea and Japan might also reduce pressure on these US allies to "go nuclear," thus forestalling wider Asian proliferation and the more complex web of deterrence relationships that would result.

Conclusion

It is, of course, impossible to predict precisely how China's nuclear weapons policy and strategic arsenal will develop in the coming decades. A dizzying array of technological, demographic, economic, and internal and external political trends are likely to exert force on Chinese strategic planners, pulling them in different directions.

There are, fortunately, a couple of things that we do know for certain. First, there is an ongoing debate among China's military thinkers about how and when to use nuclear weapons. Old logic is not being blindly accepted; traditional policies are being rethought. Second, in the nearer term, as the demographic crunch and pension crisis worsen and before China has closed its military gap with the United States, the PRC will feel pressure to increase its reliance on nuclear weapons. This is a worrying prospect for China's neighbors as well as for the United States, and it is a prospect the Obama administration should keep in mind as it works to reduce nuclear arsenals worldwide.

Endnotes

1. Robert G. Loewenthal, "Cold War Insights into China's New Ballistic-Missile Submarine Fleet," in Andrew S. Erickson, Lyle J. Goldstein, William S. Murray, and Andrew R. Wilson, eds., *China's Future Nuclear Submarine Force,* Annapolis, MD: Naval Institute Press, 2007, p. 299.

2. Alastair Iain Johnston, "China's New 'Old Thinking': The Concept of Limited Deterrence," *International Security*, Vol. 20, No. 3, Winter 1995/96, p. 5.

3. *Ibid*., p. 12.

4. Larry M. Wortzel, *China's Nuclear Forces: Operations, Training, Doctrine, Command, Control, and Campaign Planning*, Carlisle, PA: Strategic Studies Institute, US Army War College, 2007, p. 6.

5. Huan Yang, "China's Strategic Nuclear Weapons," in Michael Pillsbury, ed., *Chinese Views of Future Warfare,* Honolulu, HI: University Press of the Pacific, 2002, p. 134.

6. *Emphasis added.* Jianguo Wu, "Nuclear Shadows on High-tech Warfare," in Michael Pillsbury, ed., *Chinese Views of Future Warfare,* p. 144.

7. Carl von Clausewitz, *On War*, Michael Howard and Peter Paret, eds. and trans., Princeton, NJ: Princeton University Press, 1984, p. 77.

8. Johnston, p. 35.

9. Wortzel, pp. 15-16.

10. *Emphasis added.*
11. Zhenqiang Pan, "On China's No First Use of Nuclear Weapons," Pugwash Conferences on Science and World Affairs, available from *www.pugwash.org/reports/nw/zhenqiang.htm.*
12. "Communication of 1 August 1996 Received from the Permanent Mission of the People's Republic of China to the International Atomic Energy Agency," International Atomic Energy Agency, available from *www.iaea.org/Publications/Documents/Infcircs/1996/inf522.shtml.*
13. Quoted in Office of the Secretary of Defense, "Annual Report to Congress: Military Power of the People's Republic of China 2009," Washington, DC: Department of Defense, available from *www.defense.gov/pubs/pdfs/China_Military_Power_Report_2009.pdf.*
14. *Ibid.*
15. "Nuclear Posture Review [Excerpts]," *GlobalSecurity.org*, available from *www.globalsecurity.org/wmd/library/policy/dod/npr.htm.*
16. *Ibid.*
17. Zhenqiang Pan, "China's Nuclear Strategy in a Changing World Strategic Situation," in Barry Blechman, ed., *Unblocking the Road to Global Zero: Perspectives of Advanced Nuclear Nations: China and India,* Washington, DC: The Stimson Center, 2009, p. 44.
18. Dan Twining, "Could China and India Go to War over Tibet?" The German Marshall Fund of the United States, available from *www.gmfus.org/news_analysis/news_article_view?newsarticle.id=669*; "After LAC Incursions, China Now Violates International Border in Ladakh," *The Times of India*, available from *timesofindia.indiatimes.com/india/After-LAC-incursions-China-now-violates-Intl-Border-in-Ladakh/articleshow/4978371.cms.*
19. Twining.
20. *Ibid.*
21. Nicholas Eberstadt, "Strategic Demography: China Some Initial Findings and Implications," PowerPoint presentation, American Enterprise Institute for Public Policy Research, October 2009.
22. "World Population Prospects: The 2008 Revision," United Nations, available from *www.un.org/esa/population/publications/wpp2008/wpp2008_highlights.pdf.*
23. *Ibid.*
24. Tamara Trinh, Maria L. Manzeni, eds., "China's Pension System: Caught between Mounting Legacies and Unfavourable Demographics," *Deutsche Bank Research*, February 17, 2006.

25. Keith Crane, Roger Cliff, Evan Medeiros, James Mulvenon, and William Overholt, *Modernizing China's Military: Opportunities and Constraints*, Santa Monica, CA: The RAND Corporation, 2005.

26. Kristen Gunness and Fred Vellucci, "Reforming the Officer Corps: Keeping the College Grads in, the Peasants out, and the Incompetent down," *The 'People' in the PLA: Recruitment, Training, and Education in China's Military,* Roy Kamphausen, Andrew Scobell, and Travis Tanner, eds., Carlisle, PA: Strategic Studies Institute, US Army War College and Washington, DC: National Bureau of Asian Research, September 2008, p. 193.

27. Nikolai Sokov, "Russia's Nuclear Doctrine," *The Nuclear Threat Initiative*, available from *www.nti.org/analysis/articles/russias-nuclear-doctrine/.*

28. See, for example, Lawrence Freedman, Chap. 6, *The Evolution of Nuclear Strategy,* New York: Palgrave Macmillan, 2003.

29. Mark Stokes, "China's Evolving Conventional Strategic Strike Capability," *Project 2049 Institute,* September 14, 2009, p. 2.

Chapter 4

Plutonium, Proliferation, and Radioactive-Waste Politics in East Asia

Frank von Hippel

Depending upon how negotiations between the United States and South Korea, France and China, and the United States and Vietnam turn out, chemical reprocessing of spent nuclear fuel and recycling of recovered plutonium, which has been in decline in Europe, may make a resurgence in East Asia. Unfortunately, East Asia has not created a security architecture such as has been created in Europe, where a major conflict is now unthinkable. In fact, East Asia today is characterized by rising tensions, as North Korea threatens its neighbors and continues to expand its nuclear weapon capabilities, and China becomes increasingly assertive about its sovereignty over the resources under the seas whose shores it shares with Japan, South Korea, the Philippines, Indonesia, Brunei, Malaysia, and Vietnam. There is also the unresolved issue of the future of Taiwan. The spread of reprocessing in East Asia could therefore create the basis for a proliferation chain reaction that could make the region much more dangerous. Today, Japan is the only non-nuclear weapon state in the world that reprocesses. It has built up a domestic stockpile of about 10 tons of separated plutonium. This is a modest amount when measured in terms of fuel value but sufficient for more than 1,000 nuclear warheads. That amount will become much larger if and when the Rokkasho Reprocessing Plant goes into operation. The idea of producing nuclear weapons has come up a number of times in Japan's security debate but has never been pursued seriously.

Nevertheless, Japan's nearest neighbors regard it as a "virtual" nuclear weapon state, a country that could quickly acquire nuclear weapons if it felt threatened.

South Korea's nuclear-energy establishment feels that it has reached maturity, as demonstrated by the smooth operation of its 20 nuclear-power reactors and its 2009 success in beating out French and US-Japanese consortia for a contract to sell the United Arab Emirates (UAE) four nuclear power reactors. Its nuclear-energy establishment chafes at the United States refusing to grant South Korea the same rights to reprocess and enrich as Japan. This became a popular issue, following North Korea's nuclear test of May 9, 2010, when some South Korean politicians began calling for "nuclear sovereignty" for South Korea.[1] The timing suggests that they see some deterrence value in South Korea becoming a virtual nuclear weapon state like Japan. South Korea's nuclear-energy establishment denies such an interest, but argues that re-processing is the only way for South Korea to manage its spent fuel problem. This issue has arisen at a time when South Korea and the United States have begun to renegotiate their current agreement for nuclear co-operation, which expires in 2014.

In the 1970s and again in the 1980s, Taiwan launched clandestine reprocessing programs aimed at providing it with its own nuclear deterrent against Mainland China. Both times, the United States forced Taiwan to abandon these programs. Today, Taiwan's interest in nuclear weapons appears quiescent, but its agreement for nuclear cooperation with the United States also is due for renegotiation in 2014.

Meanwhile, China has built a pilot civilian reprocessing plant next to one of its military reprocessing plants and is considering acquiring a large facility like Japan's Rokkasho Reprocessing Plant from France. But France's Foreign Ministry is worried about the fact that China has not, like the other four permanent members of the United Nations Security Council, committed itself to end production of plutonium for weapons.

Finally, the United States is negotiating an agreement of nuclear cooperation with Vietnam, and a debate has broken out within the US Government over whether or not to try to persuade Vietnam to join the UAE in renouncing its rights to acquire national enrichment or reprocessing facilities.

The most bizarre aspect of all of these developments is that reprocessing is uneconomical and unnecessary for current generation nuclear-power reactors. Countries are justifying their pursuit of reprocessing for reasons that appear to be discredited or subjective, and therefore suspect: either the dream of commercializing plutonium breeder reactors, which failed in the United States, Western Europe, and Japan, or the claim that reprocessing will ameliorate domestic political problems with regard to the disposition of spent fuel.

The Dream Of A 'Plutonium Economy'

The US World War II Manhattan project spawned nuclear weapons. It also spawned the dream that fission could power human civilization for millennia. Enrico Fermi, the scientific leader of the US wartime plutonium-production program, and his co-workers thought that uranium was scarce and that therefore chain-reacting U-235, which makes up only 0.7 percent of natural uranium, would not be abundant enough to fuel fission power on a large scale. They therefore invented the plutonium-breeder reactor, whose ultimate fuel would be uranium-238, which comprises 99.3 percent of natural uranium.[2]

U-238 is not chain-reacting, but can be converted into chain-reacting plutonium-239 by the absorption of neutrons. A fast-neutron reactor fueled by plutonium could breed more plutonium out of U-238 than it consumed. With the resulting hundred-fold increase in the amount of energy extractable from natural uranium, even the three grams of U-238 in a ton of average crustal rock would, if converted into plutonium and fissioned, release the energy equivalent of several tons of coal.

According to his junior colleague, Alvin Weinberg, Fermi worried, however, that "It is not clear that the public will accept an energy source that produces this much radioactivity and that can be subject to diversion of material for bombs."[3]

Glenn Seaborg, a co-discoverer of plutonium, had no such doubts and, while Chairman of the US Atomic Energy Commission (AEC) from 1961 till 1971, relentlessly promoted the idea of a "plutonium economy." In a visionary speech on "The Plutonium Economy of the Future" at the end of his tenure as AEC chairman, Seaborg predicted that, by the year 2000, plutonium "can be expected to be a predominant energy source in our lives." The AEC staff projected that US nuclear power-generating capacity that year would be 1,100 billion Watts (gigawatts [GWe]). It is actually about 100 GWe today. Seaborg also projected that the United States would be increasing its stock of separated plutonium by more than 100,000 kilograms (kg) each year.[4]

Seaborg did not mention the implications of the fact that the predominant use of plutonium at the time was for nuclear weapons. The United States had already produced about 80,000 kg, enough to make the fission triggers for 30,000 nuclear weapons. Obviously, the diversion to weapons of only a miniscule rivulet from the plutonium river that Seaborg was looking forward to would transform the global security situation.

Concerns About Reprocessing and Proliferation

Under Seaborg's leadership, the AEC promoted the vision of a plutonium economy worldwide through the US Atoms for Peace program. In 1974, 3 years after Seaborg stepped down as AEC chairman, however, India used the first plutonium separated from the fuel of its first research reactor for a "peaceful nuclear explosion" that turned out to be its first step toward becoming a nuclear-armed state.[5]

India's nuclear test drew the attention of the White House and the State Department to the security implications of the AEC's promotion of plutonium as the commercial fuel of the future. President Gerald Ford and then President Jimmy Carter launched reviews that concluded that breeder reactors would not be economical for the foreseeable future. After some delay, the US Congress, faced with the skyrocketing costs of the US Clinch River demonstration breeder reactor, agreed with this reversal of policy and cancelled the project in 1983.[6]

In the meantime, the United States had succeeded in winning the cancellation of France's contracts to sell reprocessing plants for separating plutonium from irradiated uranium fuel to South Korea, Pakistan, and Taiwan. Ultimately, with the assistance of the democratic opposition to Brazil's then military government, Germany's contract to provide a reprocessing plant to that country was cancelled as well. The United States did not try to stop the entrenched reprocessing programs in the three states whose nuclear-weapon programs had spawned civilian reprocessing programs—France, the Soviet Union, and the United Kingdom (UK).

The judgments by the Ford and Carter Administrations of the poor economic prospects of the breeder reactors that were being used to justify plutonium separation have been vindicated by the abandonment of breeder-commercialization programs in Germany and the UK, and the postponement of those programs for 80 years by France and Japan.[7] India and Russia are both building liquid-sodium-cooled "demonstration" breeder reactors, but it is extremely unlikely that they will demonstrate economic competitiveness with today's water-cooled reactors. As Admiral Hyman Rickover concluded after trying a sodium-cooled propulsion reactor in a submarine, such reactors are "expensive to build, complex to operate, susceptible to prolonged shutdown as a result of even minor malfunctions, and difficult and time-consuming to repair."[8]

Reprocessing in Japan

Japan started the construction of a pilot-reprocessing plant at Tokai-mura village in 1971.[9] This plant, although small on the scale that Seaborg had envisioned, was designed to separate 2,000 kg of plutonium per year, enough for more than 250 Nagasaki bombs.[10] The Carter administration tried to persuade Japan not to start up the Tokai Reprocessing Plant. The United States was Japan's main supplier of reactor technology and fuel at the time, and their 1968 Agreement of Cooperation Concerning Civil Uses of Atomic Energy gave the United States veto power over reprocessing in Japan. The debate quickly escalated, however, to the tops of the two governments, and Prime Minister Takeo Fukuda declared Japan's right to reprocess a matter of "life or death" for Japan.[11]

It is interesting to speculate about the reasons Japan's government felt so strongly about this issue. The primary reason probably was related to the fact that the 1973 Arab oil embargo had dramatized Japan's vulnerability to a cutoff of its imported oil. This caused Japan, like many other major industrialized countries, to invest heavily in nuclear power. But, for Japan, which, unlike the United States, had no domestic uranium resources, the nuclear power plants brought a new potential vulnerability: a cutoff of imported uranium fuel. Indeed, the rise of demand for uranium after 1973 outpaced the rise in supply, and the price of natural uranium on the spot market increased six-fold by 1975.[12] This would have made breeder reactors appear more attractive. By the 1980s, however, the price of uranium in constant dollars had fallen back to its 1973 level.

There was also a second reason Japan's security establishment embraced reprocessing. Even though Japan relied primarily on the US "nuclear umbrella" against nuclear and other threats from the Soviet Union and China, reprocessing would provide Japan with its own nuclear-weapon option, "just in case."[13] In any case, the Carter administration backed down and agreed to the operation of the Tokai Pilot Reprocessing Plant and, in 1988, the Reagan administration signed a new Agreement of Cooperation that gave Japan blanket "prior consent" for the reprocessing of its spent fuel.[14]

By that time, however, breeder reactors were fading rapidly into the more distant future. Originally, Japan's nuclear-energy establishment, like the AEC, had planned to commercialize breeder reactors in the 1970s. But, in 1987, the commercialization target was pushed back to after 2020 and, in 2006, until after 2050.[15] Nevertheless, Japan shipped some of its spent fuel to France to be reprocessed and built a full-scale reprocessing plant in Rokkasho-mura, with a design capacity of 800 tons of spent light-water reactor fuel per year. Reprocessing at that rate would result in the annual separation of about eight tons of plutonium—enough for about 1,000 Nagasaki-type nuclear weapons.[16]

In the absence of breeder reactors, Japan decided to recycle the separated plutonium back into the fuel of the light-water reactors from which it had been separated. Japan's Atomic Energy Commission estimated in 2004 that this would increase the cost of nuclear power in Japan by about 0.6 yen (0.7 cents) per kilowatt-hour, relative to the direct underground disposal of the unreprocessed spent fuel.[17] Although the reprocessing plant was completed in 2001,[18] it has not yet gone into regular operation because of a seemingly unending series of technical problems.

Recycling plutonium and uranium recovered from spent fuel in light-water reactors would reduce Japan's uranium imports by 25 percent, at most. In any case, however, Japan's concern about its uranium import dependence, unlike its concern about its dependence on imported oil, appears to have dissipated. Japan has a strategic reserve of 6 months of oil imports but no strategic uranium reserve, although it would be 30 times less costly on an energy-equivalent basis.[19]

Nevertheless, Japan's commitment to reprocessing remains undiminished. A new rationale was given in the Japan Atomic Energy Commission's 2004 cost-benefit analysis. It argued that, if Japan gave up its reprocessing program, the reactors would have to shut down as their on-site storage facilities filled up:

> If we make a policy change from reprocessing to direct disposal, it is indispensable for the continuation of nuclear power generation to have communities that up until now have accepted selection as a site for nuclear facility, based on the assumption that spent fuel would be reprocessed, understand the new policy of direct disposal and accept the temporary storage of spent fuel at the site. It is clear, however, that it takes time to do so, as it is necessary to rebuild relationships of trust with the community after informing them of the policy change. It is likely that the nuclear power plants that are currently in operation will be forced to suspend operations, one after another, during this period due to the delay of the removal of spent fuel.[20]

The cost of replacing the power from Japan's nuclear power plants was estimated as being up to twice as great as the cost of reprocessing.[21]

Reprocessing is therefore kept alive in Japan in good part by concerns about the disposition of spent fuel. Local governments that host nuclear power plants want assurance that their spent fuel will not accumulate indefinitely on-site. At the same time, other local governments are reluctant to host interim central storage sites for spent fuel, for fear that they will become permanent. These governments are reluctant to host even 500-meter-deep geological repositories for radioactive waste for fear that natural processes or human intrusion could pollute the surface millennia hence.

Reprocessing plants are, in effect, interim central storage sites, but they bring enough economic benefits to the isolated poor communities that host them that those communities are willing to accept government guarantees that the radioactive waste will stay there only temporarily. In Japan, the government has guaranteed Aomori Prefecture, which hosts the Rokkasho Reprocessing Plant, that no radioactive waste will stay on its soil for more than 50 years. This sets a deadline for Japan to begin moving the high-level waste from reprocessing to an underground repository by 2045.

The estimated cost of reprocessing and associated activities, excluding transport and radioactive waste disposal, over the 40-year life of the Rokkasho Reprocessing Plant was estimated in 2003 as about 9 trillion yen ($100 billion).[22] That is obviously significant for a prefecture that in 2004 had an annual gross domestic product (GDP) of about 4.3 trillion yen ($50 billion) and was the second to the poorest of Japan's 47 prefectures measured in terms of GDP per capita.[23] The prefecture's government will receive about $200 million per year directly when the reprocessing plant is operating at full capacity.[24]

The Rokkasho Reprocessing Plant is not operating, however, and its 3,000-ton storage pool is virtually full. This means that Japan's nuclear utilities have to devise other forms of interim storage, and they are doing so. An interim storage facility is being built by Tokyo Electric Power and the Japan Atomic Power in Aomori Prefecture near the reprocessing plant, with an ultimate capacity of 5,000 tons. The first module, with a capacity of 3,000 tons, is scheduled to begin operation in 2012.[25] Chubu Electric Power, which operates the Hamaoka Nuclear Power plant, has proposed—as part of a plan to replace the two oldest nuclear units on the site—to build dry storage to accommodate the spent fuel that has accumulated in the storage pools that are to be decommissioned.[26] Kyushu Electric Power, which has 5 GWe of nuclear capacity, is looking for a site for an interim dry-cask storage facility.[27] If such efforts succeed, they could provide a relief valve for the pressures that have sustained Japan's reprocessing.

Changing Japan's reprocessing policy will be very difficult, however, because so many legal and political commitments have been attached to it. Aomori Prefecture accepted the Mutsu spent-fuel storage facility, for example, only after the governor had been ensured that there would be a second reprocessing plant to which the spent fuel would be shipped. And, as local governments are being canvassed about their willingness to accept a geological radioactive waste repository, they are being ensured that only high-level reprocessing waste from which the plutonium has been separated will be buried there. The implication is that plutonium dominates the long-term hazard of spent fuel. In fact, that is not necessarily true. In the US Department of Energy's Yucca Mountain Feasibility Study, the calculated doses to people who used aquifer water downstream from the mountain are dominated for the initial 50,000 years by technicium-99, a 210,000-year half-life fission product, and thereafter by neptunium-237, a 21-million-year half-life transuranic element.[28]

Thus, due to a combination of Japan's commitment to breeder reactors in the 1960s, problems of public acceptance with regard to interim storage of spent fuel, and a growing web of legal and political commitments, the country has trapped itself in a reprocessing program that generates huge stocks and flows of weapon-usable plutonium and sets a dangerous example for its neighbors.

South Korea's Push for the Right to Reprocess

South Korea's nuclear power program is about 25 years behind Japan's, but the storage pools for its heavy water reactors (HWRs) have long since filled up, and the storage pools at its three pressurized water reactor (PWRs) sites—Kori, Ulchin, and Yonggwang—are projected to be full by 2016, 2018, and 2021, respectively.[29] Dry-cask storage is being built for the heavy water reactor (HWR) fuel, but the Korea Atomic Energy Research Institute (KAERI) argues that such storage is politically unfeasible at the PWR sites and proposes instead to build a reprocessing plant using pyroprocessing technology[30] and fast-neutron reactors to fission the plutonium and other transuranic elements separated from the PWR fuel.[31] The design of KAERI's proposed fast-neutron transuranic burner reactors would be basically the same as those of the breeder reactors that several countries have tried unsuccessfully to commercialize.[32]

South Korea has a long history of interest in reprocessing. During the 1970s, the interest was briefly in a nuclear-weapon program, triggered by President Richard Nixon's decision that US allies in Asia should take more responsibility for their own defense. The United States decided to keep its military forces in South Korea and succeeded in persuading South Korea to cancel its order for a pilot reprocessing plant from France.[33] In 2004, however, South Korea's government informed the International Atomic Energy Agency (IAEA) that, from 1979 through 2000, KAERI had continued to conduct secret laboratory-scale enrichment and reprocessing experiments.[34]

In 1992, South and North Korea agreed not to enrich uranium or reprocess spent fuel. After North Korea conducted its second nuclear test in May 2009, however, that agreement lost its remaining credibility. South Korea's 1974 Agreement of Cooperation with the United States expires in 2014, and South Korea's government is pressing the United States for a new agreement that would give it the same blanket prior consent for reprocessing as Japan.

KAERI's pyroprocessing "solution" to South Korea's spent-fuel storage problem has its own credibility problems, however. First, it would come to fruition decades after the crisis it is proposed to solve. KAERI proposes to put into operation in 2025 a prototype facility capable of reprocessing 100 tons of spent fuel a year and, in 2028, a prototype 0.6 GWe fast-neutron reactor able to fission annually the transuranics from 50 tons of spent fuel.[35] By 2030, however, South Korea's light-water reactors are projected to be discharging about 800 tons of spent fuel annually.[36] Obviously, for the foreseeable future, South Korea will have to depend upon interim storage.

With regard to this mismatch of timing and capacity, KAERI argues that:

> To win public acceptance [South Korea's authorities] need to show that pyroprocessing or other long-term storage options are viable. Otherwise, local communities will not be convinced that any interim storage facilities will in fact be temporary.[37]

Even if full-scale pyroprocessing took place and South Korea succeeded in deploying tens of full-scale fast reactors, however, an underground repository would be required for the reprocessing waste and for the spent fuel being discharged by the heavy water reactors. KAERI argues, however, that, without fast-neutron reactors, the footprint of the underground repositories would be too large for South Korea:

> By the end of the century (assuming the new planned reactors come online), the cumulative amount of spent fuel produced by South Korean reactors is expected to exceed 110,000 tons. To dispose of such a large amount of spent fuel at a single site,

> an underground repository (and an exclusion zone surrounding the site) would need to cover as much as 80 square kilometers, an area considerably larger than Manhattan. Finding that much free space in South Korea would be enormously difficult. The country is approximately the size of Virginia [110,000 sq km] and is home to about six times as many people.[38]

A technical KAERI study finds, however, that the area underlain by tunnels would be about 20 square kilometers.[39] This area could be reduced by a factor of two if the spent fuel were cooled on the surface for 100 instead of 40 years. Use of fast reactors to fission the transuranics would not accomplish more at 40 years than aging the spent fuel for 100 years.[40] In any case, there is not much competition for real estate at a depth of 500 meters, and the area required for the surface facilities associated with an underground repository would be small in comparison with the area of, for example, a nuclear power plant.

It is the proliferation implications, however, that make this an issue of international concern. Although it would take a long time to deploy the pyroprocessing and fast reactor capacity required to keep up with the rate of discharge of transuranics in South Korea's PWR spent fuel, even the engineering prototype pyroprocessing plant that KAERI hopes to bring online in 2016 would be of proliferation concern. It would be able to separate 100 kg of plutonium, or enough for more than 10 nuclear bombs per year. KAERI argues pyroprocessing's "proliferation resistance has been internationally recognized due to the impossibility to recover plutonium."[41] The US Department of Energy did, in fact, promote the "proliferation-resistance" of pyroprocessing during the George Bush Administration. A 2009 interlaboratory review reported, however, the results of an:

> assessment [that] focuses on determining whether three alternative reprocessing technologies—COEX, UREX+, and pyroprocessing—provide nonproliferation advantages relative to the PUREX technology because they do not produce separated plutonium. [We] found only a modest improvement in reducing proliferation risk over existing PUREX technologies and these modest improvements apply primarily for non-state actors.[42]

KAERI therefore would be creating a nuclear-weapon option for South Korea in 2016, while its proposed costly approach might begin reducing the transuranics in South Korea's spent nuclear fuel after 2050. India followed this path and implemented its nuclear-weapon option in 1974. Only now, more than 35 years later, is India building its first demonstration breeder reactor, which may or may not work. South Korea may not today have any more intention than Japan to actually exploit a nuclear-weapon option, but, if a future government wished, it could do so quickly and secretly within weeks before domestic or international opposition could stop it.

On October 25, 2010, US and South Korean officials met for the first session of their negotiations on a new Agreement of Cooperation. The South Korean negotiators accepted the US proposal to do a joint study on the "feasibility" of pyroprocessing. The study is expected to take up to several years. Most likely, this means that negotiations on pyroprocessing in South Korea will be taken up after the new Agreement of Cooperation is negotiated.

It appears that KAERI will not be able to do experiments with spent fuel during the negotiation period. The Bush administration did not approve such experiments in South Korea, but allowed joint experiments with spent fuel at the Idaho National Laboratory. That could only be accomplished within the strictures of the 1978 Nonproliferation Act, however, with the legal subterfuge of defining pyroprocessing as "not reprocessing" and therefore not a "sensitive nuclear technology" subject to export controls. Late in the Bush administration, a rebellion by nonproliferation experts in the Departments of Energy and State forced a reversal of this position, which has resulted in a cutoff of US cooperation with KAERI on pyro-processing.

Taiwan: Dry-cask Interim Storage for Now

Taiwan, like Japan and South Korea, is trying to find its way forward with regard to spent-fuel management. Like South Korea, Taiwan has security concerns that led it twice to launch secret reprocessing programs. The first, launched in the 1960s, was shut down under US pressure in 1976; the second, launched in 1987, was shut down in 1988—again at US insistence.[43]

Taiwan built three 2-unit nuclear-power plants (Chinsan, Kuosheng, and Maan Shan) during 1978-1985 and has one under construction (Lungmen). As of 2006, the spent-fuel pools of the three operating power plants had all been re-racked once or twice to increase their storage density, but the oldest plant, Chinsan, was expected to run out of storage capacity in 2011, and the second oldest, Kuosheng, in 2016.[44] After looking into reprocessing in Europe, Taiwan opted for on-site dry-cask storage for the mid-term while an attempt is made to site a geological repository.[45]

Taiwan has an Agreement of Cooperation with the United States that gives the United States prior consent rights with regard to the reprocessing of Taiwan's spent fuel. This agreement will expire in 2014, and therefore, like South Korea's Agreement of Cooperation, must be renegotiated.

China: Committed to Reprocessing?

China's initial source for nuclear-energy technology was France. France reprocesses, and China announced that it would do so too, in 1987, 7 years before its first nuclear power plant went into operation. As of 2010, China had built a pilot reprocessing plant in Gansu Province, with a capacity of 50 tons of spent fuel per year, expandable to 100. China was also discussing with France the acquisition of an 800-ton-per-year plant, which, like Japan's Rokkasho Reprocessing Plant, would be based on the design of France's UP-3 plant. The new plant would have a spent-fuel storage capacity of 3,000-6,000 tons and would begin receiving spent fuel in 2018. Reprocessing would begin in 2025.[46]

China does not appear to have done a cost-benefit analysis on reprocessing vs. storage. Also, unlike Japan and South Korea, which are having trouble getting agreements from local governments to allow the siteing of central spent-fuel interim storage or a geological repository, there is no indication that China will encounter resistance to its proposal to site a repository in a remote area of Gansu Province next to the Gobi Desert. China's plans for reprocessing appear to be driven more by a concern that it may become difficult to obtain enough domestic and imported uranium to fuel the immense nuclear capacity it plans to build. This is the classic argument for plutonium breeder reactors, and China is indeed in discussions with Russia over the possibility of buying one or two copies of the BN-800 demonstration breeder reactor that Russia is currently completing.

Both the China National Nuclear Corporation (CNNC) and France's Foreign Ministry have reservations about the proposed sale of a French reprocessing plant to China, however. CNNC is concerned about the price that AREVA reportedly wants to charge for the plant: 20 billion Euros, according to a CNNC expert. For its part, France reportedly is concerned that China has not renounced the production of further plutonium for weapons and that China wishes to locate the reprocessing plant next to one of its military reprocessing plants.[47]

In the late 1970s, after India's 1974 nuclear test, the United States argued in effect, when pressing Japan, South Korea, and Taiwan to abandon their reprocessing programs: “We don’t reprocess; you don’t need to either.” When asked about the example China’s decision to reprocess might have on its neighbors such as South Korea, Vietnam, and Indonesia, Chinese officials respond that Japan has already set the reprocessing precedent and that, in any case, it is the United States, not China, that is currently negotiating Agreements of Cooperation on nuclear energy and therefore has influence on the nuclear policies of countries such as Vietnam.

Is there an Alternative to the Spread of Plutonium Separation in East Asia?

South Korea and China are both at critical junctures in their spent-fuel policies. If South Korea succeeds in persuading the United States to acquiesce to its right to reprocess, it will be the second nonweapon state to do so, and it will become correspondingly more difficult to persuade other countries not to acquire national reprocessing plants. If China continues forward to actually implement its reprocessing plan, the increasing weight of its example may help legitimize reprocessing as a standard part of the nuclear power fuel cycle. Japan is continuing with its reprocessing program even though its costs continue to mount and it continues to encounter technical problems. Is there an alternative scenario in which the building momentum toward plutonium economies and latent proliferation in East Asia might be reversed? This last section of the chapter considers the possibilities.

South Korea

The justification being put forward for South Korea’s interest in reprocessing has been developed by the KAERI. KAERI, by virtue of its technical expertise, has been able to largely monopolize the debate in South Korea—and, to a considerable extent, in Washington, DC, through the employees that it has stationed at nongovernmental organizations, think tanks, and universities there.

KAERI’s primary interest is in research and development (R&D). It has been interested in reprocessing since the 1960s and has pursued it to the extent allowed by the United States. During the Bush administration, KAERI focused on pyroprocessing after Vice President Dick Cheney’s Energy Commission embraced pyroprocessing as proliferation resistant and not reprocessing, which opened the door for the Department of Energy’s national laboratories to pursue pyroprocessing R&D in cooperation with KAERI.

To justify the funding of its pyroprocessing R&D to the South Korean government, however, KAERI has had to argue that the interim storage and geological disposal of spent fuel, although probably less costly, are unfeasible in South Korea. This is not implausible, since South Korea, like other countries—including the United States—has encountered political problems siting central spent-fuel interim storage and underground radioactive-waste disposal facilities.

The United States has gone to extended interim storage at its nuclear power plants while it works out the politics of its siting policy. South Korea should try seriously to do the same. In fact, it has no alternative. South Korea nuclear power plants will have used up their current on-site storage capacity by 2021, and the "solution" that KAERI is offering would be deployed only after 2050.

KAERI argues that, by embracing pyroprocessing and fast-neutron reactors, South Korea would make expanded on-site storage more feasible politically, because the local governments will see that there is a plan beyond interim storage. But the fast-neutron reactors that are the linchpin of KAERI's strategy could fail economically and technologically in South Korea, as they have elsewhere. It is at least as credible that South Korea could site a geological repository by 2050.

The joint South Korean-US "feasibility study" on pyroprocessing could provide a broader set of policy options for both countries to consider. It will only do so, however, if KAERI's grip on South Korea's spent-fuel policy can be broken. This would require involving officials from South Korea's responsible Ministries in the feasibility study so that they can be educated about the alternatives and empowered to develop their own views.

China

China's government similarly needs to question the precipitous pace at which the China National Nuclear Corporation proposes to move toward reprocessing and breeder reactors. That strategy is 50 years old, and has not worked well for the other countries that have pursued it. As did France, India, Japan, Russia, and the UK in the past, China has premised its reprocessing plans on the expectation of rapid commercialization of breeder reactors. Not having a design of its own, the CNNC plans to start building BN-800 reactors at a rate of one per year starting in 2013.[48] China is building light-water reactors at this rate, but their basic designs have been proven in other countries over decades. There is no such experience base for sodium-cooled reactors. Indeed, after failed attempts, plans to commercialize them on a large scale were abandoned in Germany, the UK, and the United States and postponed until after 2050 by France and Japan.

Construction of the Soviet Russian prototype of the BN-800 was begun in 1986, suspended in 1990, resumed in 2002, and currently is to be completed in 2014.[49] The BN-800 is an 800-megawatt-electric (MWe) sodium-cooled design that builds on the BN-600 reactor, which has operated in Russia since 1980—with a cumulative capacity factor as of the end of 2009 of 74 percent.[50] The BN-600 is the only sodium-cooled prototype reactor that has not been a total failure, but most countries would not judge it a full success either. As of 1997, it had experienced 14 sodium fires—some of them quite substantial.[51] Also, Russia has not yet established a plutonium fuel cycle for breeder reactors. Thus far, the BN-600 has been fueled with highly enriched uranium.

Given the historic problems of sodium-cooled reactors, China should treat the BN-800 as an experiment and not a prototype ready for mass production. If China committed only to a single BN-800 for now, there would be no need to build a large-scale reprocessing plant. Russia could provide the startup fuel and first few fuel reloads out of its stockpile of 46 tons of separated reactor-grade plutonium.[52] The core of the BN-800 requires 2.1 tons of plutonium and, assuming a 75-percent capacity factor—about 1.4 tons of plutonium annually thereafter until recycling of plutonium from its spent fuel can commence.[53] Russia has no current need for this plutonium because, under an agreement with the United States, it has committed to fuel its BN-600 and BN-800 reactors with 34 tons of excess weapon-grade plutonium.[54]

Japan

Japan is already deeply committed to reprocessing, but this has been costly both economically and to the public credibility of Japan's nuclear establishment. At least as far back as 1993, the fuel-cycle managers of Japan's three largest nuclear utilities told the author that, knowing what they did at that point, they wished that Japan had pursued a once-through fuel cycle with interim storage of spent fuel like the United States. But they described their companies as "trapped" into reprocessing by the commitments that had been made to the local governments that host their nuclear power plants.[55] Japan's Atomic Energy Commission made the same argument publicly in 2005 (see above). Japan should not trap itself more deeply.

Japan has already postponed for decades the construction of a second reprocessing plant, which was originally to have been put into operation in 2010. The current plan is to bring it into operation around 2050,[56] but that would be after the proposed opening of the geological repository, currently planned for around 2035.[57] Japan should reserve for itself the option of not building the reprocessing plant but simply emplacing in the repository spent fuel not reprocessed by the first plant.

Endnotes

1. Lee Jong-Heon, "South Koreans Call for Nuclear Sovereignty," *United Press International*, June 15, 2009; Jungmin Kang, "The North Korean Nuclear Test: Seoul Goes on the Defensive," *Bulletin of the Atomic Scientists*, June 12, 2009. For a subsequent, skeptical South Korean view, see Kim Young-hie, "The Case against Reprocessing," *JoongAng Daily*, January 23, 2010, available from *joongangdaily.joins.com/article/view.asp?aid=2915656*.

2. Thomas Cochran *et al.*, "Fast Reactor Development in the United States," *Fast Breeder Reactor Programs: History and Status,* Princeton, NJ: Princeton University, International Panel on Fissile Materials, 2010, p. 89.

3. Alvin Weinberg, *The First Nuclear Era: The Life and Times of a Technological Fixer,* New York: Springer, 1994, p. 41.

4. Glenn Seaborg, "The Plutonium Economy of the Future," paper presented at the Fourth International Conference, "Plutonium and Other Actinides," Santa Fe, NM, October 5, 1970, US Atomic Energy Commission press release S-33-70.

5. George Perkovich, *India's Nuclear Bomb,* Berkeley, CA: University of California Press, 1999, pp. 27-31.

6. Anthony Andrews, *Nuclear Fuel Reprocessing: US Policy Development,* Washington, DC: Congressional Research Service, March 27, 2008, available from *www.fas.org/sgp/crs/nuke/RS22542.pdf.*

7. Cochran *et al.*

8. Richard G. Hewlett and Francis Duncan, *Nuclear Navy: 1946–1962,* Chicago, IL: University of Chicago Press, 1974, p. 274.

9. *History of Japan Nuclear Cycle Development Institute,* Ibaraki, Japan: Japan Nuclear Fuel Cycle Development Institute, 2005, p. 19, available from *www.jaea.go.jp/jnc/siryou/skikoushi/pdf/e_jnc.pdf.*

10. The IAEA assumes that 8 kilograms (kgs) of reactor-grade plutonium is sufficient to make a nuclear weapon, including production losses. The Nagasaki bomb contained 6 kg of weapon-grade plutonium.

11. Charles S. Costello III, "Nuclear Nonproliferation: A Hidden but Contentious Issue in US-Japan Relations During the Carter Administration (1977-1981)" *Asia-Pacific Perspectives,* May 2003, p. 1. I have been informed by Dr. Fumihiko Yoshida that, although the translation "a matter of life and death" is literally correct, the sense in Japanese is less dramatic, i.e., "a critical matter."

12. Cochran *et al.*, Figure 1.2.
13. See, for example, "Declassified Documents Show Japan Balked at Signing Nuclear Weapons Treaty in 1970," November 30, 2010, available from *mdn.mainichi.jp/mdnnews/news/20101130p2a00m0na012000c.html.* The documents include draft "diplomatic policy guidelines in September 1969 [that] pointed to the need for Japan to have the capability to convert its nuclear technology into nuclear weapons while promoting the peaceful use of nuclear energy."
14. Agreement for Cooperation Between the Government of the United States of America and the Government of Japan Concerning Peaceful Uses of Nuclear Energy, available from *nnsa.energy.gov/sites/default/files/nnsa/inlinefiles/Japan_123.pdf.*
15. Tatsujiro Suzuki, "Japan's Plutonium Breeder Reactor and Its Fuel Cycle," *Fast Breeder Reactor Programs: History and Status, International Panel on Fissile Materials, 2010*, p. 56.
16. Used in the Nagasaki design, reactor-grade plutonium would most likely produce a yield of 1,000 tons of chemical explosive equivalent, vs. the 20,000-ton yield of the Nagasaki bomb. More advanced designs are insensitive to the grade of plutonium.
17. Citizen's Nuclear Information Center, "Long-Term Nuclear Program Planning Committee Publishes Costs of Nuclear Fuel Cycle," *Nuke Info Tokyo,* No. 103, November-December 2004, available from *www.cnic.jp/english/newsletter/nit103/.*
18. "History of Japan's Reprocessing Policy," Tokyo, Japan: Citizens Nuclear Information Center, available from *cnic.jp/english/newsletter/nit111/nit111articles/nit111rokkasho.html.*
19. At $130 per kilogram, the average price during 2009-2010, uranium contributed about $0.003 to the cost of a kilowatt hour. At $70/barrel, the cost of oil would contribute $0.085 to the cost of a kilowatt hour generated by an oil-fired power plant operating with 50-percent heat to electricity conversion efficiency.
20. *Framework for Nuclear Energy Policy*, Tokyo, Japan: Japan Atomic Energy Commission, 2005, p. 33, available from *www.aec.go.jp/jicst/NC/tyoki/taikou/kettei/eng_ver.pdf.*
21. "Long-Term Nuclear Program Planning Committee Publishes Costs of Nuclear Fuel Cycle."
22. "Report of Cost Estimate by the Federation of Electric Power Companies," *Nuke Info Tokyo,* No. 98, November 2003- February 2004, p. 10, available from *cnic.jp/english/newsletter/pdffiles/nit98.pdf.*

23. "Investing in Japan: Regional Information, Aomori Prefecture," Tokyo, Japan: Japan External Trade Organization (JETRO), available from *www.jetro.go.jp/en/invest/region/aomori/.*

24. The payments to Aomori Prefecture include 23,800 yen ($270) per kg of spent fuel imported into the prefecture. At 800 tons/year, that comes to about $200 million/year. Masafumi Takubo, "Wake Up, Stop Dreaming: Reassessing Japan's Reprocessing Program," *Nonproliferation Review,* Vol. 15, No. 1, 2008, p. 71.

25. *Japan's Spent Fuel and Plutonium Management Challenges,* Princeton, NJ: Princeton University, International Panel on Fissile Materials, 2006; Hisanori Nei, "Back End of Fuel Cycle Regulation in Japan," session 2A; and M. Kato, *et al*., "Activities Related to Safety Regulations of Spent Fuel Interim Storage at Japan,"Session 5A, "International Conference on Management of Spent Fuel from Nuclear Power Reactors," Vienna, Austria: IAEA, May 31–June 4, 2010, available from *www-ns.iaea.org/meetings/rw-summaries/vienna-2010-mngement-spent-fuel.htm.*

26. "Hamaoka Nuclear Power Station Replacement Plan," Chuden, Japan: Chubu Electric Power Co, 2008.

27. "Activities Related to Safety Regulations of Spent Fuel Interim Storage at Japan."

28. "Viability Assessment of a Repository at Yucca Mountain," *Total System Performance Assessment,* DOE/RW-0508/V3, Washington, DC: US Department of Energy, 1998, pp. 4-23.

29. Ki-Chul Park, "Status and Prospect of Spent Fuel Management in South Korea," *Nuclear Industry*, August 2008 (in Korean).

30. Conventional PUREX reprocessing dissolves spent fuel in acid. Pyroprocessing dissolves it in molten salt.

31. Park Seong-won, Miles Pomper, and Lawrence Scheinman, "The Domestic and International Politics of Spent Nuclear Fuel in South Korea: Are We Approaching Meltdown?" Academic Paper Series, Washington, DC: Korea Economic Institute, March 2010. Dr. Park is a former vice president of KAERI. Pomper and Scheinman are with the James Martin Center for Non-proliferation Studies.

32. The cores would be more pancake-shaped than cylindrical and would not be surrounded by uranium blankets to minimize the breeding of plutonium.

33. Jungmin Kang and H. A. Feiveson, "South Korea's Shifting and Controversial Interest in Spent Fuel Reprocessing," *Nonproliferation Review,* Spring 2001, p. 70.

34. Jungmin Kang *et al*., "South Korea's Nuclear Surprise," *Bulletin of the Atomic Scientists*, January/February 2005, p. 40.

35. For the proposed dates of the pyroprocessing facilities, see Korea Atomic Energy Research Institute, Nuclear Fuel Cycle Process Development Division, available from *www.kaeri.re.kr/english/sub/sub01_04_02_02_01.jsp*. For the proposed date of the fast reactor demonstration plant, see Fast Reactor Technology Development Division, available from *www.kaeri.re.kr/english/sub/sub01_04_02_01_01.jsp*. For the capacity of the demonstration plant, I assume 0.6 GWe as proposed by KAERI in its KALIMER-600 design and a very low "conversion ratio" of 0.25, i.e., of production of new transuranic atoms per transuranic atoms fissioned.

36. Based on 40 GWe of light-water-reactor capacity projected for 2030, National Energy Committee, *The 1st National Energy Basic Plan* (2008-2030), 2008 (Korean). South Korea currently has 15 GWe of LWR capacity and 10 GWe under construction.

37. "The Domestic and International Politics of Spent Nuclear Fuel in South Korea: Are We Approaching Meltdown?"

38. *Ibid.*

39. Won Il Ko *et al.*, "Implications of the New National Energy Basic Plan for Nuclear Waste Management in Korea," *Energy Policy,* Vol. 37, 2009, p. 3484.

40. KAERI's notional repository design is based on that of the Swedish Nuclear Fuel and Waste Management Company (SKB), which has copper canisters surrounded by bentonite clay emplaced in granite along tunnels spaced equal distances apart. Preserving the radioisotope retardation properties of the bentonite requires that it be wet, i.e., kept below a temperature of 100° C. Both SKB and KAERI analyses show that the temperature peaks about 20 years after emplacement. Jan Sundberg *et al.*, "Modeling of Thermal Rock Mass Properties at the Potential Sites of a Swedish Nuclear Waste Repository," *International Journal of Rock Mechanics and Mining Sciences*, Vol. 46, 2009, p. 1042; and S. K. Kim, "A Comparison of the HLW Underground Repository Cost for the Vertical and Horizontal Emplacement Options in Korea," *Progress in Nuclear Energy,* Vol. 49, 2007, p. 79. The thermal power output of spent fuel drops by a factor of more than 2 between 40 and 100 years after discharge. Roald A. Wigeland, "Separations and Transmutation Criteria to Improve Utilization of a Geologic Repository," *Nuclear Technology,* Vol. 154, April 2006, p. 95.

41. "Pyroprocess Technology," Daejeon, South Korea: KAERI, available from *www.kaeri.re.kr/english/sub/sub04_03.jsp*.

42. Robert Bari and L-Y Cheng (Brookhaven National Lab.), J. Phillips and M. Zentner (Pacific Northwest National Lab.), J. Pilat (Los Alamos National Lab.), G. Rochau (Sandia National Lab.), I. Therios (Argonne

National Lab.), R. Wigeland (Idaho National Lab.), and E. Wonder (QuinetiQ North America), "Proliferation Risk Reduction Study of Alternative Spent Fuel Processing Technologies," Annual Meeting of the Institute of Materials Management, Tucson, AZ, July 12-16, 2009.

43. Derek Mitchell, "Taiwan's Hsin Chu Program: Deterrence, Abandonment, and Honor," Kurt Campbell, Robert Einhorn and Mitchell Reiss, eds., *The Nuclear Tipping Point: Why States Reconsider Their Nuclear Choices,* Washington, DC: Brookings, 2004.

44. Chin-Shan Lee, "Current Status of Taipower's Radwaste Management Program," Taipei, Taiwan: Taiwan Power Company, December 5, 2006, no longer available on the web; and Chih-tien Liu, "Management of Spent Nuclear Fuel Dry Storage in Taiwan," Taipei City, Republic of China: Atomic Energy Council, October 26, 2007, available from *open.nat.gov.tw/OpenAdmin/robta/show_file.jsp?sysId=C09602868&fileNo=003*.

45. Mark Hibbs, "Long-term Spent Fuel Dilemma at Issue in Taiwan-US Renegotiation," *Nuclear Fuel,* June 1, 2009; "Taiwan Looks to GNEP for Answers to Threatening Spent Fuel Dilemma," *Nuclear Fuel,* May 7, 2007.

46. Dai Yunxiu, "Introduction of the Large Scale Reprocessing Plant in China," China National Nuclear Corporation, International Conference on Management of Spent Fuel from Nuclear Power Reactors, Vienna, Austria, May 31–June 4, 2010.

47. Mark Hibbs, "China Should Remain Prudent in Its Nuclear Fuel Path," Washington, DC: Carnegie Endowment for Peace, November 2010.

48. "Nuclear Power in China," London, UK: World Nuclear Association, available from *www.world-nuclear.org/info/inf63.html*.

49. For the start and suspension of construction of the BN-800, see "Overview of Fast Reactors in Russia and the Former Soviet Union," Lemont, IL: Argonne National Laboratory. For the restart of its construction, see the IAEA's fast reactor database. For the current plan for completion, see "Nuclear Power in Russia," London, UK: World Nuclear Association, available from *www.world-nuclear.org/info/inf45.html*.

50. IAEA, *Power Reactor Information System.*

51. O. M. Saraev, "Operating Experience with Beloyarsk Power Reactor BN600 NPP, Beloyarsk Sverdlovsk Nuclear Power Plant," IAEA FBR database, available from *www.iaea.org/inisnkm/nkm/aws/fnss/fulltext/1180_4.pdf*.

52. "Communication Received from the Russian Federation Concerning its Policies Regarding the Management of Plutonium," INFCIRC/549/Add.9/12, Vienna, Austria: IAEA, August 16, 2010.

53. "Fast Reactor Database, 2006 Update: Part 3. Core Characteristics," Vienna, Austria: IAEA, states 2.71 tons of total plutonium in the core and a mean residence time for the fuel of 420 full-power days.

54. *Agreement Between the Government of the United States Of America and the Government of the Russian Federation Concerning the Management and Disposition of Plutonium Designated as No Longer Required for Defense Purposes and Related Cooperation*, 2000, *www.state.gov/documents/organization/18557.pdf*; as amended by its 2010 *Protocol*, available from *www.state.gov/documents/organization/140694.pdf.*

55. Interviews by the author, Tokyo, Japan, March 1993.

56. T. Fukasawa *et al.*, "LWR Spent Fuel Management for the Smooth Deployment of FBR," International Conference on Management of Spent Fuel from Nuclear Power Reactors, Vienna, Austria: IAEA, May 31-June 4, 2010.

57. Hisanori Nei, NISA, METI, Government of Japan, "Back End of Fuel Cycle Regulation in Japan," presentation at the International Conference on Management of Spent Fuel from Nuclear Power Reactors, Vienna, Austria: IAEA, May 31-June 4, 2010, available from *www-ns.iaea.org/meetings/rw-summaries/vienna-2010-mngement-spent-fuel.asp.*

Chapter 5

China and the Emerging Strategic Competition in Aerospace Power

Mark Stokes
Ian Easton

Introduction

Competition is emerging over efforts to secure access to and control of the air and space mediums in the Asia-Pacific region. This competition is being driven in large part by the Chinese development of military capabilities and strategies, which increasingly challenge the ability of regional air-, missile-, and space-defense programs to keep pace. The emergence of aerospace power as a key instrument of Chinese statecraft has implications for the strategic landscape of the region and well beyond.

The military modernization campaign being undertaken by the People's Republic of China (PRC) and the Chinese development, testing, and deployment of advanced aerospace capabilities are eroding the confidence of other regional actors that they will have ensured access to and control of the air and space mediums in the event of a conflict. This is of crucial importance, because the Asia-Pacific region, defined by its vast distances and long-time horizons, is an aerospace theater by its very nature, and access to and control of the air and space dimensions of any future conflict will be critical to achieving political and military successes on the land and the sea.

The rise of China as a major economic, technological, military, and political player is changing the dynamics within the Asia-Pacific region and the world at large. Uncertainty over Chinese intentions is creating anxieties. As Richard Bush of the Brookings Institute notes, "A rising power poses a challenge to the prevailing international system and to the states that guard that system, because the new power's intentions are usually unclear."[1] Against the backdrop of ambiguity and uncertainty of the future, China's aerospace developments merit further examination.

The latest Quadrennial Defense Review (QDR), in reference to China, states: "Future adversaries will likely posses sophisticated capabilities designed to contest or deny command of the air, sea, space, and cyberspace domains."[2] Indeed, the People's Liberation Army (PLA) is rapidly advancing its capacity to apply aerospace power to create effects across domains in order to defend against perceived threats to national sovereignty and territorial integrity. Influential Chinese strategists argue that modern conventional aerospace capabilities transcend the nuclear threshold, in that they are powerful enough to deter and defeat formidable enemies without having to resort to the threat of using nuclear weapons.[3] Constrained by a relatively underdeveloped aviation establishment, the PLA is investing in aerospace capabilities that may offset shortcomings in the face of a more technologically advanced adversary. Whoever dominates the skies over a given territory—such as Taiwan; disputed territories in northern India or Japan, and the South China Sea—has a decisive advantage on the surface.

This chapter addresses trends in PRC force modernization intended to exploit weaknesses in regional air, missile, and space defenses, including a growing ability to maintain persistent surveillance around China's periphery. Included is a brief overview of China's expanding short- and medium-range ballistic missile and ground-launched cruise missile infrastructure. The subsequent section outlines trends in missile defense and long-range precision strike modernization in Taiwan, Japan, India, and the United States. The final section addresses the implications of China's growing aerospace power for regional strategic stability.

Aerospace Campaign Theory and China's Force Modernization

One of the most significant aspects of China's military modernization program is Beijing's expansion of, and growing reliance on, conventional ballistic and ground- launched cruise missiles as the centerpiece of the PRC's political and military strategy. Large-scale theater missile raids—combined with other enablers, such as anti-satellite (ASAT), cyber, and electronic attacks directed against selected critical nodes within an opponent's command and control structure or air defense system—can enable conventional air operations to be carried out at reduced risk and cost.

Barring the fielding of effective countermeasures, Chinese conventional theater missiles—specifically short- and medium-range ballistic and extended- range land attack cruise missiles (LACMs)—may over time give the PLA a decisive advantage in future conflicts around China's periphery. Ballistic and ground-launched cruise missiles are an attractive means of delivering lethal payloads due to the inherent difficulties in defending against them. Ballistic missiles themselves have a strong coercive effect, as potential adversaries around the PRC periphery have limited defensive countermeasures.

The PRC also is focused on developing the means to deny or complicate the ability of the United States to intervene in a regional crisis. Authoritative Chinese writings indicate research into, and development of, increasingly accurate and longer-range conventional strategic strike systems that could be launched from Chinese territory against land-, sea-, and space-based targets throughout the Asia-Pacific region in a crisis situation.

Extended-range conventional precision strike assets could be used to suppress US operations from forward bases in Japan, from US aircraft battle groups operating in the Western Pacific, and perhaps, over the next 5 to 10 years, from US bases on Guam. The development and deployment of an anti-ship ballistic missile (ASBM) is an example of an emerging capability. China's research and development community is expanding the nation's capacity for regional maritime surveillance in support of the PLA's missile-centric strategy. Most noteworthy is the development of constellations of intelligence-gathering satellites for the tracking and targeting of ships and mobile air defense systems.

The Centerpiece of China's Coercive Aerospace Power: Conventional Ballistic and Land Attack Cruise Missiles

The PRC's growing arsenal of increasingly accurate and lethal conventional ballistic and land-attack cruise missiles has rapidly emerged as a cornerstone of PLA warfighting capability. Since the official establishment of the PLA's first short-range ballistic missile (SRBM) brigade in 1993, ballistic missiles have been a primary instrument of psychological and political intimidation, but also potentially devastating tools of military utility. Over the last 2 decades, the Second Artillery's conventional ballistic and land attack cruise missile force—a form of aerospace power that will be critical for achievement of information dominance and air superiority in the opening phase of a conflict—has expanded significantly.

Short-Range Ballistic Missile Infrastructure. The Second Artillery's SRBM infrastructure is a central component of the PRC's coercive political and military strategy. In 2000, China's SRBM force was limited to one "regimental-sized unit" in southeastern China. Today, the force has grown to at least seven SRBM brigades. Among these, five are subordinate to the Second Artillery's 52 Base, and the remaining two units report directly to military regions.[4] The number of missiles in the Second Artillery is widely cited as exceeding 1,300 (inclusive of tactical missiles assigned to ground forces).[5] According to reports, the quantity, range, precision, and lethality of China's SRBMS are increasing over time.[6] One example can be seen in the recently deployed DF-16, a new SRBM variant with a range of up to 1,000 kilometers (km) that is reportedly designed for greater penetration of Taiwan's missile defense networks.[7]

Medium-Range Ballistic Missiles. Having established a solid foundation in conventional SRBMs, the PLA has begun to extend and diversify the warfighting capacity of the Second Artillery's ballistic missile force. The centerpiece of the Second Artillery's regional mission is the two-stage, solid-fueled DF-21 (CSS-5) medium-range ballistic missile (MRBM). Currently, the terminally guided DF-21C can deliver a 2,000 kiloton (KT) warhead to a range of at least 1,750 km, with a circular error probable (CEP) of less than 50 meters. The system could be used for conventional strikes against targets throughout Japan from east and northeast China; New Delhi, if based in Xinjiang; and western India, if based in Yunnan.[8]

Ground Launched Cruise Missiles (GLCMs). To augment its ballistic missile arsenal, the Second Artillery is steadily expanding its ground-launched LACM infrastructure. GLCMs are powerful instruments of military and political utility, because of the inherent difficulty in defending against them. Within only a few years of initial deployments, the PRC today has the world's largest inventory of extended-range GLCMs. Able to penetrate defenses and strike critical targets on land, out to a range of at least 2,000 km, the Second Artillery's DH-10 GLCMs appear to have enjoyed a relatively high acquisition priority.[9]

Anti-Satellite Weapons

China successfully tested a direct-assent, kinetic-kill ASAT missile on January 11, 2007. The test was followed with revelations that China had conducted ASAT missile tests on three previous occasions and had reportedly tested a high-powered laser ASAT weapon system on US satellites during the previous year.[10] On January 11, 2010, 3 years to the date of its successful direct-ascent ASAT test, China tested a midcourse interceptor, which represented an inherent leap forward in its ASAT capability.[11] China is also reportedly developing other ASAT weapons that could also be potentially difficult to detect and defend against, such as co-orbital micro satellite weapons (also known as parasite satellites); high-powered microwave and particle beam weapons; high-performance radar and electronic jammers; and cyber attack capabilities that could be directed against satellite tracking and control stations. In short, China's ASAT weapons programs are of a broad nature and are expanding in scope.[12]

Anti-Ship Ballistic Missiles and Beyond. China's ASBM program was officially confirmed to be in the testing phase in March 2010,[13] and ASBMs were reported to have been deployed in Southeastern China in December 2010.[14] Barring deployment of effective defenses, an initial ASBM would give the PLA a precision strike capability against aircraft carriers and other US and allied ships operating within 1,500-2,000 km from China's coast. Over the longer term, Chinese technical writings indicate the preliminary conceptual development of a conventional global precision strike capability. The accuracy and range of the PLA's conventional ballistic missile force is also expected to improve significantly over the next 10-15 years, as missiles incorporate more advanced inertial and satellite-aided navigation systems, sophisticated terminal guidance systems, and increasingly powerful solid rocket motors.[15]

Sensor Architecture for Regional Surveillance

The PLA's ability to conduct strategic and operational strike missions is likely to be restricted by the range of its persistent surveillance. To expand its battlespace awareness, the PLA is investing in at least three capabilities that could enable it to monitor activities in the Western Pacific, South China Sea, and Indian Ocean.

Space-Based Surveillance

Increasingly sophisticated space-based systems are expanding the PLA's battlespace awareness and supporting potential strike operations further from Chinese shores.[16] Space assets enable the monitoring of naval activities in surrounding waters and the tracking of air force deployments into the region. Space-based reconnaissance systems also provide imagery necessary for mission planning functions, such as navigation and terminal guidance for ASBMs and cruise missiles. Satellite communications also offer a survivable means of transmission, which will become particularly important as the PLA operates further from its territory.

China's regional strike capability appears to rely heavily on high-resolution, dual-use space-based synthetic aperture radar (SAR), electro-optical (EO), and electronic intelligence (ELINT) satellites for surveillance and targeting.[17] In a crisis situation, China may have the option of augmenting existing space-based assets with microsatellites launched on solid-fueled launch vehicles. Existing and future data-relay satellites and other beyond line-of-sight communications systems could transmit targeting data to and from the theater and/or the Second Artillery's operational-level command center.[18]

Persistent Near-space Surveillance. Chinese analysts view the realm between the atmosphere and space—"near-space"—as an area of future strategic competition.[19] Over the decade, near-space flight vehicles[20] may emerge as a dominant platform for a persistent region-wide surveillance capability during crisis situations. "Near-space" is generally characterized as the region between 20 and 100 km (65,000 to 328,000 feet [ft]) above the earth's surface.[21]

While technical challenges exist, the Second Artillery and China's defense research and development (R&D) community have become increasingly interested in near-space flight vehicles for reconnaissance, communications relay, electronic countermeasures, and precision strike operations.[22] In order to overcome technical challenges, China's aerospace industry—specifically the China Aerospace Science and Technology Corporation (CASC) and the China Aerospace Science and Industry Corporation (CASIC)—have established new research institutes dedicated to the design, development, and manufacturing of near-space-flight vehicles. Establishment of a dedicated research institute for leveraging the unique characteristics of near space signifies the importance that China places on this domain.[23]

Over-the-Horizon Radar

In addition to space-based and near-space sensors, over-the-horizon backscatter (OTH-B) radar systems would be a central element of an extended-range air and maritime surveillance architecture.[24] Managed by the PLA Air Force (PLAAF), an over-the-horizon (OTH) radar system could define the range of China's maritime precision strike capability. Skywave OTH radar systems emit a pulse in the lower part of the frequency spectrum (3-30 megaherz [MHz]) that bounces off the ionosphere to illuminate a target—either air or surface—from the top down. As a result, detection ranges for wide-area surveillance can extend out to 1,000 to 4,000 km.

Regional Impact

The PRC's expanding capacity for conducting an aerospace campaign in the Asia-Pacific region would likely be a variable of its territorial disputes with states around its periphery. As its military strength increases relative to those of its neighbors, the PRC could feasibly become more assertive in its claims. Along this trajectory, miscalculations, accidents, disputes over sovereignty, or other unforeseen events have the potential to escalate into armed conflict between the PRC and its neighbors. Each defense establishment in the region appears to be approaching the challenges differently, although most are attempting to balance interests in maintaining healthy relations with Beijing while at the same time hedging in the event of a future conflict.

United States. There are indications that the United States views China's aerospace power capability developments as its most challenging long-term conventional military threat, and is seeking ways in which to ensure an adequate defense for its forward-deployed troops in the West Pacific and its allies in the region. According to the 2010 Ballistic Missile Defense Review (BMDR), "One regional trend that particularly concerns the Unites States is the growing imbalance of power across the Taiwan Strait in China's favor. China is developing advanced ballistic missile capabilities that can threaten its neighbors and ASBM capabilities that can attempt to target naval forces in the region." Chinese ballistic missiles "will be capable of reaching not just important Taiwan military and civilian facilities but also US and allied military installations in the region."[25] As such, the United States is seeking to strengthen its missile defense partnerships in the region, most notably with Japan, while also developing and deploying a range of land-, sea-, and air-based missile defense systems supported by space-based early warning and missile tracking sensors. At the high end of the spectrum, the United States is deploying a space-based ballistic missile defense (BMD) system in the form of the Space-based Infrared System (SBIRS) and its integrated ground components. When complete, SBIRS will consist of four SBIRS-high satellites in geosynchronous orbit (GEO) high over the equator and two in highly elliptical orbits (HEO) that provide for coverage of higher latitudes.[26] These satellites provide a revolutionary early warning system that is sensitive enough to detect and target mobile missile launchers from their engines' heat signatures and will have a crucial role to play in missile defense.[27] SBIRS satellites are currently augmenting the Defense Support Program (DSP) satellites in GEO, which they are designed to eventually replace.[28] This combination of SBIRS and DSP satellites has been utilized in the creation of the theater event system (TES) in order to increase defense against growing theater ballistic missile (TBM) threats, of which China represents the largest in terms of size and sophistication.

In the Asia-Pacific region, space-based BMD systems are augmented by long-range ground-based warning sensors such as the Perimeter Acquisition Vehicle Entry Phased Array Weapons System (PAVE PAWS) sensor site at Beale Air Force Base, California,[29] and the mobile Sea-Based X-band radar in Alaska.[30] The US Navy is also deploying Aegis BMD cruisers and destroyers with advanced surveillance sensors and missile interceptors.[31] On Guam, the US Army Air and Missile Defense Command is in the process of deploying a missile defense task force for the Pacific region. This would include a Terminal High Altitude Area Defense (THAAD) battery and a Patriot Advanced Capability-3 (PAC-3) battery for ballistic missile defense, along with a surface-launched advanced medium-range air-to-air missile (SLAMRAAM) battery for cruise missile defense.[32]

US Forces Japan (USFJ) has been increasing its deployment of BMD units to Japan. USFJ deployed a mobile X-band radar system to Shariki Air Base in Aomori Prefecture in June 2006, and, in September 2006, deployed a PAC-3 battalion to Kadena Air Base on Okinawa.[33] In August 2006, the United States began forward deploying BMD capable, Aegis destroyers armed with Standard Missile-3 (SM-3) interceptors in and around Japan.[34] In October 2007, a Joint Tactical Ground Station (JTAGS) was established at Misawa AB in Aomori Prefecture.[35]

The US missile defense buildup in the Asia-Pacific region is being driven primarily by the potential threat that China's ballistic and cruise missiles present to US forces and allies in the region, most acutely illustrated by China's development of an ASBM system. China's ASBM program could jeopardize US ability to conduct air operations in the West Pacific in the near-to mid-future, potentially challenging US defense commitments in the region.[36] China's long-range anti-ship cruise missile (ASCM) and LACM programs could also have similar effects.[37] For this reason, the United States is developing a number of potential solutions to this unprecedented challenge that go beyond the current BMD architecture. Potential missile defense capabilities under development include air-launched hit-to-kill interceptors, directed energy systems, and land-based SM-3 interceptors.[38]

Taiwan. Taiwan faces the most difficult ballistic and cruise missile threat in the world. Despite a recent warming in cross-strait relations, Mainland China continues to increase its missile buildup vis-à-vis Taipei, both quantitatively and qualitatively.[39] Underscoring this point, the head of Taiwan's National Security Bureau has stated that a significant majority of China's military exercises continue to be directed against Taiwan.[40] A senior Taiwan intelligence official has also stated that China plans to increase the number of missiles deployed against Taiwan to at least 1,800.[41] As a result, Taiwan continues to build upon its existing missile-defense infrastructure comprised of both US missile defense systems obtained through Foreign Military Sales (FMS) channels and indigenous missile-defense systems developed with US assistance.

Taiwan currently fields three PAC-2 air defense batteries with 200 missiles deployed around Taipei and has developed a number of road-mobile Tien Kung-II (TK-II) air-defense missiles with a 300-km engagement range. These systems augment Taiwan's static, silo-based Tien Kung-I (TK-I) air-defense missiles, and 13 batteries of aging Improved-Homing All-the-WAY Killer (I-HAWK) missiles. Taiwan intends to begin replacing some I-HAWKs with TK-II systems.[42] To improve its missile-defense posture, Taiwan is upgrading its PAC-2 batteries to PAC-3 configuration, and purchasing new PAC-3 batteries. This could provide Taiwan with around 400 PAC-3 missiles.[43] These will augment Taiwan's approximately 500 TK-I and TK-II missiles, as well as its next-generation TK-III system, which is under development and scheduled to be deployed in 2012.[44]

Taiwan is also investing in early warning and upgrading its missile-defense sensors and command and control systems to undercut the coercive utility of China's theater and cruise missiles. Taiwan's initial step has been procuring a long-range early warning radar able to detect both air-breathing[45] and ballistic targets at extended ranges through US FMS channels. Building on existing PAVEPAWS technology, the radar system is to be situated on a peak in the Central Mountain range and will be able to provide early warning of ballistic missile launches at distances of as far as 3,000 km. The radar is also designed to monitor air targets over the Taiwan Strait and beyond at ranges of less than 200 km, depending on the target's altitude and radar cross-section.[46] The radar will augment existing and new radar systems deployed throughout Taiwan and its off-shore islands.[47] These systems will provide early warning against threats to the new Anyu-4 air defense system, comprised of regional operations control centers (ROCCs). In the event of a threat, the ROCCs will select the appropriate interceptor from a menu of air defense systems.[48]

In addition, Taiwan has long maintained an ability to carry out deep strike missions against military targets in southeast China. To counter PRC coercion, Taiwan stresses maintenance of the necessary military strength, the ability to survive a first-strike attack, and an ability to carry out a second-strike retaliation.[49] In the past, the Taiwan air force has earmarked a limited number of its fighters for strike missions, should a decision be made to do so. However, with PLA air defenses growing increasingly sophisticated, Taiwan has been developing other means to maintain a limited strike option. PRC sources indicate that Taipei has been developing its own answer to the Second Artillery's DH-10 GLCM—a land attack variant of the HF-2 anti-ship cruise missile, the HF-2E.[50]

For space-based surveillance, Taiwan has co-developed and operated two dual-use imagery satellites, the now-retired Formosat-1 and the Formosat-2. Taiwan also purchases commercial satellite imagery from a number of sources to augment its space-based reconnaissance program. However, Taiwan currently faces a gap in domestic satellite imagery coverage because its next-generation imagery satellite, Formosat-5, has suffered repeated delays and will not be launched until the end of 2013 or the first part of 2014.[51] Revelations that Mainland China exploited a commercial Singaporean communications satellite that the Taiwanese military was using during exercises have prompted Taiwan to consider building its own communications satellite to guarantee secure communications. However, for budgetary and technical reasons, it appears unlikely that such a satellite would be developed in the near- to mid-future.[52] Taiwan is currently seeking to establish the technical foundation to conduct its own satellite launches. As part of this program, Taiwan began launching sounding rockets in 1998, with seven launches having been conducted as of 2010.[53]

Japan. Unlike those of Taiwan, Japan's security concerns are primarily directed at North Korea. The chances for armed conflict between the PRC and Japan are relatively slim, despite historical animosity and budding nationalist sentiments. However, unresolved territorial disputes and a more assertive China could lead to a crisis in the future. According to Japan's White Paper on defense, "In the event of an armed attack on Japan, such attacks are likely to begin with surprise air attacks using aircraft and missiles."[54] North Korea is viewed as representing an increasingly dangerous ballistic missile threat to Japan, and China's long-range ballistic and cruise missile developments are viewed with growing concern. As such, Japan has been taking a number of steps to improve its air defense posture, which includes upgrading its air defense radars, deploying a space-based intelligence network, integrating itself in the US BMD shield, and centralizing its air defense command headquarters. Japan's Air Self Defense Force (JASDF) maintains 28 ground-based, air defense radar sites.[55] Japan in recent years has begun the deployment of four FPS-5 next-generation missile defense radars, and seven improved FPS-3 radars. These radar sites and their associated air defense units are organized into six air defense missile groups, which are grouped geographically with their associated air wings and central aircraft control and warning wings into four air defense forces—each of which will maintain one advanced FPS-5 missile defense radar site.[56] These four Air Defense Forces are unified at Japan's Air Defense Command Headquarters, which will complete its move from Fuchu Air Station to Yokota Air Base in 2011.[57]

Japan has been actively integrating itself into the US BMD shield, co-developing and deploying ballistic and cruise missile defense systems. Japan has begun equipping its Aegis destroyers with SM-3s for upper-tier ballistic missile interception. Japan is also deploying PAC-3s to various strategic locations around the country.[58] Looking ahead, Japan's Ministry of Defense (MOD) intends to link four BMD-capable Aegis destroyers[59] and 16 PAC-3 Fire Units (FUs) to its new FPS-5 radar sites and upgraded FPS-3 radar sites via a command, control, and communications (C3) network known as the Japan Aerospace Defense Ground Environment (JADGE).[60] Eventually, Japan plans to have eight Kongo-class Aegis destroyers equipped with SM-3 missiles.[61]

In a move strengthening the US-Japanese missile defense partnership, all elements of Japan's air defense network will be unified at Japan's Air Defense Command (ADC) Headquarters at Yokota Air Base by the end of 2011, when JASDF's ADC completes its move from Fuchu Air Station. About 800 Japanese personnel will transfer to the new ADC headquarters building, which will be the supreme command authority for Japanese air and ballistic missile defense.[62] The JADGE C3 network and other advanced communications links will be used by the command when the relocation is complete.[63]

This move strengthens early warning and bilateral command and control, and the relocation will help facilitate joint cooperation between US and Japanese forces, as the new bilateral air operations center will link up with the 613th Air and Space Operations Center (AOC) at Hickham Air Force Base, Hawaii, which synchronizes all US air, space and cyberspace missions in the theater.[64] The JASDF ADC complex will also be physically linked by a tunnel to a basement control hub under the headquarters of the USFJ. The Bilateral Joint Operations Coordination Command Center (BJOCC) under the USFJ headquarters building can hold up to 150 people in wartime, and every position on the main floor has a Japanese counterpart working alongside US personnel to foster bilateral cooperation and augment bilateral operability.[65]

Japan began a space-based satellite reconnaissance program in response to North Korea's test firing of a short-ranged ballistic missile over Japanese territory in 1998. Currently, Japan is believed to operate three electro-optical (EO) reconnaissance satellites, and plans to launch two next-generation synthetic aperture radar imagery (SAR) satellites in 2011 and 2012, respectively, as well as two next-generation EO satellites in 2011 and 2014, respectively.[66] Japan is also seeking to develop a number of other space-based command, control, communications, computers, and intelligence surveillance and reconnaissance (C4ISR) capabilities—such as a dedicated military communications satellite, an infrared early warning satellite, a signals intelligence (SIGINT)-collection satellite, and an independent navigation and positioning satellite network.[67]

India. While India and China today maintain cordial official relations, tensions simmer under the surface. The PRC's territorial dispute with India is over two tracts of land in eastern and northern India-Aksai Chin, which is currently administered by the PRC under the Xinjiang Uyghur Autonomous Region (UAR); and Arunachal Pradesh, which is currently administered by India. While competing claims are unlikely to erupt in a future conflict, the two nations did fight a war over these claims in 1962, and that experience has severely conditioned Indian threat perceptions of China. For all the PRC's attempts to resolve border disputes with its neighbors, the one with India is still outstanding. India is enhancing its aerospace power with significant investments into air force, theater missile, and missile defense modernization.

The Indian Air Force (IAF) is developing a layered, hardened air defense C3 network called the integrated air command, control, communications system (IACCCS), which draws from reconnaissance satellites, early warning radars, unmanned aerial vehicles (UAVs), and Airborne Warning and Control Systems (AWACS). By 2016, the IAF plans to acquire 67 low-level air transportable radars; 18 long-range active phased array surveillance radars; and 12 aerostat-mounted active phased array radars. These radars will be deployed with the IAF's existing 32 mobile control and reporting centers; 12 air defense control centers; and approximately 40 base air defense zones on India's western and northeastern borders. These will progressively replace current radars, which were acquired during the 1970s and 1980s. The IAF also acquired two long-range tracking radars in 2001. Three AWACS, modified Ilyushin IL-76, were delivered in May 2009, with two more expected sometime in 2010.[68] When complete, this radar surveillance network will be linked to joint air traffic control and reporting centers that will be operational at 29 IAF air bases.[69] The IAF is currently looking to upgrade 39 of its 80 strategic air fields along India's borders with China and Pakistan to improve network centricity and mobility.[70]

India's IACCCS will support the nation's air and missile defense architecture. The IAF plans to acquire 2,000 long-range (120 km variant) Barak-2 surface-to-air missiles (SAMs), beginning in 2011. The Indian Army plans to acquire up to 1,500 medium-range (70 km variant) Barak-2 SAMs. Each launcher will have 12 missiles.[71] IAF also expects 18 Spyder SAM systems to be delivered by the end of 2012.[72]

Starting in 2006, India has conducted a series of high-altitude interceptor tests and intends to build a multi-tiered BMD system around its mobile, indigenously built advanced air defense (AAD) or "Prithvi" interceptor missile system.[73] Four of India's initial five BMD interceptor tests were successful, with one test, on March 14, 2010, having been aborted due to technical problems.[74] India plans to conduct a total of 10 interceptor tests—five endo-atmospheric (below 30 km) and five exo-atmospheric (up to 80 km)—with the AAD interceptor missile system beginning initial deployment by 2013.[75] A next-generation version of the system is under development for the interception of intercontinental ballistic missiles (ICBMs). India is also developing a laser-based BMD system for the interception of ballistic missiles, as well as lower-level air-breathing targets, and is planning on deploying space-based radars to support the nation's BMD architecture.[76]

India has a modest but growing military space program, and some influential Indian thinkers have advocated the development of an Indian ASAT weapons program in the wake of China's 2007 ASAT test. The director of India's Defense Research and Development Organization (DRDO), General V. K. Saraswat, has stated: "India is putting together building blocks of technology that could be used to neutralize enemy satellites."[77] Air Chief Marshal P. V. Naik, speaking in a clear reference to China, stated, "Our satellites are vulnerable to ASAT weapon systems because our neighborhood possesses one."[78] However, India is not expected to test a direct-ascent ASAT system in the near future, and instead plans to further develop its BMD interceptor system, based on Agni-III technology, so that it could leapfrog technology in order to field an ASAT weapon rapidly if needed.[79] India has tested exo-atmospheric ballistic missile interceptors, which could be evolved into kinetic-kill ASAT weapons, and India is also investing in laser weapons that could be applied to an ASAT mission as well.[80]

India operates one dedicated military EO imaging satellite, the CARTOSAT 2A, and three other dual-purpose EO satellites.[81] India also launched its first SAR imaging platform, RISAT-2, on April 20, 2009, to monitor its borders with China, Bangladesh, and Pakistan.[82] The IAF has long been trying to establish an Aerospace Command at Thiruvananthapuram, without success to date.[83]

PRC Aerospace Modernization and Regional Stability

The Asia-Pacific region is in the midst of fundamental change, with significant implications for long-term strategic stability. The gradual expansion of China's long-range precision strike capabilities, especially its increasingly sophisticated conventional ballistic and cruise missile infrastructure, is altering the regional strategic landscape. Due to their speed, precision, and difficulties in fielding viable defenses, these systems—if deployed in sufficient numbers—have the potential to provide the PRC with a decisive military edge in the event of conflict over territorial or sovereignty claims. Reliance on ballistic missiles and extended-range cruise missiles also incentivizes other militaries to develop similar capabilities. Beyond force modernization programs in Taiwan, Japan, and Taiwan, the PRC's expansion of its aerospace capabilities is at least a partial driver for a shift in US defense policies.[84]

The PLA's expanding capacity to deny the United States access to bases and the ability to project power into the region figured prominently in the 2010 QDR.[85] Augmenting the QDR are a number of analyses outlining ways to manage the dynamic shifts underway in the region. With concerns mounting over the anti-access challenge to utilizing bases in the Western Pacific and area denial capabilities that could restrict US naval operations, pressure to reduce the US footprint in Japan and elsewhere could mount. Noting the emergence of an arms race, Robert Kaplan of the Center for a New American Security foresees a shift in US basin— moving away from allied territories to Guam and the South Pacific Islands—and a greater US naval presence in the Indian Ocean.[86]

To counter the PLA's growing capacity to carry out an extended-range aerospace campaign, one detailed study suggests investing in the ability to withstand initial strikes and limit damage to US and allied forces and bases; neutralize PLA command and control networks;

suppress the PLA's theater sensor architecture and theater strike systems; and sustain initiative in the air, on the sea, in space, and within the cyber domain.[87]

In short, the PRC's expanding aerospace capabilities are influencing the development of similar capabilities in other defense establishments, including the United States. However, they may also have another effect. PLA successes in fielding advanced long-range precision strike systems dilute international efforts to stem proliferation of the means of delivery for weapons of mass destruction. This may encourage other countries to follow suit, especially as China's global leadership and standing increases. In particular, long-range cruise missiles have emerged as another proliferation concern. In light of Russia's threats for withdrawal, partially due to the global proliferation of short-and medium-range ballistic and ground-launched cruise missiles, the PLA's selection of these systems to defend its territorial claims could also undermine one of the most successful and enduring arms control agreements to date—the Intermediate Nuclear Force (INF) Treaty.[88]

Conclusion

The Asia-Pacific region is witnessing increasing competition over the air and space domains, as evidenced by regional missile defense and space capability acquisitions. China's development, testing, and deployment of advanced missile and emerging capabilities, such as ASAT, cyber, and advanced electronic warfare weapons, are the primary driver behind the competition. This competition could intensify over time, should the regional actors' sense of vulnerability continue to increase. The countries around China's periphery have a growing appreciation for key strategic importance of the air and space domains. This could lead to a proliferation of long-range precision strike and ASAT capabilities, and could have a highly detrimental effect on regional stability.

China's successes in designing, developing, and producing the world's largest and most sophisticated arsenal of medium- and intermediate-range ballistic missiles create a demand for similar capabilities around the world. Thus, the PLA's conventional missile-centric strategy potentially weakens international efforts to curb the proliferation of the means of delivery for weapons of mass destruction.

Looking ahead, it will be of critical importance to seek various means by which to mitigate the potential arms race brewing in the Asia-Pacific. A Chinese willingness to increase engagement and transparency with regional stakeholders in the Asia-Pacific as it continues to modernize its military air and space capabilities will be needed for putting the region on a course toward a future defined by greater strategic stability and prosperity.

Endnotes

1. Richard C. Bush III, "China and the US-Japan Alliance," *Yomiuri Shimbun*, June 6, 2009, available from *www.brookings.edu/opinions/2009/0606_china_japan_bush.aspx*.
2. *Quadrennial Defense Review Report*, Washington DC: Department of Defense, February 2010, p. 9, available from *www.defense.gov/qdr/images/QDR_as_of_12Feb10_1000.pdf*.
3. Jiang Guocheng, "Building an Offensive and Defensive PLAAF: A Critical Review of Lieutenant General Liu Yazhou's *The Centenary of the Air Force*," *Air and Space Power Journal*, Summer 2010, p. 87, available from *www.airpower.maxwell.af.mil/airchronicles/apj/apj10/sum10/2010-2%20Summer%20English%20ASPJ.pdf*.
4. One unit is under the Nanjing Military Region in the area of Xianyou (73661 Unit), and there is another in the area of Puning, Guangdong Province (75810 Unit).
5. *Military and Security Developments Involving the People's Republic of China 2010,* Washington DC: Department of Defense, 2010, p. 66.
6. *Ibid.*, p. 2.
7. J. Michael Cole, "PRC Missile Could Render PAC-3 Obsolete," *Taipei Times*, March 18, 2011, available from *www.taipeitimes.com/News/front/archives/2011/03/18/2003498473*.
8. *Ibid.*, pp. 38, 66. For an excellent overview, see "The DF-21 Series Medium Range Ballistic Missile," *KKTT Blog*, August 23, 2009, available from *liuqiankktt.blog.163.com/blog/static/121264211200972375114290/*.
9. As of December 2009, the PLA had 200-500 ground-launched DH-10s. See *Military and Security Developments Involving the People's Republic of China 2010,* Washington, DC: Department of Defense, 2010, p. 31. For an overview of the DH-10 program, see Ian Easton, "The Assassin under the Radar: China's DH-10 Cruise Missile Program," *The Project 2049 Institute Futuregram*, October 1, 2009.
10. See Ian Easton, "The Great Game in Space: China's Evolving ASAT Weapons Programs and Their Implications for Future US Strategy," Arlington, VA: The Project 2049 Institute, June 24, 2009.
11. Wendell Minnick, "China Missile Test Has Ominous Implications," *Defense News*, January 19, 2010, available from *www.defensenews.com/story.php?i=4460204*. See also Jeffery Lewis, "Chinese Missile

Defense Test," *Arms Control Wonk*, January 12, 2010, available from *lewis.armscontrolwonk.com/archive/2588/chinese-missile-defense-test*.

12. Easton, "The Great Game."

13. Wendell Minnick, "Chinese Anti-ship Missile Could Alter US Power," *Defense News*, April 5, 2010, p. 6. For an excellent overview, see Mark Stokes, "China's Evolving Conventional Strategic Strike Capability: The Anti-ship Ballistic Missile Challenge to US Maritime Operations in the Western Pacific and Beyond," Arlington, VA: *The Project 2049 Institute Occasional Paper*, September 14, 2009.

14. See Andrew Erickson and Gabe Collins, "Ballistic Missile (ASBM) Reaches Equivalent of Initial Operating Capability (IOC)," December 30, 2010, *China Sign Post*, available from *ship-from-to.com/324285/ballistic-missile-asbm-reaches-equivalent-of-initial-operational-capability-ioc-where-it-s-going-and-what-it-means*; and J. Michael Cole, "NSB Director Confirms PRC Deployment of 'New' Missile Unit in Guangdong Province," *Taipei Times*, May 27, 2011, available from *www.taipeitimes.com/News/taiwan/archives/2011/05/27/2003504271*.

15. For detailed assessments of China's ASBM program, see Andrew Erickson and David Yang, "On the Verge of a Game-Changer: A Chinese Anti-ship Ballistic Missile Could Alter the Rules in the Pacific and Place US Navy Carrier Strike Groups in Jeopardy," *US Naval Institute Proceedings*, Vol. 135, No. 3, May 2009, pp. 26-32. See also Andrew S. Erickson, "Chinese ASBM Development: Knowns and Unknowns," Jamestown Foundation *China Brief*, Vol. 9, Issue 13, June 24, 2009, pp. 4-8. For a broader summary, see Andrew S. Erickson and David D. Yang, "Using The Land To Control The Sea? Chinese Analysts Consider the Anti-ship Ballistic Missile," *Naval War College Review*, Vol. 62, No. 4, Autumn 2009, pp. 53-86. Additionally, see Eric Hagt and Matthew Durnin, "China's Anti-ship Ballistic Missile: Developments and Missing Links," *Naval War College Review*, Vol. 62, No. 4, Autumn 2009, pp. 87-115; and Stokes, "China's Evolving Conventional Strategic Strike Capability."

16. For examples of US overviews of China's space modernization, see Andrew S. Erickson, "Eyes in the Sky," *US Naval Institute Proceedings*, Vol. 136, No. 4, April 2010, pp. 36-41; Gregory Kulacki and Jeffrey G. Lewis, *A Place for One's Mat: China's Space Program, 1956–2003*, Cambridge, MA: American Academy of Arts and Sciences, 2009, available from *www.amacad.org/publications/spaceChina.pdf*; Kevin Pollpeter, "The Chinese Vision of Space Military Operations," in James Mulvenon and David Finklestein, eds., *China's Revolution in Doctrinal Affairs: Emerging Trends in the Operational Art of the Chinese People's Liberation Army*, Alexandria, VA: CNA Corporation, December 2005,

pp. 329-369, available from *www.defensegroupinc.com/cira/pdf/doctrinebook_ch9.pdf*; and Larry M. Wortzel, *The Chinese People's Liberation Army and Space Warfare: Emerging United States-China Military Competition,* Washington, DC: American Enterprise Institute, 2007, available from *www.aei.org/paper/26977*.

17. Ian Easton and Mark A. Stokes, "China's Electronic Intelligence (ELINT) Satellite Developments: Implications for US Air and Naval Operations," Arlington, VA: Project 2049 Institute, February 23, 2011.

18. See "China Blasts off First Data Relay Satellite," *Xinhua News Agency*, April 26, 2008, available from *news.xinhuanet.com/english/2008-04/26/content_8052455.htm*.

19. See Li Yiyong and Shen Huairong, "发展近空间飞行器系统的关键技术" ["Key Technologies for Developing Near Space Flight Vehicles"], *Journal of the Academy of Equipment Command & Technology,* October 2006, pp. 52-55.

20. In Chinese writings, near-space vehicles are referred to as *jinkongjian feixingqi* (近空间飞行器).

21. Guo Weimin, Si Wanbing, Gui Qishan, and He Jiafan,"导弹作战中临近空间飞行器与航天器的协同应用" ["Coordination and Applicability of Near Space Flight Vehicles in Missile Warfare"], 飞航导弹 [*Winged Missiles Journal*], May 2008.

22. For a representative Second Artillery overview, see Li Chao, Luo Chuanyong and Wang Hongli, "近空间飞行器在第二炮兵部队的应用研究" ["Research into Near Space Flight Vehicle Applications for the Second Artillery"], *Journal of Projectiles and Guidance,* January 2009; Tang Jiapeng, Guan Shixi, Ling Guilong, and Duan Na, "Study on Propulsion System of Near Space Vehicles," *Journal of Projectiles, Rockets, Missiles, and Guidance,* June 2009, pp. 145-148.

23. See Yang Jian, "航天一院10所揭牌成立" ["CASC First Academy 10th Research Institute Established"], *China Space News*, October 24, 2008, available from *www.china-spacenews.com/n435777/n435778/n435783/49822.html*.

24. See Sean O'Connor's excellent summary of the ASBM and OTH-B programs, available from *geimint.blogspot.com/2008/11/oth-radar-and-asbm-threat.html*.

25. *Ballistic Missile Defense Review Report*, Washington DC: Department of Defense, February 2010, p. 7, available from *www.defense.gov/bmdr/docs/BMDR%20as%20of%2026JAN10%200630_for%20web.pdf*.

26. Edward P. Chatters IV and Bryan Eberhardt, "Missile Warning Systems," in *AU-18 Space Primer*, Prepared by Air Command and Staff College

Space Research Seminars, Air University Press, Maxwell Air Force Base, Alabama, September 2009, p. 228, available from *space.au.af.mil/au-18-2009/au-18-2009.pdf*; "SBIRS Team Completes Critical Design Reviews for Follow-on Production Program for HEO and GEO Payloads," *Los Angeles Air Force Base News*, January 4, 2010, available from *www.losangeles.af.mil/news/story.asp?id=123184063*; and Amy Butler, "Classified Satellite Failure Led to Latest SBIRS Delay," *Aerospace Daily and Defense Report*, October 15, 2007, available from *abcnews.go.com/Technology/story?id=3732391&page=1*.

27. Jeremy Singer, "Downshifting in Space," *Airforce Magazine*, April 2009, available from *www.airforce-magazine.com/MagazineArchive/Pages/2009/April%202009/0409space.aspx*.

28. Chatters and Eberhardt, "Missile Warning Systems."

29. *Ibid*, p. 332.

30. "Sea-Based X-Band Radar," *Missile Defense Agency Factsheet*, February 2010, available from *www.mda.mil/global/documents/pdf/sbx.pdf*.

31. "Aegis Ballistic Missile defense (Aegis BMD)," *Lockheed Martin Corporation*, 2010, available from *www.lockheedmartin.com/products/AegisBallisticMissileDefense/index.html*.

32. Luo Hui/Si Wei, "US Deploys Three Missile Defense Systems on Guam to Defend against Chinese Cruise Missile Attack," ("Mei zai guan bushu 3 zhong fangkong daodan fang wo xunhang daodan gongji"), *Huanqiu*, December 2, 2009, available from *mil.huanqiu.com/Exclusive/2009-12/648403.html*; David W. Eastburn, "Island Paradise at Forefront of Missile Defense," *Army.Mil News*, November 16, 2009, available from *www.army.mil/-news/2009/11/16/30499-island-paradise-at-the-forefront-of-missile-defense/*.

33. Ministry of Defense (MOD), *Japan's BMD*, (Ministry of Defense, Tokyo, February 2009), p. 17, available from *www.mod.go.jp/e/d_policy/bmd/bmd2009.pdf*.

34. The USS *Shiloh* was first deployed with midcourse interception capabilities to Yokosuka Naval Base in August 2006.

35. Ministry of Defense (MOD), Defense of Japan 2009, (Ministry of Defense, Tokyo, 2009), Chap.1, Sec. 2, p. 190, available from *www.mod.go.jp/e/publ/w_paper/pdf/2009/28Part3_Chapter1_Sec2.pdf*.

36. Minnick, "Chinese Anti-ship Missile Could Alter US Power," p. 6. For an excellent overview, see Stokes, "China's Evolving Conventional Strategic Strike Capability."

37. See Vitaliy O. Pradun, "From Bottle Rockets to Lightening Bolts: China's Missile Revolution and PLA Strategy against US Intervention,"

Naval War College Review, February 24, 2011, available from *www.usnwc.edu/getattachment/23a01071-5dac-433a-8452-09c542163ae8/From-Bottle-Rockets-to-Lightning-Bolts—China-s-Mi*; and Easton, "The Assassin Under the Radar."

38. However, it must be noted that these systems are as yet far from deployment-ready, and none offers an ensured measure of improvement in terms of mitigating the relative disadvantages missile defense systems face when compared with offensive missile systems.

39. For an excellent overview, see Dan Blumenthal, Michael Mazza, Gary J. Schmitt, Randall Schriver, and Mark Stokes, "Deter, Defend, Repel, And Partner: A Defense Strategy For Taiwan," *Taiwan Policy Working Group*, July 2009, available from *www.aei.org/docLib/20090803-Deter-Defend-Repel.pdf*. See also Stokes and Easton, "Evolving Aerospace Trends in the Asia Pacific Region."

40. See "70% of China's Military Drills Last Year Aimed at Taiwan: Liberty Times," *Taiwan News*, March 18, 2010, available from *www.etaiwannews.com/etn/news_content.php?id=1206110&lang=eng_news&cate_img=logo_taiwan&cate_rss=TAIWAN_eng*.

41. Russell Hsiao, "Taiwan's Military Shores Up Indigenous Capabilities," *China Brief*, September 10, 2010, *www.jamestown.org/single/?no_cache=1&tx_ttnews[tt_news]=36808*.

42. *Taiwan Air Defense Status Assessment*, Washington DC: Defense Intelligence Agency, January 21, 2010, available from *www.defensestudies.org/wp-content/uploads/2010/02/dia-taiwan-air-power-assessment.pdf*.

43. Wendell Minnick, "Taiwan's BMD Coming Online," *Defense News*, March 22, 2010, available from *www.defensenews.com/story.php?i=4547996*.

44. Wendell Minnick, "Taiwan Missile Base Identified Near China," *Defense News*, February 22, 2010, available from *minnickarticles.blogspot.com/2010/02/taiwan-missile-base-identified-near.html*.

45. In air-defense terminology, "air breathing" refers to cruise missiles, fighter aircraft, bombers, and UAVs.

46. Shirley A. Kan, "Taiwan: Major US Arms Sales since 1990," *Congressional Research Service Report for Congress*, Washington, DC, February 16, 2010, pp. 16-17, available from *www.fas.org/sgp/crs/weapons/RL30957.pdf*.

47. *The Balance of Air Power in the Taiwan Strait*, Arlington, VA: US-Taiwan Business Council, 2010, p. 25.

48. Minnick, "Taiwan's BMD Coming Online."

49. For an overview of interdiction operations, see Tony Mason, "Air Power in Taiwan's Security," in Martin Edmonds, Michael M. Tsai, eds., *Defending Taiwan: The Future Vision of Taiwan's Defence Policy And Military,* New York: Routledge Curzon Publishing, 2003, p. 151.

50. See "Taiwan to Deploy LACM," *Taiwan Defense Review*, September 6, 2005; Mark A. Stokes, "The Chinese Joint Aerospace Campaign: Strategy, Doctrine, and Force Modernization," in James Mulvenon and David Finkelstein, eds., *China's Revolution in Doctrinal Affairs,* Alexandria, VA: CNA Corporation, 2005, pp. 291-302. Also see "传台湾将试射可攻大陆雄2E导弹年底产80套" ["Taiwan to Produce At Least 80 Hsiungfeng-2E Cruise Missiles That Can Hit Mainland China"], *Global Times*, March 25, 2010, available from *news.qq.com/a/20100325/001200.htm*.

51. Peter B. de Selding, "SpaceX Falcon to Launch Taiwan's Formosat-5 Craft," *Space News*, June 15, 2010, available from *www.spacenews.com/contracts/taiwan-orders-spacex-falcon-launch-for-formosat-5.html*.

52. Lin Xiuhui, "Turning to Develop Remote Sensing Satellites, Taiwan Leaps to Asia's Number One" ("Zhuanxiang fazhan yaoce weixing Taiwan yuewei yazhou diyiming"), *New Taiwan*, October 13, 2005, available from *www.newtaiwan.com.tw/bulletinview.jsp?bulletinid=22863*.

53. "Sounding Rocket 7 Completes Science Experiment," *National Space Organization (NSPO)*, May 5, 2010, available from *www.nspo.org.tw/2008e/news/news_content.php?id=000311*.

54. Ministry of Defense (MOD), *Defense of Japan 2009*, Chap. 1, Sec. 3, Tokyo, Japan: Ministry of Defense, 2009, p. 212, available from *www.mod.go.jp/e/publ/w_paper/pdf/2009/29Part3_Chapter1_Sec3.pdf*.

55. *Ibid*., reference section, available from *www.mod.go.jp/e/publ/w_paper/pdf/2009/45Location.pdf*.

56. Japan's Air Self Defense Force (JASDF) is organized into four regional air defense forces. The Northern Air Defense Force, headquartered in Misawa, is comprised of the 2nd Air Wing and the 3rd Air Defense Missile Group at Chitose, and the 3rd Air Wing, the 6th Air Defense Missile Group, the Airborne Early Warning Group, and the Northern Aircraft Control and Warning Wing at Misawa. The Central Air Defense Force, headquartered in Iruma, is comprised of the 6th Air Wing at Komatsu; the Tactical Reconnaissance Group and the 7th Air Wing at Hyakuri; the 1st Air Defense Missile Group, the Air Defense Command Headquarters Flight Group and Central Aircraft Control and Warning Wing at Iruma; the Airborne Early Warning Group at Hamamatsu; and the 4th Air Defense Missile Group at Gifu. The Western Air Defense

Force, headquartered in Kasuga, is comprised of the 5th and 8th Air Wings at Nyutabaru and Tsuiki, respectively, and the 2nd Air Defense Missile Group, the Western Air Defense Force Headquarters Support Flight Squadron, and Western Aircraft Control and Warning Wing at Kasuga. The Southwestern Composite Air Division, headquartered in Naha, is comprised of the 83rd Air Wing, the 5th Air Defense Missile Group, and the Southwestern Aircraft Control and Warning Wing at Naha, Okinawa.

57. Charlie Reed, "Japanese Air Defense Command Center Set to Open on Yokota This Spring," *Stars and Stripes*, February 2, 2011, available from *www.stripes.com/news/pacific/japan/japanese-air-defense-command-center-set-to-open-on-yokota-this-spring-1.133536*; and Leandra D. Hernandez, "Ceremony Marks Japan's Air Defense Command Move to Yokota," *Yokota Air Base News*, February 20, 2008, available from *www.yokota.af.mil/news/story.asp?id=123088254.*

58. MOD, *Defense of Japan 2009*, Chap. 1, Sec. 2, p. 185, available from *www.mod.go.jp/e/publ/w_paper/pdf/2009/28Part3_Chapter1_Sec2.pdf.* Japan's PAC-3 Battalion 1 was first deployed to Iruma Air Base in March 2007; Battalion 3 was deployed to Hamamatsu Air Base around 2008 (as a part of the Air Missile Defense Training Ground, 2nd Technical School); Battalion 4 was reportedly deployed to Gifu Air Base around 2009, and Battalion 2 was reportedly deployed to Kasuga Air Base around 2010. In 1995, JASDF first decided to acquire 24 enhanced Patriot Advanced Capability-2 (PAC-2) (or PAC-2 Plus) fire units, which are effective against theater ballistic missiles (TBMs) and land attack cruise missiles (LACMs) with slow re-entry speeds. The delivery of these PAC-2 Plus missiles began in 1998. Each of the PAC-2 Plus fire units (four per air defense missile group) has eight launch stations, for a total of 768 missiles. Three more fire units (with 96 missiles) were purchased around 2000-2001, for a total of 27 PAC-2 Plus FUs and 864 missiles.

59. Aside from the *Aegis* DDGs Kongo and the Chokai, the DDGs Myoko and the Kirishima will also be modified for Standard Missile-3 (SM-3) capability.

60. MOD, *Defense of Japan 2009*, Chap. 1, Sec. 2, p. 185, available from *www.mod.go.jp/e/publ/w_paper/pdf/2009/28Part3_Chapter1_Sec2.pdf.*

61. Desmond Ball, "Whither the Japan-Australia Security Relationship?" *Austral Policy Forum 6-32A Report*, September 21, 2006, available from *www.nautilus.org/~rmit/forum-reports/0632a-ball.html.*

62. Reed, "Japanese Air Defense Command Center Set to Open on Yokota this Spring."

63. Rita Boland, "Partnership in the Pacific," *Signal*, June 2008, available from *www.afcea.org/signal/articles/templates/SIGNAL_Article_Template.asp?articleid=1614&zoneid=164.*

64. General Howie Chandler (USAF), "An Airman's Perspective: Air, Space, and Cyberspace Strategy for the Pacific," *Strategic Studies Quarterly*, Summer 2008, p. 15, available from *www.au.af.mil/au/ssq/2008/Summer/chandler.pdf.*

65. Vince Little, "Control Hub Used to Direct Exercise," *Stars and Stripes*, November 17, 2007, available from *www.stripes.com/article.asp?section=104&article=50313.*

66. *Basic Plan for Space Policy*, Tokyo, Japan: Secretariat of Strategic Headquarters for Space Policy, June 2009, p. 7, available from *www.kantei.go.jp/jp/singi/utyuu/keikaku/pamph_en.pdf.*

67. Paul Kallender-Umezu, "Japan Outlines Military Space Strategy Guidelines," *Defense News*, February 23, 2009, p. 29.

68. "India Gets First AWACS," *Defense Technology International*, June 2009, p. 8.

69. Prasun K. Sengupta, "Double-Digit Growth: By 2016, IAF Will Be Acquiring 67 New Low-level Air Transportable Radars (LLTR)," *Force*, February 12, 2009, p. 32. See also Rahul Bedi, "Country Briefing: India," *Jane's Defence Weekly*, January 21, 2009, p. 24.

70. Bedi, "Country Briefing: India," p. 26.

71. Prasun K. Sengupta, "Shield in the Air: Series Production of MR-SAM Expected to Begin in 2011," *Force*, February 12, 2009, pp. 42-43.

72. Bedi, "Country Briefing: India," p. 26.

73. "Test-fire of India's Interceptor Missile Postponed," *NDTV*, March 14, 2010, available from *www.ndtv.com/news/india/test-fire-of-indias-interceptor-missile-postponed-17691.php.*

74. "India Successfully Test-fires Interceptor Missile," *Indian Express*, July 26, 2010, available from *www.indianexpress.com/news/india-successfully-testfires-interceptor-missile/651741/1.* See also "India's Interceptor Missile Test Failed," *CCTV News*, March 16, 2010, available from *english.cctv.com/program/worldwidewatch/20100316/100971.shtml*. "New Interceptor Missile Fails to Take off," *The Times of India*, March 15, 2010, available from *timesofindia.indiatimes.com/india/New-interceptor-missile-fails-to-take-off/articleshow/5684974.cms.*

75. "India Plans Radars in Space to Boost Missile Defense System," *Thaindian News*, March 9, 2010, available from *www.thaindian.com/newsportal/uncategorized/india-plans-radars-in-space-to-boost-missile-defence-system_100164598.html.*

76. *Ibid*. See also Vivek Raghuvanshi, "India Developing Laser-based Anti-Missile Systems, *Defense News*, August 25, 2010, available from *www.defensenews.com/story.php?i=4757079&c=ASI&s=TOP*.

77. Sagar Kulkarni Thiruvananthapuram, "India Readying Weapon to Destroy Enemy Satellites: Saraswat," *Indian Express*, January 3, 2010, available from *www.indianexpress.com/news/india-readying-weapon-to-destroy-enemy-satel/562776/*.

78. Victoria Samson, "India's Missile Defense/Anti-satellite Nexus," *The Space Review*, May 10, 2010, available from *www.thespacereview.com/article/1621/1*.

79. *Ibid*.

80. James Carafano, "US-India Strategic Partnership on Laser-based Missile Defense," *Family Security Matters*, January 29, 2009, available from *www.familysecuritymatters.org/publications/id.2393/pub_detail.asp*. See also A. S. Joshi *et al*., "Development of High Powered Laser and Relevant Technology in India," *Fusion Engineering and Design*, February 1999, pp. 67-70.

81. "India in Multi-satellite Launch," *BBC News*, April 28, 2008, available from *news.bbc.co.uk/2/hi/south_asia/7370391.stm*. See also D. S. Madhumathi, "ISRO Arm May Get More Satellite Launch Contracts," *The Hindu Business Line*, January 23, 2008, available from *www.thehindubusinessline.com/2008/01/23/stories/2008012350332800.htm*.

82. Rahul Bedi, "India Launches Border-control Imaging Satellite," *Jane's Defence Weekly*, April 29, 2009, p. 15.

83. Radhakrishna Rao, "Establishing an Indian Space Command," New Delhi, India: Institute of Peace and Conflict Studies, August 27, 2009, available from *ipcs.org/article/defence/establishing-an-indian-space-command-2958.html*. See also "Aerospace Command Soon, Says IAF Chief," *The Hindu*, January 29, 2007, available from *www.thehindu.com/2007/01/29/stories/2007012914880100.htm*.

84. Andrew Erickson and David Yang, "On the Verge of a Game-Changer: A Chinese Anti-ship Ballistic Missile Could Alter the Rules in the Pacific and Place US Navy Carrier Strike Groups in Jeopardy," *US Naval Institute Proceedings*, Vol. 135, No. 3, May 2009, pp. 26-32; Paul S. Giarra, "A Chinese Anti-Ship Ballistic Missile: Implications for the USN," testimony before the US-China Economic and Security Commission, June 11, 2009, available from *www.uscc.gov/hearings/2009hearings/written_testimonies/09_06_11_wrts/09_06_11_giarra_statement.pdf*; Andrew F. Krepinevich, *Why AirSea Battle?* Washington, DC: Center for Strategic and Budgetary Assessments, 2010, available from *www.csbaonline.org/publications/2010/02/why-airsea-battle/*;

and Roger Cliff, Mark Burles, Michael S. Chase, Derek Eaton, and Kevin L. Pollpeter, *Entering The Dragon's Lair: Chinese Antiaccess Strategies and Their Implications For The United States,* Arlington, VA: RAND Corporation, 2007, available from *www.rand.org/pubs/monographs/2007/RAND_MG524.pdf.*

85. *Quadrennial Defense Review Report*, Washington, DC: Department of Defense, 2010, p. 31, available from *www.defense.gov/qdr/images/QDR_as_of_12Feb10_1000.pdf.*

86. See, for example, Krepinevich, *Why AirSea Battle?*; and Robert D. Kaplan, "The Geography of Chinese Power: How Far Can Beijing Reach on Land and at Sea?" *Foreign Affairs,* May/June 2010.

87. See Jan van Tol, Mark Gunzinger, Andrew Krepinevich, and Jim Thomas, *AirSea Battle: A Point-of-Departure Operational Concept,* Washington, DC: Center for Strategic and Budgetary Assessments, 2010, p. xiii. For an excellent overview of Prompt Global Strike, see Bruce M. Sugden, "Speed Kills: Analyzing the Deployment of Conventional Ballistic Missiles," *International Security*, Vol. 34, No. 1, Summer 2009, pp. 113-146.

88. Luke Harding, "Putin Threatens Withdrawal from Cold War Nuclear Treaty," *The Guardian*, October 12, 2007, available from *www.guardian.co.uk/world/2007/oct/12/russia.usa1*. Also, see Joint US-Russian Statement on the Treaty on the Elimination of Intermediate-Range and Shorter-Range Missiles at the 62nd Session of the UN General Assembly, October 25, 2007, available from *merln.ndu.edu/archivepdf/russia/State/94141.pdf.*

Part 2

Middle East

Chapter 6

The Middle East's Nuclear Future

Richard L Russell[1]

Introduction

Tehran's suspected pursuit of nuclear weapons is poised to fuel a regional nuclear arms race in the Middle East over the next 25 years. In fact, nation-states in the Middle East already are hedging their bets that Tehran will one day harbor a nuclear weapons arsenal even if it is an undeclared one, much like that of Israel.

We are already seeing preliminary signs that an arms race is getting underway in the Persian Gulf area. The Gulf Cooperation Council (GCC), led by Saudi Arabia, has publicly announced plans to invest in the nuclear power industry. The GCC members claim they are hedging their energy needs against the days in the future when their oil reserves are depleted. The GCC, however, probably has in mind sending a not too thinly veiled threat to Iran that it too can follow suit with nuclear weapons programs under the guise of a civilian nuclear program if Tehran does not cease its uranium enrichment activities. The United Arab Emirates (UAE) has been particularly active in soliciting nuclear power bids from the United States and France.

Elsewhere in the Middle East, other countries are leaning toward nuclear power programs that would lay foundations for military nuclear weapons programs in the next 25 years. Turkey, a state with one geopolitical foot in Europe and the other in the Middle East, has showed renewed interest in its nuclear power infrastructure. Egypt, too, has publicly declared its revamped interest in nuclear power technology. Syria appeared to have been harboring a clandestine nuclear program until Israel, the first nuclear weapons-capable state in the Middle East, launched airstrikes in October 2008 to destroy Syria's North Korean-supplied nuclear reactor.

While Iran's pursuit of nuclear weapons is a key determinate of the looming Middle East nuclear arms race, it is not the only one. There are five overarching key determinants fueling the Middle East appetite for nuclear weapons. These determinants are the desire for nuclear weapons to deter adversaries, compensate for conventional weapons shortcomings, fight wars, garner domestic political power, and win international political power, especially to leverage against the United States. Given this powerful array of key determinants for nuclear weapons present and pervasive in the Middle East, the current Western push to market and sell nuclear power infrastructure and capabilities to the region is dangerously short-sighted. These capabilities pose likely risks to be converted to military nuclear weapons programs in some shape or form in the next generation.

Deter Adversaries

Middle Eastern states will look to nuclear weapons to deter regional adversaries in the next 25 years. Israel's nuclear weapons program is a prime regional example of this driving determinant for nuclear weapons, and other states will likely follow suit in the years ahead. Israel has long had a nondeclared nuclear weapons program in the Middle East, which has been a security concern for Arab states. The Israelis, who leveraged their French-provided nuclear power plant at Dimona for its clandestine nuclear weapons program, sought nuclear weapons to deter and offset the numerical military superiority of conventional Arab military forces.

Tel Aviv publicly neither confirms nor denies its nuclear weapons capabilities. As Avner Cohen and William Burr explain, the Israelis have steadfastly maintained that they would not be the "first country in the region to introduce nuclear weapons into the region"—a diplomatic nuance meaning openly testing and publicly declaring nuclear weapons.[2] This posture allows the Israelis to have plausible deniability about their nuclear weapons capability, while at the same time influencing the strategic thinking of Arab leaders on decisions of war and peace with the threat of Israeli nuclear weapons.

The idea that nuclear weapons afforded Israel a deterrent against conventional war has been problematic. Contrary to expectations by deterrence theory enthusiasts, Israel's thinly veiled nuclear weapons capabilities did not deter Egyptian and Syrian forces from attacking Israel in the 1973 Middle East war.[3] The Israelis in the earliest stages of the 1973 clash suffered severe battlefield losses to Egyptian forces on the Sinai. Reports have circulated for years that the Israelis were so alarmed they were about to be defeated by Egyptian forces that they had readied their nuclear weapons, which Israel had clandestinely developed and acquired. Israeli nuclear forces in 1973 consisted of French-built Mirage aircraft capable of delivering nuclear bombs and a small force of ballistic missiles armed with nuclear weapons.[4] The Israelis, however, were able to marshal an impressive conventional military turnaround and would have nearly routed Egyptian forces had it not been for American diplomatic intervention to stop the war. Israel's impressive conventional military reversal alleviated its need to resort to nuclear weapons against Egyptian forces to defend Israel proper.

Even though Arab regimes routinely and loudly denounce Israel's nuclear weapons inventory, Middle Eastern states—aside from Saddam Hussein's Iraq and Syria's recent flirtation with a nuclear program—have not perceived an immediate and grave threat from Israel's nuclear weapons. Israeli nuclear weapons have more been an affront to Arab prestige than an acute security threat and have not sparked a nuclear arms race in the Middle East.

In marked contrast, the public revelation that Iran had a clandestine uranium enrichment program sent shudders down the backs of Arab Middle Eastern states. For nearly 2 decades, Iran was working on and off its uranium enrichment capabilities. The program, which began in the mid-1980s with centrifuge parts and drawings from the "Father" of Pakistan's nuclear weapons program, Abdul Qadeer Khan, was revealed to the world in 2002 by Iranian dissidents. The Iranians had built a facility at Natanz, with plans for installing 50,000 centrifuges.[5] The Iranians failed to notify the International Atomic Energy Agency (IAEA) of this program, despite the country's obligation to do so under the terms of the Nonproliferation Treaty (NPT), to which Iran is a signatory.

It probably is no coincidence that after Iran's uranium enrichment centrifuge program was publicly exposed in 2002, in relatively short order the most oil-wealthy states in the world—joined by other states in the Middle East—suddenly decided to diversify their sources of energy and invest in nuclear power plants.

- The GCC under the Saudi leadership tasked a team in May 2009 to begin to study the peaceful purposes of nuclear power.[6]

- The Saudis are negotiating with France for the purchase of nuclear technology, and Paris already has signed civilian nuclear deals elsewhere in the Middle East, including Algeria and Libya.[7]
- The UAE is energetically working with both France and the United States on developing its nuclear power industry.[8] South Korea too will be providing aid to the UAE's nuclear power program.[9]
- Kuwait also has shown interest in nuclear power cooperation with France, and Kuwait's Emir in February 2009 said that Kuwait was "seriously considering joining the nuclear club but only for peaceful purposes."[10]
- Jordan in May 2009 signed a nuclear energy cooperation agreement with Russia in which Moscow would provide Amman with power plants, research facilities, and training centers.[11]
- President Mubarak in 2007 announced that Egypt would redouble investment in its nuclear power infrastructure.[12] Mubarak signed a nuclear energy deal with Russian President Putin in March 2008, giving Russia the go-ahead to bid for building the first of four new nuclear power plants in Egypt.[13]

The relatively sudden surge in Arab state interest in nuclear technology after the exposure of Iran's clandestine centrifuge program suggests that these states perceive a more acute threat stemming from Iranian nuclear weapons in the future than they do from Israel's nuclear weapons today. The Arab states, after all, have lived with Israel's veiled nuclear weapons capabilities for decades, but it was only after Iran's nuclear efforts became public that they moved from the rhetoric of denouncing Israel to concrete nuclear capabilities. The Arab Gulf states would be especially eager to have nuclear weapons to deter the use of Iranian ballistic missile and nuclear weapons against them.

The Arab states undoubtedly fear that nuclear weapons in Iranian hands will further bolster Iranian power and influence in the Gulf and Middle East. Nuclear weapons would enable Tehran to support even more aggressively and energetically its growing surrogate influence through Shia militias in Iraq, Hezbollah in Lebanon, and Hamas in the Palestinian community. The Arab states probably calculate that they would be exceedingly vulnerable to Iranian political coercion and military intimidation in the future if Iran has nuclear weapons. Part and parcel of the Arab states' sudden and sharp focus on nuclear technology is an effort to signal to Tehran that they, too, could follow Iran's path toward nuclear weapons under the guise of a civilian nuclear power production infrastructure.

Turkey is probably also thinking strategically much like the Arab states. Ankara has a working relationship with Iran, but it too will probably want to hedge its bets against an Iran armed with nuclear weapons in the not-too-distant future. The Turks may very well have this set of calculations in the back of their minds with their recent renewed interest in revamping their nuclear power infrastructure.[14] Again, it probably is no coincidence that Turkey publicly announced plans to reinvest in its nuclear power infrastructure not too long after the exposure of Iran's uranium enrichment plant at Natanz.

The Turkish General Staff would not want to be in an inferior bargaining position should relations with an Iran armed with nuclear weapons deteriorate. Some observers might argue that Turkey could rely on its North Atlantic Treaty Organization (NATO) membership for a nuclear security umbrella to deter Iranian aggression, but that suggestion is likely to be less than satisfactory comfort to the Turkish military. Turkey remembers well that when it prudently turned to NATO for protection from potential Iraqi retaliation in the run-up to the American-British 2003 War against Iraq, Turkey was sternly rebuffed. That experience was a bitter pill to swallow for the Turks,who would want their own nuclear deterrent against Iran's nuclear stockpile.

Backstopping Conventional Military Shortcomings

Another key driver for nuclear weapons in the Middle East will be the desire to plug holes in defenses because of conventional military shortcomings. Even though the Arab states are plush with the most advanced ground, naval, and air weaponry, their conventional military capabilities suffer from numerous problems. The Arab Gulf states, for example, lack strong population bases from which to draw educated and technologically capable soldiers, sailors, and airmen to man their expensive weapons systems and train for modern mobile-conventional warfare. These traits leave the Arab Gulf states excessively reliant on foreign contractors to maintain and field their military forces. Family and tribal ties, moreover, trump military competence for high command in the Arab Gulf states.

The Arab Gulf states likely would look to nuclear weapons as the "quick fix" for all of their conventional military shortcomings. They might even calculate that nuclear weapons in the future would relieve

Arab Gulf states from the arduous and long-term work needed to improve their conventional military forces, which, more often than not, are reflections of the shortcomings of their own cultures, histories, and societies.[15]

Gulf state regimes would be drawn to the allure of nuclear weapons as the ultimate guarantee of their survival in a future military crisis with larger Iranian conventional military forces. The Gulf state regimes might calculate that in a future crisis with an Iran armed with nuclear weapons, the United States would be deterred from entering the fray, leaving the Arab Gulf states to fend for themselves.

To ensure that they could hold Iranian targets at risk, the Arab Gulf states are likely to be interested in acquiring and modernizing their now-limited ballistic missile holdings. The Saudis clandestinely procured intermediate-range CSS-2 ballistic missiles from China in the mid-1980s, and the UAE clandestinely procured Scud missiles from China in 1989.[16] These missiles are old, though, and the UAE and Saudi Arabia no doubt would like to modernize their ballistic missile holdings. Pakistan, China, North Korea, and Russia would be the places for them to shop, and they could offer lucrative sales to countries willing to skirt the Missile Technology Control Regime (MTCR), a voluntary cooperative effort by Western states to stem the flow of ballistic missile-related technology to states trying to buildup their ballistic missile capabilities.

Syria also has an acute interest in nuclear weapons to compensate for its conventional military shortcomings in its rivalry with Israel. Syrian conventional military forces have been consistently bested by Israel's conventional forces in the Arab-Israeli wars as well as in clashes in and around Lebanon. Syria's conventional military capabilities eroded even more when the Soviet Union collapsed and the Moscow arms pipeline dried up. Moscow under Putin's muscular foreign policy might yet renew major conventional arms supplies to Syria to revamp its conventional military forces in the not-too-distant future. But modern Russian arms alone would not be sufficient by themselves to redress Syria's conventional military shortcomings against Israeli forces.

The Syrian regime apparently decided to look to nuclear weapons to make up its conventional military shortcomings. Damascus ran the risk of detection by Israel and was clandestinely assembling a North Korean-supplied nuclear reactor until the Israelis mounted an airstrike and destroyed it in September 2007. The Syrians spent months razing and cleaning up the site before allowing international inspectors to investigate.[17] The Israelis have neither confirmed nor denied the airstrike, a posture that helped keep the strike from spiraling into a broader Middle East war. Had Israel publicly and blatantly lauded the strike, the bravado might have so humiliated the Damascus regime that it might have lashed out militarily with retaliation against Israel.

Egypt, too, might make a similar strategic calculus in the future to guard against the possible political collapse of its peace treaty with Israel. A political convulsion in the region or in Egypt itself could one day lead to the breakdown of the Egyptian-Israeli peace treaty to reawaken the bitter security rivalry that was the core of the Arab-Israel wars in the last century. The most well-organized Egyptian political opposition and the most likely to assault the Cairo regime would be the Muslim Brotherhood. In July 2006, the Muslim Brotherhood publicly called on the Mubarak regime to develop a nuclear deterrent,[18] which suggests that a nuclear weapons capability would be high on the policy agenda for a Muslim Brotherhood-led government in Cairo. Egypt, unlike Syria, is well equipped with modern conventional weaponry, thanks to decades of American security assistance. But Egyptian society and its armed forces suffer from shortcomings that prevent the full exploitation of the modern weaponry's capabilities, leaving Egypt's conventional forces outclassed by Israel's conventional forces.

Egypt could turn to nuclear weapons in the first instance to deter Israeli nuclear forces and in the second instance to counterbalance Israeli conventional military capabilities. In a future regional security environment mired with Egyptian and Israeli tensions, Cairo would want nuclear weapons to reassure itself that the Israelis could not use the threat of nuclear and conventional military superiority to coerce Egypt politically. Cairo would see nuclear weapons as the ultimate security guarantee, should push come to shove in a regional crisis. Egyptians would want nuclear weapons to deter Israeli conventional forces from again storming over Egyptian military forces, flooding the Sinai Desert, and threatening to cross the Suez Canal to challenge the survival of Egypt's regime.

Fighting Wars

Another key determinant for nuclear weapons proliferation in the Middle East is the desire for nuclear weapons to wage war. This view may be startling to some readers, because many observers commonly judge that nuclear weapons are good only for deterrence and not for warfighting. The history of nuclear weapons development shows otherwise, however. The United States and its NATO allies during the Cold War procured and deployed nuclear weapons in Europe not as some grand deterrent bluff, but because they intended to use the weapons if the Warsaw Pact forces invaded Western Europe with conventional forces. The United States and its NATO Allies worried that Warsaw Pact forces outnumbered and outgunned NATO forces, so that the alliance would have had to resort to tactical nuclear weapons to blunt a Warsaw Pact conventional military invasion.[19] Pakistan probably makes a similar strategic calculation today in seeing the numerical superiority of Indian conventional forces and the close geographic proximity of Pakistan's capital, Islamabad, to the border.

Middle Eastern states in the next 25 years might make similar strategic calculations. Saudi Arabia, for example, might come to think that the early use of nuclear weapons against Iranian forces invading through Kuwait would be wiser statecraft than letting Iranian forces get an operational foothold in the oil-rich Eastern Province of Saudi Arabia, where a largely Shia population is alienated from the Sunni Saudi regime and is sympathetic to Iran. Kuwait itself has no geopolitical buffer zone separating it from the numerically superior Iranian forces and might want to resort to nuclear weapons against Iranian forces before they cross into Kuwaiti territory. If the Kuwaitis were to hesitate to use future nuclear weapons, they would risk losing their country—much as they had in Saddam Hussein's 1990 invasion and occupation of Kuwait. The Saudis and the Kuwaitis, on top of these calculations, might judge that they themselves would need to resort to nuclear weapons to blunt an Iranian invasion, because the United States would not want to put its forces in the line of fire—as it did against Iraq in 1991 and 2003—because of the threat of Iran targeting American forces with nuclear weapons.

The Iranians certainly are aware of American conventional military prowess and would not seek a fair fight in a future military clash with the United States. Tehran watched American and British military forces dispatch Saddam Hussein's regime in 3 weeks—an impressive task that Iran was not able to accomplish after 8 brutal years of war with Iraq, which sapped Iran's national strength. The Iranians in the future, especially the Revolutionary Guards, might use nuclear weapons against American conventional military forces should they fear for the survival of the Tehran regime. They might calculate that Iranian nuclear weapons use would shock the Americans and compel them to stand down their military operations. The Iranians might additionally figure that the United States would exercise restraint and not retaliate against Iran with nuclear weapons, given Washington's political interest in maintaining the nonuse of nuclear weapons and the American preference not to inflict massive Iranian civilian casualties.

Syria and Egypt too might find themselves embroiled in a future Arab-Israeli war. If faced with a stark choice of allowing Israeli forces to capture Damascus or Cairo, the Syrian and Egyptian regimes would prefer to bludgeon Israeli conventional military advances with nuclear weapons. They might calculate that their use of nuclear weapons against Israeli conventional forces would not cross the threshold for Israeli retaliation with nuclear weapons against their capitals and population centers. These would be risky calculations, to be sure, but they are plausible ones, especially during crises in which authoritarian regimes believe their survival is at stake.

Political Power at Home

Another key determinant for nuclear weapons is domestic politics and the struggle for power inside Middle Eastern nation-states. Often overlooked is the fact that armed forces and domestic communities and interest blocks become influential advocates for nuclear weapons programs in nation-state decisionmaking circles. As Scott Sagan points out, in examining cases of nuclear proliferation, a state's nuclear energy establishment includes civilian reactors and laboratories, military elements, politicians, and the public, who strongly support nuclear weapons acquisition. These are all important drivers of proliferation.[20] India's decision to test a nuclear device in 1974, for example, appeared to be due more to internal domestic politics than external threats.[21]

The Revolutionary Guard in Iran is undoubtedly a powerful domestic advocate for Iranian nuclear weapons. Iranian President Mahmoud Ahmadinejad is a Revolutionary Guard veteran, and, under his leadership, Guard commanders have filled increasingly important domestic political and economic posts to increase the institution's overall influence in government decisionmaking. Although not much is known about Iran's nuclear weapons program, the Revolutionary Guard would likely be in control of Iran's future nuclear weapons. The Revolutionary Guard operates most of Iran's ballistic missiles and would likely control Iran's future nuclear weapons, and most or all of its chemical and biological weapons.[22] When push comes to shove in government power corridors, the Revolutionary Guard has vested interests in seeing that the nuclear weapons program proceeds and, along with it, the Revolutionary Guard's status and prestige in Tehran.

Wide swaths of Iranian public opinion also support Iran's pursuit of nuclear technology. It would not be too much of a leap in reasoning to assume that public opinion would be proud of an Iranian government in the future that demonstrates Iran's technological prowess with the detonation of a nuclear device or devices. Iran's development of nuclear power and potentially a nuclear weapons infrastructure is a source of great domestic Iranian pride and nationalism. As Iran scholar Ray Takeyh observes, "Far from being a source of restraint, the emerging popular sentiment is that, as a great civilisation [sic] with a long history, Iran has a right to acquire a nuclear capability."[23] The pride that swells from Iran's nuclear activities helps to temper Iranian public frustrations with Iran's deteriorating economy and lack of political freedoms. Takeyh notes on this score that the "Recent disclosures of the sophisticated nature of Iran's nuclear program have been a source of pride for a citizenry accustomed to the revolution's failures and setbacks."[24]

Iran's pursuit of nuclear weapons also has other powerful domestic constituencies. Takeyh elaborates:

> Alongside this popular sentiment is the emergence of a bureaucratic and scientific establishment with its own parochial considerations. Under the auspices of the Revolutionary Guards, an entire array of organizations such as the Defense Industries Organization, university laboratories, and a plethora of companies (many of them owned by hard-line clerics) have provided the impetus for Iran's expanding and lucrative nuclear efforts.[25]

Iranian public and government pride in the country's nuclear accomplishments mirrors the swells of national pride witnessed in South Asia's nuclear weapons arms race. Mass public outpourings of support were shown for the governments in New Delhi in 1974 and 1998, as well as in Islamabad in 1998, after these countries detonated nuclear explosions. Indian public opinion in June 1974, for example, showed that 91 percent of the adult literate Indian population knew about the explosion, and of those, 90 percent were "personally proud of this achievement."[26]

Regimes in the Middle East also would lean on nuclear weapons programs to hedge against internal threats to their rule. Many regimes in the Middle East over the next 25 years are likely to feel threatened by potential internal political convulsions and would view nuclear weapons as a hedge against succumbing to mob civil violence and coups. Syria's minority Alawite regime, for example, might have had an internal security threat contingency on its mind in working on its clandestine nuclear program with North Korea. Saudi Arabia might become gravely threatened by al Qaeda Sunni-based insurgents or Hezbollah Shia insurgents in its heavily Shia-populated Eastern Province. The royal families in the small Arab Gulf states, especially those like the UAE and Kuwait with deep financial pockets, could see nuclear weapons as their "ace in the hole" to guarantee their survival and control over their countries against the political weight of even larger populations of expatriots and foreign workers on which many government and private sector functions depend. Egypt could face a tumultuous political transition after President Mubarak's eventual death, and nuclear weapons would be useful instruments to rally Egyptian nationalism to garner internal political support for a new regime in Cairo.

Regional Political Power and Leverage on Washington

A determinant that looms large behind Middle Eastern aspirations for nuclear weapons is power and influence—beyond deterrence—in regional and international politics. The Iranians would want to parlay a nuclear weapons inventory to coerce Saudi Arabia and the Arab Gulf states politically to make them appease Iranian security policy and distance themselves from American power in the Gulf and Middle East. Saudi Arabia would want to tap a nuclear stockpile to counterbalance Iran's nuclear weapons inventory to maintain its political stature as leader of the Sunni Muslim world against Iran, as the leader of the Shia Muslim world. The smaller Arab Gulf states—the UAE and Kuwait in particular—would want to use nuclear weapons inventories to maintain their political autonomies from both Saudi Arabia and Iran in the event that the United States is compelled to lessen its military and political presence in the region in light of the proliferation of nuclear weapons.

Egypt, as well as Syria and Algeria, would see nuclear weapons as instruments for stopping the erosion of Arab political power in regional and international politics. They have been especially frustrated to see power shifting from northern Africa and the Levant to the Gulf. Egypt has long seen itself as the center of Arab politics, but frets that it is being eclipsed by Saudi and Gulf power. Egypt would look to nuclear weapons to reassert its stature as the preeminent Arab power. Cairo, too, would not want to be eclipsed by Shia power bolstered by Tehran's nuclear weapons, which could be parlayed into more aggressive Iranian support for Hezbollah and Palestinian militant Islamists such as Islamic Jihad and Hamas to put Iran front and center of Middle Eastern politics. Algerian officials reportedly considered nuclear power as part of a plan to transform Algeria into a regional superpower, and nuclear weapons could have played a part in this strategy, according to nuclear weapons expert David Albright.[27]

Middle Eastern states would be especially keen to parlay nuclear weapons into influence abroad with the United States, which is a final determinant for regional nuclear weapons proliferation. Middle Eastern states have no doubt noticed that what captures acute American attention is nuclear weapons proliferation. They see, for example, that two of the poorest per capita countries in the world, Pakistan and North Korea, are able to seize the attention of American policy makers and exert an influence on international politics well above their economic "throw weights."

North Korea and Iran in particular are able to capture American policymakers' attention, largely because of their nuclear weapons-related activities. If not for their ambitions and nuclear weapons activities, these countries would not merit the extraordinary American attention that they do. As for Iran, Iran expert Karim Sadjadpour notes a private conversation he had with a former member of Iran's nuclear negotiating team in which he expressed the opinion that Iran's nuclear program was not so important until it became important to the United States. The Iranian official responded, "That's absolutely right."[28]

Syria, with a bleak economic picture comparable to those of Pakistan and North Korea, probably harbored illusions of one day presenting the world with a nuclear weapons capability fait accompli. Damascus could have parlayed nuclear weapons capabilities for the attention of and influence on American policy in the Middle East. That tact would have been in keeping with Syria's longstanding regional role as the "spoiler," with its support to Palestinian and Shia Hezbollah opposition, and more recently of Sunni jihadists in Iraq—to make sure that no major regional agreements could go through without Syria's approval.

Egypt could think along similar lines. Cairo sees its self-image as the power center of Arab politics deteriorating as Jordan plays a greater role in regional issues, Saudi Arabia increasingly exerts a leadership role in Arab politics based on wealth and stature, and Iran strengthens its regional role in the Gulf and in the Levant. Cairo could parlay its nuclear power infrastructure into a military nuclear weapons program to redress Egypt's sliding prestige in the region against Israel, the Arab states, and Iran. Egyptian leaders might calculate that the peace treaty with Israel would protect it from Israeli military strikes should a clandestine Egyptian nuclear weapons program be exposed. The Egyptians could present the United States with a fait accompli nuclear weapons capability and use it as leverage to gain more American security assistance to Egypt. Cairo could argue that unless Washington rackets up its military security assistance, Egypt would have to move from a minimalist to a maximalist nuclear weapons inventory.

Algeria, too, could reawaken its nuclear weapons program to extract American policy attention. Algiers might find itself in the next generation under renewed and even more strident militant Islamic opposition than in the 1990s. Algerian officials could argue that they need major infusions of American military and security assistance to make sure that nuclear weapons remain secure in secular Arab political hands in Algiers, and not fall into the hands of the likes of al Qaeda of northern Africa. The Algerians might take pointers on this score from Pakistan's extraction of generous economic, military, security, and intelligence assistance from the United States, because Washington is increasingly uneasy about the security of Pakistan's nuclear weapons inventory in light of the Taliban and al Qaeda inroads in Pakistan.

Non-proliferation Policy Implications

The great danger is that the United States is "cutting off its nose to spite its face" with nuclear weapons proliferation in the Middle East. Washington has shown an eagerness to support nuclear power infrastructure in the Gulf based largely on commercial interests. It is actively marketing nuclear plants and assistance to the UAE and Kuwait. The United States no doubt wants American industry to win regional commercial competition against French and other foreign firms that are aggressively marketing their nuclear wares in the region. The American, French, and European commercial perspectives on nuclear power in the Middle East, however, neglects the stubborn key determinants of nuclear developments discussed in this chapter.

Middle Eastern states will be under heavy pressure in the future to convert ostensibly civilian nuclear power programs into clandestine military nuclear weapons programs, given the key determinants at play in the region. The Western community is putting itself at risk by essentially replaying the French mistake of supplying Israel and Iraq with ostensibly civilian nuclear power reactors that in the last century were clandestinely harnessed for military nuclear weapons programs.

Even if Western nuclear technology is not directly harnessed for military nuclear weapons programs, the expertise and technology could be easily diverted to the military. The United States, France, and other Western countries, for example, made that mistake in supplying South Africa with civilian nuclear technology and assistance. Although that assistance did not directly build South Africa's nuclear weapons before the 1990 abandonment, the assistance substantially increased the technical competence of Pretoria's nuclear engineers, technicians, and scientists, who made up South Africa's nuclear weapons intellectual capital.[29]

Some observers might argue that Arab states would not dare risk jeopardizing their bilateral security relationships with the United States by embarking on clandestine nuclear weapons programs. But these programs could be very small and difficult to detect. The South African case is illustrative of how medium-sized powers like the Arab states could nurture nuclear weapons programs that could go undetected. The South African bomb program in the 1980s employed only 100 people, of whom about 40 were directly involved in the weapons program and only 20 built South Africa's small nuclear arsenal. By the time the program was cancelled in 1990, the work force still had only about 300 people.[30]

International safeguards under the auspices of the IAEA would be little more than speed bumps for determined Middle Eastern proliferators to overcome. North Korea has set a model of behavior in which nation-states could ostensibly comply with IAEA safeguards for years until their nuclear capabilities have sufficiently matured to allow them to go it alone without international community assistance, after they had withdrawn from the NPT. Or, if they were the least bit cunning, they could play along with IAEA inspections and hide military nuclear weapons programs for as long as possible, much as Iraq had done prior to the 1991 war.

IAEA safeguards would hamper, but not stop, determined Arab efforts to shift or divert civilian nuclear power infrastructure toward military nuclear weapons programs. Arab states, for example, might acquire large uranium holdings from the international market and then give formal notice and withdraw from the treaty and its inspection requirements. Uranium stocks could then be run through reactors and reprocessed for weapons-grade plutonium, perhaps by parallel and clandestine plutonium-reprocessing facilities purchased from China or other states. Uranium stocks too could be run through clandestine centrifuges—perhaps acquired from Pakistan, much like North Korea appears to have done—and refined to weapons grade.

The Arab Gulf states are relying on international technical assistance from France, the United States, China, and Russia, to name just a few, to get their nuclear power infrastructure foundations laid and then up and running. In the meantime, the Arab Gulf states are training a cadre of domestic talent, which over a generation could be ready to fill foreign shoes and assume the reigns of the nuclear power infrastructure, especially if these states withdrew from IAEA safeguards and the NPT and shifted their civilian programs to wartime-like military nuclear weapons programs. Emirati officials, for example, readily admit today that they are developing domestic talent to run and maintain nuclear reactors by creating nuclear science and engineering degree programs at Khalifa University, the country's largest technical school.[31] One cannot help but suspect that UAE officials look to how far Iran has progressed with its nuclear program, and are determined to keep pace—even though the Emirates got a late start.

One of the delivery vehicles of choice for nuclear weapons in the Middle East would be combat aircraft. The West has been gracious in selling high-performance aircraft too, such as Mirage and F-16s, which could be modified to carry nuclear payloads. The Pakistanis appear to have "wired" their American-built F-16s to carry nuclear payloads.[32] It would be a fair bet that Pakistan could contract, for the right price, its expertise to the oil-rich Gulf States to help them modify their F-16s to do likewise.

Middle Eastern states would be concerned that air defenses of adversaries could stop many of their combat aircraft from arriving over targets. They would be keen to upgrade now-limited ballistic missile capabilities to ensure that nuclear payloads would get through enemy air defenses and in less time than combat aircraft. The Arab states would be eager to purchase solid fuel and longer-range and more modern and reliable ballistic missiles, and would look to Pakistan, China, and Russia as the most likely sources of modern ballistic missiles. Middle Eastern states would entice Pakistan, China, and Russia to break international restrictions for providing renewed ballistic missiles and technologies to the region with lucrative "cash on the barrelhead" offers. Islamabad, Beijing, and Moscow would be interested in shunning international arms restrictions to gain strategic footholds in the region and to offset the American hegemony there.

Pakistan and India are setting the pace for the Arab states to move beyond combat aircraft and ballistic missiles and into cruise missiles as a delivery means for nuclear weapons. Pakistan is producing streams of plutonium for nuclear warheads for cruise missiles launched from ships, submarines, and aircraft, while India is designing cruise missiles with nuclear warheads by relying on Russian missile design assistance.[33] Middle Eastern states would likely follow suit and begin moving into cruise missile technologies for future nuclear weapons inventories in the next 25 years.

Endnotes

1. The views in this chapter are not those of the US Government, the Department of Defense, or the National Defense University. They are the author's alone.

2. Avner Cohen and William Burr, "The Untold Story of Israel's Bomb," *The Washington Post*, April 30, 2006, pp. B1 & B3.
3. Ward Wilson, "The Myth of Nuclear Deterrence," *Nonproliferation Review,* Vol. 15, No. 3, November 2008, p. 434.
4. Patrick Tyler, *A World of Trouble: The White House and the Middle East—from the Cold War to the War on Terror,* New York: Farrar Straus Giroux, 2009, p. 141.
5. William J. Broad and David E. Sanger, "As Crisis Brews, Iran Hits Bumps in Atomic Path," *The New York Times*, March 5, 2006.
6. "GCC Work Team on Peaceful Nuclear Energy Use Meets," *Oman Daily Observer*, May 20, 2009.
7. "Saudi-French Civil N-Pact 'Soon,'" *Saudi Gazette*, May 11, 2009.
8. James Kanter, "France Set to Announce UAE Nuclear Deal," *International Herald Tribune,* January 14, 2008; Jay Solomon and Margaret Coker, "Oil-rich Arab State Pushes Nuclear Bid with US Help," *The Wall Street Journal*, April 2, 2009.
9. "South Korean Cabinet Approves Peaceful Nuclear Accord with UAE," *Kuwait News Agency*, June 17, 2009.
10. "Kuwait Eyes Civilian Nuclear Power Project with French Help," *The Peninsula*, February 19, 2009.
11. "Russia, Jordan Sign Nuclear Cooperation Agreement," *Haaretz*, May 23, 2009.
12. "Egypt Unveils Nuclear Plants Plan," *BBC News*, October 29, 2007.
13. "Russia-Egypt Nuclear Deal Signed," *BBC News*, March 25, 2008.
14. Karl Vick, "Energy, Iran Spur Turkey's Revival of Nuclear Plants," *The Washington Post*, March 7, 2006.
15. For a comprehensive analysis of Arab military shortcomings, see Kenneth M. Pollack, *Arabs at War: Military Effectiveness, 1948-1991,* Lincoln, NE: University of Nebraska Press, 2002.
16. Richard L. Russell, *Weapons Proliferation and War in the Greater Middle East: Strategic Contest,* London, UK, and New York: Routledge, 2006, p. 64.
17. Jay Solomon, "Syria Signals It Will Stop U.N. Nuclear Inspectors," *Wall Street Journal*, October 4, 2008.
18. James A. Russell, "A Tipping Point Realized? Nuclear Proliferation in the Persian Gulf and Middle East," *Contemporary Security Policy,* Vol. 29, No. 3, December 2008, p. 530.
19. For an insightful treatment of nuclear weapons strategy in Cold War

Europe, see Lawrence Freedman, *The Evolution of Nuclear Strategy,* New York: St. Martin's Press, 1983, pp. 288-293.

20. Scott D. Sagan, "Why Do States Build Nuclear Weapons? Three Models in Search of a Bomb," *International Security,* Vol. 21, No. 3, Winter 1996/97, pp. 63-65.

21. *Ibid.*, pp. 67-68; and Tanya Ogilvie-White, "Is There a Theory of Nuclear Proliferation? An Analysis of the Contemporary Debate," *Nonproliferation Review,* Fall 1996, pp. 46, 58, Endnote 58.

22. Anthony H. Cordesman and Martin Kleiber, *Iran's Military Forces and Warfighting Capabilities: The Threat to the Northern Gulf,* Westport, CT: Praeger Security International, 2007, p. 73.

23. Ray Takeyh, "Iran Builds the Bomb," *Survival,* Vol. 46, No. 4, November 2004, p. 58.

24. Ray Takeyh, *Hidden Iran: Paradox and Power in the Islamic Republic,* New York: Henry Holt and Company, 2006, p. 154.

25. *Ibid.*, p. 156.

26. Sagan, "Why Do States Build Nuclear Weapons?" p. 68.

27. David Albright and Corey Hinderstein, "Algeria: Big Deal in the Desert?" *Bulletin of the Atomic Scientists,* Vol. 57, No. 3, May/June 2001, p. 47.

28. Quoted in Theodoros Tsakiris, ed., "Iranian-American Relations under the Early Obama Administration: Virtual Dialogue," *Middle East Economic Survey Research Special Report,* April 15, 2009.

29. J. W. de Villiers, Roger Jardine, and Mitchell Reiss, "Why South Africa Gave up the Bomb," *Foreign Affairs,* Vol. 72, No. 5, November/ December 1993, p. 105.

30. David Albright, "South Africa and the Affordable Bomb," *Bulletin of the Atomic Scientists,* Vol. 50, No. 4, July 1994.

31. Jay Solomon and Margaret Coker, "Oil-rich Arab State Pushes Nuclear Bid with US Help," *The Wall Street Journal*, April 2, 2009.

32. Sharon Squassoni, *Indian and Pakistani Nuclear Weapons*, Congressional Research Service Report for Congress, Washington, DC: Congressional Research Service, February 17, 2005, p. 3; Bruce Riedel, "Pakistan and the Bomb," *The Wall Street Journal*, May 30, 2009.

33. R. Jeffrey Smith and Joby Warrick, "Nuclear Aims by Pakistan, India Prompt US Concern," *The Washington Post*, May 28, 2009.

Chapter 7

Alternative Proliferation Futures for North Africa

Bruno Tertrais

Of "Cascading" Effects in the Middle East

The Iranian nuclear program has led to renewed fears of a "cascade" of proliferation in the Middle East: a rapid and almost mechanical process through which a country crossing the threshold would lead others to follow suit. Some claim these fears are overblown. They note that they are a recurring feature of Western strategic analysis, which have not been proven by subsequent developments.[1] So why would a nuclear Iran trigger a cascade of proliferation in the Middle East, the argument goes, whereas a nuclear Israel has not produced that effect for more than 40 years? The answer is fourfold:

- Iran's in-your-face nuclear policy poses a real political challenge to Arab states in terms of prestige and legitimacy. Israel never publicly acknowledged its nuclear capability, and it is much more an adversary than a competitor vying for influence in the region.
- Iran is seen as a potential security threat by the Gulf States, but also by many in Egypt, given its increasing influence in the Gaza strip. By contrast, a stable "cold peace" continues to prevail with Israel.

- In the context of an ongoing worldwide nuclear "renaissance"—which is likely to continue, albeit at a slower pace, after the Fukushima catastrophe—ambitious, ostensibly civilian nuclear programs justified by the need to preserve hydrocarbon resources could provide an excellent cover for dual-use or military-related activities.
- Some of the actors in the region are losing confidence in the United States as a security guarantor. Washington's longstanding motto is that a nuclear Iran is "unacceptable." Thus, if Iran became nuclear, it will be seen throughout the Middle East as a failure of US policy. This logic may be applicable in particular to Saudi Arabia, whose relations with the United States degraded significantly in 2011.

This chapter will assess the probability of "tertiary" proliferation; that is, the scenario whereby an Arab country—in this case, Algeria—would be reacting to an Egyptian nuclear option, which itself would be largely a reaction to Iran's program.[2] Cairo and Algiers, whose political regimes are dominated by the armed forces, are rivals on the Arab scene, and have always had difficult relations. Their respective nuclear programs resemble each other, and Algeria—which enjoys good relations with Iran—seems to be watching very closely what Egypt is doing to make sure that it does not appear to fall behind the coming Middle Eastern nuclear "race."

Of all the Middle East countries, Egypt may be the most likely to go nuclear if the Iranian program continues unabated. Egypt has significant nuclear expertise and is likely to be attracted by both the political and strategic advantages of a nuclear option. The fact that other Middle East countries—Saudi Arabia and Turkey—are also reported to be tempted to go in that direction will be an added incentive. Egypt may not seek at all costs to be the first Arab nuclear state. But it is almost certain to do what it must to avoid being the second one.

The Egyptian Option

As the most populated Arab state, with a long tradition of intellectual supremacy in the region, Egypt considers itself to have a particular status in the Middle East and in the Muslim world. At the domestic level, Egypt has entered a phase of transition whose outcome is uncertain. Two things were apparent in the Fall of 2011: first, the military does not intend to completely relinquish its grip on power; second, the Muslim Brotherhood increasingly appears to be the best-organized political force in the country.

The Egyptian announcement of the revival of its nuclear program in 2006 raised concerns in the nonproliferation community. Egypt—the "usual suspect"—has regularly aroused suspicions concerning its nuclear intentions.[3] While Libya has demonstrably renounced the nuclear option, Egypt has never really come to terms with Israel's possession of nuclear weapons. But most important, the emergence of Iran as a potential nuclear power leads one to wonder if the nuclear military option could be reconsidered by Mubarak's successors.

Egypt's longstanding ambitions in the field of nuclear energy have been stymied for decades due to lack of funds and political will, poor management, and little enthusiasm by potential Western nuclear providers. However, under Hosni Mubarak, the country's nuclear research activities had significantly increased. As a result, Egypt today has probably the most mature nuclear research program in the Arab world (along with Algeria, as will be seen below).

The Egyptian Atomic Energy Authority (EAEA) has two major research centers located at Inshas, near Cairo. The first is the Nuclear Research Centre (NRC), Egypt's main nuclear facility. It includes a 10 MeV (million electron volts) cyclotron provided by Russia through a 1991 agreement, a Nuclear Fuel Research Laboratory, and a Fuel Manufacturing Pilot Plant, as well as two research reactors:

- ETRR-1 (EG-001), a small Warm Water Reactor (WWR) tank reactor (2 megawatt thermal [MWth]), which was built in 1958 by the Soviet Union and became critical in 1961. The fuel (10-percent enriched uranium) was also provided by Moscow. It is used for solid state, nuclear, and reactor physics; chemical research; isotope production; and biological irradiation. After an in-service inspection by the International Atomic Energy Agency (IAEA) in 1992, the EAEA started to modernize instrumentation and safety systems, fission chamber assemblies, and other equipment. ETRR-1 has been used less after the commissioning of ETTR-2.
- ETRR-2 (EG-002), an open pool-type light-water reactor (22.5 MWth) built by the Argentine firm INVAP (Investigaciones Aplicadas), was inaugurated in 1998. Its fuel elements were made by Argentina, using 19.75-percent enriched uranium from Russia. The last shipment of fuel was delivered in 1997. It is primarily used for radioisotope production, medical and nuclear solid-state research, nuclear engineering experiments, material fuel tests, and various other fields to train scientists

> and technical personnel. This fuel is of the same type as the one previously provided by INVAP to Algeria (see below). The ETRR-2 could produce more than 6 kilos of plutonium a year.[4]

The other key node in the Egyptian nuclear program is the Hot Laboratories and Waste Management Centre (HLWMC), also located at Inshas. It includes a Radioisotope Production Facility, a Low- and Intermediate-Level Liquid Waste Station, and a Radioactive Waste Disposal Site. The HLWMC aims, inter alia, at developing Egyptian expertise in the back end of the fuel cycle: the site also hosts a Nuclear Chemistry Building and a Hydrometallurgy Pilot Plant.

Egypt does not report any conventional uranium resources. There is, however, speculation about possible resources amounting to up to 15,000 tons. Unconventional resources of uranium are found in phosphate and monazite deposits. The Nuclear Material Agency has established a pilot-scale extraction plant to exploit the Egyptian black sands at Rosetta Beach on the Mediterranean coast.

Anwar el-Sadat's decision to ratify the Non-proliferation Treaty (NPT) in February 1981 symbolized the abandonment of the military nuclear option. A Comprehensive Safeguards Agreement with the IAEA came into force in June 1982. Today, all known Egyptian nuclear facilities are safeguarded.

At the turn of the century, Egyptian attempts to acquire nuclear weapons seemed to belong to the past. Writing in 2002, a well-known Israeli expert said:

> As far as entering the nuclear arms race itself, the consensus in Israel today is that Egypt continues to uphold its strategic decision of 1981 (when it ratified the NPT) not to pursue this option.[5]

It was also widely believed that Egyptian dependence on US assistance would be a serious de facto deterrent to any violation of the NPT by Cairo.

But the Egyptian nuclear picture has significantly changed in the past 5 years. On March 28, 2006, during the 18th annual Arab Summit, Amr Musa, the Secretary General of the 22-nation Arab League and former Egyptian Foreign Minister, called on all Arab countries "to respond to societal energy needs by aggressively pursuing peaceful nuclear energy programs and, in the words of one report, thereby joining the 'nuclear club'."[6] A few months later, Gamal Mubarak, the then-President's son and Assistant Secretary of the National Democratic Party (NDP), announced during a conference of the party in September 2006 that Egypt planned to restart its nuclear energy program.[7] This was confirmed 2 days later by the President, who emphasized that nuclear energy would allow Egypt to meet its energy needs in the face of a shortage in national oil and gas reserves.[8] The higher ministerial council for energy reconvened for the first time in 20 years: it created an ad hoc committee comprised of five ministries (including electricity and energy, oil, and defense) to explore the nuclear option.[9] Electricity Minister Hassan Yunis announced a global plan that consisted of the building of three plants, generating a total of 1,800 megawatts (MW) until 2020. He said that Egypt would build its first power plant (a 1,100 MW station) at El-Dabaa.

In 2007, Yunis confirmed the government's aim of more than doubling the country's power generation capacity by 2027 from 23,000 MW to 52,000 MW. This plan was also intended to reduce dependence on natural gas and petroleum for electricity generation by using alternative energy sources, including renewable ones.[10] Egyptian experts say the plan's rationale is "purely economic."[11] Egyptian power generation relies on oil and natural gas. It is argued that indigenous reserves are expected to be depleted in 30-40 years, and that generating electricity through nuclear energy would allow Egypt to export more of its own natural resources. Former Minister of Electricity and Energy (1968-70) and current head of the Energy Committee at the National Specialized Councils, Mustafa Kamal Sabry, affirmed that: "The fact that our other energy sources are either too expensive or not everlasting means that the nuclear energy option is inevitable for Egypt."[12] There are also clearly status and domestic legitimacy dimensions in Cairo's nuclear bid. As claimed by Minister Yunis:

> The people are searching for a dream, a national project that proves to us that we are strong and capable of doing something fitting of the grandeur of a country that some have begun to doubt.[13]

Egypt has a high number of nuclear cooperation agreements in force, and signed a new one with Russia in 2008.

The political turmoil in Egypt and the Fukushima catastrophe have not diminished Cairo's nuclear ambitions. The tender for the future Egyptian power plant to be issued in early 2011 was delayed for obvious political reasons. But in July, it was reported that the process would be launched after the presidential elections.[14] Amr Moussa, then a main presidential hopeful, insisted that the program should and will go ahead.[15] A conjunction of several elements has come to cast serious doubts upon the strictly peaceful nature of Egypt's nuclear intentions.

Egypt persistently refuses to bolster its nonproliferation credentials. It does not want to subscribe to an Additional Protocol. It does not want to exclude the option of building enrichment or reprocessing facilities, arguing "against any attempt to limit the right of state-parties to the NPT to the full fuel cycle" and refusing new commitments as long as Israel's facilities are not put under safeguards.[16] Egypt has not ratified the Pelindaba Treaty (signed in April 1996) establishing a Nuclear-Weapon-Free Zone (NWFZ) in Africa. It has failed to ratify the Comprehensive Test Ban Treaty (CTBT, signed in October 1996). While Cairo claims that matters of status and principle explain its position, the fact is that Egypt seems to behave like a typical "hedging" state.

It is now known that Egypt has conducted significant undeclared activities in the past. A February 2005 report by the IAEA Director General identified multiple failures to report to the IAEA a number of activities related to conversion, irradiation, and reprocessing. Regarding uranium conversion, Cairo had failed in 1982 to report the possession of approximately 67 kilos of imported UF4, 3 kilos of uranium metal (some of which had been imported, the rest had been produced from imported UF4), 9.5 kilos of imported thorium compounds, and small amounts of domestically produced UO2, UO3, and UF4. Between 1990 and 2003, Cairo had conducted uranium and thorium irradiation experiments, as well as preparatory activities related to reprocessing (including undeclared imported non-irradiated fuel rods containing 10-percent enriched uranium). Egypt had also avoided providing initial design information for the Hydrometallurgy Pilot Plant and the Radioisotope Production Facility, and modified design information for the two reactors.[17] As some experts have emphasized:

> The work itself was not illegal, but the failure to declare it to the IAEA raises questions about Egypt's intentions, the true extent of their nuclear infrastructure and capabilities, and whether it carried out other, undeclared activities related to nuclear weapon development.[18]

During IAEA investigations, Egypt claimed its innocence and reaffirmed its continued commitment to its obligations. Cairo denied allegations of a secret program and declared that the failures were not intentional. Subsequent to the IAEA Director General report, IAEA board members qualified the violations as minor. The United States even praised Egypt's cooperation, saying that its example clearly demonstrated the "appropriate means for resolving outstanding safeguards issues, specifically, full cooperation with the IAEA on steps to address all concerns."[19] This led experts to conclude that "Egypt's infractions do not show a methodical build-up of a latent weapons capability."[20]

However, the subsequent discovery of traces of highly enriched uranium in the country has led to new questions about Egypt's activities and imports. As stated in the IAEA Safeguards Statement for 2008:

> In 2007 and 2008, some high enriched uranium (HEU) and low enriched uranium (LEU) particles were found in environmental samples taken at Inshas. Egypt stated that, as a result of an investigation carried out to identify the source of the particles, it believed the particles could have been brought into the country through contaminated radioisotope transport containers.[21]

According to AEAE officials, such containers had been imported for research in the areas of medicine and agriculture.[22] This record and the absence of an Additional Protocol naturally raise questions about whether the full range of Cairo's nuclear activities is publicly known. For instance, given the longstanding involvement of Egyptian scientists and technicians in the small Libyan nuclear research program, one would like to be certain that none had been involved in Kaddafi's secret effort to acquire a uranium enrichment capability.[23]

As in the case of some Gulf States, the timeline of Egypt's rejuvenation of its nuclear energy program suspiciously coincided with Iran's acceleration of its nuclear effort (in particular, the start of uranium enrichment at Natanz in early 2006). The two countries have had difficult relations since the assassination of President Sadat. A Tehran street has been named in honor of his murderer. Iran's growing prestige and influence in Iraq, Lebanon, and, most importantly, in the Gaza Strip, are seen with increasing discomfort in Cairo. In February 2006, Egypt voted in favor of the IAEA Board of Governors' resolution that transferred the Iranian file to the United Nations (UN) Security Council. As noted by some observers:

> Egypt's announcement [in September 2006] that it will revive its dormant nuclear program—coupled with similar statements from Morocco, Saudi Arabia, and other Arab governments—is a direct consequence of Iran's budding nuclear program and the international community's inability to stop it.[24]

Dr. Mohamed Kadry Said, an advisor at Cairo's Al Ahram Center for Political and Strategic Studies, stated that "for our people here to feel some sort of inferiority with regard to the Iranians or Israelis this affects their morale very much."[25] This simultaneous reference to Israel and Iran has become a standard in Egyptian debates—implicitly giving ground to suspicions, considering that Israel's nuclear civilian activities are quite modest. While President Mubarak alluded several times in the 1990s to the possibility of a nuclear weapons program and/or to a withdrawal from the NPT, such statements by Egyptian officials now seem to be increasingly frequent and explicit. In January 2007, Mubarak affirmed: "We don't want nuclear arms in the area but we are obligated to defend ourselves. We will have to have the appropriate weapons."[26] In April 2010, Foreign Minister Ahmad Abu Al-Gheit alluded to the possibility that Iran would be "forcing the Arabs to engage in a [nuclear arms] race."[27] In another interview, he, too, referred simultaneously to Iran and Israel, and refused, when asked to say that Egypt would not build nuclear weapons.[28] In June 2010, Ambassador Maged Abdul Aziz, the Egyptian head of delegation to the NPT Review Conference, said:

> If others will acquire nuclear weapons—and if others are going to use these nuclear weapons to acquire status in the region of the Middle East—let me tell you, we are not going to accept to be second-class citizens in the region of the Middle East. . . . If the Iranian program proves to be a military program and [if] Israeli nuclear capabilities [are maintained], both are going to be a threat to . . . Egypt and to all the countries in the Arab world. That will make a lot of countries of the Arab world change their mind.[29]

In September 2011, a retired Egyptian general openly called for Cairo to follow Tehran's example.[30]

Despite such insistence on external drivers, an Egyptian nuclear military option would doubtlessly also have an important domestic political component. As a commentator put it shamelessly 15 years ago, nuclear weapons could be:

> . . . the most cost-effective means available to Egypt for improving her intrinsic strength and relative power . . . [and would] revitalize Cairo's political and cultural leadership role in the region. It will also help disseminate a moderating and democratizing Arab vision. This can only serve the interests of peace and stability in the region.[31]

The Muslim Brotherhood—who is now the dominant political force in the country, having won both parliamentary and presidential elections—praise a nuclear weapons option to counter Israel's nuclear capabilities.[32] Several members of the Shura Council (the consultative Upper House) have also called for a nuclear weapons program.[33] It is a sign of the times that even Mohamed El-Baradei, the former Director General of the IAEA and a former presidential hopeful, refused to discard a nuclear weapons option for Egypt—perhaps seeking support from the Muslim Brotherhood.[34] Finally, a nuclear weapons program could bolster the domestic and regional status of Mubarak's successors.

Since it became a member of the NPT in 1981, Egypt has actively promoted, through national means as well as through the League of Arab States and the Non-Aligned Movement (NAM), the idea of a Nuclear-Weapon-Free Zone in the Middle East. Egypt rightly assesses that consensus at the 1995 NPT Review and Extension Conference was made possible only by the adoption of a specific resolution on the Middle East. In recent years, the idea of a Weapons of Mass Destruction (WMD)-free zone in the Middle East has become a useful vehicle for Egyptian diplomacy to challenge the Iranian nuclear program under the disguise of a project historically aimed primarily at the denuclearization of Israel.[35]

At the May 2010 NPT Review Conference, Cairo was a key participant as the chair of the NAM and of the New Agenda Coalition. Egypt's diplomacy was instrumental in ensuring that the idea of a conference on the establishment of a WMD-free zone in the Middle East obtained consensus. The conference is to be held in or after 2012. Presumably, a perceived failure to make progress in this regard could be used as a pretext by those Egyptians who are pushing for a nuclear weapons option.

Finally, an official acknowledgment by Israel of its nuclear weapon capability would be an extraordinarily strong incentive for Egypt to push for its own nuclear weapons option. While nothing suggests that today Israel is ready to change its longstanding declaratory policy on the subject, an openly nuclear-armed Iran might lead Israel to reconsider its position if it was judged necessary to ensure deterrence vis-à-vis Tehran and the reassurance of its own population.

If Egypt was to visibly take steps in that direction, it is not certain that the threat of cutting off Western assistance to the country would be enough of a deterrent. An Egyptian government that decides to build nuclear weapons might also be one that has decided to distance itself from the West. This could happen, for instance, if the Muslim Brotherhood grew in power and influence within the new regime. Moreover, as it happened in the past for Pakistan, Gulf countries could step in and assist Egypt—and perhaps even become stakeholders in a de facto multinational Arab nuclear program.

An Algerian Option?

When it comes to assessing prospects for nuclear proliferation, Algeria is usually not on the radar screen of most Western analysts. This is a mistake. Algeria has the technical means and potentially the political will to be at least a "nuclear hedging" country.

Since the late 1980s, Algeria has had a very significant nuclear program, which includes in particular now-safeguarded nuclear facilities on two different sites.

- The Nur research reactor (DZ-0001) is located at the Draria nuclear complex, about 20 kilometers (km) east of Algiers. It is owned and licensed by the Research and Higher Education Ministry, and operated by the Unité de Recherche en Génie Nucléaire (URGN).[36] The reactor's construction by the Argentinian firm INVAP began in 1987, under a contract signed in May 1985. This was not a "turnkey" operation: the construction involved a significant number of Algerian firms and technicians.[37] The small pool-type, light-water reactor of 1 MWth went critical in 1989. Its fuel (20-percent LEU) was provided by Argentina. Its stated goal is research and the production of isotopes.
- Algeria also has a pilot fuel fabrication plant, UDEC, located at the Drania nuclear complex. It was built by INVAP under a 1985 agreement. Even though the plant was 90 percent completed in mid-1991, domestic security conditions hampered further work on the project. It was fully completed only in mid-2000.[38]
- The Es Salam research reactor (DZ-0002) is located in Ain Oussera, in the Saharasert, 140 kilometers south of Algiers. It is owned by the Research and Higher Education Ministry, licensed by the Algerian Nuclear Safety Commission, and operated by the Centre de Développement des Systèmes Energétiques (Centre for the Development of Energy Systems, CDSE).[39] The construction began in 1988, and went critical in 1992, before being inaugurated in 1993—after a controversy arose about the nature of Algeria's program (see below). The reactor was a heavy water-type, reported to the IAEA to be designed to produce 15 MWth. The reactor was built following the signing of a nuclear cooperation agreement with China in February 1983. The builder was Zhongyuan Engineering Corporation (a subsidiary of China National Nuclear Corporation), the same company that built the Pakistani Chashma nuclear power

plants. Beijing stated in 1991 that under this agreement, it had also delivered to Algeria 11 metric tons of heavy water and 216 fuel modules, totalling 909 kilos of 3 percent LEU.[40] (It seems that the Algerian government had envisioned cooperating with France, but ended up turning to Beijing at the end of 1982.)[41] The reactor's fuel was also provided by China.

- The Ain Oussera site also hosts various facilities, including an isotope production plant, hot cell laboratories, and waste storage tanks. These are collectively mentioned in the IAEA list of safeguarded installations as AURES-1.

Algeria today has one of the best and most developed nuclear complexes of the whole Arab world; it also has vast deposits of uranium in the southeast part of the country, near Tamanrasset. In addition, the country has considerable amounts of phosphate ore from which uranium could be recovered.[42] Concerns about Algeria's nuclear intentions surfaced in 1991, as US satellite observation revealed the existence and nature of the Ain Oussera project. The US State Department reportedly did not believe that Algiers was seriously considering a program of a military nature. In fact, it turned out that a senior State Department official had been informed as early as 1988 of the nature of the contract by the Chinese government.[43] The story became public through an article in The Washington Times.[44] (The day before, Algiers had expelled the United Kingdom [UK] military attaché for having been found with a camera on the site.)

That the Algerian nuclear complex resembled Egypt's program fueled suspicions. Not unlike Egypt's, Algeria's nuclear infrastructure is significantly developed and includes a fairly large research reactor. Proliferation concerns stemmed from the combination of several factors. First, Algeria had not signed the NPT, and its facilities were not safeguarded. (In 1991, many nonaligned states had yet to sign the NPT, since they viewed it as an instrument of domination by industrialized nations.) Algeria had signed an INFCIRC/66-type agreement in 1989, which covered only the Argentine-supplied reactor.

Second, the El Salam complex, which is fairly large and well protected for a research facility, is of a type that would potentially allow for the production of weapon-grade plutonium, and satellite observation of the site raised many questions. Several foreign experts believed that a heavy-walled building near the reactor was intended to be a full-scale reprocessing plant. The size of the cooling towers was said to exceed the requirements of a 15 MW reactor and to be consistent with a 40- or even 60-MWth reactor.[45] Finally, the site was well protected, including through Soviet-made SA-5 surface-to-air missiles.[46]

Estimates regarding the quantity or plutonium that could be generated by the reactor at 15 MW vary between three and five kilograms (kg) a year.[47] However, in June 1995, it was reported—consistently, as is now known, with US intelligence estimates at the time—that the reactor was in fact fueled with 3-percent LEU instead of natural uranium. This lessened the quantity of plutonium possible to produce annually with the reactor, which was evaluated at one kilogram, assuming a power of 15 MW.[48] There are, however, several options for producing weapon-grade plutonium from such a reactor. One would be to increase significantly the number of reloads of LEU; another would be to switch to natural uranium fuel. A third option would be to irradiate natural uranium targets—a process through which it would be possible to obtain about 1.5 kg of plutonium a year.[49] A European expert estimated in 2009 that the Ain Oussera reactor had produced 50 kilos of plutonium since its inauguration—a very high estimate, but, nevertheless, a not implausible one.[50]

A prominent member of the then-Algerian government has stated in a 2009 conversation with this author that the project had entirely been run by the military, and that the civilian leadership had been kept in the dark.[51] Algeria faced no direct military threat at the time. A nuclear option could have been motivated by one of several of the following factors: recurring tensions with its two main neighbors, Morocco and Libya (which entertained a nuclear weapons option, as Algiers probably knew); a "prestige" dimension, which certainly would have mattered to a country that is one of the biggest in Africa, has been a leading member of NAM and sees both Libya and Egypt as competitors in both North Africa and in the Arab world; or domestic balance-of-power considerations, if the armed forces were looking to bolster their grip on power. There is also the possibility that Algiers's past military-oriented nuclear activities were conducted on behalf of, or in cooperation with, another country.

At a press conference on April 29, 1991, a spokesman for the Algerian Ministry of Scientific Research said that the El Salam reactor's purpose was the production of isotopes and electricity.[52] In May, the government claimed that it was preparing for the "post-oil" era.[53] The government gave technical details about the reactor and announced that it would be put under safeguards once completed.[54] An official TV report included government comments to the effect that the reactor's power could not be increased beyond 20 MW, and that the Ain Oussera site was chosen only because of its geological stability.[55]

The role of international pressure was probably important in leading Algiers to accept NPT ratification and IAEA safeguards. At that time, the Algerian government was isolated and needed to consolidate its relations with the West. Following the aborted December 1991 elections that had given victory to the Islamic Salvation Front, a coup had taken place on January 11, 1992, and a state of emergency had been declared on February 9, 1992.[56]

The first IAEA inspections to El Salam took place in January 1992, thus in the midst of the political crisis.[57] A few days later, a temporary facility-specific safeguards agreement was signed with the IAEA, allowing for inspection of the Ain Oussera complex; it came into force in June 1992.

Algeria officially announced its decision to join the NPT on December 21, 1993, on the occasion of the inauguration of the El Salam reactor.[58] Algiers deposited its instruments of ratification of the NPT in January 1995. A full-scope safeguards agreement with the IAEA came into force in January 1997. (Inspections reported minor discrepancies with Algeria's initial declarations, namely small quantities of undeclared materials—three kg of enriched uranium, several litres of heavy water, and several pellets of natural uranium provided by China.[59]) Algiers also signed the CTBT in October 1996 and ratified the Pelindaba Treaty in February 1998.

At the same time, Algiers sought to reinforce its cooperation with China through a series of next-steps agreements in 1996 and 1997, which covered the completion of a hot-cells facility (phase two), the building of facilities for the production of isotopes (phase three), as well as the construction of underground waste-storage tanks. There have been reports of Algeria's unwillingness to open the Ain Oussera hot cells facility to inspections, as well as of an undeclared removal of two fuel rods from the reactor.[60] Algerian claims that the isotope facility is to be used for the production of Cobalt-60 have been met with suspicion.[61] However, in 2002, the United States was said to have been satisfied with IAEA surveillance of the Ain Oussera complex.[62]

Concerns resurfaced in the late 1990s, as a report from the Spanish intelligence service, Centro Superior de Información de la Defensa (CESID), allegedly claimed that even though there was currently no evidence of a political will by Algiers to undertake nuclear military applications:

> ... The knowledge acquired by a notable team of technicians and scientists, with the availability of the facilities that it will

have at the end of the century, puts this country in a privileged position to restart the programme's military character if the political decision is made.[63]

In this regard, it is noteworthy that there was a significant transfer of "nuclear know-how" by INVAP during the construction of the Nur reactor and the UDEC pilot fuel fabrication plant (which was then being built).[64] It is noteworthy that experts from the Institute for Science and International Security (ISIS), after extensive research, have found that there was a discrepancy between the 300 highly qualified engineers claimed to be working in the Algerian nuclear program—and the low number of Algerian publications in the field, furthering suspicions that some of the scientists may have been involved in classified work.[65]

As in many other states in the region, the idea of developing nuclear power has attracted interest. Algeria's scarcity of water resources and the benefits of reserving an increasing share of the country's oil and gas for exports, given the rising prices of such commodities, have frequently been cited as economic incentives. There is also clearly a prestige factor at play, as in many other countries. In November 2006, the Minister of Energy and Mining announced that a significant nuclear power program would be launched, taking advantage of the country's abundant resources in uranium.[66] In December, a security and safety institution was established. Algiers would like to have its first nuclear power plant running in 2020. Algeria seems to consider that it is a natural leader in Africa's development of indigenous energy programs. It hosts the African Union Energy Commission (AFREC)[67] and, in January 2007, hosted the first Africa-wide conference devoted to nuclear energy.[68]

During the French presidential election campaign, then-candidate Nicolas Sarkozy launched the idea of an energy partnership with Algeria, which would include investment in gas exploitation in return for nuclear cooperation.[69] However, as of the Fall of 2011, this proposal had not been translated into concrete action by the two countries except for a generic nuclear cooperation agreement signed in 2008. The French firm AREVA is said to be uninterested in selling a reactor to Algeria.[70]

So Algiers seems keen to multiply and diversify its options. In May 2006, an 11-strong delegation visited South Korea to explore bilateral nuclear cooperation, with reportedly a strong interest in facilities such as hot cells.[71] In November 2006, Algiers expressed interest in Iran's offer of sharing its expertise.[72] In 2007-2008, Algeria also signed various new nuclear cooperation agreements with a number of countries, including Argentina, China, France, and the United States.

Algiers ratified the CTBT in July 2003. Under pressure from the United States and Europe, it negotiated with the IAEA an Additional Protocol (AP) to its Safeguards Agreement. The IAEA Board of Governors approved the Algerian AP in September 2004. However, as of August 2010, Algeria had yet to sign it. Whether Algeria is using the coming into force of the AP as a political tool to advance the cause of a NWFZ in the Middle East, to appear as the champion of nonaligned countries' right to peaceful use of nuclear energy, or it is seriously hesitating before giving up a potential military option remains unclear. Algeria has been a long-standing proponent of the idea of a NWFZ in the Middle East. More recently, it has consistently supported the Iranian position as to its "right" and intention to pursue a full nuclear fuel cycle, abstaining in several votes on the Iranian issue at meetings of the IAEA Board of Governors.[73] (Algerian-Iranian relations had been restored in 2002, after a decade-long freeze—due to Tehran's alleged support for Algerian extremists.) Bouteflika's support for the Iranian position was reiterated at the occasion of Ahmadinejad's visit to Algiers in August 2007, saying it was:

> unacceptable that countries which are members of the Nuclear Non-Proliferation Treaty are constrained, because of selective and unilateral interpretations, to renounce their normal and legitimate right to acquire these technologies for purely peaceful purposes.[74]

In some respects, Algeria's contemporary situation could be compared with Pakistan's: a military-dominated Muslim-majority state with a serious terrorism problem, which enjoys good relations with the United States, but has received important nuclear assistance from China. After the aborted elections of December 1991, Washington benefited from a cold in French-Algerian relations, and the US-Algeria relationship has been made stronger in the post-September 11, 2001, environment. At the same time, cooperation with China has continued and expanded in the economic field.[75] Meanwhile, the terrorist Groupe Salafiste de Prédication et de Combat (GCSP) continues to be very active in the country, threatening both national and international interests—French ones, in particular. Since 2006, the group has been officially designated as al Qaeda's affiliate in the region ("Al Qaeda in the Islamic Maghreb" [AQMI]). A radicalization of the country remains a very hypothetical scenario. The current system—partly democratic with a strong military influence—looks strong. However, the aborted 1991 elections showed that the population was ready to give a majority to political forces perceived as being less corrupt than the old guard that had run the country since the 1962 independence, and more in tune with its day-to-day needs.

An Algerian nuclear military option remains a real possibility.[76] The probability of such an option being realized would dramatically increase if three conditions were met: a rebirth of nuclear weapons options or "hedging" strategies in the Arab world; a further weakening of the nuclear nonproliferation regime, particularly if Iran were to continue to proceed on the nuclear path; and a growing tension between Algeria and the West, be it under the current regime or after a "regime change"—leading the country to be governed, for instance, by an Adalet ve Kalkınma Partisi (AKP)-type Islamist-oriented political force. Given Algeria's membership in the NPT and the Pelindaba Treaty, any nuclear option would have to be developed either in secrecy—for instance, through a uranium enrichment program, possibly with Iranian or North Korean assistance—or after a withdrawal from such treaties.

The main obstacle to a possible Algerian nuclear option is that the country does not have ballistic missiles or even a missile industry. This would not be an issue for a "hedging" option with primarily political goals. A more ambitious nuclear program would have to be accompanied by foreign procurement of missiles, probably in Iran or North Korea.

Algeria, whose institutions have been dominated by the National Liberation Front since its 1962 independence, has enjoyed a growing relationship with Iran since the resumption of diplomatic relations in 2000.[77] Tehran could be a conduit for the acquisition not only of ballistic missiles, but of nuclear-related technology. In fact, Algiers would be almost an ideal candidate if Tehran was looking for partners in its own nuclear weapons drive.[78] Algeria could be, for instance, an alternative source of weapons-usable plutonium for Iran.

Regional Dynamics and the Risk of Action-Reaction

From a technical standpoint, Egypt and Algeria have largely similar nuclear programs, and doubts linger in both countries regarding the existence of undeclared nuclear activities (notably in the field of uranium enrichment or plutonium separation), especially given that neither of the two has brought an Additional Protocol into force. According to a European expert, Algerian expertise and know-how are actually superior to Egypt's.[79] For Algeria, an Egyptian drive for nuclear weapons would undoubtedly be a trigger to restart (or accelerate) its dual-use or military-related nuclear activities.

It is not widely appreciated that the two countries have an extraordinarily bitter relationship, made up of resentment and jealousy with deep historical roots. In particular, despite the fact that Nasser openly supported the Algerian independence movement, there is the feeling in Algiers that the self-appointed leader of the Arab world did not do its best to support the insurgency (or alternatively, that Egypt exaggerates its contribution to the independence of Algeria).[80] After Algeria's independence, Egypt touted itself as a model and a tutor for the young Republic, an attitude that many Algerians saw as condescending and involving undue meddling into internal affairs. Among the grudges that Algeria holds over Egypt are its alleged lack of recognition for the military and financial support given to Cairo in its wars against Israel between 1967 and 1973, and its subsequent separate peace with Israel. In the debate over the reform of the UN Security Council, Algeria has made it clear that it will not accept Egypt being conferred a permanent seat at the UN Security Council. Also in 2004, Algeria challenged Cairo's leadership over the League of Arab States.[81]

At the risk of oversimplification, there is an Egyptian "superiority complex" over Algeria, and a corresponding Algerian "inferiority complex" over Egypt. This rivalry was exposed to the limelight in recent years at the occasion of the 1990 and 2010 Soccer World Cup Playoffs. In 1989, Egypt qualified by winning over Algeria.[82] In 2009, the reverse happened: Algeria qualified by winning over Egypt. At both occasions, passions ran high, and violence erupted after the games, with significant diplomatic and economic consequences.[83]

The contract with INVAP to build the ETRR-2 reactor was signed in September 1992, 18 months after the revelation of the existence of the Algerian reactor.[84] Algeria's attitude regarding Egypt was made clear in 2006, when it announced its nuclear energy program just a few weeks after Egypt's own announcement. Just like Cairo, Algiers would like to have its first nuclear power plant operating around 2020. These plans have not been altered by the Fukushima accident.

In the Spring of 2010, the Algerian press published a declassified US document reporting a May 1991 State Department request for Egyptian assistance in gathering information about the Ain Oussera reactor.[85] Unsurprisingly, this created a furor in Algeria.

In sum, there is enough evidence to suggest that Algeria's conduct in the nuclear field should be monitored as carefully as Egypt's. "Tertiary proliferation" might not be the end of the proliferation game in the Middle East. If both Egypt and Algeria were showing signs of going nuclear, should one expect the new Libyan regime, for instance, to stand idle?

Endnotes

1. See, for instance Moeed Yusuf, "Predicting Proliferation: The History of the Future of Nuclear Weapons," *Policy Paper No. 11*, Washington, DC: The Brookings Institution, January 2009.
2. It could be argued that Pakistan's nuclear program was also a case of "tertiary" proliferation, since it was a reaction to India's program, which itself was largely a response to China's own program. However, in the case of Asia, the trauma of military defeats (1962 for India, 1971 for Pakistan) was arguably as important as the existence of neighboring nuclear programs. By contrast, in the Middle East, the 1967 defeat against Israel did not lead to a rush to go nuclear in Arab countries.
3. The expression "the usual suspect" comes from Mark Fitzpatrick, ed., *Nuclear Programmes in the Middle East: In the Shadow of Iran*, London, UK: International Institute for Strategic Studies, 2008, p. 17.
4. Wyn Bowen and Joanna Kid, "The Nuclear Capabilities and Ambitions of Iran's Neighbors," in Henry Sokolski and Patrick Clawson, eds., *Getting Ready for a Nuclear-Armed Iran*, Carlisle, PA: Strategic Studies Institute, US Army War College, 2005, p. 64.
5. Emily B. Landau, "Egypt's Nuclear Dilemma," *Strategic Assessment*, Vol. 5, No. 3, November 2002.
6. Sammy Salama and Gina Cabrera-Farraj, "Secretary General of Arab League Urges Arab Countries to Exploit Nuclear Power, Enter 'Nuclear Club'," *WMD Insights*, May 2006.
7. "Mubarak's Son Proposes Developing Nuclear Energy," *The Associated Press*, September 19, 2006.
8. "Egyptian President Discusses Reform Plans, Nuclear Energy at Party Conference," BBC, September 22, 2006.
9. "Time for the N word," *Al-Ahram Weekly*, No. 814, 2006.
10. "Egypt Aims to Double Power Generation Capacity within 20 Years," *Global Insight*, August 3, 2007.
11. Dr. Abdel Hakim Kandil, Professor of Nuclear and Inorganic Chemistry at Cairo's Helwan University, quoted in "Inside Egypt's Nuclear Debate," *International Security Network*, March 26, 2007.
12. Quoted in "Dumping the Nuclear Option?" *Al-Ahram Weekly*, No. 713, 2004.
13. Quoted in Sammy Salama and Gina Cabrera-Farraj, "Renewed Egyptian

Ambitions for a Peaceful Nuclear Program," *WMD Insights*, November 2006.

14. "N-power Tender after Presidential Polls," *The Egyptian Gazette*, July 3, 2011.

15. See, for instance, Amr Moussa, "Egypt Must Turn Over New Leaf with All Countries, Including Iran," Interview with *Khabar Online*, MEMRI Special Dispatch, No. 3994, July 12, 2011.

16. Miles Pomper and Peter Crail, "Interview with Nabil Fahmy, Egyptian Ambassador to the United States," *Arms Control Today*, July 21, 2008. A more precise, official description of the Egyptian position by Egyptian Deputy Foreign Minister Ramzy Ezzedine Ramzy is: "Egypt rejects any attempts to impose additional obligations on non-nuclear weapon states, which are already in compliance with their commitments pursuant to the Treaty, if they are not reciprocated by equal and commensurate measures by states that still lie outside the treaty and are not bound by Comprehensive Safeguards Agreements." Statement at the NPT PrepCom 2008 General Debate, New York, April 29, 2008.

17. *Implementation of the NPT Safeguards Agreement in the Arab Republic of Egypt*, GOV/2005/9, Vienna, Austria, International Atomic Energy Agency, February 14, 2005.

18. Jack Boureston, Yana Feldman, and Mary Beth Nikitin, "Egypt—New Revelations about Past Activities?" *First Watch International*, March 4, 2005.

19. Ambassador Jackie Sanders, "US Praises Egypt's Nuclear Openness," *Reuters*, March 2, 2005.

20. Boureston *et al*., "Egypt—New Revelations about Past Activities?"

21. *The Safeguards Implementation Report for 2008*, p. 11.

22. Gamal Essam El-Din, "An Old Story Made New," *Al-Ahram Weekly*, No. 947, 2009.

23. Some Israeli experts claim that there are a high number of Egyptian publications related to uranium enrichment (interviews in Tel-Aviv, Israel, January 2007). It is widely suspected that Egyptian officials met with representatives of the A. Q. Khan network in the past.

24. Sammy Salama and Heidi Weber, "Arab Nuclear Envy," *Bulletin of the Atomic Scientists*, September-October 2007.

25. Quoted in "Inside Egypt's Nuclear Debate."

26. "Egypt May Develop Nuclear Weapons," *United Press International*, January 20, 2007.

27. "Egyptian Foreign Minister Ahmad Abu Al-Gheit Warns that a Nuclear

Iran Would Force the Arabs to Join the Nuclear Race," Special Dispatch No. 2929, *The Middle East Media Research Institute*, April 30, 2010.

28. Quoted in "Obama Pushes For Cuts to Nuclear Arsenals During Global Summit," *PBS NewsHour*, April 12, 2010.

29. Quoted in Elaine M. Grossman, "Egypt Plays Key Nonproliferation Role, But Keeps Nuclear Options Open," *NTI Global Security Newswire*, June 10, 2010.

30. "Retired Egyptian General Abd Al-Hamid Umran Calls for an Egyptian Nuclear Program: We Should Follow the Iranian Model and Deceive the International Community," MEMRI Special Dispatch No. 4142, September 16, 2011.

31. Adel Safty, "Proliferation, Balance of Power, and Nuclear Deterrence: Should Egypt Pursue a Nuclear Option?" *International Studies*, Vol. 33, No. 1, 1996, pp. 32-34.

32. Sammy Salama and Khalid Hilal, "Egyptian Muslim Brotherhood Presses Government for Nuclear Weapons," *WMD Insights*, November 2006. The Brotherhood is not overtly opposing Iran's nuclear drive.

33. Gamal Essam El-Din, "'No Need for Nukes,'" *Al-Ahram Weekly*, No. 977, 2009.

34. In an April 2010 interview, when asked, "Can you say that your country, Egypt, will never acquire nuclear weapons even if its neighbor Israel possesses them?" El-Baradei replied: "The solution would be that Israel gives up its arsenal. But if instability continues, if we continue to see Palestinians being killed, if the wars in Afghanistan, in Iraq or in Somalia continue, then all scenarios are possible." Antoine Malo, "Nous ne pouvons pas attendre une explosion au milieu de Manhattan" ("We Cannot Expect an Explosion in the Middle of Manhattan"), *Le Journal du Dimanche*, April 11, 2010.

35. Nevertheless, the Egyptian-dominated League of Arab States has opposed the Gulf Cooperation Council's idea of pushing first for a "Gulf WMD-free zone"; that is, to give priority to Iran over Israel.

36. "Nur" means "light" in Arabic. The URGN is the Draria Nuclear Centre.

37. "Reactor Nur (Algeria)—Introduction," available from *www.invap.net*.

38. Roberto Mario Ornstein, "Argentina as an Exporter of Nuclear Technology—Past, Present and Future," Buenos Aires, Argentina: Consejo Argentino Para Las Relaciones Internacionales, 2001, pp. 25-26.

39. "El Salam" means "peace" in Arabic. The Center for the Development

of Energy Systems (CDSE) is now commonly referred to as the Birine, or El Salam Nuclear Research Center.

40. "China-Nuclear Cooperation Agreements," Washington and Lee University, Lexington, VA: NTI Research Library. See also a collection of declassified documents in William Burr, ed., "The Algerian Nuclear Problem, 1991: Controversy over the Es Salam Reactor," Electronic Briefing Book No. 228, Washington, DC: George Washington University, National Security Archive, September 10, 2007 (Hereafter: Burr, "The Algerian Nuclear Problem").

41. Ann MacLachlan, "Algerian Leader Asserts Good Faith in Nuclear Research Reactor Plans," *Nucleonics Week*, May 23, 1991, pp. 11-12.

42. Jeffrey Fields and Jack Boureston, "Algeria Country Profile," Stockholm, Sweden: Stockholm International Peace Research Institute (SIPRI), July 2004. Regarding the country's uranium resources, official Algerian estimates vary between 29,000 and 56,000 tons.

43. David Albright and Corey Hinderstein, "Algeria: Big Deal in the Desert?" *Bulletin of the Atomic Scientists*, May-June 2001, p. 47.

44. Bill Gertz, "China Helps Algeria Develop Nuclear Weapons," *The Washington Times*, April 11, 1991.

45. Mark Hibbs, "Cooling Towers are Key to Claim Algeria Is Building Bomb Reactor," *Nucleonics Week*, April 18, 1991, pp. 7-8; MacLachlan, "Algerian Leader Asserts Good Faith," pp. 11-12. In 1991, US Intelligence assessed that the reactor's power could be increased to 50 megawatts (MW), see Burr, "The Algerian Nuclear Problem." Some analysts pointed out that China had a history of building research reactors with "disproportionate cooling." See Albright and Hinderstein, "Algeria: Big Deal in the Desert?" p. 47.

46. The US Government noted in 1991 that the site had been defended by anti-aircraft batteries and early warning radar from mid-January to mid-March of that year, that is, during Operation DESERT STORM. See Burr, "The Algerian Nuclear Problem."

47. "Algeria," in Joseph Cirincione, Jon B. Wolfstahl, and Miriam Rajkumar, *Deadly Arsenals: Tracking Weapons of Mass Destruction*, Washington, DC: Carnegie Endowment for International Peace, 2002, p. 299; and "Algeria: Nuclear Reactor Update," *Wisconsin Project on Arms Control*, The Risk Report, Vol. 1, No. 5, June 1995, p. 12. US intelligence estimated in 1991 that if the reactor's power was increased to 50 MW, its plutonium production capability would be approximately 10 to 13 kilograms (kg), See Burr, "The Algerian Nuclear Problem."

48. "Algeria: Nuclear Reactor Update," p. 12. US Intelligence noted in 1991 that a power increase to 50 MW would imply a capability to produce three kg of plutonium (Pu) a year. See Burr, "The Algerian Nuclear

Problem."

49. "Algeria: Nuclear Reactor Update," p. 12; Albright and Hinderstein, "Algeria: Big Deal in the Desert?" p. 50.

50. Friedrich Steinhäusler, "Infrastructure Security and Nuclear Power," paper prepared for the seminar on Extended Deterrence, Security Guarantees, and Nuclear Proliferation: Strategic Stability in the Persian Gulf, Dubai, United Arab Emirates, Gulf Research Center, October 4-5, 2009.

51. Interview in Paris, January 2009.

52. "El Salam Reactor—Ain Oussera," available from *www.globalsecurity.org*.

53. See Burr, "The Algerian Nuclear Problem."

54. MacLachlan, "Algerian Leader Asserts Good Faith," pp. 11-12; Albright and Hinderstein, "Algeria: Big Deal in the Desert?" p. 48.

55. See Burr, "The Algerian Nuclear Problem."

56. Reports in early 1992 that Iraq had transferred nuclear material and scientists to Algeria were found unsubstantiated. Albright and Hinderstein, "Algeria: Big Deal in the Desert?" p. 49.

57. *Ibid.*

58. See "Address by the Minister for Foreign Affairs of Algeria on the Occasion of the Inauguration of the 'Es Salam' Reactor on December 21, 1993," INFCIRC/429, February 18, 1994.

59. Albright and Hinderstein, "Algeria: Big Deal in the Desert?" p. 49.

60. *Ibid.*

61. *Ibid.*, p. 50.

62. See Cirincione, *et al.*, *Deadly Arsenals*, p. 301.

63. Quoted in M. Gonzales and J. M. Larraya, "El Cesid Warns that Algeria Can Have the Capacity to Produce Military Plutonium in Two Years," *El Pais*, August 23, 1998 (English translation by ISIS).

64. "Reactor Nur (Algeria)—Introduction"; Ornstein, "Argentina as an Exporter of Nuclear Technology—Past, Present and Future."

65. Albright and Hinderstein, "Algeria: Big Deal in the Desert?" p. 50.

66. Khalid Hilal, "Algeria Announces Plans for Expanded Nuclear Energy Programme; Iran Offers to Help," *WMD Insights*, February 2007.

67. An "African Regional Cooperative Agreement for Research, Development and Training Related to Nuclear Science and Technology" (AFRA) was signed in 1990. See INFCIRC/377, April 2, 1990.

68. The Conference adopted on January 14, 2007 a "Final Declaration of

Algiers" and a "Plan of Action."

69. Discours de Nicolas Sarkozy—Conférence de presse sur la politique internationale, Paris, France, Méridien Montparnasse (Speech by Nicolas Sarkozy at a Press Conference on International Policy in Paris, France, Le Meridien Montparnasse), February 28, 2007.

70. Interviews in Paris, France, August 2007.

71. See Daniel A. Pinkston, "Algeria Seeks Nuclear Cooperation with South Korea as Seoul Prepares New Nuclear Plans," *WMD Insights*, June 2006.

72. Hilal, "Algeria Announces Plans."

73. *Ibid.*

74. Reuters, "L'Algérie marque son appui à l'Iran sur le nucléaire civil" ("Algeria Marks its Endorsement Iran on Civil Nuclear"), *Le Monde*, August 7, 2007.

75. In addition, Russia has become a significant strategic partner of Algeria, through important conventional weapons sales, including a 2006 $8-billion deal.

76. This author wrote about Algeria's possible nuclear intentions in a 2009 book entitled *Le Marché Noir de la Bombe (The Black Market of the Bomb)*, Paris, France: Buchet-Chastel, 2009. A flurry of headlines ensued in Algeria (as well as in Morocco). Many officials and journalists suggested that the author had a political agenda and was possibly acting on France or Israel's behalf. More interestingly, Energy and Mining Minister Chakib Khelil was led to claim that Algeria "is currently setting up measures that will allow it to sign the Additional Protocol." See "Les précisions de Khelil" ("The Details of Khelil"), *Le Temps d'Algérie* (*The Times of Algeria*), September 25, 2009. Nearly 1 year later, the AP had still not been signed by Algiers.

77. The two countries had severed diplomatic relations in 1993, following accusations of Iranian support for the Islamic Salvation Front.

78. In 2000, two commentators noted that "The Sahara desert sites . . . might be ideal for testing an Iranian-built atom bomb." Al J. Venter and Pat Lancaster, "A Nuclear Newcomer," *The Middle East*, June 1, 2000. This remains an improbable scenario, given the constant Algerian complaints about the alleged consequences of French nuclear testing on Algerian territory from 1960 to 1966.

79. Steinhäusler.

80. Nasser's support for the Algerian insurgency was a key reason behind France's decision to go to war, along with the United Kingdom, against Egypt in 1956.

81. The Arab League has been located in Cairo since its creation in 1945,

and its Secretary General has always been an Egyptian (except between 1979 and 1990, when the League was moved to Tunis with a Tunisian Secretary General, because of Arab challenges to the Egyptian peace with Israel.

82. Egypt refused to send a team to the 1990 Africa Cup held in Algeria.
83. Egypt is the largest foreign investor in Algeria.
84. Available from *www.invap.net*.
85. See Ian Allen, "US Asked for Egypt's Spy Help on Algerian Nuclear Reactor," available from *intelNews.org*, May 5, 2010; and "Amr Moussa dément: L'Egypte accuse d'espionnage en Algérie" ("Insane Amr Moussa: Egypt Accused of Spying in Algeria"), May 8, 2010. Given that the Egyptian foreign minister at the time was the current Secretary of the League of Arab States, this episode was widely seen in Cairo as an attempt to weaken Egyptian influence in the League.

Chapter 8

Casting a Blind Eye:
Kissinger and Nixon Finesse Israel's Bomb

Victor Gilinsky

It is now widely accepted that 1969 marked a turning point in US policy regarding Israeli nuclear weapons. A "stopping point" may be a better description. The pivotal moment appears to have come in a private, unrecorded September 1969 meeting between Richard Nixon and Golda Meir: She is supposed to have owned up to having the bomb, and Nixon is supposed to have promised that as long as Israel kept its bomb under wraps, the United States would not ask questions about it.

Up to that point, the United States had been urging Israel to join the Nonproliferation Treaty (NPT).[1] After the 1969 meeting, as General Yitzhak Rabin (the Israeli Ambassador at the time) put it, the subject "dropped off the agenda." In fact, the entire subject of Israeli nuclear weapons dropped off the US foreign policy agenda.

This history is still important today, because the subject is still off the US agenda. In fact, the US Government is still committed to keeping Israel off the international nonproliferation agenda.[2] But the pretense of ignorance about Israeli bombs does not wash anymore. President Barack Obama looked foolish, or worse, when he said he did not want to "speculate" whether any countries in the Middle East had nuclear weapons.[3] The evident double standard undermines efforts to control the spread of nuclear weapons worldwide.[4]

It is useful, therefore, to try to understand the 1969 origins of the current approach toward Israeli nuclear weapons and to inquire about the continuing validity of US promises at the time. We have more material to work with, since the Nixon Library released a few years ago many Nixon-era White House documents related to Israeli nuclear weapons, including recommendations to the President from his national security advisor, Henry Kissinger. The released documents—some of them formerly Top Secret—provide a fascinating glimpse into the White House policy reviews before the critical meeting with Meir.

The story has now been told in some detail, most recently by Avner Cohen, who used the 1969 Nixon-Meir meeting as the point of departure for his critique of Israel's policy of "opacity," or total secrecy about its bomb.[5] What strikes me about this, and other accounts of the 1969 US policy shift, is that, however interesting they are, these accounts are focused mainly on the Israeli side of the interaction. From my own brief look at the documents, there is rather more to the story of interest from the US point of view.

Let me sketch some points that strike me about: (1) the Kissinger-directed White House policy analyses and recommendations; (2) Nixon's own handling of the Israeli nuclear issue; and, (3) the current weight of Nixon's promises to Meir, including any promise to shield Israel from the NPT.

Nixon Submits NPT For Approval

It was President Nixon, by the way, who ratified US membership in the NPT after President Lyndon Johnson had negotiated it and signed it. Nixon had no particular attachment to the Treaty—it does not even rate a mention in his memoirs—and neither did Kissinger.6 Still, Nixon submitted the NPT to the Senate soon after he entered office, and received its approval in March 1969. Apparently Nixon was persuaded the United States did not thereby give up any freedom of action. In any case, he had no intention of pressing other countries to adhere to it.[7]

However little Nixon thought of the NPT, other senior officials did take it seriously, and the ratified Treaty formed part of the backdrop to dealing with Israel's rapidly evolving nuclear weapons project. Since Israel was not one of the NPT-authorized five nuclear powers, the confrontation with Israel was to be the first test of the universality of the new Treaty.

Decision on Phantom II Aircraft Left from the Johnson Administration

The immediate nuclear-related Israeli question Kissinger had to address actually had to do with conventional arms—whether to permit delivery of 50 F-4 Phantom aircraft that Israel had bought in the last days of the Johnson administration. The F-4 was the top fighter-bomber in the world, and the Israelis wanted it badly. The outgoing administration had written into the F-4 contract the possibility of cancellation if it appeared Israel was getting nuclear weapons.

The Defense and State Departments had wanted, as a condition of the F-4 sale, an explicit Israeli pledge not to build nuclear weapons.[8] Israel offered instead its standard declaration that it would "not be the first country to introduce nuclear weapons into the Middle East."[9] The US interpretation of this was that not "to introduce" nuclear weapons meant not to obtain them. But Rabin would not agree, nor would he provide an alternative definition. When Defense Assistant Secretary Paul Warnke, who was handling the plane sale, asked, "What do you mean by 'introduce'?" Rabin responded with, "What do you mean by 'nuclear weapon'?"[10] The discussion went round and round until finally Rabin allowed—and this stuck as the Israeli interpretation—that an unadvertised and untested nuclear device would not be a nuclear weapon. This made explicit that Israel's declaration did not exclude physical possession of nuclear weapons.

Warnke would not yield on the F-4 sale, so Rabin found ways to get around the Defense Department.[11] Seventy senators signed a letter to the President supporting the sale. Arthur Goldberg and others spoke directly to President Johnson, who then ordered the Defense Department to approve the F-4 sale without conditions.[12] Despite this order, Defense Secretary Clark Clifford permitted Warnke to say in his approval letter to Rabin that the United States retained the option to withhold delivery if Israel was not complying with its pledge not to introduce nuclear weapons—as the United States understood it.[13] Since the planes were not yet built, the final decision on their delivery was left to the incoming Nixon administration.

Kissinger Launches Policy Review on Israeli Nuclear Weapons

To make the new administration's decision more difficult, intelligence indicated the Israeli nuclear weapons project was advancing rapidly, and possibly had already succeeded in producing bombs. (US experts had been visiting Dimona more or less annually since the early 1960s, supposedly to ensure the work there stayed "peaceful," but the Israelis had easily hoodwinked them.)[14] Israel was also producing Jericho missiles, which because of their low accuracy could only have been intended for carrying nuclear warheads. Additionally, as Kissinger later informed the President, there was "circumstantial evidence that some fissionable material available for Israel's weapons development was illegally obtained from the United States by about 1965."[15]

It was against this background that Kissinger ran a White House study (NSSM 40) in mid-1969 on responding to Israeli nuclear weapons. The principal participants were the Departments of State and Defense, the Joint Chiefs of Staff, and the Central Intelligence Agency (CIA). They all agreed that Israeli acquisition of nuclear weapons raised the prospect of a more dangerous Middle East and undermined efforts to control proliferation worldwide. They also agreed that a major US effort to stop the Israelis was justified. But they did not agree on what that meant.

In truth, it was too late to stop the manufacture of Israel's first bombs. Any possibility of keeping Israel from going any further depended entirely on the United States—on which Israel depended for advanced weapons—making this a firm condition of the weapons supply. But as the Johnson administration history showed, this condition would not be easy to make stick in the US domestic political environment.

The Defense Department and the Joint Chiefs, as they did under the previous administration, advocated withholding delivery of the F-4 Phantom jets to gain an Israeli commitment not to build nuclear weapons or nuclear missiles, or at least not to deploy them. The State Department, on the other hand, wanted to avoid a confrontation with Israel, in part to preserve political capital for Arab-Israeli peace negotiations. It advocated keeping weapon sales and nuclear issues on separate tracks, and proposed a series of well-meaning but ineffectual steps to deal with the nuclear issue.[16] The State Department rationalized that there was still time for negotiations over the issue, that the Israelis had still not completed nuclear weapons, and that, in fact, they really only wanted a nuclear option and might stop on their own. If the Israelis did not stop, the State Department advised, we should at least "make a record for ourselves" of having tried to stop them.

In the hope of facilitating Israeli adherence to the NPT, the State Department offered the view that reasonable interpretation of the NPT's Article III would draw the difference between maintaining and exercising the option to manufacture nuclear explosives. In other words, State was saying that so long as a country had not taken the last step in nuclear weapon manufacture, it could be judged to be in conformance with the Treaty.

In his recommendation to the President on possible Israeli adherence to the NPT, Kissinger went even further in watering down the meaning of the Treaty. He wrote:

> The entire group agreed that, at a minimum, we want Israel to sign the NPT. This is not because signing will make any difference in Israel's actual nuclear program because Israel could produce warheads clandestinely. Israel's signature would, however, give us . . . a way of opening the discussion. It would also publicly commit Israel not to acquire nuclear weapons.

Kissinger apparently believed that the Israelis might actually sign the NPT—a course they pretended to be evaluating—with the thought of still keeping clandestine bombs. And he was willing to go along with that arrangement.

In the end, the touchstone of US seriousness about stopping Israel's nuclear weapons program was still a willingness to tie delivery of the F-4 Phantoms to the nuclear issue. This Kissinger did not propose to do—it seems, on the basis of Nixon's guidance—although he kept the door open to doing so at a later stage. He concluded that holding the planes back would unleash a fierce political response against the administration from Israel's domestic supporters, and that this was too high a price for the administration to pay to uphold the principle of nonproliferation.[17] Without the leverage of the fighter aircraft deal, however, there was no chance of gaining Israeli agreement on the nuclear issue. The only option left was to see what could be salvaged in terms of appearances.

In writing to the President about what the United States really wanted, Kissinger subtly shifted the ground away from trying to stop the Israelis from accepting their nuclear weapons but trying to: (1) avoid the appearance of US complicity in Israel becoming a nuclear power; and, (2) keep Israel's bomb from leading to Arab pressure on the Soviets to match it.[18] "While we might ideally like to halt Israeli possession," Kissinger wrote, "what we really want at a minimum may be just to keep Israeli possession from becoming an established international fact." In other words, if no one knew that Israel had bombs, that was almost as good as if they didn't exist—and it was a lot cheaper in political capital.

To make this work, both the United States and the Soviet Union had to pretend total ignorance. In the case of the US Government, with its difficulty in keeping secrets, it would be best if the government really was ignorant of the truth and so should stop asking questions. The Israelis had to go along with this by keeping their bomb under wraps, but of course, they were going to do so anyway. In short, after all the high-level White House analyses of what to do about Israeli nuclear weapons, the recommended option was for the US Government to stick its head in the sand.

Kissinger and the top US diplomats still pursued Israeli adherence to the NPT, just as had their predecessors in the Johnson administration, and continued fencing with Rabin over the meaning of "introduce" in the Israeli nuclear mantra—again, without result. The fact was that by August, the first of the F-4s were already getting delivered to the Israelis. They didn't have to give in on anything.

Nixon Decides

Since we have Kissinger's memoranda and his formal recommendations, it is tempting to see in them the intellectual lineage of the President's decision. There is, however, a tendency to exaggerate the importance of the written bureaucratic record—and the work of advisors altogether. High-level decisions often move on other tracks. In the end, it appears that Nixon did in his private meeting with Mrs. Meir on the nuclear issue—the meeting on that day covered other important topics—what he would have done anyway, quite apart from any advice he got. He gave the Israelis a pass on their nuclear weapons program primarily because he wanted them on his side in what he saw as his worldwide struggle with the Soviets. He did not care about the NPT and ignored Kissinger's (seemingly genuine) recommendation to pursue an Israeli signature.[19] Nixon seems to have decided the United States would not pursue the question of Israeli nuclear weapons, would not press Israel to join the NPT, and would end the by-then farcical US "visits" to Dimona.[20]

It would also have been natural for Nixon to want to keep the entire arrangement secret, for one thing, to avoid charges of complicity in Israel's nuclear program. Similarly, Meir agreed to keep, or acquiesced in keeping, the existence of her weapons secret, which she had every incentive to do, anyhow.[21]

Nixon had already set his course in favor of providing Israel with advanced weapons during the 1968 presidential campaign. He said:

> The United States has a firm and unwavering commitment to the national existence of Israel . . . as long as the threat of Arab attack remains direct and imminent . . . the balance must be tipped in Israel's favor.[22]

In speaking to a Jewish group, Nixon explicitly promised that, if elected, he would send the 50 Phantoms, and he told Rabin the same in a private meeting.[23]

A March 1970 memorandum written by the President to Kissinger provides further insight into Nixon's thinking underlying the 1969 Nixon-Meir deal.[24] Nixon wrote the memorandum after his decision in early March 1970 to delay delivery of a later batch of F-4 Phantoms provoked a storm of protest from Israel's US supporters.[25] He had held up the planes because, with an eye on possible Soviet reaction, he did not want to tip the military balance in the Middle East too far in favor of Israel. His willingness to hold up delivery of the F-4s is interesting in itself. This is the same act that Kissinger earlier judged as too risky politically for reasons related to nuclear proliferation or the NPT. But Nixon was prepared to make it for reasons he thought important enough.[26]

In the March 1970 memorandum, Nixon told Kissinger that, in further talks with Meir and Rabin, Kissinger needed to "lay it on the line." Nixon said the key to his own pro-Israel stance was opposition to Soviet expansion. He was counting on Israel to stand with the United States. The Israelis had to understand that their "only reliable friends are the hawks in this country," not the liberals. RN (as Nixon referred to himself) "does not want to see Israel go down the drain and makes an absolute commitment that he will see to it that Israel always has 'an edge'." Nixon pointed out that he did not get many Jewish votes in New York, Pennsylvania, California, or Illinois—the implication of which was pretty clear.[27] At the same time, he said, his "silent majority" voters would expect Israel to oppose Soviet expansion everywhere. He also stated:

> will not stand for a double standard . . . it is a question of all or none. This is cold turkey and it is time that our friends in Israel understood this. . . . Unless they understand it and act as if they understood it beginning now they are down the tubes.

Nixon was irked that US Jews were hawks when it came to Israel but doves on Vietnam, and he obviously wanted the Israelis to help straighten out his domestic political opponents. But what mattered to Nixon most was that Israel stand fast with him against Soviet expansion. That is what the 1969 Nixon-Meir deal was mainly about.

What US Obligations Remain from the Deal?

That 1969 deal still casts a shadow over US-Israeli relations. There are reports that in 2009, President Obama provided Prime Minister Netanyahu with a letter that was said to "reaffirm" the 1969 agreement in writing.[28] In light of this, it is worthwhile to reconsider the assumptions of the original 1969 deal and to ask to what extent they are still valid today.[29]

In their dealings with both the Johnson and Nixon administrations, the Israelis accepted that not being "the first to introduce nuclear weapons into the Middle East" meant keeping their weapon's existence secret and not performing nuclear tests. By Kissinger's account, Nixon emphasized these conditions to Meir as the "primary concern."[30] Despite this, the Israelis conducted a nuclear test in 1979 in the oceans below South Africa.[31] More importantly, everyone now knows about the existence of Israel's nuclear weapons. There is no longer even any ambiguity.

There were a number of reasons the United States worried in the past about public knowledge of Israel's nuclear weapons: One was that the Soviets might then have had to help the Arab countries in some way that increased the risk of a US confrontation with the Soviets. But now the Soviets are gone. Another reason was the fear that public knowledge of the Israeli nuclear weapons program would undermine the NPT, especially in the Middle East, by forcing Arab governments to respond with nuclear programs of their own. Well, now everyone outside Israel already knows and talks freely about Israeli nuclear weapons. Still another reason was the concern that knowledge about the Israeli weapons might expose the United States to charges of complicity in the Israeli nuclear program. But it is precisely the current policy of pretended ignorance about Israel's weapons that makes the United States look foolish, hypocritical, and complicit to boot.

In the end, it is up to the Israelis to decide how they want to deal with their half of the 1969 deal—whether to stick with "opacity." But it is up to the United States to decide how to deal with our half—whether to continue the US Government's taboo on discussing Israel's nuclear weapons. Whatever reasons there may be to continue to do so, they do not include obligations flowing from the 1969 Nixon-Meir deal.

Endnotes

1. As early as 1960, President Dwight Eisenhower met with his top Cabinet officials and military leaders to discuss the problems raised by information that the Israelis, in Secretary of State Christian Herter's words, were "operating a plutonium production plant." Defense Secretary Thomas Gates said, "Our information is that the plant is not for peaceful uses." The President made clear that the issue went beyond the Middle East. He said, "We are now faced with the question of what to do as further countries become atomic producers." He told the group the United States needed to tell the Israelis that we wanted the International Atomic Energy Agency (IAEA) to inspect the plant "as a matter of course." See General A. J. Goodpastor's January 12, 1961, Memorandum regarding a December 9, 1960, conference with the President.

2. Consider, for example, the Obama administration's hostile reaction to the proposal, coming out of the 2010 NPT Review Conference, for a 2012 meeting to discuss a nuclear-free Middle East, a goal the United States claims to support. Although the US delegation had voted for the entire document—presumably to avoid an embarrassing conference failure—the Obama White House immediately thereafter attacked the language of the meeting proposal.
3. Helen Thomas, at the President's first televised news conference, February 9, 2009.
4. Israel was not the only country whose nuclear weapons program was eased by *ad hoc* considerations that overwhelmed US support for the Nonproliferation Treaty (NPT). This also happened in US interactions with India and Pakistan over their nuclear programs, and, at one point, even with North Korea. In fact, US policy toward India's nuclear program is surely a close second to that toward Israel's nuclear program in its glaring inconsistencies with stated nonproliferation policy. Israel was, however, the first country to face down US nonproliferation policy—immediately after the signing of the Treaty—which created a precedent for US acquiescence in NPT holdouts that was later exploited by other countries.
5. Avner Cohen, *The Worst Kept Secret: Israel's Bargain with the Bomb*, New York: Columbia University Press, 2010. See also the article by William Burr and Avner Cohen in the May 2006 issue of *Bulletin of the Atomic Scientists*: "As long as Israel kept the bomb in the basement—which meant keeping the program under full secrecy, making no test, declaration, or any other visible act of displaying capability or otherwise transforming its status—the United States could live with Israel's 'non-introduction' pledge. . . ."
6. Nixon's memoirs contain no index entry for the NPT and apparently no reference to the Treaty in the book. See Richard Nixon, *RN: The Memoirs of Richard Nixon*, New York, Grosset & Dunlop, 1978. Kissinger's memoirs make two glancing references, one to the 1968 signing by Johnson, and the second to German concerns about discriminatory treatment under the Treaty. See Henry Kissinger, *White House Years*, Boston, MA: Little, Brown and Co., 1979.
7. After deciding to back the Treaty, Nixon instructed US diplomats not to push it too hard, and especially not to lean on the Germans. See also Robert Dallek, *Nixon and Kissinger: Partners in Power*, New York: HarperCollins 2007, p. 136: "In [early] 1969, Nixon . . . urged the Senate to approve a nuclear nonproliferation treaty (NPT) signed by Johnson. Nixon's commitment to an NPT carried no political or economic costs. His internal directive supporting ratification emphasized that adherence

to the treaty neither created new commitments abroad nor broadened existing ones. Nor would the treaty cause any international difficulties for the United States, since Nixon had no intention to pressure other countries to follow America's lead."

8. An indication of this comes through in a 1966 cable from Secretary of State Dean Rusk to the US Ambassador in Israel. Rusk described his conversation with the Israeli Ambassador, who repeated what was by then the formulaic "[Israel] would not be first to introduce nuclear weapons in the Near East." Rusk told him, "Nothing would be more disastrous" for Israel than to get nuclear weapons, and he urged the Israelis to accept international inspection. Rusk noted, "If Israel is holding open the nuclear option, it should forget US support. We would not be with you. . . ." Telegram from the Department of State to the Embassy in Israel, Washington, DC, July 28, 1966.
9. A formulation usually attributed to Shimon Peres, who improvised it in response to an unexpected question from President John Kennedy.
10. Memorandum of conversation, "Negotiations with Israel—F-4 and Advanced Weapons, November 12, 1968," approved by Paul Warnke.
11. In his memoirs, Rabin comments on getting involved in US campaign politics:

    Sensitive souls may find the notion of setting a Democratic president against his Republican successor distasteful. If so, they will only be demonstrating their ignorance of the ways and means of American politics. It is not enough to say that in pursuing his country's welfare an ambassador to Washington is entitled to take advantage of the ongoing rivalry between the two parties. The fact is that for his efforts to bear fruit, he is obliged to do so; and any ambassador who is either unwilling or unable to maneuver through America's political landscape to advance his country's interests would do well to return home.

    Yitzhak Rabin, The Rabin Memoirs, Berkeley: University of California Press, 1979, p. 142.

12. It is hard to know what Johnson really thought about Israel getting the Bomb. He seemed to genuinely care about the NPT and getting Israel to sign it. But there seems to have been another side, too, as indicated by a story Arnold Kramish told. In 1967, Kramish had somehow gotten an invitation to visit Dimona. Before leaving, he called US Ambassador Walworth Barbour in Tel-Aviv. "Oh, no," Barbour shouted. "If you learn anything about Dimona, I'd have to tell the President, and then he would have to do something, and he doesn't want to." T. C. Reed and Danny Stillman, The Nuclear Express: a Political Examination of the Bomb and its Proliferation, Minneapolis, MN: Zenith Press, 2009, p. 119.

13. Letter, Paul Warnke to Yitzhak Rabin, November 27, 1968. This arguably still conformed to Johnson's instructions, in the sense that the Israelis were not asked to agree beforehand with the US interpretation.

14. The arrangement was first worked out during the Kennedy administration, but it soon deteriorated. Here is an account provided by former Ambassador Barbour:

    . . . We had considerable difficulty making arrangements for periodic visits which was a window-dressing exercise. The Israelis tried to be as forthcoming, or to appear as forthcoming as possible, at the same time without revealing anything to us. This wining them and dining them and taking them down there with, under great secrecy, sometimes even meeting them at the airport when they arrived, and taking them off the plane, and over around the back, and then clearing them through customs with Russian names and so forth [Laughs], it was all a very unrealistic exercise which went on for many, many years and then finally just petered out when even the United States realized it wasn't getting anywhere. And it became ridiculous.

    See May 22, 1981, interview, Kennedy Library Oral History Project. One is left with the impression that the State Department, which coordinated the "visits" (specifically, not inspections), was not especially keen on having the experts learn anything. They apparently did not receive intelligence briefings.

15. This refers to the suspicion that Israel stole highly enriched uranium from the Nuclear Materials and Equipment Corporation (NUMEC) fuel plant in Apollo, PA, whose owners had close Israeli ties. A 1965 inventory found that a loss of about 100 kilograms (kg) could not be explained after accounting for all possible industrial loss pathways. By the time of Kissinger's memorandum, a further loss of 150 kg remained unaccounted for. The CIA had by then concluded that the material ended up in Israel's bomb program. In the early part of the Nixon administration, all the top national security officials, including Kissinger and the President himself, were involved in one way or another in the NUMEC case. See: Victor Gilinsky and Roger Mattson, "Revisiting the NUMEC Affair," *Bulletin of the Atomic Scientists*, March-April 2010, p. 61.

16. National Security Study Memorandum No. 40, "Israeli Nuclear Weapons Program—Issues and Courses of Action," Rodger P. Davies State/NEA to Dr. Kissinger, undated but evidently mid-1969, formerly Top Secret ("sanitized").

17. Dallek, *Nixon and Kissinger*, p. 176: "The White House considered tying arms shipments to Israeli promises not to go nuclear, but concerns about domestic political opposition deterred it from making the connection."

Kissinger barely mentioned the concern about opposition from domestic Jewish groups, even though that was obviously a major factor. This omission is not surprising, since Nixon had earlier instructed his national security staff not to mention domestic political considerations, so as to maintain an illusory separation. See Richard Reeves, *President Nixon Alone in the White House*, New York: Simon & Shuster, 2001, p. 42, describes a February 22, 1969, Nixon memo to Rogers and Kissinger regarding Middle East papers from State and the National Security Council (NSC): "In the future, I want no references to domestic political considerations to be included in any papers. . . ." It is a reminder to be cautious in relying on the written record. One is dealing with people who operate on several levels, and who use their writings for multiple purposes.

18. "(1) Israel's secret possession of nuclear weapons would increase the potential danger in the Middle East, and *we do not desire complicity* in it. (2) In this case, *public knowledge is almost as dangerous as possession itself.* This is what might spark a Soviet nuclear guarantee for the Arabs, tighten the Soviet hold on the Arabs, and increase the danger of our involvement. *Indeed, the Soviets might have an incentive not to know*." Henry Kissinger, Memorandum for the President, "Israeli Nuclear Program." The copy in the Nixon Library is undated, but it refers to a Tab A dated July 19, 1969. Emphasis added.

19. Kissinger did not attend Nixon's private meeting with Meir and, hard as it is to believe, he seems not to have immediately taken in the change in policy. In an October 8, 1969, memorandum to the President, he reports on, among other things, Rabin's answer regarding the prospects for Israeli NPT adherence, that the next Israeli government will decide after the upcoming elections. Kissinger commented: "This formulation strikes me as unacceptably weak. It seems to me that signature of the NPT with its loopholes and escape clause would not jeopardize Israel's potential nuclear capability or diminish Arab recognition of its conventional military superiority." He recommended that Nixon press Meir to make a "vigorous personal effort" to gain Cabinet support for an Israeli signature and ratification. This was 2 weeks after the Nixon-Meir private meeting. Perhaps the meeting left the NPT issue up in the air, with Nixon leaving it to Meir to decide.

20. The last "visit" took place in July 1969. The Israelis rushed the US team, as usual. Meir refused a later US request from US Ambassador Barbour for an extra daylong visit. As much as the Israelis controlled the visits, they involved a lot of preparation, and there was always the chance of a slipup that revealed too much. In reality, the Israelis did not have much to worry about—the Americans apparently never sent anyone who knew Hebrew, and were used to getting the runaround.

21. Kissinger seems to allude to this in his memoirs: "It would be too much to claim that Mrs. Meir agreed; more accurate to say she acquiesced in a formulation whose meaning *only the future would reveal.*" Kissinger, *White House Years*, p. 371, emphasis added. Nixon does not mention the September 1969 meeting in his memoirs. Meir was obviously the cleverest of the lot. Of course, it is possible that she may have been reluctant to agree not to test warheads.

22. Statement by Richard Nixon, *The New York Times*, September 9, 1968.

23. Rabin, *The Rabin Memoirs*, pp. 131, 133.

24. Memorandum for Henry Kissinger from the President, March 17, 1970. In his memoirs, Nixon quotes at length from this memorandum, so it seems to reflect his considered views.

25. Nixon quotes at length from it in his memoirs and describes the background as follows:

    At the beginning of March I decided to postpone our delivery of Phantom jets to Israel. I had heard that the Soviets had come under renewed pressures from their Arab clients to surpass the new American deliveries to Israel, and I hoped that since Israel was already in a strong military position, I could slow down the arms race without tipping the fragile military balance in the region. I also believed that American influence in the Middle East increasingly depended on our renewing diplomatic relationships with Egypt and Syria, and this decision would help promote that goal. . . . One of the main problems I faced in this regard was the unyielding and shortsighted pro-Israeli attitude in large and influential segments of the American Jewish community, Congress, the media, and in intellectual and cultural circles. . . . There was a wave of criticism in the media and in Congress when my decision to postpone the Phantom deliveries was announced...I was annoyed that a number of the senators who were urging that we send more military aid to save Israel were opposing our efforts to save South Vietnam from Communist domination. I dictated a memorandum to Kissinger describing my feelings. . . .

26. Ultimately, of course, the Israelis got the planes. Another angle on the plane delivery decision is presented in a recent biography of John Mitchell, Nixon's Attorney General:

    Max Fisher, the late Jewish industrialist, philanthropist, and pro-Israel lobbyist, remembered pleading with Kissinger in 1970 to speed up American delivery of a few dozen *Phantom* fighter jets for which Israel had paid, but, owing to pressure from Arab states, never received.

    Completion of the deal would mark a decisive shift in American policy towards Israel: from neutrality to the guarantee of military supremacy Nixon had advocated as a candidate. . . . Who could convince the President? 'Go see John Mitchell,' Kissinger said . . . Fisher did as he was told—and got what he wanted.

See James Rosen, *The Strong Man: John Mitchell and the Secrets of Watergate*, New York: Doubleday, 2008, p. 127.

27. Although earlier in the memorandum, he says he is not motivated by the "Jewish vote."

28. See Eli Lake: "Exclusive: Obama Agrees to Keep Israel's Nukes Secret," *The Washington Times,* October 2, 2009: "President Obama has reaffirmed a 4-decade-old secret understanding that has allowed Israel to keep a nuclear arsenal without opening it to international inspections. . . ."

29. In any case, the United States is not obligated to observe an informal private agreement of which there is no written record.

30. Kissinger wrote to Nixon in an October 7, 1969, memorandum: "During your private conversation with Golda Meir, you emphasized that our primary concern was that the Israelis make no visible introduction of nuclear weapons or undertake a nuclear test program."

31. President Carter's Science Advisor Frank Press commissioned a panel of academic scientists who devised an ingenious alternative scientific explanation about how the satellite might have been fooled. But every expert intelligence body in the government regarded the satellite signal as a valid indication of a test. Incidentally, such a test was also a violation of the Limited Test Ban Treaty, to which Israel is a party. Reed and Stillman, *The Nuclear Express*, p. 180.

Part 3

South Asia

Chapter 9

Nuclear Weapons Stability or Anarchy in the 21st Century: China, India, and Pakistan

Thomas W Graham

Introduction

During the 20th century, the dominant nuclear weapons competition was between the Soviet Union and the United States. The United Kingdom (UK), France, and Israel were loosely allied with the United States, and China was allied with Russia until the Sino-Soviet split. However, the UK, France, China, and Israel played a relatively minor role in the 20th-century nuclear competition and in the development of global nuclear strategy.[1] Terminology describing nation-state nuclear weapons status and the elaborate nuclear doctrines built by the superpowers had a dominant bipolar perspective.[2] Both superpowers engaged in massive overkill, producing tens of thousands of nuclear weapons with yields from tons to megatons.[3] Both superpowers designed, built, deployed, and exercised nuclear forces to conduct a first strike. However, they described their nuclear doctrines in terms of second strikes planned to be launched only after they were attacked out of the blue by their mortal Cold War enemy.[4] Both superpowers spent trillions of dollars on their nuclear infrastructure, weapons, and delivery systems.[5] The Soviet Union was driven to ruin by its inability to keep up with US high-technology precision strike capabilities and massive over-investment in nuclear weapons. Such expenditures provided relatively few positive economic or technical spin-offs. This 20th-century nuclear narrative is not likely to be repeated in the 21st century. However, these important lessons are not being learned by an increasing number of 21st-century nuclear actors.

Only at the end of the Cold War did one American President mention the impossibility of achieving a military victory in fighting a nuclear war.[6] Memoirs or editorials written by American atomic scientists or former US decisionmakers that attempt to put the actual utility of nuclear weapons into context have been largely ignored.[7] Dramatic reductions in US and Russian nuclear forces took place only after the end of the Cold War, the dissolution of the Union of Soviet Socialist Republics (USSR), and the relegation of Russia to second- or third-power status.

Partisan and bureaucratic politics in the United States and Russia are driven by 21st-century nuclear postures, North Atlantic Treaty Organization (NATO) Alliance relations, and Russia's fear that it cannot defend itself without the threat to use nuclear weapons early in a conflict.[8] However, what is missing is a realistic political rationale for the use of nuclear weapons to protect either country's vital national interests.[9]

Both the UK and France have reduced their nuclear forces to the point that the logical next step is to go to zero, a move inconceivable as long as their world status continues to be associated with 20th-century nuclear norms.[10] Most countries are content to ignore Israel's unsafeguarded nuclear program, whose original strategic rationale died with the end of the Cold War.[11] North Korea, an exceedingly poor but tough nation with a tiny nuclear force, appears on the surface to be immune from either pressure from or the promise of cooperation with the global community.[12]

If today's business-as-usual paradigm continues, the next 2 decades of the 21st century will look very different than the 20th century with respect to nuclear weapons. Current conventional wisdoms suggest change in nuclear status, and politics will be incremental. This may turn out to be tragically wrong if global nuclear dogma is influenced strongly by the unstable triangular nuclear weapons competition among China, India, and Pakistan.[13] Three indicators are worth watching to foreshadow whether the world will move toward nuclear stability or anarchy in South West Asia. First, will countries stabilize their operationally deployed nuclear forces at the approximate level of 150-200, 300-500 or larger? Second, will these three countries adopt compatible and increasingly stable nuclear postures, or will they continue to cling to three divergent nuclear postures? Third, will future military crises be resolved with or without use or threatened use of nuclear weapons? By and large, the United States, Russia, the UK, France, Israel, Iran, and the Democratic People's Republic of Korea (DPRK) will be bystanders in this Southwest

Asian nuclear drama. As a result, to help assess forthcoming global nuclear stability, it is imperative to take a fresh look at the dynamics that are driving contemporary nuclear force structures and modernization in Southwest Asia.

To describe more accurately 21st-century nuclear proliferation, this chapter introduces a 10-stage categorization of nuclear weapons status. This conceptual framework combines elements from both vertical and horizontal dimensions of nuclear proliferation popularized in the 1960s.

Subsequent sections of this chapter will describe the emergence of five incompatible nuclear dogmas that seem to be driving approximately 20 countries in the 21st century. This chapter then describes the evolution of nuclear doctrines in China, India, and Pakistan. The next section will assess heuristic drivers of Chinese, Indian, and Pakistani nuclear proliferation and force modernization. These factors will influence whether these Southwest Asian countries move toward excessive expansion of their nuclear forces or the politically risky path toward greater stability in both numbers and doctrine. The final analytical section will discuss the quantitative growth potential of nuclear forces in Southwest Asia over the next 2 decades. This chapter ends with a challenge to current conventional wisdoms with respect to Southwest Asia's role to foster or undermine global nuclear stability.

Vocabulary for 21st Century Nuclear Proliferation

In this century, old vocabulary used to categorize nuclear weapons status is inadequate to describe the evolution and complexity of the nuclear environment. The old terms were relevant for the 20th century. The terms "Nuclear Weapons States (NWS), de facto nuclear weapons states, threshold nuclear weapons states, and Non-Nuclear Weapons States (NNWS)" are not adequate to describe meaningful differences in the nuclear status of countries today. To solve this problem, a 10-stage categorization of nuclear weapons status has been developed. It draws on 70 years of nuclear history (see Appendix 9-1). Stage 1 (Watch List Nations) and Stage 2 (Threshold Nations) describe nation-states that are beginning to walk down a path that could lead to three different end points: nuclear weapons, latent nuclear weapons capability, or robust use of nuclear power. Many states in these first two categories may be hedging against growing nuclear infrastructure being developed by their neighbors.[14]

Crossing the nuclear weapons threshold occurs between Stage 2 and Stage 3 (Tiny Nuclear Forces). At the other end of this categorization,

Stage 10 (Superpower Nuclear Forces) describes the United States and the USSR, who had tens of thousands of nuclear weapons and sophisticated associated capabilities. These two countries largely defined the vocabulary of nuclear weapons status. No country in the 21st century is likely to repeat the process that led to the creation of similar gargantuan nuclear forces. Over the next 2 decades, it is conceivable both the United States and Russia will reduce their nuclear forces to the level of approximately 1,000 operationally deployed nuclear weapons.[15] If they do so, this would move them down to Stage 9 (Massive Nuclear Forces).

During the Cold War, British, French, and Chinese nuclear forces had characteristics associated with Stage 8 (Mature Nuclear Forces). Over the last decade, British nuclear forces have dropped to Stage 7 (Large Nuclear Forces).

Nations that have developed first-generation nuclear weapons vary from Stage 3 (Tiny Nuclear Forces) to Stage 6 (Medium Nuclear Forces). Virtually all open source or academic literature on nuclear proliferation puts countries that have passed the nuclear weapons threshold into one category, de facto nuclear weapons states. This chapter argues the degree of nuclear weapons production, development, and deployment of delivery systems, and the creation of nuclear doctrine and postures cannot be described in a single category. This 10-stage categorization is capable of being used to describe more precisely where countries stand and how each might change in the future.

For the countries in Southwest Asia—China, India, and Pakistan—the key question is whether each country decides its end point to be nuclear forces and postures associated with Large, Mature, or Massive Nuclear Forces. It is the thesis of this chapter that all three stages are credible under realistic assumptions for China, India, and Pakistan. The implications for the world will be profound, depending on which end point each country chooses or is forced to choose.

As countries in the Middle East develop nuclear research and development programs as a hedge against Iran's move toward nuclear weapons, characterizing their nuclear activities will place them into either Stage 1 or Stage 2. If history is any guide, by the time a country crosses from Stage 2A to Stage 2B, it becomes virtually impossible for external powers to turn it around (see Appendix 9-2). If a nuclear proliferation cascade takes place in the Middle East or East Asia, it will reinforce, not create, more pressing negative trends that are already evident in Southwest Asia.[16] If hedging in the Middle East and East Asia and modernization in Southwest Asia take place, the prediction that 20 states will obtain or maintain nuclear weapons, which President John Kennedy feared in 1960, may become true in the 21st century.[17] If this occurs, it will be a truly historic and bipartisan accomplishment over the next two decades.[18]

Nuclear Doctrines and Functions of Nuclear Weapons in the 20th Century

During the Cold War, nuclear dogma of the five declared nuclear weapons states can be placed along a continuum (see Figure 9-1). Countries on the right, such as the USSR/Russia and the United States, built excessive nuclear forces for nuclear warfighting. China, the country on the extreme left, built a small number of relatively crude operationally deployed nuclear weapons devoted to deterring an attack on their country.[19] Countries in the middle had capabilities associated with both nuclear warfighting and deterrence, but their modest nuclear forces played a marginal role in the 20th-century nuclear balance of power.

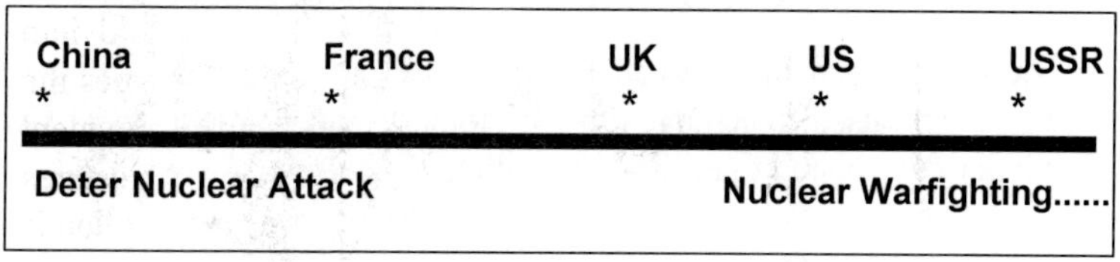

Figure 9-1. Nuclear Dogma for the 20th Century

In retrospect, Cold War history demonstrated that nuclear weapons served many different functions in addition to deterring the use of nuclear weapons (see Figure 9-2). During the Cold War, nuclear weapons were utilized not only to deter the use of nuclear weapons, but for several other purposes as well. In terms of military policy, they were used to deter the use of other weapons of mass destruction (WMD) and to deter an opponent with superior conventional forces. The classic NATO-Warsaw Pact standoff was characterized by the United States and NATO attempting to deter perceived overwhelming conventional forces from the USSR and Warsaw Pact with nuclear weapons. This was called "extended deterrence." No such Soviet attack on Western Europe took place, so advocates of nuclear weapons argue nuclear deterrence worked. However, despite massive spending, force preparations, exercises, and war gaming, it is not clear from the historical record whether these specific NATO nuclear forces deterred a Soviet attack or whether Soviet decisionmakers never anticipated authorizing a first strike despite their considerable preparations to do so.

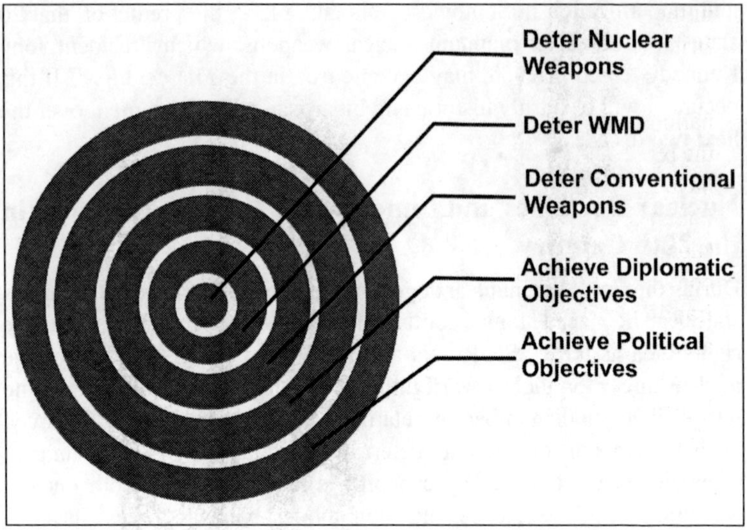

Figure 9-2. Functions of Nuclear Weapons in the 20th Century.

Less described in the academic literature is the fact that nuclear weapons were used to achieve other diplomatic and political objectives only indirectly related to military operations.[20]

Emerging 21st Century Nuclear Dogma

During our contemporary era, approximately 20 countries have had nuclear programs that can be described as Stage 1 to Stage 10.[21] They seem to fall into five not mutually exclusive groups. The first group consists of the "declining nuclear powers." The United States, UK, and France are reducing their nuclear forces and are de-emphasizing their role in military strategy. However, even in these declining nuclear countries, the function of nuclear weapons remains broad. Nuclear weapons continue to play an important role in domestic and bureaucratic politics. For example, the Obama administration's US Nuclear Posture Review saw a limited reduction in nuclear force size and a small narrowing of nuclear weapons use doctrine.[22] In the United States, even this incremental change triggered dramatic increases in spending on offensive nuclear weapons and infrastructure and intense partisan political struggle over ratification of nuclear arms control treaties.[23] Ironically, one distinguished participant in decades of nuclear politics, Brent Scowcroft, has argued the intense partisan politics associated with nuclear weapons are more extreme today than they were during the Cold War.[24] This suggests that in political terms, the movement toward zero nuclear weapons is dead in the United States. In the UK, controversy continues over the size of Britain's remaining sea-based leg of its nuclear force, the Trident.[25]

The second group consists of "maximalist" countries. Four such nations—Russia, Pakistan, the DPRK, and Iran—seem to be embracing the broadest possible function for nuclear weapons. At least two of them have adopted doctrines that emphasize nuclear warfighting. Russia and Pakistan are treating nuclear weapons as the single essential military capability that allows them to defend their territory against the superior conventional forces of NATO and India, respectively. The DPRK and Iran have incorporated nuclear weapons into the hypernationalism associated with the protection of their countries' national security and sovereignty. Both countries assume hostile neighbors and foreign powers intent on fomenting regime change.[26] Both countries paint a picture of being threatened by the United States in ways that seem laughable to anyone who is living in an increasingly divided, inward-looking, and budget-cutting-obsessed America of 2012.

Countries in the third group include China, Israel, and India. For different reasons, these three countries seem to be engaged in limited nuclear weapons modernization. They seem to be waiting to see which way the world nuclear order will move before deciding on the final end point for their nuclear forces and postures.

A fourth group consists of countries that seem to be using nuclear weapons to strengthen their legitimacy, resist internal reforms, and guarantee regime survival. If one looks at the countries associated with Stage 1, Stage 2, or Stage 3, more than a few appear to be thinking about nuclear weapons as the new "weapons of the weak."[27] Burma, Iran, North Korea, and Syria, to name a few, are fragile countries without much stake in the existing world order. These countries reject interaction with the rest of the world and perceive that nuclear weapons will allow their regimes to continue on their present course. These nations are placing a bet that nuclear weapons will provide them with total security, internal as well as external. Thus, they are under investing in other tools to maintain their sovereignty and secure their prosperity. If this model gains traction, one of the most important functions of nuclear weapons in the 21st century may become to secure regime survival among totalitarian governments (see Figure 9-3).

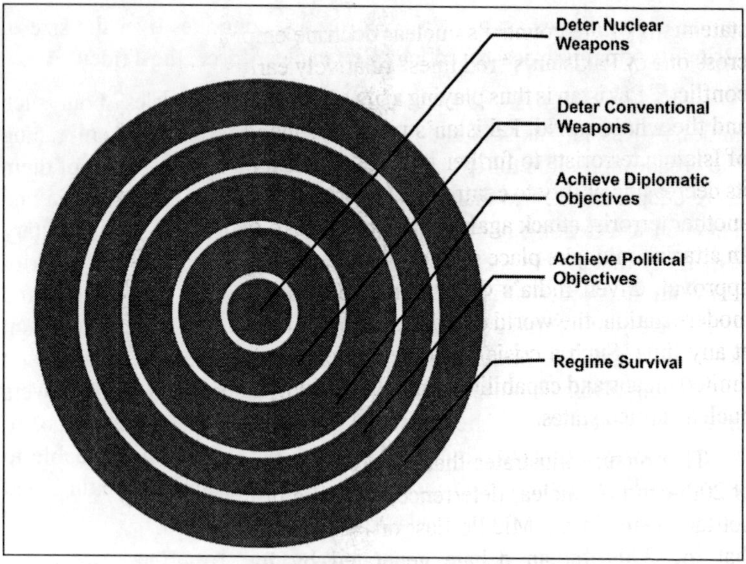

Figure 9-3. Functions of Nuclear Weapons in the 21st Century

Countries in a fifth category seem to be hedging against the prospect that Iran and North Korea's nuclear weapons program continues to gain strength and triggers a nuclear proliferation cascade, primarily in the Middle East and North East Asia.

Nuclear Dogma in Southern Asia

Equally important as the steady, quantitative grown of nuclear forces that has taken place in Southwest Asia is the existence of three mutually incompatible nuclear doctrines in the region.[28] For over 5 decades, China has maintained a nuclear posture that has been built around a relatively small, operationally deployed force and no first use. China deterred both the Soviet Union and the United States with medium-sized nuclear forces in the Cold War. During the 1970s through at least 2010, China has maintained a robust nuclear research, development, testing and evaluation (RDT&E) system, but it has deployed relatively few nuclear weapons.[29] While academic debates in China can be identified—advocating larger and more offensively oriented nuclear forces and doctrine—such debates seem to be theoretical at present.[30]

In contrast, Pakistan has an openly first-strike-oriented nuclear force. Its nuclear weapons must be dispersed very early during a military crisis with India.[31] It is during movement that Pakistan's nuclear weapons may be most vulnerable to theft from terrorists.[32] Authoritative Pakistani statements of the country's nuclear doctrine emphasize that India could cross one of Pakistan's "red lines" relatively early during a conventional conflict.[33] Pakistan is thus playing a big game of chicken with itself, India, and the whole world. Pakistan's refusal or inability to terminate its use of Islamic terrorists to further its goals in Kashmir and Afghanistan and its decreasing ability to control the terrorist groups it created suggest that another terrorist attack against India could take place at any time.[34] Such an attack could take place with or without explicit Pakistani government approval. Given India's Cold Start conventional military doctrine and modernization, the world could face another nuclear crisis in South Asia at any time. Such a crisis could be started by a terrorist group that has limited means and capabilities and no proclivity to foster stability among nuclear-armed states.

This picture illustrates that we are already very far from the logic of 20th-century nuclear deterrence, even if a proliferation cascade does not take place in the Middle East or East Asia. It is within this context that the 2009 Indian debate generated by former defense scientist Dr. K. Santhanam is fascinating.[35] During this debate, a vast amount of information about India's nuclear weapons program was presented to the Indian public. Many former heads of India's Department of Atomic Energy argued that India must resume nuclear weapons testing and both develop and deploy thermonuclear weapons. In this same time frame, India announced plans to develop the Agni 5 ballistic missile, reportedly designed to have the intercontinental range to hit all targets in China.[36] India is also engaged in research on ballistic missile defense, which is already being used by Pakistani strategists to justify production of more nuclear weapons. From this perspective, Indian nuclear and missile technical elites have set the stage for a nuclear arms race with both China and Pakistan that could last decades into the future.

On the other hand, some Indian strategists who often reflect thinking within South Block, such as the late K. Subrahmanyam and Dr. VS Arunachalam—who brought Santhanam into the nuclear weapons business and was his immediate superior—argue that India can use fission weapons and accurate delivery systems to achieve the same deterrent effect that thermonuclear weapons and inaccurate intercontinental ballistic missiles (ICBMs) achieved in the 20th century.[37] It is known that current Prime Minister Manmohan Singh is a relative dove toward both Pakistan and China. When he was Finance Minister, he was skeptical of the ability of the Department of Atomic Energy to achieve results.[38] The Prime Minister's entire career has been dedicated to giving India the opportunity to compete on the global stage in terms of economics and technology. Thus, a dramatic expansion of India's nuclear weapons force under his watch would conflict with his lifelong goal to make India a major world power by using its proven comparative advantages—such as its skilled manpower, the rule of law, a vibrant civil society, and a relatively productive interaction with the global community.

These two schools of thought have existed in India for many years. Today, India seems to be unsure where it is headed. Some in India advocate renewed nuclear testing and thermonuclear weapons on ICBMs to approach capabilities associated with China. Others argue that nuclear deterrence can be achieved at lower levels, in part because Chinese nuclear forces are relatively small.[39]

If one puts the evolution of nuclear doctrines in China, India, and Pakistan into a global context, the key driver is Pakistan. All unclassified indications suggest Pakistan is expanding its nuclear weapons program, with no end in sight.[40] Whether Pakistan is ahead of India or not in terms of nuclear weapons capabilities is a debatable point. However, if the high estimates of Pakistan's nuclear force and low estimates of Chinese nuclear force are compared, it is logical to conclude Pakistan may surpass China in quantitative terms over the next decade, if not before.

Pakistani writings emphasize the need for nuclear weapons to balance India's superior conventional forces. While this logic was compelling for the United States in the Cold War, it is a hollow concept in terms of justifying how many nuclear weapons Pakistan needs to build and deploy to deter only one country, India. Does Pakistan require 50, 100, 150, 200, 250, 300, 350, 400, or more nuclear weapons? If Pakistan feels it must target India's entire military, industrial, and research complex; hold India's major cities at risk; and be prepared to fight using nuclear weapons on the battlefield, it will require at least 300-500 nuclear weapons. This would require a huge expenditure of funds with even larger opportunity costs. If Pakistan follows this path, will it essentially give up maintaining a credible conventional military force and put all of its eggs into a nuclear basket? Will the drain on Pakistan's military to fight Islamic terrorists and make up for inadequate civilian government capacity make it depend even more on nuclear weapons? Will Pakistan continue its own Cold War ideology toward India?[41] Will Pakistani military decisionmaking continue to exhibit deeply flawed logic that led it to start and lose four conflicts with India?[42] If Pakistan follows this path, the lesson of the former Soviet Union should loom large. Who in Pakistan has the courage to raise these issues?

There is no debate that China is building up its conventional military capabilities across the board.[43] China is modernizing its nuclear force, but it is also retiring old nuclear delivery systems. Some descriptions of the growth in Chinese missile systems include medium-range systems that may be armed with both nuclear and conventional warheads.[44] Thus, it is not clear whether the net increase in Chinese operationally deployed nuclear weapons is significant in quantitative terms.[45] It is clear China is replacing vulnerable liquid-fueled systems with mobile and solid-fueled systems. This means China's nuclear force of the future will be more stable, not less. However, China's large (1,000-plus) ballistic missile and cruise missile force, armed with conventional weapons, gives it a massive breakout potential in terms of nuclear-capable delivery systems.[46] As a result, Chinese perceptions of the legitimate role for nuclear weapons and Chinese perceptions of how the United States targets China are extremely important. This, in turn, relates to the debate over the legitimate role for nuclear weapons in the 21st century. Will it be narrowed in the 21st century to the innermost circle shown in Figure 9-2, or will it be expanded to the outer-most circle in Figure 9-3?

Beginning in 1970, China has embarked on the largest expansion of nuclear power in the world.[47] In 2010, China has 13 operating nuclear power plants, 62 nuclear power plants under construction or firmly planned, and an additional 76 units proposed. It plans to have 80 Giga-watts electric (GWe) by 2020, 200 GWe by 2030, and 400 GWe by 2050. A close reading of construction schedules reveals that China is proceeding from first pouring concrete to hooking up a reactor to the grid in approximately 5 years. China has imported nuclear reactor technology and equipment from Canada (AECL), France (Framatome/ AREVA), the United States/Japan (Westinghouse/Toshiba), and Russia (Atomstroyexport). It is starting to manufacture major components of its nuclear power reactors. China also has ambitious plans for 18 high temperature gas-cooled reactors (HTGR) and breeder reactors. [48]

The magnitude of this expansion has several implications for nuclear proliferation on a global basis.

First, it may create financial pressure on the International Atomic Energy Agency (IAEA) if safeguards are going to be applied to all these nuclear power plants. Second, in terms of the world export market, once China firmly establishes which reactor will become its dominant third-Generation model and proves its indigenous construction capabilities, it will become a major potential exporter of nuclear power reactors. At that stage, China will have one simple sales pitch: We have built more modern nuclear reactors than any other country in the world over the last decade. Western companies that have sold China their nuclear power reactor technology may have sealed their own fate. Third, China has ambitious plans to utilize recycled reactor-grade plutonium (RGPu).[49] Associated reprocessing and fuel fabrication facilities will stress the state of the art for safeguarding bulk handling facilities. The combination of a large future stockpile of RGPu and significant error margins in outside knowledge of China's past production of weapons-grade plutonium (WGPu) and highly enriched uranium (HEU) suggests China may have a huge potent breakout capability of up to 800 nuclear weapons.[50] While this scenario is just a scenario, these theoretical projections indicate just how important China will be to the global nuclear balance of power in the 21st century.

For the present, the technical, management, capital, materials, and diplomatic requirements for this peaceful nuclear program and the lack of an acute national security threat suggest a major expansion in China's nuclear weapons force is not likely in the immediate future. China faced more acute nuclear threats during the Cold War and reacted by deploying a relatively small nuclear force. However, most unclassified publications continue to describe the growth in China's military and its lack of transparency. Most assessments assume China's nuclear force will be on the rise in a big way. The view that China may be a smaller nuclear threat than advertised is clearly a minority perspective in the US strategic community.

What Drives Chinese, Indian, And Pakistani Nuclear Force Development?

For purposes of this chapter, it is assumed China has 150 operationally deployed nuclear weapons plus or minus 50.[51] It is assumed that both India and Pakistan have approximately 80 nuclear weapons plus or minus 20.[52]

These numbers differ from conventional wisdom in several ways. First, China's operationally deployed nuclear forces may be significantly smaller than the oft-quoted number of 400 nuclear weapons.[53] Second, most assessments of the India-Pakistan nuclear balance have argued India has been ahead of Pakistan for several decades.[54] This may or may not be correct today. Based on the assumptions used in this chapter, three possibilities exist for the Indo-Pak nuclear balance. India and Pakistan may be approximately equal. India may be ahead by as much as 100 to 60. Alternatively, Pakistan may be ahead by as much as 100 to 60.

Two important conclusions can be drawn from this assessment. First, if India is ahead of Pakistan or Pakistan is ahead of India in quantitative terms, the differences are relatively small. They are insignificant in terms of military power or deterrence impact. Second, when viewed in terms of the history of nuclear weapons, China, India, and Pakistan all have relatively modest nuclear forces at present. However, this situation may not remain static for the future. China and India have significant breakout potential if they decide to use RGPu in their nuclear weapons. Pakistan has a huge appetite for nuclear weapons and has publicized no statements that provide any suggestion that an end point is yet in sight.[55]

A review of the history of Chinese, Indian, and Pakistani nuclear weapons programs reveals that each started with multiple drivers (see Appendix 9-3). These drivers have changed over time. Today, we find that the primary driver for China is a fear of a conventional or nuclear attack on its nuclear forces by the United States. For India, the primary pressure seems to be from its nuclear and defense scientists, who want to prove against most evidence to date that they are world class. For Pakistan, the primary driver appears to be a fear of India's superior conventional force. For each of these three countries, one could see a future with two dramatically different nuclear futures. One would feature a nuclear arms race that takes place for several decades, leading to several hundred nuclear weapons. The other would be relatively stable nuclear forces maintained close to current levels. The key will be elite decisionmakers within each country. If senior leaders want nuclear weapons to play a limited role in their national security to deter the use of nuclear weapons, then medium-sized and stable nuclear forces are compatible with their countries' national security interests and targeting requirements. On the other hand, if senior leaders believe their national survival rests on nuclear warfighting capabilities to deter superior conventional forces, then large nuclear forces and hair-trigger nuclear postures will be required. These key decisions will be made in Southwest Asia, not in the Middle East or Northeast Asia.

A close examination of the drivers of proliferation in each country suggests that Indian scientists have a major influence on government decisionmaking. Drawing on the excellent article in this volume by Mian and Ramana, Indian policymakers have always sought to maintain the capability to use the country's civilian nuclear power program for weapons purposes. Not only does India have an estimated 6.8 ton-stockpile of mostly unsafeguarded RGPu, but it has the potential to produce WGPu in its eight unsafeguarded power reactors and its breeder reactors. Figures calculated by Mian and Ramana suggest India could have an arsenal of over 850 nuclear weapons using these sources.

Quantitative Growth Potential for Nuclear Weapons in Southwest Asia

A review of Appendix 9-4 reveals that even a relatively small monthly production of nuclear materials used for weapons purposes could lead to potential growth of hundreds of nuclear weapons over a period of 2 decades. Unclassified assessments of China, India, and Pakistan show that each country has the technical infrastructure to produce unsafeguarded nuclear material at this level of magnitude.[56] On the high end of the scale, if China were to determine as a matter of urgent national priority it needed to approach quantitative parity with the United States and Russia, it could reach the level of approximately 1,000 nuclear weapons within 2 decades. This would probably require it to resume production of fissionable material for weapons purposes or use RGPu to produce nuclear weapons.[57]

The primary conclusion from this theoretical mathematical projection is to alert global decisionmakers that the range of future nuclear force sizes and postures in Southwest Asia is extremely broad. There are no technical or institutional controls capable of preventing China, India, and Pakistan from developing substantial nuclear forces over the next 2 decades. Thus, the primary driver will be the direction in which the world moves in terms of the perceived legitimate function of nuclear weapons. If the United States, China, and other major powers are able to convince the world that the sole legitimate function of nuclear weapons is to deter the use of nuclear weapons, then it is plausible nuclear forces in China, India, and Pakistan could stabilize around 150-200. From Pakistan's perspective, this would require that its legitimate security concerns vis-à-vis India are addressed by creative solutions involving both China and the United States.

Conclusion

The world faces a stark choice between business as usual and a concerted effort to deal with the root causes of serious national security threats seen by decisionmakers in China, India, and Pakistan. As recommended by Mian and Ramana and supported by this author, "A basic reordering of priorities in each of these countries is long overdue."

All governments are forced by events to manage short-term crises and thus give lower priority to long-term problems. From an American perspective, there are more than enough reasons to avoid addressing the nuclear weapons challenge in the context of US bilateral relations with China, India, and Pakistan. However, if this proclivity persists among

US decisionmakers, the result is likely to be both larger nuclear forces and nuclear postures that shift toward nuclear warfighting over the next 2 decades.

This business-as-usual approach is likely to yield the following: China, India, and Pakistan will continue to maintain three mutually incompatible nuclear doctrines. Multiple drivers for nuclear force modernization in each country will provide sufficient domestic and bureaucratic political pressure to expand and modernize nuclear weapons for decades to come.

Given this situation, proposed arms control treaties such as the Comprehensive Test Ban Treaty (CTBT) and Fissile Material Cutoff Treaty (FMCT) will not be implemented. Both proposed agreements are opposed by all three countries to varying degrees. The roots of their opposition are not being addressed seriously with policy research, strategic planning, or diplomacy.

The Obama administration's rhetoric associated with nuclear weapons sounds idealistic.[58] However, its actions reflect a business-as-usual proclivity. The administration is acting as if nuclear weapons represent one issue that can be partitioned into its own narrow policy lane and managed by mid-level officials within the US Government. This is understandable, given the pressing economic, environmental, terroristic and Afghanistan-Pakistan war agendas the Obama administration inherited and has created for itself.

The United States has adopted a neo-Cold War nuclear posture to keep a few European allies quiet and to avoid a major bureaucratic fight between the White House and a few civilian Pentagon officials who work closely with Republican allies on Capitol Hill. How US nuclear weapons based in Europe will translate into greater security in Europe is never discussed with any degree of rigor or intellectual honesty. Perhaps the administration's logic was that it perceived the demonstration effect of a fundamentally new American nuclear posture would have little significant impact on thinking in China, India, and Pakistan. So why pay a short-term domestic political price for the prospects of marginal increases in long-term stability? However, absent such a fundamental change and serious discussions between the United States and China, one can predict with a high degree of confidence that business as usual will produce nuclear arms races in Southwest Asia for decades.

Other reasons to sustain a business-as-usual approach are obvious. America will continue to spend approximately $10 billion per year on national missile defense to neutralize potent domestic constituencies regardless of its technical feasibility and negative impacts on Russia and China.[59] The United States does not want to think seriously about steps it could take to address the Kashmir conflict because it is so complex; India's position has been set in stone for decades, and it is easier to think of India as a global economic power sympathetic to American values. The United States has not invested in civilian governance and rebuilding civil administrative capability in Pakistan because the military is the only functioning entity in the country in the short term.[60] Honest and capable civilian political leadership in Pakistan is almost entirely lacking and will take many years to develop and mature, if it ever occurs. Pakistani-born Islamic terrorists and the "India-phobic and paranoid"[61] Pakistani strategic culture is acknowledged by American decisionmakers as a key problem, but American decisions and actions are focused almost exclusively on the War on Terror.[62] (To date, even after Osama bin Laden was killed, no significant policy changes seem to be taking place in Washington or Islamabad.)

The perception persists in both Washington and Islamabad that the United States needs Pakistan more than Pakistan needs the United States. In this context, adding the nuclear weapons issue to an overly crowded policy agenda with Pakistan will definitely overload the circuits. The net result is probably that Pakistan leaders have concluded they can build as many nuclear weapons as they can produce plutonium and HEU. They will take symbolic steps to appear to secure nuclear materials and weapons better, but the question of "how much is enough" is off the table.[63]

If this business-as-usual situation continues, the world should ready itself for a very rough ride in terms of nuclear weapons in the next 2 decades of the 21st century. Southwest Asia will be the dominant driver to the unstable world our children will rightly accuse us of having ignored to their peril. American decisionmakers in the 1980s chose to ignore realities on the ground after the Soviets were defeated in Afghanistan. The blowback next time will be orders of magnitude larger and more tragic.

Endnotes

1. Lawrence Freedman, *The Evolution of Nuclear Strategy,* New York: St. Martin's Press, 1981; Richard Rhodes, *The Making of the Atomic Bomb*, New York: Simon & Schuster, 1986; Richard Rhodes, *Dark Sun: The Making of the Hydrogen Bomb,* New York: Simon & Schuster, 1995; Richard Rhodes, *Arsenals of Folly: The Making of the Nuclear Arms Race*, New York: Alfred A. Knopf, 2007; Richard Rhodes, *The Twilight of the Bomb,* New York: Alfred A. Knopf, 2010; Margaret Gowing, *Independence and Deterrence: Britain and Atomic Energy, 1945-1952,*

Vol. I, Policy Making, New York: St. Martin's Press, 1974; David S. Yost "France's Evolving Nuclear Strategy," *Survival*, Vol. 47, Issue 3, 2005; Avner Cohen, *Israel and the Bomb*, New York: Columbia University Press, 1983, Stephen M. Millett, "Soviet Perceptions of Nuclear Strategy and Implications for US Deterrence," *Air University Review*, March-April 1982; David Holloway, *Stalin and the Bomb,* New Haven, CT: Yale University Press, 1994.

2. Fred Kaplan, *The Wizards of Armageddon*, New York: Simon and Schuster, 1983.

3. *America's Strategic Posture: The Final Report of the Congressional Commission on the Strategic Posture of the United States*, Washington, DC: United States Institute of Peace, 2009, p. 111.

4. Morton H. Halperin, *Nuclear Fallacy: Dispelling the Myth of Nuclear Strategy,* Cambridge, MA: Ballinger, 1987.

5. Stephen I. Swartz, *Atomic Audit: The Costs and Consequences of US Nuclear Weapons since 1940,* Washington, DC: Brookings Institution Press, 1998; Stephen I. Schwartz and Deepti Choubey, *Nuclear Security Spending: Assessing Costs, Examining Priorities*, Washington, DC: Carnegie Endowment for International Peace, 2009.

6. On April 30, 1994, President Reagan stated in a speech delivered in China:

   We live in a troubled world, and the United States and China, as two great nations, share a special responsibility to help reduce the risks of war. We both agree that there can be only one sane policy to preserve our precious civilization in the modern age. A nuclear war cannot be won and must never be fought. And no matter how great the obstacles may seem, we must never stop our efforts to reduce the weapons of war. We must never stop at all until we see the day when nuclear arms have been banished from the face of this Earth.

   Peter Lettow, *Ronald Reagan and His Quest to Abolish Nuclear Weapons*, New York: Random House, 2005.

7. Vannevar Bush, *Modern Arms and Free Men: A Discussion of the Role of Science in Preserving Democracy,* New York: Simon and Schuster, 1949; George F. Kennan, *The Nuclear Delusion: Soviet-American Relations in the Atomic Age*, New York: Pantheon Books, 1976; James R. Killian, *Sputnik, Scientists, and Eisenhower: A Memoir of the First Assistant to the President for Science and Technology,* Cambridge, MA: MIT Press, 1982; McGeorge Bundy, William T. Crowe, Jr., Sidney Drell, *Reducing Nuclear Danger: The Road Away from the Brink,* New York: Council on Foreign Relations, 1983; Robert S. McNamara, *Blundering Into Disaster: Surviving the First Century of the Nuclear Age,* New

York: Pantheon Books, 1986; Morton H. Halperin, *Nuclear Fallacy: Dispelling the Myth of Nuclear Strategy,* Cambridge, MA: Ballinger, 1987; Herb York, *Making Weapons, Talking Peace: A Physicist's Odyssey from Hiroshima to Geneva*, New York: Basic Books, 1987; McGeorge Bundy, *Danger and Survival: Choices About the Bomb in the First Fifty Years,* New York: Random House, 1988; Sidney D. Drell, *In the Shadow of the Bomb: Physics and Arms Control*, New York: American Institute of Physics, 1993; Graham Allison, *Nuclear Terrorism: The Ultimate Preventable Catastrophe*, New York: An Owl Book, 2004; George P. Schultz, William J. Perry, Henry A. Kissinger, and Sam Nunn, "A World Free of Nuclear Weapons," *The Wall Street Journal*, January 4, 2007.

8. Daryl G. Kimball and Greg Thielmann, "Obama's NPR: Transitional, Not Transformational," *Arms Control Today*, Vol. 40, No. 5, May 2010; Morton H. Halperin, "A New Nuclear Posture," *Arms Control Today*, Vol. 40, No. 5, May 2010; Jacob W. Kipp, "Asian Drivers of Russia's Nuclear Force Posture," Arlington, VA: Nonproliferation Policy Education Center, Unpublished Essay, 2010.

9. David E. Sanger, *The Inheritance: The World Obama Confronts and the Challenges to American Power,* New York: Harmony Books, 2009, p. 176.

10. "British Nuclear Arsenal Stands at 225 Warheads," *Nuclear Threat Initiative: Global Security Newswire*, available from *www.nti.org/gsn/article/british-nuclear-arsenal-stands-at-225-warheads/*; see United States Institute of Peace, p. 111.

11. Exceptions to the proclivity to ignore Israel's nuclear weapons program can be seen in Avner Cohen, *Israel and the Bomb,* New York: Columbia University Press, 1983; Victor Gilinsky, "Sometimes We Don't Want to Know: Kissinger and Nixon Finesse Israel's Bomb," Washington, DC: Nonproliferation Policy Education Center, Unpublished Analysis, 2011; Avner Cohen, *The Worst-Kept Secret: Israel's Bargain with the Bomb*, New York: Columbia University Press, 2010.

12. Joel S. Wit, Daniel B. Poneman, and Robert L. Gallucci, *Going Critical: The First North Korean Nuclear Crisis*, Washington, DC: The Brookings Institution Press, 2004. A highly informed assessment that the Democratic People's Republic of Korea (DPRK) might be willing to give up its nuclear weapons if the United States implemented its agreements is contained in Leon V. Sigal, "Primer-North Korea, South Korea, and the United States: Reading Between the Lines of the Cheonan Attack," *Bulletin of the Atomic Scientists*, Vol. 66, No. 5, 2010, pp. 35-66.

13. This author is in agreement with a comment made by George Perkovich

that the Southwest Asia triangle of China, India, and Pakistan is influenced by a US-Russia-China triangle. This comment was made at the "Life After START: New Challenges, New Opportunities" conference held in Washington, DC, on January 27, 2011.

14. Bruno Tertrais, "After Iran: Prospects for Nuclear Proliferation in North Africa," Washington, DC: Nonproliferation Policy Education Center, Unpublished Analysis, 2010; Shraham Chubin, "Nuclear Proliferation Prospects in the Middle East to 2025," Washington, DC: Nonproliferation Policy Education Center, Unpublished Analysis, 2011.

15. McGeorge Bundy, William T. Crowe, Jr., Sidney Drell, *Reducing Nuclear Danger: The Road Away from the Brink*, New York: Council on Foreign Relations, 1983, p. 99.

16. International Security Advisory Board, "Report on Discouraging a Cascade of Nuclear Weapons States," Washington, DC: Department of State, October 19, 2007.

17. Presidential candidate John Kennedy's oft-referenced prediction about the spread of nuclear weapons: "There are indications, because of new inventions that 10, 15, or 20 nations will have a nuclear capability—including Red China—by the end of the presidential office in 1964." Cited in Joseph Cirincione, *Bomb Scare: The History and Future of Nuclear Weapons*, New York: Columbia University Press, 2007, p. 28.

18. Since the Nixon administration, both Democrats and Republicans have supported nuclear nonproliferation efforts at the rhetorical level, but they have rarely been willing to pay a significant diplomatic, economic, or domestic political price to achieve nuclear nonproliferation outcomes.

19. Robert E. Johnson, "China's Nuclear Forces and Policies," in Larry M. Wortzel, ed., *China's Military Modernization and International Implications*, New York: Greenwood Press, 1988.

20. Thomas W. Graham, *The Politics of Failure: Strategic Nuclear Arms Control, Public Opinion and Domestic Politics in the United States*, MIT Ph.D. dissertation, 1989.

21. The most interesting category is Stage One: Watch List Nations. With the prospects of Iran crossing from Stage 2 to Stage 3 and the DPRK moving from Stage 3 to Stage 4, an unusually large number of countries can be considered Watch List Nations. For purposes of this chapter, they would include Algeria, Egypt, Saudi Arabia, Syria, and Turkey (in the Middle East); Japan, South Korea, and Taiwan (in East Asia); and Burma/Myanmar (in South Asia). Unlike in the 20th century, when Watch List countries were mostly Third World countries with emerging technical capabilities, in the 21st century these countries range in technical capabilities from Japan on one end to Burma on the other.

22. United States Institute of Peace.

23. This is best demonstrated by the April 6, 2010, cover letter to the *Nuclear Posture Review* signed by Secretary of Defense Robert Gates. It committed to transferring nearly $5 billion from the Department of Defense to the Department of Energy to be used for purposes of maintaining offensive nuclear weapons. Thus, the United States will spend more money on offensive nuclear weapons research, development, testing, and evaluation (RDT&E) than it did during the Cold War. This figure increased to approximately $ 80 billion in the context of the debate over ratification of the New START treaty in 2010.

24. "John Kerry Puts off Key Vote on Arms Treaty; Hopes Dim for Quick Passage," *The Washington Post*, August 4, 2010.

25. BBC News, "Trident Scale Back Urged Amid Cost Worries," July 28, 2010.

26. It seems ironic that the "Axis of Evil" concept used by President George W. Bush in his 2002 State of the Union Address seems to continue to frame how many Americans view nuclear proliferation long after President Bush left office. Fear associated with Iran and North Korea obtaining or increasing small stockpiles of nuclear weapons dominate fear that operationally deployed nuclear forces will expand in Southwest Asia.

27. The phrase "weapons of the weak" comes from James C. Scott, *Weapons of the Weak: Everyday Forms of Peasant Resistance,* New Haven, CT: Yale University Press, 1985.

28. For a discussion of growth in nuclear forces in China, India, and Pakistan, see the excellent essay written by Zia Mian and M. V. Ramana, "Imbricated Regional Rivalries and Global Order: South Asia, China and the United States," Washington, DC: Nonproliferation Policy Education Center, Unpublished Analysis, 2010.

29. Jeffrey Lewis, "How Many Chinese Nuclear Weapons?" cited from *Arms Control Wonk*, March 7, 2004, available from *Lewis.Armscontrolwonk.com/archive/99/howmany-chinese-nuclear-weapons*; *Annual Report to Congress: Military and Security Developments Involving the People's Republic of China,* Washington, DC: Department of Defense, 2011, pp. 3-4, 34-35, 38, 78.

30. *Annual Report to Congress: Military and Security Developments,* 2011, p. 34; *Annual Report to Congress: Military and Security Developments Involving the People's Republic of China,* Washington, DC: Department of Defense, 2010, p. 35; *Annual Report to Congress: Military Power of the People's Republic of China*, Washington, DC: Department of Defense, 2006, p. 25; *Annual Report to Congress: Military Power of the*

People's Republic of China, Washington, DC: Department of Defense, 2008, pp. 26-27.

31. Vipin Narang, "Posturing for Peace? Pakistan's Nuclear Postures and South Asian Stability," *International Security*, Vol. 34, No. 3, Winter 2009/10, p. 44.
32. Sanger, p. 179.
33. Peter Lavoy, "Islamabad's Nuclear Posture: Its Premises and Implementation," in Henry D. Sokolski, ed., *Pakistan's Nuclear Future: Worries beyond War*, Carlisle, PA: Strategic Studies Institute, US Army War College, 2008; Vipin Narang, pp. 59-62.
34. Pakistan's rigid military dogma is well described in Ahmed Rashid, "And Hate Begat Hate," *The New York Times*, Sunday Review, September 11, 2011, pp. 1, 7.
35. L. K. Krishnan, "Why Pokhran Yield Does Not Matter Now," *Rediff News*, August 31, 2009; K. Santhanam and Ashok Parthasarathi, "Pokhran-II Thermonuclear Test, a Failure," *The Hindu*, September 17, 2009.
36. "What Makes 5000 km Range Agni-5 Missile Deadlier," *Rediff News*, October 12, 2009; "India's Agni-5 Can Target Our Harbin City: Chinese Daily," *The Times of India*, October 15, 2009; "Agni-5, India's Answer to China's Lethal Missile," *Deccan Herald*, February 10, 2010.
37. K. Subrahmanyam and V.S. Arunachalam, "Deterrence and Explosive Yield," *The Hindu*, September 21, 2009.
38. George Perkovich, *India's Nuclear Bomb: The Impact on Global Proliferation,* Berkeley, CA: University of California Press, 1999, pp. 320-21, 347, 351; Raj Chengappa, *Weapons of Peace: The Secret Story of India's Quest to be a Nuclear Power,* New Delhi, India: HarperCollins Publishers India, 2000, pp. 368-69, 380-81, 390-97.
39. Manpreet Sethi, *Nuclear Deterrence in Second Tier Nuclear Weapon States: A Case Study of India*, CHS Occasional Paper No. 25, Pondicherry, India: French Research Institute of India, December 2009, pp. 6, 37-9, 43.
40. David Albright and Paul Brannan, "Pakistan Appears to be Building a Third Plutonium Production Reactor at Khushab Nuclear Site," the Institute of Science and International Security, June 21, 2007; Zian Min, "Pakistan May Have Completed New Plutonium Production Reactor, Khushab-II," International Panel on Fissile Materials, February 28, 2010; Discussion at the Stimson Center on February 23, 2011, suggested the increasing conventional imbalance between India and Pakistan will result in Pakistan's building more nuclear weapons and relying more on terrorists to counter India.

41. In terms of Pakistan's strategic culture, see Husain Haqqani, *Pakistan: Between Mosque and Military*, Washington, DC: Carnegie Endowment for International Peace, 2005; Ayesha Siddiqa, *Military Inc. Inside Pakistan's Military Economy,* London, UK: Pluto Press, 2007.

42. There is an extensive academic debate about the number of wars India and Pakistan have fought. However, there is no debate that India and Pakistan have engaged in military conflicts in 1947, 1965, 1971, and 1999. Most scholarship concludes that Pakistan started each conflict with India. Most scholarship, including important research produced in Pakistan, has concluded that Pakistan's military, political, and economic position was weaker after each conflict than it was before hostilities were initiated. In addition, India and Pakistan have had several tense confrontations that could have led to war in 1986-87 (Brasstacks) and 2001-02. See P. R. Chari, Pervez Iqbal Cheema, and Stephen P. Cohen, *Four Crises and a Peace Process: American Engagement in South Asia*, Washington, DC: The Brookings Institution, 2007; Polly Nayak and Michael Krepon, *US Crisis Management in South Asia's Twin Peaks Crisis*, Report 57, Washington, DC: The Stimson Center, 2007.

43. Robert D. Kaplan, "The Geography of Chinese Power: How Far Can Beijing Reach on Land and at Sea?" *Foreign Affairs*, Vol. 89, No. 3, May/June 2010; Henry Sokolski, "Missiles for Peace," *Armed Forces Journal*, July 2010; *Annual Report to Congress: Military and Security Developments Involving the People's Republic of China*, 2011; *Annual Report to Congress: Military and Security Developments Involving the People's Republic of China*, 2010.

44. See description available from *www.deagel.com/Ballistic-Missiles/DF-21_a000859001.aspx*.

45. One article that assumes the Chinese nuclear buildup is substantial and is having an increasing impact on Russian threat perceptions can be found in Jacob W. Kipp, "Asian Drivers of Russia's Nuclear Force Posture," Washington, DC: Nonproliferation Policy Education Center, Unpublished Analysis, 2010.

46. *Annual Report to Congress: Military and Security Developments Involving the People's Republic of China,* 2011, pp. 30, 33, 78; *Military and Security Developments*, 2010, p. 35; Ian Easton, "The Asia-Pacific's Emerging Missile Defense and Space Competition," Washington, DC: Nonproliferation Policy Education Center, Unpublished Analysis, 2010; Mark Stokes and Ian Easton, "Evolving Aerospace Trends in the Asia-Pacific Region," Washington, DC: Nonproliferation Policy Education Center, Unpublished Analysis.

47. Yun Zhou, "The Security Implications of China's Nuclear Energy Expansion," *Nonproliferation Review*, Vol. 17, No. 2, July 2010.

48. "Nuclear Power in China," *World Nuclear Association,* pp. 10, 13-14, available from *www.world-nuclear.org/info/inf63.html.*

49. AFP, "China Needs 10 Years for Nuclear Fuel Recycling: CNNC," January 17, 2011.

50. The initial "guesstimate" of China's weapons-grade plutonium (WGPu) production was included in David Albright, Frans Berkhout, and William Walker, *Plutonium and Highly Enriched Uranium 1996: World Inventories, Capabilities and Policies*, 1997, pp. 76-77. A more recent estimate, with lower figures for the estimated production of weapons-grade material by China, can be found in Hui Zhang, "China," *Global Fissile Material Report*, 2010. The figure of 800 weapons was used by Mian and Ramana.

51. The assumption China has approximately 150, plus or minus 50, operationally deployed nuclear comes from multiple public estimates. A comprehensive nongovernment assessment concluded in 2006 that China had 93 land-based nuclear-armed ballistic missiles, 12 JL-1 SLBMs, and 40 aircraft-delivered nuclear weapons, for a total of approximately 145 operational warheads. Hans M. Kristensen, Robert S. Norris, and Matthew G. McKinzie, *Chinese Nuclear Forces and US Nuclear War Planning,* Washington DC: The Federation of American Scientists and the Natural Resources Defense Council, 2006, p. 202. A retired Indian military intelligence officer associated with the Chennai Centre for China Studies assessed that China has around 130 nuclear warheads deployed on missiles and aircraft. See Colonel R. Hariharan, "Nuclear Capability of India and China," *The Island*, July 13, 2010. On February 28, 2006, the Director of the DIA, Lieutenant General Michael D. Maples, presented before the Senate Armed Services Committee the following prepared statement: "It is likely the number of deployed Chinese nuclear-armed theater and strategic systems will increase in the next several years. China currently has more than 100 nuclear weapons." Michael D. Maples, Lieutenant General USA, Director DIA, *Current and Projected National Security Threats to the United States*, Statement for the Record before the Senate Armed Services Committee, February 28, 2006, p. 4. Jeffrey Lewis concluded China has around 100 nuclear weapons in "How Many Chinese Nuclear Weapons?" March 7, 2004, cited from *Arms Control Wonk*, available from *Lewis.Armscontrol-wonk.com/archive/99/howmany-chinese-nuclear-weapons*. "The Public Estimates of the Size of the Chinese Nuclear Arsenal are Less than 200 Warheads, cited in Mian and Ramana, p. 9. Senior Colonel Yao Yunzhu, "China's Perspective on Nuclear Deterrence," *Air and Space Power Journal*, Spring 2010; Michael Wines and Edward Wong, "China's Push to Modernize its Military Is Bearing Fruit," *The New York Times*, January 6, 2011. In 2011, Hua Han stated China has approximately 150

operationally deployed nuclear weapons. Statement made at a panel called "Two Triangles: India-Pakistan-China and China-US-Russia," at the 2011 Carnegie Endowment International Nuclear Policy Conference, Washington, DC; "China Least Potent among N-powers, Says Harvard Study," *Times of India*, May 8, 2011. "The military's nuclear deterrent estimated by experts at no more than 160 [nuclear] warheads, has been redeployed since 2008 into mobile launchers and advanced submarines that no longer are sitting ducks for attacks," *The New York Times*, January 6, 2011, p. A4.

52. "According to open source estimates, today Pakistan has about 85 nuclear weapons, which are under the complete control of the Pakistani military," *World at Risk: The Report of the Commission on the Prevention of Weapons of Mass Destruction Proliferation and Terrorism*, New York: Vintage Books, 2008, p. 67. Pakistan has 70 to 90 strategic nuclear weapons as opposed to India's 60 to 80. "Pakistan Has More Nukes and Fissile Materials than India," *Economic Times*, August 2, 2010.

53. Robert S. Norris, Andrew S. Burrows, and Richard W. Fieldhouse, eds., *Nuclear Weapons Databook* Vol. V, "British, French and Chinese Nuclear Weapons," Boulder, CO: Westview Press, 1994, pp. 324, 359; United States Institute of Peace, p. 111.

54. Leonard S. Spector, *Nuclear Proliferation Today,* New York: Vintage Books, 1984; Leonard S. Spector, New York: Vintage, 1985; Leonard S. Spector, *Going Nuclear,* Cambridge, MA: Ballinger Publishing Company, 1987; Leonard S. Spector, *The Undeclared Bomb,* Cambridge, MA: Ballinger Publishing Company, 1988; Leonard S. Spector with Jacqueline R. Smith, *Nuclear Ambitions,* Boulder, CO: Westview Press, 1990; Rodney W. Jones and Mark G. McDonough with Toby F. Dalton and Gregory D. Koblentz, *Tracking Nuclear Proliferation: A Guide in Maps and Charts*, Washington, DC: Carnegie Endowment for International Peace, 1998; Joseph Cirincione, Jon B. Wolfsthal, and Miriam Rajkumar, *Deadly Arsenals: Nuclear, Biological, and Chemical Threats*, 2nd Ed., Washington, DC: Carnegie Endowment for International Peace, 2005; Jeffery T. Richardson, *Spying On The Bomb: American Nuclear Intelligence From Nazi Germany to Iran and North Korea*, New York: W. W. Norton, 2006; Joseph Cirincione, *Bomb Scare: The History & Future of Nuclear Weapons,* New York: Columbia University Press, 2007.

55. David E. Sanger and Eric Schmitt, "Pakistani Arms Pose Challenge to US Policy," *The New York Times*, January 31, 2011, p. A1, 7.

56. Alexander Glaser, "Weapons-grade Plutonium Production Potential in the Indian Prototype Fast Breeder Reactor," December 13, 2006, p. 38.

57. Hui Zhang.

58. Remarks of President Barack Obama, Prague, Czech Republic, April 5, 2009.

59. George N. Lewis and Theodore A. Postal, "A Flawed and Dangerous US Missile Defense Plan," *Arms Control Today*, Vol. 40, No. 4, May 2010. To date, the United States has spent approximately $100 billion on missile defense. Steven A. Hidreth and Amy F. Woolf, "National Missile Defense: Issues for Congress," Washington, DC: Congressional Research Service, July 17, 2001; Joseph Cirincione, "Brief History of Ballistic Missile Defense and Current Programs in the United States," Washinton, DC: Carnegie Endowment for International Peace, July 1998; Sanger, p. 188.

60. Sanger, pp. 175-344.

61. Feroz Hassan Khan, "Prospects for Indian and Pakistani Arms Control and CBMs," Washington, DC: Nonproliferation Policy Education Center, Unpublished Analysis, 2010, p. 5.

62. Bob Woodward, *Obama's Wars,* New York: Simon & Schuster, 2010, pp. 3, 89, 99, 101, 108-9, 111, 187-88, 194, 203, 208-10, 214-16, 284-89, 296, 302-3, 328, 330, 355, 363-69, 379.

63. Sanger, p. 219.

Chapter 10

Nuclear Missile-Related Risks in South Asia

RN Ganesh

Introduction

In April 2000, a few days before embarking on the first visit in 22 years by an American President to India and Pakistan, President Bill Clinton referred to South Asia as "the most dangerous place in the world." More than 10 years down the line, many would still consider that description apt. South Asia is the only region in the world where there are serious disputes involving the risk of war between three contiguous nuclear-armed countries with a history of military conflict.[1]

The history of India's relations with China and Pakistan is characterized by conflicts and animosity. This chapter will lay out the historical background that has brought the three countries to their respective current strategic perspectives. The differing world views of the three countries have molded their individual strategic postures, and each has come to adopt nuclear weapons as a security imperative for differing reasons. Based on their strategic perceptions, the nature and quantum of their nuclear arsenals, too, are widely disparate. China views its main threat as the United States, against which its nuclear deterrent is designed. India views its major strategic threat as emanating from China, though its immediate concern is Pakistan's support of cross-border terrorism and the Pakistan military's periodic attempts to change the agreed lines of control on its borders. Pakistan views India as its major threat, whose aim is to destroy the Pakistan state. The nuclear equation between China, India, and Pakistan is often characterized by the analogy of a triangle; it would be more apt to compare it to a vicious circle, in which an action by one results in an escalatory reaction from the other two.

The chapter will then take a brief overview of the nuclear forces of the three countries, highlight the main features of each, and examine the linkage between force architectures and the respective strategic postures. The missile defense policies of each country will be discussed, and their current and potential capabilities assessed.

In the unbalanced nuclear situation that exists among the three countries, there is a risk of missile competitions acquiring their own dynamic. The chapter looks at current and possible future missile rivalries, and the possibility and effects of some kind of offensive missile restraint regime as in the Intermediate-Range Nuclear Forces (INF) Treaty. The recent implosion of the Union of Soviet Socialist Republics (USSR) under the burden of its calamitous arms race with the United States carries too grave a lesson for any of these countries to ignore. The chapter suggests that both India and China have similar approaches in that they do not believe that parity of nuclear forces is a prerequisite for deterrence. Discussing the risk factors in the India-Pakistan context, the chapter concludes that the main threat of unintended or uncontrolled nuclear conflict is from short-range ballistic missiles (SRBMs), and this is possibly due to escalation triggered by their employment as a battlefield weapon. The chapter also argues that ambiguity in nuclear doctrine carries the danger of wrong interpretation of intentions and is a risk-prone strategy.

The chapter concludes with some suggestions for risk reduction, including the possibility of moves toward recessing the deterrent and elimination of SRBMs.

Historical Background

India and Pakistan

The sustained hostility between India and Pakistan has existed since the two countries became independent, and the reasons are deep-rooted. In the princely state of Jammu and Kashmir, whereas the Jammu District had a preponderance of Hindus, Kashmir had a Muslim majority. When India and Pakistan became independent, the erstwhile Indian princedoms were given the choice of accession, and the Hindu ruler of Jammu and Kashmir opted to join India. For Pakistan, which was founded on the basis of religious identity, this was a negation of the basis of its creation.

In 1948, Pakistan sent in its troops along with tribal militants to seize Kashmir, and India sent in its army. Both countries heeded a ceasefire call by the United Nations (UN), but each held on to the territory it had under its control. That situation continues to this day.

As the years passed, the differences between the two countries widened. India is a secular democracy; Pakistan has been ruled by military dictators for about 30 of its 63 years of statehood. In the general elections held in Pakistan in 1970, West Pakistan rulers were stunned when Shaikh Mujib-ur-Rehman, the Bengali leader of East Pakistan, won an overwhelming majority and claimed the Prime Ministership. General Yahya Khan, the Chief Martial Law Administrator, refused to accept the election result, and Mujib was put in prison.[2] Following Mujib's imprisonment and transfer to a prison in West Pakistan, a group of rebel officers declared Bangladesh independent on March 26, 1971. In response, the Pakistani Army launched bloody reprisals (Operation SEARCHLIGHT), killing almost a million Bengalis. Over 10-million refugees fled across the border for sanctuary in Indian refugee camps.[3] When the December 1971 war broke out between India and Pakistan and with India's victory, East Pakistan became Bangladesh.

These seminal events—the accession of Kashmir to India, Pakistan's loss of its eastern territory, and the overwhelming defeat in the war (which ended with 90,000 Pakistani troops in Indian prisoner-of-war camps)—have deeply affected the national psyche, which now blames India for all the nation's problems. Pakistan still thirsts for revenge.

Immediately after the war ended, Zulfikar Ali Bhutto, who had replaced Yahya Khan as the President of Pakistan, launched his program to acquire a nuclear bomb, which he termed the "Islamic bomb." India demonstrated its nuclear capability by exploding a subterranean nuclear device in 1974, and, with China's assistance, Pakistan accelerated the progress of its nuclear quest. In 1998, India exploded several nuclear devices and declared itself a weapons state. Days later, Pakistan followed suit.

India and China

India inherited its troubled relations with China from its former British rulers. Ironically, independent India had been among the first countries to recognize the new government of China in 1949, when the rest of the world still recognized Chiang Kai-Shek's Formosa as the real China. But the very next year, Chinese troops occupied Tibet, and India extended shelter to the Dalai Lama, who formed a government-in-exile in the Indian state of Himachal. Thousands of Tibetan refugees crossed over into India and live there to this day. The core issues between the two countries are the status of Tibet, Chinese territorial claims on the northern and eastern borders of India, and India's sympathy toward and protection of the Dalai Lama. The territorial claims by China vary in force from time to time; indeed, China uses the border issue to regulate the temperature of its relations with India, depending on its interests in the issues current at any given time.

While the Indian Government does not allow the Dalai Lama to engage in political activity and has accepted Tibet as an autonomous region under China, there is still great Chinese mistrust of India's position on this issue. The prickly relations between the two are exacerbated by China's support to Pakistan and its covert transfer of nuclear technology and nuclear materials, as well as conventional weapons, to that country. In an act that impacted Indian security, Pakistan ceded part of the disputed territory under its control north of Kashmir to China, which gave China direct access from Sinkiang to Tibet.

While the main causes of poor relations between China and India can be identified and resolved, given political will on both sides, there are some less tangible reasons. China is on the rise; its long-nurtured global ambitions are now beginning to reach a stage that it can brook no impediments, and it views India as a challenge to its aspirations to be the foremost power in Asia.

Pakistan and China

Pakistan has built up close relations with China across the spectrum of military, economic, and political cooperation. It was among the earlier countries to accord recognition to the communist government in 1950, but later opposed the entry of China into the UN out of deference to the United States. For many years, Pakistan's attitude to China mirrored that of the United States, with which it was allied in the Central Treaty Organization.

The US military assistance to India after the Chinese attack in 1962 and the US refusal to intervene militarily on Pakistan's side in the wars against India in 1965 and 1971 were probably influential in bringing Pakistan much closer to China. China began to support Pakistan against India on Kashmir. China has made huge investments in Pakistan, particularly in Gwadar and northern Baluchistan, to the extent of nearly \$20 billion.[4] The United States has applied sanctions on Pakistan sporadically; the on-again off-again pattern of economic and military aid has been determined by its perceived need for Pakistan's assistance in the Afghanistan imbroglio.

Most importantly, from the 1980s to the 1990s, China supplied Pakistan with nuclear technology and missiles, as well as equipment and facilities for uranium enrichment. Currently, two more reactors are being built with Chinese assistance to produce weapon-grade plutonium. With its growing international footprint, China is today able to defy the United States and is in the process of continuing and expanding its nuclear cooperation with Pakistan.

For its part, Pakistan has provided China with access to the Indian Ocean, has made territorial "adjustments" to enable China to build a highway connecting Sinkiang to Tibet and to Pakistan, and has supported China on all international disputes. Each country uses the other for its own reasons involving India. China uses Pakistan as a cat's paw to slow India's growth and development, complicate its security environment, and act as a strategic distraction. Pakistan uses China to get political support, military hardware, and nuclear weapons and technology.

Strategic Perceptions

China

China sees itself as surrounded on all sides by unfriendly states aligned to prevent its rise to a position of eminence, and, in response, has acted vigorously to provide its armed forces with adequate retaliatory and offensive capability. It considers the United States its major adversary, which has declared its intention to prevent the re-absorption of Taiwan. China also views Japan and South Korea as willing allies of the United States in any conflict situation, and is particularly concerned about the American plans for missile defense cooperation with these countries.

China's relations with Russia have been uneasy in the past, but there has been a quantum increase in their mutual cooperation since the collapse of the USSR and America's emergence as the sole superpower. However, underlying the good relations is still an element of suspicion that makes the two countries wary of each other.

China's relations with India swing from cold to overtly hostile, with sporadic thaws. While full-scale military action is an unlikely option, China skilfully manipulates the long-standing claim on India's northeastern and western borders issue to extract diplomatic mileage, and even engages in minor border incidents to keep the "pot boiling." India's growth and progress have created a southern flank situation for China, which it has factored into its defense posture by the militarization of Tibet and by establishing missile bases within striking range of Indian targets.[5]

The US threat, however, is the main driver of its security strategy and the predominant factor in China's strategic calculus, which subsumes all other threat considerations.

Pakistan

Pakistan's threat perception and defense posture are entirely Indo-centric. The country began its military nuclear program as a sequel to the defeat in the 1971 war with India. By 1979, Pakistan had already set up its facilities for producing weapons-grade uranium, when it incurred US punitive action. In the 1990s, plutonium production was operationalized with the commissioning of the Chinese-designed and supplied Khushab reactor,[6] and China still continues to play a major role in Pakistan's nuclear program.

When the United States launched its War on Terror, Pakistan had little choice but to fall in line and support the US campaign in Afghanistan against al Qaeda and the Taliban. With its own military heavily under attack by the Taliban, the Pakistani Government is hard pressed to balance the conflicting demands of its Army, the Islamic fundamentalists, and the Baluchistan secessionists on the one hand, and America's operational dictates on the other. There is a great deal of sympathy for the Islamist cause among sections of the military and the population, and resentment against the government for acting against the Taliban at the behest of the Americans. China is viewed as a staunch and permanent ally, whose friendship with Pakistan is "as high as the mountains and as deep as the ocean."[7]

India

India perceives a military threat on two fronts. The threat from Pakistan has persisted since both countries became independent in 1947. While the central issue according to Pakistan is the dispute over Kashmir, India's view is that this may have been true until some years ago, but the situation now has gone beyond Kashmir to one of Pakistan's support and exploitation of nonstate militancy, which uses terrorist-type tactics. India has been attacked by Pakistan-based terrorists seven or eight times in the last 8 years; on every occasion, it has been persuaded and pressured by the international community led by the United States to exercise restraint.

China blows hot and cold on the border issue, using it as a regulator to manipulate Indian and regional attitudes. Having fought wars with both countries, India views their close relations and China's supplies of nuclear technology and weapons to Pakistan with concern. In recent times,

China's rising prosperity has resulted in a new expansionist approach, both in foreign economic policies (trade and acquisition of oil and other commodities), as well as in its strategic expansion into the Indian Ocean region. These factors impelled the Indian Defence Minister, George Fernandes, to state publicly that China was India's major threat.[8] India's major strategic concern is China, but its short-term security preoccupations are completely dominated by Pakistan-related issues.

Linkages Between Strategic Perceptions and Strategic Force Structures

In classical national security planning, nations define their national objectives and their vital national interests. Based on these, nations develop a grand strategy to safeguard those interests. From there flow the security architecture and force levels, depending on the technological and economic strength of the country. It is also a historical phenomenon that as the resources and capabilities grow, the expanding military potential fuels higher national ambitions, and national interests and strategy are modified to meet the changed aspirations.

China

Although China is being discussed along with the other two South Asian powers because of the geo-political framework of this book, this chapter does not view it solely within this narrow power grouping. China is an aspiring superpower, and in many ways already has a power status that is second only to that of the United States. As has been amply emphasized, China's main threat is the United States, and its immediate security concern is to prevent international (read: American) legitimization of an independent status for Taiwan. While China will not act precipitately to bring about Taiwan's reunification, it views that as an inevitability, and has worked steadfastly toward that goal. In 1999, China had about 150 deployable SRBMs in the Taiwan theater, which grew to about 650 in 2005; the number is currently over a thousand. Similarly, the number and the capability of China's intermediate-range ballistic missiles (IRBMs) have increased, and the current accuracies of these longer-range missiles are aimed at restricting US logistic and support capabilities in Japan and the Pacific. China's DF 21D has already generated more articles, especially in US naval circles, than any other single weapon in recent times, because of its purported ability to target US carrier battle groups in the Asian Pacific. China's growing intercontinental ballistic missile (ICBM) arsenal, too, makes the retaliatory capability against mainland United States increasingly credible. China is acting logically and consistently to attain its strategic aims of preventing the de jure independence of Taiwan, and building its might, slowly, to be able to challenge the United States.

India

India has often been accused of lacking in strategic vision, and as, many Indians believe, not entirely without reason. Although there has been a recent increase in the general discourse in matters concerning security and strategy, the amount of attention that the Indian polity devotes to these vital aspects needs to be far greater than it is. India has identified its threats in general terms as emanating from the possession of nuclear weapons by both its neighbors and their active mutual collusion. It has, accordingly, embarked on a program to be able to retaliate against an attack by China, though the progress is rather slow. To meet its perceived threats, India needs not large numbers, but adequate missiles with the capability to cause unacceptable damage at a range of between 4,000 and 5,000 kilometers (km). This perception has led naturally to the development of SRBMs, medium-range ballistic missiles (MRBMs), and, as recently announced, the 5,000-km range Agni. Most of India's operational missiles are of short range, which might lead one to the conclusion that its main preoccupation is with Pakistan. However, this must be looked at as being more due to the developmental process than an indicator of India's strategic priorities. India's progress can be flagged by the steady increase in the ranges of its missiles, and the preponderance of SRBMs is only partially due to its perceived requirements. This proportion is likely to change as the longer-range missiles are improved, and their serial production gathers momentum. A major reason for India's missile inventory not yet reflecting its strategic imperatives is the narrow design and engineering base for military armament production. This is restricted to just one government organization, which is responsible for the design and the development of short-, medium-, intermediate- and long-range missiles, cruise missiles, submarine-launched ballistic missiles (SLBMs), and missile defence. The planned Indian missile force architecture is rational and in line with strategic needs, but it is a few years behind the stage where it could have been, because of inadequate human and material resource utilization; the private sector has still to be brought meaningfully into the design and production chain.

Pakistan

Pakistan's force planning is facilitated by its relatively uncomplicated strategic threat evaluation. Pakistan's single-point focus and the ease with which it has circumvented international laws to acquire its missile force have enabled it to meet its basic strategic requirements in a very short time, and Pakistan's acquisition of longer-range missiles has expanded and improved its capability.

In contrast to India, Pakistan's missile force is wellmatched with its needs. Pakistan has missiles of the ranges required, and its medium-range missiles are ready to be operationalized. The development of the country's short- and medium-range missiles has progressed almost in parallel, giving the overall system structure a balanced look. Simultaneously, Pakistan is developing (acquiring) land attack cruise missiles of both the ground- and air-launched variety, and a sea-based version is reportedly planned. A major factor is that Pakistan's missiles were supplied wholesale by China and Korea, and even the production factories were built by them. Also, Pakistan seems to have had no economic problems, since these supplies come under special financial arrangements with China—not to mention the generous aid given by the United States for its War on Terror and the clandestine financial support from several Arab states. Pakistan's missile forces closely match its strategic needs, and it is currently engaged in expanding its cruise missile capability.

Nuclear and Missile Forces

China

China's military strategy underwent a significant change after the 1991 Gulf War. The lessons that the Chinese People's Liberation Army (PLA) drew were profound:

- The pace of modern war demands long-range offensive capability.
- Missile defense is crucial to the outcome of the war.
- Air power is central to the success of land- and sea-based operations.
- Information technology is no longer an adjunct, but the most vital component of the military's operational and technical resources.

The PLA's modernization drive was a direct outcome of the analysis of the Gulf War. At the center of the modernization was the development of long-range missiles as well as missile defense, air power, and information technology.[9]

Mark Stokes and Ian Easton, in their "Evolving Aerospace Trends in the Asia-Pacific Region," emphasize that it is the organization and structure of the force, rather than just numbers, that give it its relevance. Unlike in any other country, the centerpiece of China's deterrent is a force of nuclear-armed missiles with a core of conventional ballistic missiles under the integrated command of the Second Artillery. The authors sum up the thrust of China's aerospace strategy thus:

> Increasingly accurate conventional ballistic missiles and ground launched cruise missiles (GLCMs) are the optimal means for suppressing enemy air defense and creating a more permissive environment for subsequent conventional air operations due to their relative immunity to defense systems. In a conflict, they can be supported by electronic attack assets which reduce early warning and confuse enemy commanders. In addition, space-based, airborne, and ground-based sensors can facilitate command and control, and provide crucial strategic intelligence, theater awareness, targeting, and battle damage assessment information.[10]

China's all-round force modernization is far more ambitious than is realized by many in all respects—in numbers, in variety, in quality, and in strategic innovativeness. To cite Stokes and Easton again, the Chinese approach to the Taiwan issue is an example of what other countries with which China has had historical territorial disputes might expect. In the case of Taiwan, China has adopted a posture of continuous and low-level coercion—having established aerospace superiority and displaying the capability to blockade and invade over water. To deal with the expected US sea-based intervention, China has publicised the capability of its DF 21-D missile with a payload of over 500 kg and a range of over 2,000 km, with a circular error probable (CEP) of just 50 meters.[11]

Main Features of China's Missile Inventory

Details of China's missile force are given in Appendix 10-1, Tables 1 and 2. The important features are:

a. Of a total estimated number of about 1,300 missiles, about 1,150 are SRBMs, for which there are about 150 nuclear warheads; the rest of the SRBMs are conventionally armed. Almost all the SRBMs are ranged on the coast to meet a Taiwan contingency.

b. The remaining inventory consists of about 90 MRBMs, 20 IRBMs, and 40 ICBMs, with about 100 plus nuclear warheads between them. It is assumed that all IRBMs and ICBMs would be nuclear-armed.

c. China has built and acquired a large number of cruise missiles, including land attack cruise missiles (LACMs) and anti-ship cruise missiles (ASCMs) to cater for a confrontation with the United States over Taiwan. Some of the cruise missiles are long-range (2,000 to 3,000 km) and are nuclear capable.

d. To maintain military as well as political pressure on Taiwan, China has deployed heavy concentrations of short- and medium-range missiles in the coastal region adjacent to the Taiwan Straits.

e. Missile bases in northeastern, western, and southern China (Appendix 10-4) are equipped with MRBMs, IRBMs and LACMs that can target Japan and South Korea, Russia, and India respectively.

f. China has instituted a comprehensive modernization of its missile forces, and wherever newer versions have or are being developed, it may be presumed that progressive replacement of the older version is being undertaken.

g. China still does not have an operational sea-based deterrent. The JL 2 SLBM is under development and will have to wait for the Jin class nuclear-powered ballistic missile submarines (SSBN) to complete sea trials before it can itself undergo submerged launch tests.

Pakistan

Pakistan began its nuclear program soon after the disastrous Bangladesh war of 1971, and it has created a missile force that will reach practically the whole of India when operationalized. In the early stages, American-supplied F-16s were the primary delivery vehicles. Later, Pakistan changed over to missiles as the main delivery system, when the United States applied sanctions under the Pressler Amendment. With Pakistan now an ally of the United States in the War against Terror, F-16s are again being supplied (16 aircraft up to 2008), and the older aircraft have been taken up for refurbishing in the United States. However, ballistic and cruise missiles remain the preferred choice as nuclear weapon delivery vehicles, since they have definite advantages, not the least of which is India's lack of an operational missile defense capability.

Pakistan's acquisition of missiles began in the mid-to-late 1980s. It has been supplied a range of solid-fueled SRBMs by China. North Korea, too, has provided Pakistan with liquid-fueled missiles, reportedly in exchange for uranium enrichment technology. During the mid-1990s, a complete missile manufacturing plant was transferred to Pakistan by China, and:

> Chinese assistance most likely encompassed equipment and technology transfers in the areas of solid-fuel propellants, manufacture of airframes, re-entry thermal protection materials, post-boost vehicles, guidance and control, missile computers, integration of warheads, and the manufacture of transporter-erector launchers (TELs) for the missiles.[12]

China's assistance continued and even accelerated after the 1998 nuclear tests. It now nominally observes the Missile Technology Control Regime (MTCR) guidelines, but makes important exceptions, such as excluding cruise missiles and not counting the supply of weapons in a dismantled state that enable China to continue business as usual with Pakistan.

Main Features of Pakistan's Missile Inventory

Details of Pakistan's missile force are in Appendix 10-2, Tables 3 and 4. Its main features are:

a. The missile inventory is estimated to consist of about 85 Hatf 3 (Ghaznavi) SRBMs of 280-km range, about 40 Hatf 4 missiles of about 800-km range, and about 10 to 15 Hatf 5 (NODONG) MRBMs with a 1000-km range.

b. The Babur is a ground-launched LACM, probably the Chinese DF 10, which itself is a derivative of the US Tomahawk.[13]

c. An air-launched cruise missile, the Hatf 8, has been test-launched from a Mirage aircraft. The Hatf 8 ("Ra'ad") reportedly has a range of about 350 km. The air-launched version of the Babur is also being planned to be developed.

d. While as far as is known Pakistan does not have plans for a sea-based ballistic missile deterrent, it plans to develop a submarine-launched version of the Babur missile subsequently, to give it a sea-based deterrent in the form of an SLCM.

e. Pakistan's missiles are all of Chinese or Korean origin and design, and the country still depends heavily on China and the Democratic People's Republic of Korea (DPRK) for missile technology and hardware.

f. The Ghaznavi (M11) and Shaheen (probably M9), both SRBMs, are believed to be operational.

g. The Shaheen II (MRBM) development is complete, and induction and service trials may soon commence. Ghauri II (MRBM) development may be completed soon. Ghauri III (IRBM) is still estimated to be about 5 years further away.

The current Pakistan inventory, when fully operational, will have ground-, air- and submarine-launched components (the latter two being purely cruise missile equipped) with sufficient reach to strike any point in India.

India

After the Chinese border attack in 1962 and the nuclear test by China in 1964, India began work on nuclear explosive devices. This culminated in its "peaceful nuclear explosion" in 1974. After this bold step, India relapsed into inactivity for no known reason. About India's confused and indecisive approach to nuclear matters, the late Indian Army Chief, General Sundarji, sardonically wrote: "Between the mid-seventies and the mid-eighties India's decision-making in this regard appears to have enjoyed something halfway between a drugged sleep and a deep post-prandial slumber."[14] In the 1980s, Indian intelligence finally became aware of Pakistan's efforts to acquire nuclear weapons from China. After oblique threats by Pakistan during the Brasstacks crisis in 1982, the Indian government seemed to have been shaken into wakefulness and reviewed its options for weaponization. In 1983, Dr. Abdul Kalam, the head of the Defence Research and Development Organisation (DRDO), was tasked to develop two types of strategic ballistic missiles and three types of battlefield tactical missiles (an anti-tank missile and two anti-aircraft missiles—one short-range and one medium-range).

The program, called the Integrated Guided Missile Development Program, made progress in the next decade, and produced the 150-km SRBM Prithvi ("Earth") and the 1,500-km range IRBM Agni ("Fire"). The latter was particularly important, since it proved India's "re-entry vehicle" technology and formed the basis for longer-range Agnis of 2,000 and 3,000 km, as well as the 5,000-km range Agni that is to be developed. A supersonic cruise missile, BrahMos, has been produced by Russia and India in a joint venture. The missile, with a range of 750 km, will have all three variants (ground/air/sea launched) and is expected to enter operational service with the Army and Air Force in the near future. The naval version is still to be developed. In the last 10 years, India has made visible progress in ship- and submarine-launched missiles, and currently a 1,000-km cruise missile (Nirbhay) is also under development.[15]

Main Features of India's Missile Inventory

Details of India's missile force are in Appendix 10-3, Tables 5 and 6. The main features are:

a. Over time, India has achieved a certain degree of invulnerability to technology denial.

b. The latest test of the Agni III, specifically to test its range capability of 3,500 km, was successfully carried out on February 8, 2010. The missile is soon to be delivered to the Army.

c. Russia is collaborating with India for the production of the supersonic cruise missile BrahMos.

d. There are reports that the DRDO has completed development of the Agni IV IRBM and is going ahead directly with the Agni V, with a range of over 5000 km.[16]

e. The development of a cruise missile, Nirbhay, with a range of 1,000 km is also reported to be in progress.

South Asia and Missile Defense

The strategic implications of missile defense in relation to the stability of nuclear deterrence were a major issue of contention between the two superpowers during the Cold War, until the signing of the Anti-Ballistic Missile (ABM) Treaty in 1972. The United States withdrew unilaterally from the Treaty in 2001, causing great unease and criticism in Russia and China.

The main argument put forward in favor of missile defense is that if all countries have effective missile defense, the value of offensive nuclear weapons would be greatly diminished and would pave the way for disarmament. Another argument made was that deterrence does not work with states with irrational leaders, and their potential adversaries cannot remain defenseless.

The opponents of missile defense point out that the immediate reaction will be for the nuclear-armed countries without anti-missile defense (AMD) capability to increase their stockpiles in an effort to restore nuclear parity. Not only will the number of missiles in the total global arsenal increase, but tactics will now veer toward saturation attacks, which will present a far greater threat.[17] Russia and China strongly oppose missile defense, since they consider it a means for the United States to gain and maintain nuclear superiority, which is antithetical to nuclear stability.

There is apparent logic in the arguments of both sides, and even in the United States, the support for missile defense as a strategy is far from universal. The United States has taken the crucial step and changed its nuclear strategy to include nuclear defense as one leg of the new "strategic triad." While announcing its plans for implementation of the new strategy, the United States also simultaneously announced a unilateral reduction in its missile strength, thus dampening the validity of the argument about arms escalation.

The risk as far as South Asia is concerned is that China has already started increasing its number of deployable warheads by making its missiles multiple independently targetable, re-entry vehicle (MIRV)-capable. There is apprehension that this can cause arsenal escalation by India, and then, in response to India's, by Pakistan.[18]

The conclusion that can be drawn is not surprising: missile defense adds to the effectiveness of a country's nuclear deterrence; it is supported by states that possess or have access to the requisite technology and resources, and opposed by states that have lesser capability in these aspects. But one thing is fairly unarguable—missile defense is not a purely defensive capability, since it enhances the possessor's aggressive potential as well.

Missile Defense Policies and Capabilities

China

When the United States decided to withdraw from the ABM Treaty and embark on developing a national missile defense system, China was critical of the step for the same reasons as Russia was. But the level of protest rose sharply when the Nuclear Posture Review of the George W. Bush administration formally included nuclear defense in US strategy as one leg of the new strategic triad. China denounced this as a retrograde measure, which would increase the risk of nuclear war. There were vague rumblings that China's cooperation with the United States on issues such as the Nonproliferation Treaty (NPT), MTCR, and Fissile Material Cutoff Treaty (FMCT) would be reviewed. China's apprehension would obviously be that its small arsenal could be neutralized, leaving it completely defenseless against the United States.[19]

AMD Capability

In comparison with India, China has a head start in missile defense technology. According to an article in the website, SinoDefence.com, as early as in 1963, Mao had ordered the creation of a strategic force capable of both offense and defense.[20] A directive was issued to commence "Project 640," as it was called in 1964, and infrastructure was built in about 5 years for the design and development of anti-ballistic missiles. Considerable work was done on mono-pulse and phased array radars, and a network of early warning ground radar stations was established. The signing of the ABM Treaty by the United States and the USSR diluted the urgency of this project, which was finally cancelled in 1980 by Deng Hsiao Ping. The radar network was converted to serve the growing space program.

China later re-energized its missile defense program, probably when the United States unilaterally withdrew from the ABM Treaty in 2001. In 2004, China purchased 120 S-300P interceptor missile systems (North Atlantic Treaty Organization [NATO] designation SA-10) from Russia and soon produced its own versions—the HQ10 and HQ15 systems—as well as the HQ9 system, which is thought to have borrowed Patriot technology.

On January 12, 2011, China carried out a successful high-altitude interception of a ground-launched missile within its own territory. Analysts differ on the type of missile that was fired, but it was probably an HQ9 missile (based on the DF21 series) with kinetic kill capability. All indications, therefore, are that China is pursuing the creation of an offensive-defensive strategic capability vigorously and has capabilities across the spectrum to attack missiles in the cruise phase to the terminal defense. China historically has depended on the USSR (and now Russia) for periodic injections of new technology, which it then internalizes and is able to develop and mass-produce the end product on the acquired technology base. To accelerate the creation of its AMD base, which now appears to have become an urgent aim, China may well resort to more assistance from Russia for technological upgrades rather than depend entirely on its own research and development. China appears to have responded to the US AMD strategy with a surge in the national effort to build a modern missile defense capability, rather than just resort to increasing its missile arsenal.

Pakistan

Predictably, Pakistan has followed China's cue and opposes AMD. There are good reasons for this response. First, regardless of its being on the American side in the War on Terror, Pakistan is China's strategic ally, and it is inconceivable that it would take a contrary position on such a major issue. Second—and this would be an overriding consideration—

Pakistan considers its nuclear arsenal the equalizer in its military balance against India, and it is only to be expected that it would seek to oppose any move to change the nuclear relativities.

AMD Capability

Pakistan has made no moves toward developing a missile defense system. It already depends heavily on financial support that the United States provides for the War against Terror, and the economic burden of research, development, acquisition, and maintenance of an AMD system is not an option in its current state. Pakistan would have to depend on China for the acquisition of one, which China itself is in the early stages of developing. Pakistan is much more likely to wait for China to transfer the systems to it in the fullness of time. In the meanwhile, it continues to condemn missile defense development efforts by India.

India

After some initial reservations, India supported the US AMD strategy when the United States announced its proposed Theater Missile Defense (TMD) plans simultaneously with significant missile cuts. In the Indian perception, the US AMD policy represented a shift of emphasis to defensive deterrence, which is more in tune with India's political preferences. From India's point of view, the TMD strategy not only made it possible to avoid, or at least reduce, the enormous expense involved in building a large arsenal of IRBMs and ICBMs; the strategy also jelled with the two major precepts of India's own promulgated nuclear doctrine: no first use and a credible minimum deterrent. India's stance on the AMD policy was not without its benefits. The Bush administration cleared the Israeli Green Pine radar system for sale to India, and also entered into talks with India on cooperation in missile defense. An agreement entitled a "New Framework for the US-India Defense Relationship" was signed by Secretary of Defense Donald Rumsfeld and the Indian Defence Minister Pranab Mukherjee on June 28, 2005, which specifically mentions a commitment to collaborate in missile defense.[21] Though the agreement was signed 5 years ago, there is thus far no tangible evidence of any collaboration in this field—a fact that may be due to Pakistan's objections to the United States. There are several published reports about India's efforts to develop an anti-missile missile, and from current indications, it is clear that India has decided to build its own missile defense capability. How extensive the coverage will be is an open question.

AMD Capability

While India has had plans to develop a missile defense system for some time, progress has only been seen in the last few years. The first test was an exo-atmospheric interception at an altitude of 48 km in November 2006, followed by an endo-atmospheric launch in December 2008 at an altitude of 15 km. In March 2009, a third successful interception was carried out, reportedly at a much greater altitude than the March 2006 test.[22] A fourth test launch conducted in March 2011 failed, because of one of the missiles veering from its course. According to news reports, the test will be conducted again in June.[23]

The early warning and tracking radars that comprise other vital parts of the missile defense system were acquired from Israel. Three "Green Pine" systems have been purchased, and the missile that complements them is still under development. The Arrow 2 missile, which was part of the original system, was not cleared by the United States, since it falls in Category I of the MTCR. A compatible missile will have to be acquired or developed from within existing Indian designs. India has the developmental capability, but in the available time frame, it is likely that, while continuing with its developmental efforts, it will seek assistance in specific technology areas. India has thus embarked on a comprehensive missile defense program to cover all stages of an incoming missile's trajectory, but it will probably be some years before India can field an operational missile defense system.

Existing and Potential Missile Competitions

The missile competitions and rivalries among India, China, and Pakistan are complex: each country's missile force architecture is based on its own threat perception and world view. China has global aspirations, and the United States is its main rival and potential adversary. If China builds a capability sufficient for its objectives against the United States, then that capability will also be sufficient for it to deal with its lesser threats. China does not compete with India directly; it does this obliquely, by regulating the flow of strategic arms and material to Pakistan.

India's ambitions are less grandiose, and limited to maintaining an adequate defense capability against its hostile northern and western neighbors. The threat posed by China is the main driver that determines India's missile force architecture. An area of doubt is the quantitative interpretation of India's aim of a credible minimum deterrent.

Pakistan's view is focused on India's capability; it aspires to buildup its missile force to equal India's. As India seeks to balance its capability with China, Pakistan perceives an imbalance in relation to India and acts to rectify it. China and Pakistan are allied against India for strategic, if not military, purposes; this unusual triangle is not a stable one, with two sides pitted against the third.

The Federation of American Scientists, in its "Status of World's Nuclear Forces" for 2010 (Appendix 10-5, Table 10-7), estimates that China possesses about 240 warheads; India, 60-80; and Pakistan, 70-90.[24] The number of warheads in Pakistan's arsenal has overtaken India's.

With the commissioning of two new reactors at the Chinese-built facility at Khushab, Pakistan's plutonium production capacity is expected to rise fivefold. The motivation could be threefold: to produce a large number of compact warheads that would be needed for the new long-range cruise missiles, to build new warheads for extensive deployment as battlefield weapons, or to buildup a stockpile of fissile materials so that Pakistan can subsequently acquiesce to joining the FMCT. This combination of factors poses the very real danger of escalating stockpiles beyond the requirements commensurate with Pakistan's nuclear doctrine, which is yet to be formally declared.

Missile competition in South Asia is worrisome, because conditions are so different that harking back to history is of little benefit. The only precedent we have to go by is the US-USSR one, and that is not wholly relevant for a number of reasons. First, the two Cold War adversaries were continents apart, and that eliminated the risk caused by daily confrontations, stressed personnel, and local overreactions. Also, the rivals in that case were seasoned "Cold Warriors," with a sophisticated set of rules and layered formal and informal communication to reduce the possibility of mistaken launches. Finally, the technology in the Indo-Pakistan case is rudimentary, without multilayered fail-safe overrides.

Sino-Indian Context

The nuclear situation between India and China is presently a stable one, with neither side given to exaggerated responses or threatening postures with each other. The dialogue between these two countries is more balanced and, notwithstanding the occasional unfriendly and even hostile rhetoric, exchanges between the two countries continue at the highest political level. The risk of an unauthorized or inadvertent nuclear flare-up between India and China is therefore a remote one for the time being. But it has been the Indian experience that Sino-Indian relations have their peaks and troughs, completely dictated by Chinese tactical perceptions. At times, the Chinese adopt a reasonable attitude and suggest waiting for a "wiser generation"; at others, they raise the tempo of their rhetoric in their Government media. Chinese continuity and tenacity of purpose are proverbial, compared with other states. As Stokes and Easton have commented, China might well turn to Japan or India after having settled the Taiwan issue.[25]

The problem in the Sino-Indian context is somewhat different—it lies in the huge disparity between the force levels of the two sides, which raises the question of whether India will be sucked into an arms race.

A reference to Appendix 10-3, Table 10-5, will show that India has an estimated total of 150 missiles of which about 130 are SRBMs of the 350-km range and below. The Agni series of missiles is under production only in the shorter range (Agni II MRBM) version as the IRBMs (Agni III and Agni V) are still under development.

In comparison, China (Appendix 10-1, Table 10-1) has over 1,100 SRBMs, about 90 MRBMs, 20 IRBMs, and about 40 ICBMs. While the numerical superiority alone is vast (about 1,300 to 150), the adverse ratio (for India) in the number of missiles that each can bring to bear on the other's targets is much more pronounced—since Indian missiles that can reach Chinese targets are very few at present, and even these cannot reach the value targets in the Chinese Northeast and East. In contrast (Appendix 10-4, China - Missile Deployment), China has the DF 3, 4 IRBMs, and DF 21 MRBMs bases located in the Qinghai province of Tibet (distance to Delhi approximately 2,500 km), and the same missiles together with DF 5 ICBMs in Yunnan Province in Southern China, which is also approximately the same distance.

In short, there can be no comparison between the ballistic missile forces of the two countries. India has therefore taken the pragmatic approach that it cannot and will not seek parity with China, and that its nuclear force levels will be built up only to the extent that its "minimum credible deterrent" doctrine requires. India has declined to specify a numerical ceiling, since this would obviously be related to China's force structure, albeit at a lower level. But the fact that parity is not an objective has been stated at fairly high official levels.[26] If India were to attempt parity with China, it would set in train an arms race that would be disastrous to it from every point of view. With the Indian economy buoyant after decades of stagnation and the stated government target of a gross domestic product (GDP) growth in double digits, it is certain that no Indian Government will sacrifice the prospect of economic progress in a futile pursuit of arms parity with China. Thus, the balance of offensive ballistic missiles is likely to be retained at some notional ratio of sufficiency, whose figure would obviously not be in the public domain.

As stated above, the current situation appears stable, and there is no looming arms race between India and China on the horizon, mainly because of India's limited objectives. But there is the uneasy prospect of the border dispute being raised at some point in the future at a time of China's choosing, which will involve the kind of military and nuclear coercion that Taiwan is experiencing today. If that situation arises, India will have three options: to degrade China's offensive capability by enhancing its own air and missile defence capability, to increase its own offensive capability, or to negotiate a voluntary reduction of arsenals on both sides before matters reach a crisis point. The first option involves the creation of a wide area or several local missile shields and also the building up of a huge conventional military force. The second will result in the arms race that India seeks to avoid at all costs. So there appears to be only one viable option—to reach an agreement on missile limits.

A Global INF?

Such limits could be quantitative, as in the Strategic Arms Limitation Treaty (SALT) and Strategic Offensive Reductions Treaty (SORT), or qualitative, as in the INF Treaty. The INF Treaty served to give momentum to the considerable progress that has been made in arms reduction. Like every good treaty, it left all parties a little dissatisfied, but with much to be content with. The Soviets were able to achieve the virtual elimination of nuclear missile-borne weapons from Europe. The Europeans were happy, because they were not under threat from Soviet IRBMs, especially the SS-20 missiles. The British were relieved that ground launched cruise missile (GLCMs) were not going to be stationed in the United Kingdom (UK). The United States was pleased to have reduced the USSR's arsenal by 1,800-odd warheads against about 850 of its own, and to roll back the highly accurate MIRV SS-20 missiles at the same time. But now the Russians have repeatedly said that they do not believe that the INF Treaty is relevant anymore, since it was signed in a different era—with Europe divided into the Warsaw Pact and NATO. Now some Eastern Bloc countries have been enrolled in NATO, and Russia needs IRBMs—probably to be able to deploy them as a counter to Chinese missiles deployed against Russia. Russia is pressing for the globalization of the INF, and has expressed its intention to withdraw from the Treaty, as it is entitled to do if its national interests are threatened.[27] If a global INF were to come into being, it would mean that the embargo on missiles between 500- and 5,500-km range would apply to Britain, France, and China as well. It would make no difference to Britain and France, who do not have any land-based missiles. But the embargo applies in a big way to China, since, in their present form, the INF criteria would eliminate all but a handful of China's missiles. Clearly any scheme modeled on the INF would have to be specially tailored to make even a beginning in reducing China's threat perceptions, which cover the total range spectrum, from short (Russia, South Korea, Taiwan, and Japan) to medium and intermediate (Russia, India, and Japan), to Intercontinental (United States, Europe). In fact, the specified intermediate range of 5,500 km would mean that India and China would practically be in the "proscribed zone" from each other, and the shorter range proscription (less than 500 km) would make India and Pakistan weaponless against each other except for short-range ballistic missiles (SRBMs). The SRBMs, as is argued later in this chapter, is the category that needs to be eliminated. So there do not appear to be grounds for optimism about successfully devising range-based missile elimination criteria that will meet the security needs of the South Asian countries.

Missile Defense Competition

As far as a balance in the defensive missile force levels is concerned, one can surmise that here, too, there will be a restrained approach. The same governing factors apply—China's nuclear perceptions are not predicated on Indian actions and policies, since its threat perceptions are entirely focused on the United States. This would probably result in China concentrating its effort on building an extensive missile shield over its vital nuclear assets to keep its retaliatory capability intact. Since India cannot afford to indulge in an arms race, the same philosophy of sufficiency rather than parity will be the guide. Current Indian efforts to establish a missile defense cannot raise a shield over the entire country, and it is likely that the objective of missile defense may have to be concentrated on survival of the country's strategic leadership and retaliation capability—an approach very similar to China's vis-à-vis the United States.

Consequently, missile defense development by both sides may not change the equation very much, with missile defenses providing an added element of confidence in an ensured retaliatory capability rather than immunity from a strike.

India-Pakistan Context

The dangerous competition in the subcontinental context is the deployment of SRBMs by both sides. SRBMs, being of shorter range, would necessarily have to be forward-deployed away from the direct supervision and control of higher political and military leaders. Pakistan's doctrine, which has not been formally promulgated but has been surmised by gleaning statements from military and civilian sources, does envisage the use of nuclear weapons in a conventional scenario. Stemming from this use, it is unlikely that Pakistan will resort to a first strike "out of the blue." It envisages use of nuclear weapons as the decisive extension of the conventional battle, if that battle is going unfavorably from its point of view. In other words, risk is heightened when hostilities have broken out or are imminent.

Short-range ballistic missiles, whether nuclear or conventionally war-headed—if used to complement conventional forces—will be a major source of risk, since they may be used in the heat of battle. There is no way of distinguishing between an incoming conventionally tipped SRBM and a nuclear one. Any incoming ballistic missile will therefore be assumed to be a nuclear strike, and the defender will act accordingly, starting a nuclear exchange.

Thus, the biggest risk in the India-Pakistan context is an accidental, mistaken, or unauthorized missile launch, or the evaluation of an incoming conventional missile as a nuclear attack or the precursor of one.

Risk Factors in Indo-Pak Context

1. *Deployment and Delegation.* With a long common border and its geographic characteristics, Pakistan may choose to disperse its missiles widely, and the operational preference would be for delegative rather than assertive control. Pakistani statements emphasise that the country's nuclear weapons are its great equalizer, and that they will be brought into use in a critical situation. Over time, this military teaching can erode the inhibitive element and condition the authorized commander to err on the side of aggression.
2. *Cross-border Infiltration and Artillery Fire.* Indian and Pakistani troops are closely deployed across the line of control, and there are frequent cross-border firings (usually to cover the injection of infiltrators). This adds to the stress levels of personnel, and flash points are lowered. In a frequently crisis-ridden scenario, the cross-border firings increase the danger of an accidental or maverick launch.
3. *Exploitation of Militants and Irregulars.* From the very inception of the state, Pakistan has resorted to the exploitation of nonstate militants to conduct deniable military operations. On occasion, military personnel have conducted attacks disguised as irregulars.

This is well-known and documented, and was clearly exposed during the Kargil war, when so-called Mujahideen were found to be soldiers without uniforms.[28] While not directly presenting a missile-related risk, such incidents are a potential trigger to the outbreak of hostilities, which could escalate into missile and nuclear exchanges.

4. *Recourse to Tactical Nuclear Weapons.* The frequent statements by Pakistan about the need for nuclear weapons to balance India's conventional strength give rise to the belief that battlefield nuclear weapons may be part of the Pakistani warfighting strategy. This would considerably lower thresholds and vitiate all other nuclear restraint measures. Recourse to the use of tactical or battlefield nuclear weapons will inevitably lead to nuclear escalation, and there would be a serious risk of a full-scale nuclear exchange.

5. *Ambiguity as Doctrine.* Some Pakistani experts propagate the notion that ambiguity is a part of deterrence. They have also said that nuclear weapons may be used if certain red lines, which are not officially specified, are crossed. This is a dangerous policy: in the nuclear context, while clarity enhances deterrence, ambiguity makes risks more acute and should be eliminated.

Risk-Reduction Measures—India and Pakistan

Both India and Pakistan have shown awareness of the ever-present danger of war between them. Since 1949, a number of measures have been instituted to lessen the risk of a border incident escalating to war. There are a number of confidence-building measures (CBMs) in force, which range across a wide spectrum of subjects, from avoidance of attacks on each others' nuclear facilities to advance notification of military exercises and also of missile launches. But there is acceptance on both sides that the observance has been somewhat less than meticulous.[29] The surest way to mitigate the risk of nuclear exchanges is obviously to address the issue of the risk of war, at which many of these CBMs are aimed. But taking the situation as it is, one approach could be to focus only on those aspects that are missile-related.

Eliminate SRBMs

A major step forward could be the elimination of SRBMs. As has been argued, the very first detection of a ballistic missile launch, even conventionally tipped, will initiate an unintended nuclear exchange. It is this writer's view that these launches complicate an existing situation, and have no flexibility or graduated response capability that is so essential in the control of a nuclear situation. The elimination of SRBMs by both sides will considerably reduce the risks.

Eliminate Tactical Nuclear Weapons

Tactical nuclear weapons, including nuclear mines and other static nuclear explosive devices, must be defined, eliminated if existing, and proscribed. The countries must come to an agreement that such weapons will not be made or used.

Revisit the 'Third Way'

George Perkovich, in a 1993 article titled "A Nuclear Third Way in South Asia," had proposed a rollback to a state of nonweaponized deterrence.[30] Much water has flowed down the Ganga and the Indus since then, and many of the proposed measures are no longer possible. Weaponization has occurred, ballistic missiles have been developed and deployed, and the subcontinent is witnessing the development of anti-missile defense systems. But it may be worthwhile to revisit this subject. At the time it was published, the article had suggested that the preparation of missiles could be kept limited to a defined level. Missiles in peacetime are kept in storage separate from their warheads, and the missile airframes themselves are not ready for immediate launch. The launch of a missile from its cold, dissembled state requires several steps: The warheads and missiles have to be separately prepared and the missiles fueled before they are brought together to be mated at the launch site and loaded on the delivery system (the launcher or aircraft) and subjected to checks before and after each stage. If an agreement can be reached to pre-define a stage beyond which the missiles will not be prepared, it would eliminate much of a risk in normal times. Further, thought can be given to the introduction of time buffers, so that the entire process is deliberate, and there is the possibility of recall at each stage.

Once this is agreed upon, the question of verification can be discussed. Perhaps a separate communication channel for missile warnings can be manned or activated when needed.

Need to Work Toward Agreement on Crucial Principles

Concerted efforts are required to reach agreement on the principles that deterrence need not be "warhead for warhead" and that asymmetrical deterrence is a valid concept in the modern age. This can be a first step toward agreeing on ratios between the nuclear forces of the countries concerned. It is relevant here that any discourse on this aspect must recognize that the China-India-Pakistan equation does not stand in isolation, and must be viewed as part of the global nuclear balance.

Conclusion

Countries of the subcontinent, for better or for worse, have acquired nuclear weapons capability. This is the reality, and management of nuclear risk must proceed from this datum. Internal political stability is crucial to reach a level of mutual confidence. At present, both countries have their hands full with internal armed insurgence. In Pakistan, the threat of nuclear missiles being forcibly taken by enemies of the state cannot be disregarded, notwithstanding the conciliatory statements in this regard from US and Pakistani sources.

A major requirement is the cessation of all cross-border terrorist activity, which is aided and abetted by Pakistan. India has suffered seven heinous attacks from across the border in the last 8 years, and a repetition of such incidents may have an unpredictable response.

Transparency and clarity are the cornerstones of nuclear stability, and policies of studied ambiguity are highly risk-prone. China is playing a partisan game in South Asia, and must be involved in efforts to manage and ameliorate the critical situation in the subcontinent.

Despite enormous odds, India and Pakistan are still engaged in dialogue at the top levels of Government. These efforts lend hope and must persist if the grave risk of nuclear conflict is to be avoided.

Endnotes

1. In this chapter, China is included in the term "South Asia," because of its close proximity and involvement in the security issues of the region.
2. "Yahya and Co. feared that Mujib's ascendancy would mean far greater autonomy for the long-exploited East Pakistanis, and the Pakistani army ruthlessly moved to crush the Bengali movement." "Pakistan: Mujib's Secret Trial," *TIME magazine*, August 23, 1971, available from *www.time.com/time/magazine/article/0,9171,877251,00.html.*
3. "It is now officially estimated that refugees will swell to 12 million by the end of the year. The cost to the Indian government for the fiscal year ending next March 31 may run as high as $830 million." "East Pakistan: Even the Skies Weep," *TIME magazine*, October 25, 1971, available from *www.time.com/time/magazine/article/0,9171,877316-3,00.html.*
4. Megha Bahree, "China in Pakistan," *Forbes Magazine,* February 7, 2009, available from *www.forbes.com/2009/07/02/ruba-china-pakistan-trade-sidebar.html.*

5. Claude Arpi, "Missiles in Tibet," *Indian Defence Review,* Vol. 23, No. 3, July-September 2008.

6. "A Brief History of Pakistan's Nuclear Program," Washington, DC: Federation of American Scientists, December 11, 2002, available from *www.fas.org/nuke/guide/pakistan/nuke/.*

7. [Musharraf's] "Visit to China," *The Daily Times* (Lahore, Pakistan), November 3, 2003.

8. "China is threat No.1, says Fernandes," *Hindustan Times*, New Delhi, India, May 3, 1998.

9. You E. Ji, *The Armed Forces of China*, St. Leonards, New South Wales, Australia: Allen & Unwin, 1999, p. 11.

10. Mark A. Stokes and Ian Easton, "Evolving Aerospace Trends in the Asia-Pacific Region—Implications for Stability in the Taiwan Straits and beyond," Arlington, VA: The Project 2049 Institute, May 27 2010, available from *project2049.net/documents/aerospace_trends_asia_pacific_region_stokes_easton.pdf.*

11. Stokes and Easton.

12. "Missile," *Pakistan Country Profile*, Washington, DC: Nuclear Threat Initiative, available from *www.nti.org/e_research/profiles/Pakistan/Missile/index.html*.

13. *Ibid.*

14. General K. Sundarji, *Blind Men of Hindoostan-Indo-Pak Nuclear War,* New Delhi, India: UBS Publishers and Distributors Ltd., 1993, p. xiv.

15. Robert S. Norris and Hans M. Kristensen, "Indian Nuclear Forces, 2008," *Bulletin of the Atomic Scientists*, Vol. 64, No. 5, November/December 2008, available from *bos.sagepub.com/content/64/5/38.full.pdf+html.*

16. "India will conduct its first test of the over-5,000 km range Agni-V missile within a year's time, top Defence Research and Development Organisation (DRDO) officials said on Wednesday. . . . The DRDO director-general, Dr. V.K. Saraswat, said that the Agni-V missile is 'out of the drawing board' and that 'testing and evaluation of sub-systems' of the missile is currently on." See "Agni-V Test in a Yr, Say DRDO Officials," *The Asian* Age, February 10, 2010, available from *www.asianage.com/content/agni-v-test-yr-say-drdo-officials*.

17. Oliver Jones, "Ballistic Missile Defence in the 21st Century," *E-International Relations*, March 13, 2010, available from *www.e-ir.info/?p=3462*.

18. "Why CND Opposes Missile Defence," Campaign for Nuclear Disarmament, London, UK: Mordechai Vanunu House, available from *www.cnduk.org/index2.php?option=com_content&do_pdf=1&id=108.*

19. Dr. Dingli Shen, "A Chinese Perspective on National Missile Defense," Shanghai, China: Institute for Environmental and Energy Research, Fudan University, available from *ieer.org/resource/commentary/a-chinese-perspective-on-national-missile-defense/.*

20. "Project 640: China's National Missile Defence in the '70s," *SinoDefence.com*, April 11, 2009, available from *www.sinodefence.com/special/airdefence/project640.asp.*

21. "New Framework for the US-India Defense Relationship," Document Signed by US Secretary Rumsfeld and Indian Minister Mukherjee, June 28, 2005, Washington, DC: National Defense University, Military Education Research Library Network (MERLN), available from *merln.ndu.edu/index.cfm?secID=175&pageID=3&type=section.*

22. TS Subramaniam, *"Hat-Trick of Hits," Frontline*, Vol. 26, Issue 7, March 26, 2010.

23. "India to Re-test Ballistic Missile Defence Shield," *Thaindia News*, April 11, 2010, available from *www.thaindian.com/newsportal/sci-tech/india-to-re-test-ballistic-missile-defence-shield_100346454.html.*

24. "Status of World Nuclear Forces 2010," Arlington, VA: Federation of American Scientists, available from *www.fas.org/programs/ssp/nukes/nuclearweapons/nukestatus.html.*

25. Stokes and Easton, "Evolving Aerospace Trends," 2010.

26. Kanti Bajpai, "India's Nuclear Posture After Pokhran II," *International Studies* (New Delhi), Vol. 37, No 4, October-December 2000, citing George Perkovich, *India's Nuclear Bomb: The Impact on Global Proliferation*, Berkeley, CA: University of California Press, 1999, p. 440. Cites a "BJP official" as saying, "We do not seek parity with China; we don't have the resources, and we don't have the will. What we are seeking is a minimum deterrent." The remark may have been made by Brajesh Mishra, Principal Secretary to the Prime Minister (and later, National Security Advisor). See C. Raja Mohan's reference to a similar statement, which he attributes to Mishra, in his article, "Sino-Indian Nuclear Talks Vital," *The Hindu*, November 3, 1998.

27. "INF Treaty Developments-2010," in *Treaty between the United States and the Union of Soviet Socialist Republics on the Elimination of Their Immediate-Range and Shorter-Range Missiles (INF Treaty)*, Washington, DC: Nuclear Threat Initiative, available from *www.nti.org/treaties-and-regimes/treaty-between-the-united-states-of-america-*

and-the-union-of-soviet-socialist-republics-on-the-elimination-of-their-intermediate-range-and-shorter-range-missiles/.

There (have) . . . been continuing concerns in Russia that if no other countries join the Treaty, it may no longer prove useful. On 17 February, a diplomatic-military source in Moscow said that "Russia and the USA are planning to go back to the issue of prospects for keeping or revoking the INF treaty after a new START Treaty has been signed.

28. Seth C. Jones and C. Christine Fair, *Counterinsurgency in Pakistan*, Santa Monica, CA: Rand Corporation, Rand National Security Division, 2010. In Chap. 2 of this Rand-funded monograph published in May 2010, the authors give details of Pakistan's use of Mujahideens, militants, and irregulars to further its "Foreign Policy Objectives" in Kashmir.
29. A discussion on current CBMs is included in Neil Joecke, "The Indo-Pakistani Nuclear Confrontation: Lessons from the Past, Contingencies for the Future," in Henry Sokolski, ed., *Pakistan's Nuclear Future: Reining in the Risk*, Carlisle, PA: Strategic Studies Institute, US Army War College, December 2009.
30. George Perkovich, "A Nuclear Third Way in South Asia," *Foreign Policy*, Issue 91, Summer 1993, p. 85.

Chapter 11

Prospects for Indian and Pakistani Arms Control

Feroz Hassan Khan

The views expressed herein are solely the author's personal views and do not represent either the Pakistani Government or the US Department of Defense. The author is grateful to Nick M. Masellis, National Security Agency (NSA) Research Associate, MS in Defense Analysis, for his research assistance.

Introduction

The regional dynamic in South Asia is both extravagant and complicated. For centuries, various empires have risen, thrived, and fallen as numerous wars and clashes for control over resources spread across the geography. South Asian history writ large has seen hypothetical borders drawn several times over, leaving open the questions of the viability of state control and dealing with perpetuating ethnic tensions. Though the great partition of India in 1947 ought to have politically resolved communal disharmony, the haste of British withdrawal constituted a geopolitical quagmire that has resulted in an "enduring rivalry" between the nations of India and Pakistan that has lasted for more than 60 years.[1]

The contemporary security climate in the region has exasperated this historical precedent of protracted conflict, which has, in turn, nurtured an environment that remains immune to building trust and confidence.

Since the demonstration of their nuclear capabilities, both India and

Pakistan have increased the risk of wars, cross-border arms buildups, and the lack of sustained peace dialogue, either bilaterally or under the aegis of any third party or international organization. Moreover, the regional security environment breeds broader strategic anxieties in both India and Pakistan, which makes the likelihood of conventional war between the two nuclear-armed neighbors exponentially higher than anywhere else in the world.

Thus, the ensuing regional culture leans more toward military competition, as opposed to strategic restraint and conflict resolution (the logical course for strategic stability). Clearly, considering the prospects of arms control and confidence-building measures (CBMs) in the midst of this current regional and international climate remains problematic all to itself, but when strategic imbalances are further influenced by the singular perceptions of the predominant powers in the region, addressing the various grievances becomes ever more convoluted.

Despite these geopolitical calamities, this chapter examines the prospects of arms control and CBMs in South Asia within the next decade. To provide a sustainable and realistic effort toward the latter, the first section will examine the strategic anxieties of India and Pakistan, respectively. The second section will be an overview of treaties and CBMs that have been attempted in the past (some of which are still applicable today), reviewing a trend of crisis and bilateral missteps. The third analyzes the Lahore Memorandum of Understanding (MOU) of 1998 and the Strategic Restraint Regime (SRR) proposals, and how such measures can be more effective in the future. The fourth presents three possible trajectories that the region might take and suggests new ways forward that can create an environment malleable to pragmatic CBMs and arms control measures feasible in the foreseeable future.

Strategic Anxieties

India's Strategic Anxieties

As previously suggested, the dynamics associated with the endemic rivalry between India and Pakistan must be viewed through the broader lens of regional politics and security. This becomes more apparent when we consider India's perception of Chinese strategic objectives in the region. In order to propose any realistic CBMs for the future, such perceptions must be factored into the overall South Asian security equation.

In general, India believes China is encircling the country by establishing special partnerships with many of India's smaller neighbors.

Specifically, India is irked by the growing relationship evolving between China and Pakistan, which India believes has a singular purpose of bringing down its natural rise as an aspiring global power.

One of the more onerous issues is the perception that has come to be known as the "String of Pearls."[2] To provide a frame of reference, Pakistan's Makran coastline has strategic significance, which offers Pakistan options to counter India's projection of power in the Indian Ocean. Pakistan has already shown signs that it is moving to develop broader air and naval capabilities. The buildup of the Gwadar commercial port along this coast—assisted by China—exacerbates India's anxieties, and provides Pakistan with broader strategic utility. For the Chinese, the buildup provides a potential access to energy pipelines that would "unlock trade routes to the market and energy supplies of Central Asia," with less risk.[3]

This is significant, since India is geographically restricted in its access to the East as well as the West, due to the physical presence of Bangladesh and Pakistan, as well as the Himalayas to the North. In this regard, India's access to Southwest Asia runs into a geographical barrier because of its rivalry with Pakistan. Similarly, India succumbs to constraints from East Asia via Bangladesh/Burma, which physically block India's access to those markets. With China also entering the scene with growing presence along the Makran Coast, the situation from India's perspective becomes ever more tenuous. This, in turn, forces India to rely on its maritime capabilities in order to maintain trade routes and logistics between its continental shores and the rest of the world, making up for this strategic handicap.

As a part of its expanded naval presence, India has launched ballistic missile subs and other naval capabilities that can act as an extended security arm for protecting its various trade routes, as well as enable a third-strike capability (in addition to its land-based and air assets). India's growing presence in the maritime environment, in conjunction with its overall strategic rise, makes its smaller neighbors nervous. This strategic apprehension creates a ripple effect across the region, in which the smaller countries move closer to external alliances in order to balance India's rising power.

Additionally, India believes China is propping up Pakistan's nuclear and military capabilities in areas where Western technologies are not providing the need. In particular, India is under the impression that Pakistan is taking advantage of America's involvement in Afghanistan, which places it in a unique position to acquire strategic capabilities and other political remunerations.

Regardless of these concerns, India's strategic calculus of structural and conventional force advantages over Pakistan was neutralized (to an extent) ever since Pakistan demonstrated its nuclear capability in 1998. Many Indian strategists believe, however, that this nuclear hedge provides Pakistan with the ability to conduct asymmetric warfare against India boldly without fear of reprisal. This reinforces India's belief that as long as Pakistan can keep India engaged inwardly through insurgencies (as well as build upon its strategic alliances with the United States and China), India's rise to power will be curtailed.

Pakistan's Strategic Anxieties

Generally speaking, Pakistan's strategic anxieties in the region are a mirror reflection of India—vis-à-vis the other half of the "enduring rivalry." For Pakistan, however, the objective is threefold and simplistic in nature: national survival; remain a relevant actor in the region; and refuse to be marginalized by India.

Pakistan is also a country that wields vast manpower, with a population of 170 million; strong strategic assets in the shape of nuclear weapons and natural resources; a half million-size conventional army; and as a proactive player in the Muslim world. The latter status not only serves as a means to connect with the Muslim community on a bilateral sense, but helps Pakistan play a role in bridging Islamic countries with China and United States. Despite such macro-level accolades, the intense rivalry and competition with India over the past 60 years has made Pakistan India-phobic and "paranoid" concerning a variety of issues.

Much like India's concerns over the geographic firewall that restricts its land accessibility to the East and West, so does Pakistan interpret India's foreign policy maneuvers as geopolitically encircling the state. As India increases its influence and presence in Afghanistan through a slew of consulates, Pakistan considers these developments hostile to its interests. India has also established a strategically located air base in Tajikistan (Ayni Air Base in Dushanbe), which also adds to these suspicions. Furthermore, India's investment in the Iranian port of Chabahar—50 miles West of Gwadar Port—and construction of roads through Zahedan into Afghanistan, adds additional tension in an area that is essential for transporting goods and energy to a host of countries. All of these moves are, respectively, viewed as encircling Pakistan.

There are also operational issues that hinder Pakistan's strategic balance on its eastern and western borders. India's strategic orientation remains toward Pakistan, where the bulk of its armed forces are deployed.

As a result, since 1948, Indian and Pakistani troops remain deployed—eyeball to eyeball—along the Line of Control (LOC) in Kashmir. On the opposite side of its border, Pakistan's anxieties are no more apparent than in the quantity of internal strife that has embroiled it in multiple insurgencies and instabilities along its frontier territory. In sum, Pakistan is caught between striking a balance of dealing with India and crushing multiple insurgencies, while still retaining interests in Afghanistan.

The ultimate nightmare for Pakistan is to live with two hostile neighbors—India in the East and Afghanistan in the West. Pakistan believes that unless conflict is resolved with India, it has no choice but to seek balance with an ethnically diverse and friendly government in Kabul—a government that does not conduct negative bidding on the behest of powers hostile to Pakistan and further destabilizes the already troubled western border areas. On the contrary, if Afghanistan becomes a strategic satellite of India's geopolitical outmaneuverings, in addition to the ongoing problems in Jammu and Kashmir, a perpetual state of tension and crisis will continue to loom between the three countries.

Overarching these regional issues is Pakistan's fear that its long-term ally, the United States, may eventually turn against it under Indian influence. The US-India nuclear deal was an event that has exacerbated these anxieties, viewed by Pakistan as skewing the imbalance in greater favor of the already powerful India. In fact, since September 11, 2001 (9/11), there has been a slow erosion of overall international sympathy with Pakistan's grievances, especially over the issues of Jammu and Kashmir; the socioeconomic costs of 3 decades of Afghan wars; and daily episodes of terrorism within the country.

The prospects of such growing imbalances of political and economic disparities vis-à-vis India, coupled with mounting internal problems (especially persistent terrorism ranging from Quetta to Swat), will continue to endanger Pakistan's cumulative national power. Under consistent pressure from India, instability in Afghanistan, and a fragile domestic structure, Pakistan as a state will become significantly weak and unstable. Therefore, its aforementioned strengths could very well become its vulnerabilities and stir broad international upheaval. Under these circumstances, Pakistanis are keener to obtain a strategic peace with India, which would allow them the space and time to recover from these multiple challenges.

Breaking the Gridlock

Given both India and Pakistan's strategic anxieties, it is no wonder that they succumb to gridlock rather than a path of reconciliation and

CBMs. Further, because of blatantly conflicting objectives between the two countries—one global and the other regional—security competition and asymmetry of interests continue to grow between the two. Despite negativity and pessimism, however, there is potential for both new CBMs and arms control. A brief overview of the CBMs from 1947 to date illustrates the nature of the problem, and a conceptual framework of past initiatives is also necessary to consider—especially given that past attempts have been directly affiliated with crisis and entrenched in ulterior motives. Nonetheless, learning from these unsuccessful attempts will strengthen considerations when framing such policies in the future.

An Overview of Major Agreements and Treaties

One of the explanations attributed to such a track record has been indebted to the fact that each major treaty, or CBM, has had a high point of origin in crisis resolution. Historically, Pakistan preferred outside mediation in disputes with India, because as a smaller and weaker party with a strong sense of morality on its side, Pakistan could win justice through such means (e.g., international organizations like the United Nations [UN], or seeking alliance with major powers).

That proved to be a fallacy. Instead, Pakistan became a geopolitical pawn between great powers during the Cold War. Rather than strengthening itself by alliance and relevancy against its archrival India, it found itself in strategic competition with India in which the trajectories favored India, while the alliance did not mitigate its security concerns. This, then, became a fundamental reason for Pakistan to seek a nuclear weapons program.

India, on the other hand, has always despised outside intervention in its subcontinental affairs and has sought to address all problems to be resolved on a bilateral basis because of the asymmetric power is tipped in its favor. In general, bilateralism has suited India for strategic reasons, and conforms to its traditional nonaligned stance of keeping the superpowers away from the region.

Nevertheless, despite India's insistence on bilateralism, not a single problem has been resolved on a bilateral basis. Moreover, since 9/11, Pakistan has come under scrutiny from the international community with regard to its policy of using asymmetric force to settle the dispute of Jammu and Kashmir. In this context, outside intervention does not necessarily favor Pakistan and even could strengthen India's position. Aside from the present disparity, treaties and agreements that were brokered by outside intervention in the past have led to both India and Pakistan having a generally good record of implementation.

Major Agreements and Treaties, 1947-2004

The first agreement after the 1947-48 War over Kashmir, through bilateral talks between India and Pakistan, came about as an extension of a UN Security Council Resolution. Under this resolution, the 1949 Karachi Agreement was instituted. This initial agreement should have served as a framework for other measures in the future. To date, the Karachi Agreement does serve as the guideline for the conduct of troops deployed along the LOC in Kashmir. Monitored by UN observers, India and Pakistan have deployed forces along the LOC adhering (by and large) to the parameters set by the UN-approved agreement.

The next major agreement, the 1960 Indus Water Treaty, was also a response to crisis and brokered by a third-party mechanism—the World Bank. This agreement over water distribution had its origin in the Kashmir crisis. While former President Pervez Musharraf's "outside the box" interim solution to the Kashmir dispute went nowhere, behind-the-scenes negotiations dragged on. Meanwhile, India began constructing new dams in Kashmir, diverting authorized water resources to Pakistan in clear violation of the Indus Water Treaty. This reveals that Kashmir is not just an ideological and territorial dispute, but reflects a water resource issue with the potential for crisis and tension as well. Though India and Pakistan have had reasonable complaints, the basic tenets of the treaty have functioned despite many wars and military crises. Yet, if India's dam constructions and water diversion strategy against Pakistan persist, this could well lead to the eventual collapse of the Indus Water Treaty altogether.

The Tashkent Agreement of 1966 was brokered by the Soviets after the 1965 war, and indirectly supported by the United States. Once again, like the previous agreement in 1948, this agreement came about as a result of crisis and war. Though the Tashkent Agreement did not provide any framework for resolution of the disputes between India and Pakistan—at least for the next 25 years—the dispute over Jammu and Kashmir remained on the back burner.

After the 1971 war, however, the approach to dialogue changed. With India's primacy established, there was no further agreement that was implemented on a third-party basis. Preceding agreements would be conducted bilaterally, or with mere pressure from the international community. There are three major agreements that can be attributed to India and Pakistan's bilateral relations. Again, each of these agreements came with crisis as a backdrop:

- The Simla Agreement of 1972 was directly in response of the 1971 War.

- The Lahore Agreement of 1999 was a reaction to the crisis spawned by the 1998 nuclear tests and ongoing Kashmir issues.
- The 2004 Islamabad Accord resulted from 9/11 and the 2001-2002 military crisis and ongoing Kashmir issues.

All of these agreements from 1972 onward were bilateral and had effective frameworks to resolve conflict but no effective longevity. One after another, they were violated by either side, resulting in repeated, intensive military crises. For example, in the mid-1980s, India was undergoing a Sikh crisis in Punjab when the Indian Army assaulted a Sikh holy shrine in Amritsar (Operation BLUESTAR), which exacerbated the Sikh insurgency. Simultaneously, in a planned military operation, India decided to occupy the Siachin Glacier (Operation MEGHDOOT) in the disputed northern areas of Kashmir. This event once again brought up the issue of Jammu and Kashmir on the radar screen of the India-Pakistan dispute. Two years later, Indian Army Chief General Sundarji planned a major military exercise code-named "Brasstacks," which had a secret plan for a preventive war as a pretext to neutralize Pakistan's nuclear program.[4] These two crises occurred at a time when Pakistan was deeply involved in an asymmetric war against the Soviet Union (with the support of the United States).

In 1990, the next crisis resulted from a Kashmir uprising, in which escalation peaked to a point that India and Pakistan were once again at the brink of war. This crisis was significant from one standpoint—both India and Pakistan had a covert nuclear weapons capability, which was known to both sides. This situation prompted the United States to intervene from then on.

Additionally, the history of trust-damaging episodes in the midst of such crises has been far greater than the record of keeping faith in treaties. Again, while India has a global audience to project its position, Pakistan has typically had a smaller, regional venue in which to project its position. All these elements help explain the rise and failure of various agreements, treaties, and accords. Yet, another lens to consider toward progress on the diplomatic front is the induction of strategic CBMs.

Strategic CBMs

The notion of strategic CBM implies that nuclear CBMs and conventional military force CBMs have a symbiotic relationship. One of the foremost issues of CBMs between India and Pakistan is of a conceptual nature. The premise behind strategic CBMs is that nuclear CBMs, on their own, are meaningless if conventional force restraints are not applied.

There are four distinct areas in which India and Pakistan differ in terms of structuring and harnessing CBMs, while arms control becomes problematic.

First, India finds abhorrent anything that binds it to regional terms. From the outset, India took a position of global disarmament as a prelude to its own disarmament from nuclear weapons. Pakistan, on the other hand, insists on everything that is regional and India-specific. Based on the latter position, India does not want to be tied down to Pakistan alone, and recognizes problems with other countries (specifically China) that must also be calculated. India also only wants nuclear military CBMs that allow it to keep its conventional force supremacy intact. Meanwhile, Pakistan's insistence on regional nuclear CBMs also results from Western pressure to forgo its nuclear ambitions. Pakistan's nuclear program was nurtured under obstacles, sanctions, and other reprisals from the nonproliferation regime. Moreover, Pakistan has endured sanctions that have affected it in a negative manner, whereas India has sustained sanctions with little or no effect.

Second, any CBM that inhibits India's use of force within the region is considered to be counterintuitive to its force posture. This, then, is Pakistan's fundamental problem. Third, India insists that nuclear CBMs begin with a declared doctrine. Pakistan simply believes that real doctrines are classified, and that declared doctrines are simply "verbal posturing" meant for diplomatic consumption only.[5]

Finally, India believes that on the matters of command and control, its declared second-strike doctrine and civil supremacy of armed forces is sufficient to explain the articulation of command and control on nuclear weapons. For Pakistan, clear delineation of command channels and explicit decisionmaking bodies constitute a system that is responsible for managing command and control during peace, crisis, and war. This emphasis on command and control also reflects Pakistan's checkered history of civil-military relations.

In response, Pakistan proffered regional proposals, beginning with India's first nuclear test in 1974. Seven regional-based proposals were made, with each one automatically rejected by India.[6] This allowed Pakistan to show (the region, in its case) that India did not want to cooperate—thus placing the burden on India to defend its position. Pakistan knew that the proposals were not realistic, and the international community recognized this point as well. Not all the proposals were disingenuous, however, and had world powers not dismissed it, there might have been a different outcome. Pakistan also used these regional proposals to create the diplomatic space to develop its own nuclear program, while simultaneously shifting the pressure onto India and underscoring the responsibility of proliferation on the bigger power.

Moving forward, new military and nuclear CBMs (similar to the treaties previously discussed) came about in the wake of nuclear developments and military crises. Most of them were, once again, bilateral CBMs. For example, the 1988 prohibition against attacking nuclear installations and facilities was in response to information that was widely analyzed, showing that India would attack Pakistani nuclear installations. The precedent of preventive strikes was also established after the Israeli bombing of Iraqi nuclear facilities, and reports of India mimicking a similar attack against Pakistani centrifuge facilities surfaced during the military crisis that ensued after India occupied Siachin Glacier—an undemarcated territory above the LOC in Kashmir. India and Pakistan once again went into bilateral agreements following the major crisis in the 1980s, when political leadership under Zia-ul-Haq, and subsequent civilian leaders like Benazir Bhutto and Nawaz Sharif, also created initiatives with India's Rajiv Gandhi and other congressional leaders. Additional agreements would follow.

Notifications of military exercises and airspace violations were actually a derivative of "Brasstacks" and other minor incidents in which the Indian Army contemplated making war with Pakistan. The agreement would oblige each side to provide advanced notification of military exercises.

Another example is the bilateral, joint declaration on the complete prohibition of chemical weapons in 1992, which was in response to both sides trading allegations that the other was building a chemical weapons program. This joint agreement was also a way to deflect pressures from the international community—which was then deliberating the implementation of the Chemical Weapons Convention (CWC) that was eventually signed in 1993. When India declared possession of chemical weapons as required by the CWC, Pakistan protested, alleging violation of the bilateral, joint declaration against chemical weapons.

Last was the hotlines agreement between the director-generals of military operations (DGMOs)—the foreign secretaries and maritime security agencies—which came about as an agreed-upon mechanism for military and diplomats to communicate with each other in order to prevent the emergence of a crisis and to manage escalation. Though this agreement is a reasonable and practical means to communicate, it has not been used in such a manner. As opposed to their original intent to act as a crisis-prevention tool, hotlines have typically been used for deception at worst and post-crisis management at best.

There have been plenty of examples indicating this misuse of an otherwise productive tool, for example: hotlines were useful after the withdrawal of the Kargil Crisis, but not during the crisis; the 1999 Indian plane hijacking hotlines between the DGMOs did not work when the crisis was at its peak; and in Mumbai in 2008, the foreign secretaries' line did not prevent the India and Pakistan situation from derailing the entire peace process. Moreover, the maritime security hotline has not prevented the daily fishermen from being caught by each side; rather, it has been used after the fact when the governments decide to return them.

All of these agreements indicate that there have been thoughtful ideas, but the implementation of those ideas has been incredibly poor. Neither side has built upon such measures, but has instead used them as a means to counteract the other.

Lahore MOU and Strategic Restraint Regime

Contrary to many of the discussed agreements, the Lahore MOU is by far the most significant agreement between India and Pakistan; it not only has created a framework for new arms control and CBMs, but contains the prospects of conflict resolution as well.

The Lahore MOU came about after the famous summit between the Prime Ministers of India and Pakistan in February 1999. This agreement was the result of an intense 8-month period after the nuclear test in May 1998, in which US diplomats led by Deputy Secretary of State Strobe Talbot were actively involved to implement the UN Security Council Resolution.[7] The June 1998 UN Security Council Resolution condemned both India and Pakistan, placing stringent conditions on both countries—including the issue of Jammu and Kashmir. In fact, there were many ideas flowing between India and Pakistani diplomats during this time.[8]

India and Pakistan decided to triangulate bilateral dialogues, with the United States as the third-party player. Theoretically, this was a good way forward; however, with each side speaking separately to the United States, great suspicion ensued. Another entanglement was that the United States was approaching the issue based on its experience in Europe; this did not necessarily conform to South Asia. For example, most CBMs and agreements were in a bipolar world during the Cold War. Moreover, these agreements happened after the conflict was resolved: East-West conflict had ended. This did not conform to the strategic realities of this region.

Despite these incongruities, strategic restraint became the term du jour. The US experts team presented Pakistan with a paper called Minimum Deterrence Posture (MDP), which included concepts of how to move forward: geographical separation of major components of nuclear arsenals and delivery means; the segregation of delivery systems from warhead locations; declaring non-nuclear delivery systems with their specific locations (e.g., which squadron of aircraft would be nuclear or non-nuclear and providing the location); the establishment of a finite ceiling for fissile material production and monitoring of nuclear testing; and, lastly, limiting ballistic flight tests and production limits. This MDP was otherwise referred to as "strategic pause."

These concepts were alien to South Asian security experts. Again, the MDP was derived by Cold War concepts, which were not applicable to the regional security environment. India and Pakistan obviously did not accept them; however, the Pakistan side did recognize these concepts in principle, with a promise to return back to what they considered to be within their own regional interests.

In response, Pakistan analyzed US proposals and translated them into their own regional-based proposal, which they coined SRR.[9] The SRR was conceptually emphasized through the principle of nuclear restraint, with conventional force restraint as well—hence, a strategic CBM. It was simply not practical for a small country like Pakistan to "segregate" delivery systems as presented by the United States. This was unacceptable, because the concept undercut Pakistan's ambiguity of strategic deterrence while still allowing India to wage a conventional war against it. Lastly, Pakistan and India were not agreeing to the Comprehensive Test Ban Treaty (CTBT), but were principally agreeing to the US proposal that they would not conduct any more tests. The result was that the dialogue lost its fervor, because the United States began to mirror India's position—resulting in Pakistan losing interest.

Pakistan's fundamental problem was India's conventional threat, which remained unaddressed in every proposal given by the United States. Any CBMs not related to conventional force would be irrelevant and, therefore, the failure of acceptance of SSR in South Asia was the bedrock from which the new US policy toward the region—as well as new strategic competition between India and Pakistan—began.

What Pakistan proposed was a comprehensive conventional force restraint agreement. This proposal had three major elements: identifying the offensive forces of each country whose location and posture were to be acknowledged; the designation of geographical border areas as

Low Force Zone (LFZ), where offensive forces would be kept at bay; and the notion of a mutually balanced force reduction in the long run as conflict resolution and peace prevail in the region. As an alternative, the Pakistani side produced several proposals, and designated each side as an offensive force. By identifying the forces that were offensive to each other, there could be measures to move these formations away geographically in order to prevent tensions and armed conflict.

The LFZs would be the hallmark of this intended policy. In LFZs, the border areas and towns close by would have a defense purpose only—the number of forces in these garrisons would remain as agreed upon by both sides. In the event of changes, each side would notify the other. Moreover, the Pakistani side proposed a mutually balanced and proposed force reduction in the long run. Due to a proportional difference in force (India having a much larger military apparatus), conventional force reduction would be proportional, with force ratios equal between the two sides.

On the question of nuclear non-mating and delivery systems, Pakistan acknowledged this to be an existential nuclear posture. Pakistan was amenable to formalizing regional nondeployment of nuclear weapons in conjunction with conflict resolution and conventional force restraints. The SRR also proposed mutual missile restraints between India and Pakistan, including range-payload ceiling; flight-testing notifications; and prohibition of additional destabilizing modernizations, such as missile defense and development of submarine launched ballistic missiles (SLBMs) in order to address the issue.

Despite all of these developments in the negotiation process, however, the United States accepted India's position in not agreeing to the terms. This resulted in the derailment of the whole process. Unfortunately, US ignorance of the SSR was a historical failure, since the SSR could have produced a general peace and stability framework in the region against a trajectory of competition and conflict.

Nevertheless, the Lahore MOU framework came as a result of political will from the leadership in both India and Pakistan. The bureaucrats were pressured to reach an agreement within a span of 10 days—and they did. This not only illustrates that there is no dearth of ideas as far as CBMs are concerned, but emphasizes the importance of political will, as well. The Lahore MOU still stands as the best framework to pick up the threads of peace and security architecture in South Asia.

The next section examines the three possible trajectories India and Pakistan could take in the second decade of the 21st century, given the current course. Stability in the region would depend on the dynamics that could emerge from the following three scenarios—ideally, one that promotes peace and security through strategic CBMs.

Bad, Ugly, and Good: Trajectories in the Region

Bad

Today, the region as a whole stands in a bad position; the choice from here is to either go down a path that leads to a good scenario, or one that plummets the region into a multitude of ugly developments. The status quo between India and Pakistan is plush with tension and loss of trust (as presented throughout this chapter). There is no third-party influence that can change this inertia. The only positive influence is the United States; however, even with its nudging, India and Pakistan continue to only "talk the talk," not "walk the walk." Each failure in the dialogue process results in the stronger side learning from the weaker side's negotiating positions and vulnerabilities, so it can exploit them when tension and crises return. Therefore, whenever Pakistan tried to concede in the past, instead of converting the development into a sincere, honest proposal, India has come back with an alternative proposition—knowing full well it would be unacceptable for Pakistan to concede.

The result of the outlined posture in the region is a slow arms race that continues to push the region closer to conventional force deployments. India continues to apply coercive diplomatic pressure and suggestive doctrines like Cold Start, which has implied threatened use of force through public statements by both civilians and military leaders alike. In fact, a recent statement by former Indian Army Chief Deepak Kapur stated publicly that India can deal with Pakistan within the first 96 hours of engagement, and immediately turn to China without issue.[10] This is only one example of the aggressive posturing by the Indian military in recent years. Because Pakistani forces are deployed on multiple fronts, with the potential of political crisis, the likelihood of Pakistan pushing toward strategic weapons deployment or shifting from a recessed nuclear deployment toward an ambiguous state of deployment, is likely (in 3-5 years if the trend persists).

Every major power is dealing with India with new nuclear agreements, making India the only country in the world that is a nonmember of the Nonproliferation Treaty (NPT)—having no obligation as a nonweapons state—but, at the same time, is recognized as a de facto nuclear weapons state. This position of appeasing a state that challenged the regime and is not susceptible to the NPT is creating a sense of Western duplicity and discriminatory feelings in Pakistan. These issues, coupled with the US agenda to jump-start the global arms control process (CTBT, etc.), will force Pakistan into a position that it no longer has any incentive to cooperate.

Ugly

If this bad trend continues, then a direr scenario will ensue. Increasing tension between India and China, as well as India and Pakistan, will develop. This will lead to a heightened security environment in the region and military forces being on the alert, if not fully deployed, on the borders. This could easily become a self-fulfilling prophecy.

Technological innovation would be the acquisition or deployment of missile defenses with the transfer of technologies such as ARROW, in collaboration with Israel, etc. China may not be expected to deploy its strategic arsenal, but Pakistan cannot be expected to remain nondeployed if this arises. In return, India would have deployed strategic arsenals by more robust naval developments such as nuclear submarines, or any other mix of strategic weapons.

When such a situation happens, the possibility of hot pursuits either along the LOC by Indian ground forces and Special Forces; cross-border attacks by the Indian air force; or naval coercive deployment in the Arabian Sea by Indian forces to exploit Pakistan's vulnerabilities cannot be ruled out. Alternatively, implementing a Cold Start organizational pattern of deployment as outlined in the doctrine—through integrated battle groups (IBGs)—could also be strategically deployed in the area. This would be a clear fortification of the border, and a flagrant attempt to escalate. In response, Pakistan would break loose from all arms control discussion. This can lead to a whole meltdown of the regional situation, with the United States no longer in a position to intervene positively.

Good

The ugly scenario can be prevented if the current trajectories are reversed through cautious influence by the superpowers to end the India-Pakistan deadlock. If the dialogue process does lead in a positive and meaningful direction, there can certainly be a good option, with the potential for strategic CBMs.

India must make a conscious policy shift toward Pakistan, recognizing the two positive trends that have recently emerged. First is the success of the democratic political process; the second is the focus of the Pakistani military against violent extremism. Therefore, India must reach out through dialogue to strengthen and support these trends.

India should also revise its current security doctrine of coercion (Cold Start), exploitation (e.g., back away from its perceived negative role in Afghanistan) and aggressive diplomatic isolation of Pakistan, which were still in place at the time of this writing.

The best course for India is to pick up the threads of the Lahore MOU and Islamabad Accord, from where they were left. If India picks up what was in the framework in Lahore and gives fair consideration to the SSR (thinking through the lens of strategic CBMs) that Pakistan had offered, progress can be made.

By easing the relationship and initiating people-to-people contact, three separate endeavors could be agreed upon by India and Pakistan:

1. Promote religious tourism. Sikhs, Hindus, Muslims, and other religious sects should be afforded an opportunity to visit shrines in India, as well as the inverse in Pakistan.
2. Increase cultural tourism and sports exchanges. India has used sports as a cultural and political tool in the past, ranging from threats to not sending cricket teams for competition to openly supporting Hindu extremists who threaten Pakistani players and cultural performances. Such acts should cease, with a more positive exchange in the future.
3. Ease trade relations between the two countries. There are concerns on both sides, but there can be some linkages.

Most important is the Indus Water Treaty. For the first time, there is a sense that India is using its position to bolster water rights from Pakistan by erecting dams, etc. If the two countries move in a direction that embraces cooperation on such important strategic issues, then the prospects of CBMs can sow the seeds from this fertile soil.

A Way Forward

In the next 3 to 5 years, four key areas have prospects of launching CBMs and even rudimentary arms control measures. These are briefly mentioned here—all can be attributed to the tragic Mumbai incident in 2008. Further analysis and elaboration can be filled in during a later discussion. Yet, it is important to provide an overview of such potential measures when proposing a new way forward.

First and most immediate is a CBM for India and Pakistan to revive the Joint Anti-Terrorism Mechanism agreed on in 2006, sequential to the 2004 Islamabad Accord. This mechanism failed as a result of the Mumbai incident. It is important that both countries draw lessons from the failure and improve the mechanism to prevent derailment of relations between them as a result of a terror attack. It is unlikely that terrorism in the region will disappear any time soon, but it is important to not allow terrorists to hold two nuclear-armed states hostage.

Next, India and Pakistan should establish a National Risk Reduction Center (NRRC). In the case of Mumbai, there was a deadlock of communication at both political and military levels following this horrific event, which indicated the fragility of relations between the two countries. An institutional mechanism of reducing such risks—with a spectrum of communications and resolutions ranging from a Mumbai-type terror incident, up to a nuclear-related accident—is now essential.

The third CBM is maritime in nature. Because the Mumbai incident involved maritime transit, there is all the more reason for developing maritime CBMs between the two countries. India and Pakistan can begin under the spirit of Lahore MOU and the Incidents at Sea (INCSEA) Agreement, delineating maritime boundaries to prevent fishermen incursions, and also develop maritime cooperation in other areas such as sea piracy. A maritime hotline should be put to better use to prevent another Mumbai-like event and the abduction of innocent fishermen.

Finally, even though it may appear premature, India and Pakistan must conduct a very sober analysis of ballistic missile inventories. As widely reported and understood, the shortest-range ballistic missiles—Prithvi-I in the case of India, and HATF-I in the case of Pakistan—have little strategic utility and greater technical problems to manage. It may be wise for India and Pakistan to consider eliminating these two capabilities as a first step. This will prove to be symbolic, without impacting military stature or capabilities to address various contingencies. Similarly, in the long term, there may be a realization that the next category of ballistic missiles, Prithvi-II and HATF-II, may also be left with less military utility. The technical and strategic analysis of this proposal is not discussed here, but is again left for further analysis at a later time.

Nonetheless, if the current dialogue that has been announced to start by the end of February 2010 puts the region on the good path, with India and Pakistan commencing a meaningful CBM, there are clauses within the Lahore MOU that can be resurrected. Examples include engaging in bilateral consultations on security; disarmament and nonproliferation issues; review of the existing communications links; and periodically reviewing the implementation of existing CBMs. The Lahore MOU also promised that expert level agreements would be negotiated at a technical-expert level. It would be wise of India and Pakistan to begin a prospect of arms control and CBMs in the current decade, using the Lahore MOU as a rubric.

The first decade of the 21st century has been rife with tremendous tensions in the region, from the response to 9/11 via the War on Terror, to the lasting rivalry between India and Pakistan. This decade has shown that India and Pakistan have engaged on a pathway of competition and non-resolution that is steeped in historical precedent. The next decade should reverse this trend from competition to a cooperative security framework, redressed of new formal security threats and nontraditional security issues (e.g., water, energy, food security, and cross-border terrorism) taking a greater salience over old military issues.

Endnotes

1. The term "enduring rivalry" is borrowed from T. V. Paul, ed., *The India- Pakistan Conflict: An Enduring Rivalry*, New York: Cambridge University Press, 2005. He defines "enduring rivalry" as conflicts between two or more states, lasting more than 2 decades, with several militarized interstate disputes punctuating the relationship in between and characterized by a persistent, fundamental and long-term incompatibility of goals between the states.
2. Christopher J. Pherson, *String of Pearls: Meeting the Challenge of China's Rising Power*, Carlisle, PA: Strategic Studies Institute, US Army War College, July 2006, available from *www.strategicstudiesinstitute.army.mil/pdffiles/PUB721.pdf.*
3. Robert Kaplan, "Pakistan's Fatal Shore," *The Atlantic,* May 2009.
4. Scott D. Sagan and Kenneth N. Waltz, *The Spread of Nuclear Weapons: A Debate Renewed,* New York: W. W. Norton, 2003, pp. 92-95.
5. See George H. Quester, *Nuclear Pakistan and Nuclear India: Stable Deterrent or Proliferation Challenge?* Carlisle, PA: Strategic Studies Institute, US Army War College, November 1992, p. 12.
6. The regional proposals are as follows: the South Asian Nuclear Weapon Free Zone, November 1974; Joint Renunciation of Acquisition or the Manufacture of Nuclear Weapons, 1978; Mutual Inspections of Nuclear Facilities, 1979; Simultaneous Acceptance of International Atomic Energy Agency (IAEA) "Full Scope" Safeguards, 1979; Simultaneous Accession to the Nonproliferation Treaty (NPT) 1979; Bilateral Nuclear Test-Ban Threat, 1987; Multilateral Conference on Nonproliferation in South Asia in 1987 and 1991.

7. See Security Council Resolution 1172, 1998, available from *www.un.org/News/Press/docs/1998/sc6528.doc.htm.*

8. The author was involved as part of the expert-level dialogue with both the United States and India.

9. The author was personally responsible for the preparation of the paper that developed this concept. The paper was presented to the US team on September 15, 1998, in New York. See Feroz H. Khan, "Reducing the Risk of Nuclear War in South Asia," in Henry Sokolski, ed., *Pakistan's Nuclear Future: Reining in the Risk,* Carlisle, PA: Strategic Studies Institute, pp. 70-71.

10. Deepak Kapur, quoted by Nirupama Subramanian, "General Kapoor's Remarks Generate Heat in Pakistan," *The Hindu,* January 5, 2010, available from *www.hindu.com/2010/01/05/stories/2010010560030100.htm.*

Part 4

Post-Cold War Military Science and Arms Control

Chapter 12

To What Extent can Precision Conventional Technologies Substitute for Nuclear Weapons?

Stephen J Lukasik

Nuclear weapons technology and its related systems, doctrines, and strategies are based on what was the newest discovery of science in the 1930s. Although nuclear weapons were developed too late to have much of an impact in World War II, they did play an important role in national security during the following decades. In the intervening 70 years, new technologies have been applied to the protection of states and their populations. The proposition examined here is that these new technologies, and the demonstrated capabilities of systems and doctrines based on them, can in some cases substitute for those currently provided by nuclear weapons. The technologies seen as potentially offering these capabilities are those involving the precise and discriminate application of far smaller amounts of force to achieve militarily desirable effects than those delivered by even the lowest-yield nuclear weapons.

The replacement of nuclear weapons with more effective ways of achieving military objectives has been underway for a number of years. During the period of nuclear arms limitation negotiations between the United States and Russia, conventional military capabilities have benefited from developments in radar, stealth, precision navigation, unmanned vehicles, guidance, propulsion, computation, and networked communications linking target-acquisition sensors to national-level commanders as well as to theater forces and down to quite low organizational levels. The commonly held view is that if one can find a target and identify it, it can be dealt with quickly and effectively. With such capabilities, consideration of the potential for the substitutability of conventional for nuclear weapons is natural.

Substitutability implies trade-offs, since nuclear and discriminate conventional technologies have quite different characteristics, each having both desirable and undesirable characteristics. There are at least four relevant issues:

1. As the United States and Russia reduce their stockpiles equally and in concert to a level of roughly 1,000 warheads, they enter the range in which their stockpiles are numerically comparable to those of other nuclear states. But the downward movement in numbers of the United States and Russia is opposite to the upward trends in at least four nuclear nations. Warhead numbers do not tell the whole story, however. Strategic balance calculations on which US and Soviet net assessments were made included a number of other metrics: yield, range, accuracy, vulnerability, reliability, readiness, etc. None of these are addressed adequately by the simple matter of warhead numbers.
2. As national goals evolve over time, and as national security needs to change correspondingly, new technologies such as those noted above become important in assessing the ability of a nation to enforce its will on another. However, these substitution options are not equally accessible to all nations, because they depend on sustained long-term investments in research and development (R&D), target acquisition, delivery systems, training, employment doctrines, and conventional warhead type and design. Not all states are equally endowed with the necessary economic, technological, and production capabilities to deploy and maintain weapons based on these advances.
3. The new discriminate technologies have practical limits not shared by the nuclear weapons they could be seen as replacing. Nuclear weapons have such large areas of destruction that small errors in delivery accuracy, target identification, target vulnerability, and uncertainties in weather and visibility are unimportant, but these are central for the effectiveness of conventional discriminate technologies. Thus, nuclear weapons, however costly, could provide more effective and reliable options for the delivery of military force for some countries.
4. Understanding the equivalence between nuclear and discriminate conventional weapons depends on complex

calculations related to a nation's perceived adversaries, the nuclear and conventional capabilities of each, how the lower collateral damage of conventional weapons is valued by each, the number of aim points needed to achieve a desired effect, and the fact that the discriminate technologies must be costed on the basis of actual continued use—while nuclear deterrent forces are never to be "used" beyond being in existence and having imputed capabilities that are generally not precisely known by opposing sides. Nuclear weapons are judged on the basis of their presumed first-strike destructiveness. Conventional weapons are judged by their post-conflict outcomes. Thus, the two classes of weapons are not directly commensurate.

Nuclear Weapons in Practice

Beyond their potential military uses, nuclear weapons have some perverse characteristics not shared by discriminate conventional technologies—the most serious being accidental or unintended nuclear war. The textbook case is Cuba (1962). While a good deal of the "fog of war" is unavoidable, nuclear capabilities used will result in a large force expended in a relatively short time that does not allow any margin for error. The beginning is the end. In 1969, the Soviets went down the same path with the People's Republic of China (PRC) over several long-running border disputes, with further implications of threats to their nuclear facilities. Soviet nuclear adventurism was repeated a third time, in Afghanistan in 1982, when SCUD missiles were secretly deployed to the Wakhan Corridor to threaten PRC and Pakistani nuclear facilities.

These situations highlight the danger of the unwise deployment of nuclear weapons. Whatever weapons are available will be deployed, however low the stakes. The scale of destruction between 200 pounds (lb.) of chemical explosives and 20,000,000 lb. (20 kilotons [KT]) or 20,000,000,000 lbs. (20 megatons [MT] of trinitrotoluene [TNT] is not easily grasped.) Measuring nuclear capabilities in kilotons and megatons reduces the apparent differences to misleadingly small numbers. Putting weapons or people into situations in which such large differences in scale must be accurately understood is to invite errors in judgment.

Another difficulty is that nuclear weapons interfere with the conduct of more frequent non-nuclear military operations. In 1967 and 1968, only nuclear-armed aircraft were available to go to the aid of the USS Liberty and USS Pueblo, and they could not be used under the circumstances. The Union of Soviet Socialist Republics (USSR) found itself in a similar circumstance during the 1979 Soviet invasion of Afghanistan. Secret concentrations of forces in preparation for the invasion were made to appear as normal troop movements, so they had to take their Free Rocket Over Ground (FROG, a North Atlantic Treaty Organization [NATO] designation) mobile nuclear-capable missiles with them. The United Kingdom (UK) was forced into a similar situation in 1982, when it dispatched nuclear-armed naval forces to the Falkland Islands. The need for speed precluded offloading the UK's naval nuclear weapons before departure or en route. While no nuclear consequences resulted in these last two cases, owning nuclear weapons imbues all military operations with nuclear-use implications.

Other potential disasters follow from the accidents attending nuclear weapon deployment. It is difficult to handle nuclear weapons without something going awry, a state of affairs well known to those dealing with reliability theory.[1] The issue in reliability is not the fact of unreliability per se but the consequences of reliability failures. These depend on details of weapon design that will not be generally known to all involved: the quality and stability of the chemical explosive components, the number of detonation points required for fission yield, the design of handling equipment, the training of operational and maintenance personnel, the details of the arming and firing circuitry, etc.

Incidents at sea are another source of accidents, given that such international space is often where short-range confrontations between nuclear-armed adversaries occur.

Another emergent characteristic of nuclear arsenals is that of hoaxes, rumors, exaggeration, and fear. These are driven by perceptions—some created by a state wishing to inflate its capability to deter; others, from self-deception. Brian Jenkins makes the case, in his provocativelytitled book, Will Terrorists Go Nuclear? that al Qaeda is a nuclear power, not because it possesses nuclear weapons, but because we are as frightened of them now as we would be if they did possess them.[2] An earlier observation by Secretary of State Dean Acheson in 1951 with regard to nuclear weapon use in Korea was similar:

> The threat represented by our stockpile of atomic bombs was not a political advantage or asset, but, rather a political liability. The threat of its use by us would frighten our allies to death but not worry our enemies.[3]

Recognizing that beliefs and fear are the essence of the matter, note must be taken of the opportunities and instabilities of contemporary personal communication channels to propagate hoaxes and rumors, and thus, the fear they engender. These rumors and hoaxes supplement the mass media, especially with their 24 hours a day/7 days a week need to fill airtime with talk, images, and speculation, regardless of substance.

In view of the disadvantages of too much force for rational needs, difficult-to-arrest slides down slippery slopes to unintended conflict, accidents in handling and deployment, and the unbounded fear or anger that they generate make assessment of the value of their substitutability difficult.

Efficient Application of Minimum Force

Sun Tzu said, "Generally in war the best policy is to take a state intact; to ruin it is inferior to this." He further notes, "For to win 100 victories in 100 battles is not the acme of skill. To subdue the enemy without fighting is the acme of skill."[4] The excessive magnitude of nuclear force in even the smallest such weapon and the attendant uncertainties in the outcomes of its use makes industrial war—the application of a state's total power toward the use of force against an adversary—no longer feasible as an instrument of national policy.[5] Industrial war spawned the creation of nuclear force, which by its nature renders such conflicts too dangerous to undertake. Multiple nuclear states with multiple competing interests, global relationships across a range of economic and political domains, and the rise of both sub-state organizations and transnational institutions now channel confrontation into more local, limited, and specific directions.

Since resources are limited in practice, prudence suggests using minimal resources in the light of future needs and uncertain outcomes. Nor is there any point expending resources to destroy something of no military or economic value. Destruction must eventually be repaired, and costs and consequences are shared. An attack is a beginning, not an end. Hence, in unleashing force, one is setting sequences of unpredictable events in motion.

In this discussion, we ask if the goals of the use of nuclear force can be as satisfactorily achieved with post-nuclear technology that centers on maximum efficiency and discrimination in the delivery of minimum amounts of force. Sometimes referred to as "surgical," in practice such strikes carry the same costs as those in the medical analogy.

There are a number of technologies that can be combined to protect a nation's security that were not on the horizon when the decision to develop nuclear weapons was made. These are not matters of theory. They represent capabilities that are available today and have been integrated into force structures since the mid-1980s to achieve some efficiency and discrimination in the delivery of force. While not yet perfected, they promise alternatives to the unconstrained use of nuclear force.

Target Attacks with "Dumb" Weapons: The Issue of Collateral Damage

The first "precision" air attack took place 8 years after the first Wright brothers' flight. On November 1, 1911, Lieutenant Guilio Gavotti, commander of the Italian air fleet, directed his Bleriot X.1 fighter over a Turkish camp near Ain Zara as part of a campaign for control of Libya and Crete. He leaned over the cockpit and dropped four modified 4 lb. Swedish hand grenades. The attack set a second record when the Turks complained that the bombs hit a field hospital, thus establishing the first mention of collateral damage.[6]

Air attacks were developed by Germany in World War I and in the Spanish Civil War by the German Condor legion. The force commander made the German policy clear when he posted a "Golden Rule" for his pilots: "If for any reason, the original target cannot be attacked . . . the bombs are to be dropped blind anywhere over enemy territory, again without regard for the civilian population."[7]

Air attack was a major tactic in World War II and continued to reflect the debate over precision attacks on military targets vs. indiscriminate attacks on cities and civilian populations. Air attacks were of three types: air-to-ground tactical support for the Allied forces, for which collateral damage was not a factor; precision attacks on military and industrial targets intended to minimize collateral damage; and outright terror attacks on civilians. Precision bombardment was aided by the famous Norden bombsight, which increased accuracy by being able to compensate for the speed of the aircraft. What it could not do, and which led to circular error probable (CEPs) of several miles, was to compensate for the winds throughout the bomb's trajectory. These were exacerbated by the need to fly at high altitude to avoid anti-aircraft artillery (AAA) fire. By 1942, all reservations about collateral damage were ignored.

In Operation ROLLING THUNDER in Vietnam in 1965, the primary objective was the North Vietnamese logistics system. US policy was mindful of minimizing civilian casualties, so targets and mission details were decided in Washington. Unexpended ordnance could only be jettisoned at sea, and enemy aircraft had to be visually identified before being engaged. Two bridges, the Tanh Hoa heavy-masonry bridge over the Song Ma River and the Paul Doumer Railroad Bridge near Hanoi, were repeatedly attacked with "dumb" bombs between June 1965 and

January 1968 without success, pointing to the need for greater bombing effectiveness.

Discriminate Technologies

Radar hardly seems new, since it had far more effect on the outcome of World War II than did nuclear weapons. It can locate and track moving targets at long range, work through obscuration, filter signals to match target characteristics, and use Identification, Friend or Foe (IFF) to reduce targeting errors. Newer technology enables radar to work underground, through walls, and operate with a low probability of detection. Its competing technology is low radar cross-section platforms that can penetrate areas with less risk and thus provide better accuracy for weapons delivery and, when manned, add human judgment to the process.

Satellite-based navigation (GPS) enables platforms to know where they are and, with GPS coordinates of targets, enables weapons to be delivered with significant accuracy. Local GPS enhancements can fill in possible reception gaps and increase accuracy further. Satellite-based reconnaissance enables the location of fixed targets. Unmanned air platforms can do the same thing, with more immediacy and specificity. They can, for example, provide virtually continuous surveillance of areas at less risk than can manned aircraft or ground observers. Such platforms can have reduced observables and be configured to deliver warheads to targets. Cruise missiles, aided by GPS, inertial, or terrain matching guidance technology, constitute another type of unmanned platform with a longer range and larger payloads.

A variety of autonomous homing or manually guided warheads enable relatively small warheads to engage selected targets with effectiveness when directed to their points of greatest vulnerability. These include home-on-emitter and home-on-jammer warheads as well as those employing visual or infrared (IR) image correlation.

Ballistic missile defense is probably the most highly precise and discriminate technology available and has no downside in collateral damage.

Other precision technologies include cyber weapons, which enable networked platforms and facilities to be selectively attacked.

Special forces provide the ultimate in accurately delivering warheads or other devices, to targets with the flexibility provided by human minds, eyes, and hands.

Networks supporting software-enabled functionality provide new capabilities for information collection, collaborative analysis, distribution of information to forces for immediate use, as well as rapid and flexible command and control. Their competing technology is portable, relatively short-range emitters of high-powered focused microwave energy that can couple to electronic circuits to disable or destroy them—with little collateral damage.

While there are a number of technologies that support the precise application of force, one must ask two questions. First, how well have they met their potential capabilities? The second is whether these technologies, employed by trained forces operating under developed and tested operational doctrine, can achieve the same national objectives for security attributed to nuclear weapons.

Precise Delivery of Force to a Selected Point

The obvious characteristic, and the one technologists and military people enthuse about, is the precision delivery part. This is a matter of design, fabrication, testing, training, mission planning, and mission execution. All these facets of the problem are understood in principle, but they change in significant detail when technologies change and have to be thought out anew in each case.

The second, frequently overlooked, part of the task is to know what point to select. This is in part technical: the matter of identifying the most vulnerable points in a selected target that, when struck appropriately, will disable or destroy it. But finding the target, knowing it is the most important target at the time of attack, and doing this in the face of camouflage; deception; target mobility; and under conditions that often result in lack of information, direction, visibility, and other circumstances, is challenging. The latter are matters for the collection, analysis, and distribution of intelligence, both strategic and tactical. Without correct and timely intelligence, precision delivery is worthless. Knowledge acquisition and distribution comes before precise delivery. Precisely killing what you do not want to kill is collateral damage—a large negative on the scoreboard, especially under the conditions of 21st-century conflict among the people and public scorekeeping.

Furthermore, when directing force at a target, the target is typically not passive. It reacts to an attack by defending itself. In so doing, it degrades the performance of the attacker, sometimes successfully evading damage and sometimes causing collateral damage itself.

By 1972, electro-optical guided bombs (EOGB) and laser-guided bombs (LGB) were in the inventory, and available for another go at the two bridges that had defied serious damage 4 years earlier. On the first raid against the Tanh Hoa Bridge, weather precluded the use of the LCBs, but 12 F–4s, each carrying two 2,000-lb. weapons, severely damaged the bridge. A second strike by 8 F–4s resulted in 12 direct hits and 4 probable hits with EOGBs. A third strike by three aircraft carrying 3,000-lb. LGBs dropped the rest of the spans.

The 1981 Israeli air strike against the Iraqi Osirik reactor provides an interesting contrast to the US technology. Israel opted out of using EOGBs in its inventory. Instead, Israel used carefully selected, weighed, and balanced 2,000-lb. Mk 84 gravity bombs delivered in a dive maneuver by eight F–16s at a 3,000-ft altitude. Of the 16 bombs delivered, 15 hit the reactor dome. The attack was timed for a Sunday so that no workers would be on-site; it was at the last possible time before the reactor was in operation and would have released radioactivity when destroyed.

Operation DESERT STORM in 1991 found the US Department of Defense (DoD) better prepared to use its new technology. Again, the F–117A was chosen for its weapon delivery capability. Twenty arrived over Baghdad, Iraq, but collateral damage constraints had the effect that 20 percent of the first strike aircraft had to return with their weapons because they could not positively identify their targets. Because there were so many targets and some covered such large areas, there were many separate aim points. Because there was such a dense air defense environment, cruise missiles were employed also, but their low altitude at relatively low speeds resulted in several being shot down by ground fire.

The results were quite impressive. The 25–30 ft CEPs achieved on test and training ranges were largely achieved by the F–117As, the 104 Tomahawk land-attack missile (TLAM), and 35 air-launched cruise missiles (ALCM). The most famous was the picture of a smokestack in the crosshairs of an F–117A. The LGB went down the stack and destroyed several floors of the building. But a command and control facility in the basement was undamaged. After the war, the DoD estimated that 800 targets were attacked, and only about 50 (6 percent) were misidentified by pilots.

Precision weapons continued to be important in Iraq, with several cases of particular interest. The Amiriya bunker, a large, hardened underground structure 40 ft underground with a 10-ft reinforced concrete roof, was believed to be a part of the Iraqi command and control system. An F–117A released two LGBs simultaneously. Both homed on the same illuminated spot (which was 20 ft off from the intended ventilation shaft target.) The first weapon cratered the building roof but did not penetrate it. The second weapon easily penetrated the crater that the first weapons created and then penetrated the roof. Unfortunately, the bunker was being used as an air raid shelter. Between 300 and 400 civilians were killed, and 28 survived.

Bridges critical to supplying Iraqi forces in Kuwait continued to be important targets. Between January 16 and February 1991, of the 50 bridges in Iraq and Kuwait, 42 were attacked and 27 destroyed. Typically, there was one sortie carrying two LGBs per bridge. Collateral damage was generally light, but on one mission an LGB veered away from the target and hit a market area, killing 130 people.

Air attacks continued for the next several years to try to bring Iraq into compliance with prior agreements. As air attacks in Iraq were phasing down, the national focus shifted to events in the former Yugoslavia. Operation ALLIED FORCE was directed to stabilize the chaos following the dissolution of the communist government in 1990 and the unleashing of long-standing hatreds, underlined by the religious differences in this high-water mark of the Muslim advance into Europe in the 13th century. Ethnic cleansing in Bosnia and Kosovo of all non-Serbs ensued.

The rules of engagement to minimize collateral damage and the nature of coalition warfare proved difficult to implement to achieve the desired political objectives effectively. The air resources employed were substantial, and, at the same time, described NATO as wanting "half a war." Cruise missiles from B–52s, surface ships, and US and UK submarines attacked air defenses as a preliminary to deeper strikes. Serbian air defenses, a holdover from the USSR, were substantial: Mig–21 and -29 fighters, SAM SA–2,–3,and–6s, and AAA.

An F–1117A was lost through an effective use of radars in a bi-static mode. Substantial military damage was inflicted with minimal NATO losses, but post-conflict searches on the ground confirmed only 6 percent of the "confirmed" kills. Apparently many of the kills were against decoys or the result of pilots and photoanalysts who gave these reports the benefit of the doubt. While the precision of weapons delivery was good, some damage, such as to runways, was quickly repaired. Collateral damage was not insignificant, especially when amplified by the news media and on-the-spot reporting.

The most politically embarrassing failure was mistaking the Chinese Embassy for the Yugoslav Federal Directorate of Supply and Procurement. The error was the result of outdated maps that failed to report the new location of the embassy correctly. A lengthy investigation identified seven Central Intelligence Agency (CIA) employees responsible for the intelligence failure. The CIA Director claimed the problem was "systemic," with blame shared by the CIA and the National Imagery and Mapping Agency, but then shifted it to private contractors to whom the government's work had been outsourced.

In all, these air campaigns, however impressive in terms of previous dumb-weapon capabilities, did not clearly establish confidence in precision low-collateral damage technology. This was due to a combination of genuine technical problems in planning and executing raids in dense urban areas, failures of intelligence, and initial overoptimistic reporting of results that gave decisionmakers reason to continue. On the other hand, the Joint Direct Attack Munition (JDAM), the 5,000-lb. hard-target penetrating munition, was quite effective.

What does not come out of such sound bites as "one-shot-per-kill" is the large amount of effort involved in delivering a small number of precision weapons to targets. Omitted are the additional aircraft for refueling, defense suppression, fighter escorts, carrier protection, air defense, and the like. Also ignored in tallies of accuracy is that defensive actions damage some precision munitions and countermeasures degrade accuracy. When collateral damage is a single metric, it is not entirely under the control of the attacker.

In terms of the utility of conventional weapons delivered with precision and with regard to the minimization of collateral damage, we can conclude:

1. The technology can deliver sufficiently high accuracy such that relatively small amounts of destructive power can effectively destroy many targets if some degree of maturity in technology and doctrine has been achieved.

2. The promise of control of collateral damage is less clear, though significantly less than with nuclear weapons. Intelligence agencies and military planners devote far more time to the study of targets than they do to the comparable understanding and characterization of non-targets.

3. The delivery of conventional force for strategic purposes involves large numbers of supporting capabilities, including intelligence collection and analysis, delivery systems, mission planning technology, command and control, damage assessment, media communication, and "systems" for post-attack exploitation of the results of such operations.

4. However much one might wish the problem away, applying force under circumstances in whichtargets and non-targets are in intimate contact is not simple. There are realistic limits to what can be done to control collateral damage. These circumstances diminish the utility of discriminate weapons in some situations, especially when the use of civilian populations as a shield is adopted as a deterrent strategy.

Cyber Weapons in a Strategic Role

Strategic response cyber attacks may not have the immediacy of nuclear attacks, since they can consist of instructions for events to happen at any time in the future, or under specified circumstances. Their effectiveness will depend on the degree to which a target nation is wired with digital networks that penetrate as many aspects of its military and civilian economy as possible.[8] They are precise, because networks can only function when every person, place, or device has a network address. Thus, for a wired nation, all aspects of its activity are in the hands of whoever has the "phone book," and the possibilities open to them depend on the extent of the information technology (IT) penetration and the cleverness of the attacker. Classes of targets that can be selectively attacked or attacked as groups include:

1. *Government.* Governments are laying the foundations for e-governments, whose information networks provide the major interface between clients and service providers. By disrupting these, the essential functions of government can be interfered with on a continuing basis, reducing the trust in government that is necessary for the maintenance of order and economic functioning. Thus, strategic cyber attacks can start with massive identity manipulation to steal the identities of real people but also to create synthetic people. Trust attacks will be used to confuse records to the extent that health records, credit card records, land transfer records, stock transfer records, and the like are sufficiently distorted to the point that instead of current tolerable error rates of, perhaps 10^{-5}, they might be increased to 10^{-3}–10^{-2} or more.
2. *Infrastructure.* Cyber attacks on cities and energy infrastructures would focus on penetrating operational control centers, such as those of electric power generation, transmission and distribution; gas and oil pipelines; and rail and air systems. Trains provide an attractive kinetic energy weapon if they can be caused to derail, especially in a tunnel or in a way that destroys a bridge,

or to release toxic or inflammable cargo. The essence of all infrastructure attacks is not to disrupt operations temporarily but to do so in a way that causes physical devices to operate beyond their intended parameter ranges and destroy themselves—as by destroying bearings in generators, high-voltage transformers in transmission systems, or circuit boards in computers and switches.

3. *Military Systems.* Surveillance, intelligence, communication, weapons systems, and command and control facilities all depend, in an age of net-centric warfare, on computation and software for their functionality.

4. *Physical Objects.* For reasons such as inventory control, transportation tracking, and prevention of theft, physical objects can be tagged with a transmitter/receiver having its own Internet Protocol (IP) address such as with an Radio Frequency Identification (RFID) device. These can communicate with each other to self-organize into micro-nets to issue an alert in the event of behavior outside specified limits.

5. *Buildings.* Increasingly, buildings are internally networked to integrate occupant communications, heating, ventilation, and air conditioning (HVAC), physical access to areas, energy efficiency, fire protection, etc. As such nets become increasingly intelligent, both through pre-programmed limits and learning occupant activity patterns, they can be made more effective and contribute to environmental protection as well. The target implication is that buildings can be rendered unusable through the denial of communication, heat, water, power, and physical access.

6. *People.* Badges, biometrics, cell phones, and location tracking will enable people to be tracked for normal or emergency communications. They provide electronic identities that can be taken over at any time.

7. *Residences.* The same functions that are useful for military, commercial, and industrial buildings will be useful in residences. In addition, tasks such as ordering and cooking food; providing entertainment; and controlling the thermal, acoustic, and visual environment will add to the quality of life of its occupants. Here the implications are the same as for military, commercial, and institutional buildings. If someone takes over the command and control functions of residences, they can be rendered unusable.

8. *Vehicles.* Tracking vehicles increases the safety of the vehicle and its occupants, increases the efficiency of commercial uses, and provides for downloading vehicle software updates or uploading mechanical status information for maintenance and diagnostics. GPS already plays this role for some vehicles, and cellular tracking via Bluetooth technology can also be utilized. Control of even a small part of a vehicle fleet will enable attacks on cities by disrupting urban and intercity traffic.
9. *Robots.* Industrial production now makes heavy use of robotic devices, networked within a facility. Higher levels of manufacturing integration will see these networked more broadly. Facilities are currently networked to suppliers and shippers to support just-in-time manufacturing and custom-specified products. Similarly, manufacturing integration will be extended to the retail level for the same reasons. There is, in addition, increasing use of robots at the retail consumer level for such tasks as the delivery of meals in institutions and home cleaning. When robots can be issued arbitrary instructions, they can come under external control and be turned from helpers to saboteurs.

When nations come to depend heavily on cyber technologies, their essential functioning can be disrupted or destroyed by operating their internal controls "in reverse," instructing mechanical devices to work in ways that are beyond the operating or logic limits designed into them. Even if manual backup systems are available, having to resort to them reduces the efficiency level at which an economy operates. Moreover, such attacks are inexpensive, can be repeated until they succeed, and do not expose the attacker to harm or even identification.

The degree to which the above cyber speculations can be substantiated is not nearly as great as when we speak about the performance of nuclear or precision weapons. The Internet as a public access digital communication network did not come into effective existence until web browsers were developed in the early 1990s. In effect, cyber attack tools today are in about the same relative state of development in achieving their future effectiveness as precision weapons were in the early 1970s, with the first EOGBs and LGBs.

Nevertheless, one does see numerous well-documented cases of cyber attacks. Identity theft, spam, phishing, burglary, fraud, stalking, viruses and worms, distributed denial of service attacks, botnets, and state-sanctioned cyber attack groups worldwide are sufficiently documented in the literature that the general outlines of the capability of such weapons are becoming clear. There have been organized cyber attacks on states that occurred as isolated incidents—as against Estonia in 2007, or, in coordination with military actions, as with the Russian invasion of Georgia in 2008. State actions that are visible to date include intelligence collection that has some degree of legitimacy. Cyber attacks defeat both law enforcement and counterintelligence agencies because cyber attacks use communication facilities in numerous jurisdictions, are performed in complete anonymity, and can be repeated as often as the attacker desires, since there is no penalty imposed on an attacker for attempting an unsuccessful penetration.

Cyber attacks fall into a gray area of international law. They are not seen as "armed attacks" for which one set of remedies is available under the United Nations (UN) Charter, but jurisdiction and anonymity severely hamper domestic law enforcement.

We lack fundamental defensive capabilities such as early warning networks, situation awareness, and order of battle information, while our options for response are limited. Intrusion detectors, anti-virus software, spam filters, and encryption technology provide some defensive capabilities, but what the human mind can create, another human mind can circumvent. Informed insiders also provide attackers with a significant edge over defenders. One can expect that matters will not always be this way, but at this point rights and responsibilities for those in the global cyber commons are undefined. What is more troubling is the lack of user or market interest in network security and user protection. As a result, consumers and business organizations worldwide are busy attaching more devices to a fundamentally insecure network, all of which create new vulnerabilities and access paths for attackers.

Paths to the Future

The United States and Russia, having been reducing their nuclear stockpiles since the 1990s while at the same time developing a wide range of conventional capabilities, are driven to precision for the obvious reasons of greater efficiency and effectiveness. The two countries may be precursors to substitution by a larger number of countries. Other national stockpiles are still less than 1,000, but some nations are newer to the business and are still in the phase of developing capabilities that have been part of their national agenda since the 1960s. It is unlikely that having striven to achieve their nuclear capability, these nations would change directions so soon.

The newer nuclear nations are drawn to nuclear weapons for the power they unleash, and they have not embraced the idea of limiting damage to their enemies. An announced intention to destroy their enemies, and to benefit from the fear that intent produces is what they are about. So substitution is still a bit too avant garde. If new nuclear nations, with a more modest set of enemies, do not become mired down constructing huge stockpiles, they may be quite satisfied with a simple deterrent capability without regard to the fine points of strategic theory.

The original five nuclear states will continue to see themselves in a modified but still polarized Cold War relationship, requiring nuclear deterrence vis-à-vis each other. In this light, these five states would see missile defense as destabilizing that mutual balance. But deploying ballistic missile defenses (BMD) to protect themselves against threats from the new nuclear states makes much more sense. Anti-Ballistic Missile (ABM) deployments, designed to protect a finite number of self-identified target states from the latter states, are being designed and implemented. They could be separate systems separately administered, based on defense agreements among a limited set of states concerned with particular threats.

Such systems could be boost-phase systems—either sea-based or based in territory of the parties to the separate treaties—or they could be air attacks on soft "R&D" launch facilities during launch preparations. Such ballistic missile defense systems could be viewed as enforcing a quarantine on space launches from threatening states. Pre-launch payload inspections could ensure that peaceful access to space would not suffer interference.

A global missile defense architecture consisting of separate systems to protect group A from threat nation X, another to protect group B from Y, etc., clearly does not scale. But when the number of threat states is small and is growing slowly, one can forgo the efficiency principle in favor of limited solutions tailored to a few particular circumstances. Procurement efficiency will not be totally forgone, since there will, in such a future situation, be a growing market for missile defense systems, and it is not unreasonable to believe that, even with a small number of such systems and some commonalities among the threatened states, they can be networked to some extent.

Some of these ideas in precision conventional weapons, cyber attack and defense capabilities, and missile defense are ongoing and not revolutionary. They all depend on networked arrangements for early warning, strategic reconnaissance, and navigation—front-end systems whose output can be shared among states that feel they need defense capabilities—but do not wish to enter into binding international agreements. The Internet, Google Earth, and GPS are starts in that direction.

The technologies involved in the precise delivery of force, first introduced in this discussion in terms of offensive needs, blur the separation of offense and defense. They reflect the observation of Albert Wohlstetter in discussing deterrence and missile defense, that offense had become defense and defense had become offense.

The new nuclear weapons states are much less homogeneous than were the first five, divided as they were over Communism. The new nuclear nations are a commoditization of nuclear weapons to support the needs of regional interests. To speak of "proliferation" is to lump separate problems into one-size-fits-all prescriptions. Israel–"Palestine," Pakistan–India, Iran–Iraq, North Korea–South Korea, and possibly others to arise from new sources of tension and varied sets of constraints. It is possible that precision in physical targeting may also provide fruitful approaches to precision in political targeting as well.

Endnotes

1. Charles Perrow, *Normal Accidents: Living With High-Risk Technologies*, New York: Basic Books, 1984. An alternate body of thought in the same community holds that any desired level of reliability can be achieved—the issue being the amount of care and attention given to achieving reliability. Since investment in reliability is, of necessity, limited, given other needs, the difference between the two viewpoints is quantitative, not qualitative. Thus, the approach taken here is to examine data rather than rely on theory.
2. Brian Michael Jenkins, *Will Terrorists Go Nuclear?* Amherst, New York: Prometheus Books, 2008.
3. William C. Yengst, Stephen J. Lukasik, and Mark A. Jensen, "Nuclear Weapons that Went to War (NWTWTW)," DNA-TR-96-25, draft final report sponsored by US Defense Special Weapons Agency and Science Applications International Corp., October 1996, unclassified, available from *www.npolicy.org/article.php?aid=80&rt=&key=nwtwtw&sec=article&author=*.
4. Sun Tzu, *The Art of War*, Chap. 3, "Offensive Strategy," Samuel B. Griffith, trans., Oxford, UK: Oxford University Press, 1963.
5. Rupert Smith, *The Utility of Force: The Art of War in the Modern World*, New York: Random House/Vintage Books, 2007.
6. This and the following cases are taken from unpublished manuscripts prepared in the 1996–1998 period by William C. Yengst, as part of a preliminary study of precision weapons and their effectiveness.

7. *Ibid.*
8. The common view among cyber technologists is that interfering with computers and the processes they support is the greatest harm that can occur. In suggesting that cyber attacks are an effective application of "force," far-more-serious end results are envisaged here. Societies depend on infrastructure to deliver essential goods and services: electric power, communications, information, natural gas, crude and refined fossil fuel through pipelines, transportation of raw material, goods and people, water and waste purification and disposal, etc. These depend on rotating machinery, pumps, pipes, circuit boards, and other devices. They are all managed by computers, so they do function as intended by their designers. Cyber attackers can "get into" their computer-based command and control systems and instruct those systems to operate beyond their design limits, causing them to destroy themselves. Such physical destruction is far more serious than causing computers to stop, because the time to repair the damage depends on repair crews, the availability of spares, and the control and repair of associated damage caused when large amounts of the kinetic, electrical, and hydraulic energy involved in their operation are released in an uncontrolled manner. Such attacks are discussed in Stephen J. Lukasik, "Mass–Effect Network Attacks: A Safe and Efficient Terrorist Strategy," SAIC report to the Defense Threat Reduction Agency (DTRA), January 2007.

Chapter 13

Missiles for Peace

Henry D Sokolski

In an effort to reduce US military reliance on nuclear weapons, the Barack Obama administration is emphasizing how much more America can rely on advanced non-nuclear weapons to defend its interests, allies, and friends. There is only one problem: The White House's plans to deploy these weapons systems—including new non-nuclear missile defenses and long-range conventional missiles—do not quite add up.

The missile defense system the Obama administration has advocated may be incapable of countering the missile threat the Pentagon is projecting. Meanwhile, the long-range conventional missile system the Pentagon is working on is unlikely to be able to reach anything but a mere handful of targets.

None of this, however, is inevitable. Both programs can be enhanced, but only at the risk of upsetting America's two largest potential rivals: China and Russia. Still, enhancing these programs would limit the harm either China or Russia might otherwise be able to inflict on the United States and its allies. More importantly, it would put the United States in a far better position to get Beijing and Moscow to agree to deep ground-based, nuclear-capable missile reductions and to cooperate on missile defenses—which, in turn, would make all parties far safer.

This is conceivable if the United States had the right offensive and defensive programs in place. Unfortunately, the United States doesn't yet. Take the administration's missile defense efforts. The Pentagon announced in 2009 that it was deploying the first fully tested version of a system known as the Standard Missile-3 (SM-3) to neutralize Iran's shorter-range rockets. After 2018, the Pentagon says it will begin deploying an entirely new variant to neutralize Iran's intermediate- and intercontinental-range ballistic missiles. US intelligence agencies last fall said Iran was most likely to deploy these sometime after 2020.

This all seemed sound enough until Defense Secretary Robert Gates announced in April 2010 that, with sufficient foreign assistance, Iran's longest-range rockets could fly by 2015—5 years earlier than originally projected. Some outside experts have doubted that the much ballyhooed advanced variant of the SM-3—the SM-3 Block II B—could be effective against intercontinental ballistic missiles on any timeline. There has never been any question, though, of the Pentagon being able to field it before 2015. It cannot.

Enter the administration's critics. The fix they are pushing is to ready a two-staged missile defense interceptor derived from the fully tested US homeland defense system currently based in Alaska. This two-stage interceptor is what former President George W. Bush promised to deploy in Poland by 2017, but that President Obama unplugged last fall to mollify the Russians. Whether this system could be brought online and made to work before 2015 is open to debate.

Moscow, however, fears this system will be all too effective. It worries that it might be upgraded to intercept Russian missiles aimed at the North Atlantic Treaty Organization (NATO) and the United States. As extra insurance against this prospect or the possibility of the most robust SM-3 systems being deployed, Russia included language in the New Strategic Arms Reduction Treaty (New START) linking missile defense limits to limits on offensive missiles. Russia's foreign minister insists the New START language gives Russia the right to leave the treaty if the United States increases its missile defense capabilities significantly.

When it seemed clear that Washington would not need to upgrade the current missile defense system extensively until after the New START agreement expires in 2020, Moscow's rhetorical foot-stamping on the link between New START and missile defenses was easy to dismiss. Now, if by 2015 the Iranians field missiles that could reach America, Moscow's threat to leave the treaty would have to be taken more seriously.

In this case, the United States would face two disagreeable choices. It has 30 ground-based missile defense interceptor launchers based in the United States that can knock down a maximum of 15 incoming missiles (assuming two interceptor shots per attacking missile). It is unclear how well this system would work, however, without any ability to target offensive missiles well before they reach the United States (i.e., in midcourse). The SM-3 Block II B is supposed to afford this capability, as was the two-stage interceptor system that Bush promised Poland. Pushing these programs for deployment before 2020, though, would risk upsetting Moscow, which might react by withdrawing from the New START agreement and by fielding more ballistic missile warheads to penetrate US defenses.

The other option would be to hope for the best, blink, and hold off deploying any midcourse defense capabilities until 2020. A third option—which the White House now hopes it can pull off—is to get Moscow to agree well before 2015 to deeper nuclear ballistic missile and tactical nuclear weapons cuts and to cooperate with the United States in deploying effective missile defenses against Iran. How willing Moscow might be to reach such an agreement, though, given its long list of military grievances against NATO, is unclear.

Meanwhile, Russia is taking no risks: It is developing missiles that fly entirely or mostly in the atmosphere, making them far more difficult for US missile defenses to neutralize.

The Chinese Threat

Meanwhile, there is another missile threat on the horizon—that of highly precise, ground-based Chinese intermediate-range, conventionally armed missiles. This threat is one that the United States will need to address no matter what it is able to negotiate with Moscow. Now under development, these Chinese medium-range land-based ballistic and cruise missiles threaten to target US aircraft carrier task forces operating in the Pacific, the Indian Ocean, and the Persian Gulf. The current generation of Chinese missiles already can strike many of our fixed bases and those of our allies and friends in these regions (e.g., Taiwan, Okinawa, and Guam).

This missile threat helps explain why the US Navy is so gung-ho on hosting missile defenses on its Aegis cruisers. The Navy, though, is under no illusion: The Chinese already are deploying far more missiles than the United States or its allies have missile defenses. Certainly, in the near term, it will be far cheaper and easier for the Chinese to produce more offensive ground-based missiles and the Russians to put more nuclear warheads on their large, ground-based ballistic missiles than it will be for the United States to keep building missile defenses to knock them down.

With the production of enough SM-3 interceptors (i.e., thousands), the costs of our missile defenses could drop below that of offensive missile systems, but this would require a good number of America's allies buying large numbers of SM-3 systems. Alternatively, some technical breakthroughs might be made that would enable much smaller, drone-delivered, boost-phase interceptor systems to knock rockets out before they left the atmosphere. In either case, this will take time.

Bottom line: Unless the United States can give Iran, China, and Russia a clear military incentive now to stop building and relying so heavily on offensive ground-launched missiles for their security, Washington risks falling behind a large strategic eight ball. An additional given is that Washington will have to deploy more advanced missile defenses to deal with increasing numbers of ground-based Chinese conventional long-range missiles and Russian nuclear ballistic warheads. This is the case with the Chinese land-based conventional missile threat, even if Obama somehow eliminated all nuclear weapons. Given the current costs of missile defenses, trying to pressure China and Russia not to increase their land-based missile capabilities by simply threatening them with a major US missile defense effort alone, though, is as unlikely to work as the attempt to pressure the Soviet Union in the 1980s was. Something else will be needed.

Long-Range Strike

One idea that has support in Washington is to develop our own fleet of fast-flying, conventional, medium- and long-range strike weapons to put Russia and China's growing land-based nuclear and conventional missile fleets at risk. A clear incentive to do so is that the Russians and Chinese are worried that the United States might. Here, they have cause: China and Russia are investing in long-range missiles to threaten US and allied targets. Moscow and Beijing are fearful that if the United States deployed a fleet of accurate, land-based, fast-flying, conventional missiles of its own, Washington could threaten a vast number of key Chinese and Russian fixed military command and support targets (e.g., above ground radars, storage sites, etc.). Worse, these countries fear the United States might even be able to threaten their ground-based missile forces from their garrisons over key fixed Chinese and Russian transit choke points—i.e., select mobile missile rail lines and assigned mobile missile roads, pre-assigned launch sites, bridges, and tunnels.

Could the United States develop such a weapon system? It nearly did. In the second term of the Bush administration, the Pentagon developed and tested a conventional front end employing metal rods

("Rods from God") that could be mounted on existing US land-based ballistic missiles or on submarine-based ballistic missiles. In 2005, the Pentagon's Defense Science Board determined that highly precise, non-nuclear front ends could be substituted for the nuclear warheads on 50 existing land-based US nuclear-armed rockets for about $900 million dollars. The board determined that retrofitting these front ends could be completed in a matter of months.

What makes this earlier non-nuclear ballistic missile proposal intriguing is that the Obama administration is now sold on a concept that is somewhat similar. In 2010, Vice President Joe Biden announced the administration's support for a conventional long-range offensive weapon called Prompt Global Strike. This program has several systems under development, but the most prominent one relies on an exotic, yet-to-be-proven, hypersonic boost glide delivery system kludged onto a long-range ballistic missile. As a result, it is very expensive and technologically risky: The first test flight of the system on April 22, 2010, ended in failure, as did the second test flight on August 11, 2011. Current plans are to deploy only one launcher with one to two missiles for possible reload, but development could take years.

Why is the administration pushing such dicey, sophisticated technology? The short answer is arms control. The proposed Prompt Global Strike system is not truly a ballistic missile. More than half of its flight trajectory varies, much like that of a plane. This, White House officials note, is its key advantage: Because it does not fit the New START agreement's definition for a strategic ballistic missile, the system would not be counted against the treaty's ballistic missile limits. This argument, though, hardly makes sense. For starters, the systems have got to be far cheaper and quicker to go with existing technology, convert deployed US nuclear rockets, and make them conventional—rather than try to crash-develop a hypersonic boost glide vehicle front end. Second, given that the Obama administration is currently interested in deploying only a few of these systems, it hardly matters whether they are counted against New START limits or not.

Finally, if the Pentagon is worried about keeping US nuclear warhead deployment numbers up, it could accomplish this simply by taking whatever nuclear warheads it might remove from existing US land-based rockets and uploading them on slower- flying, recallable strategic bombers. Under the New START agreement, nuclear-capable bombers are counted as one nuclear warhead, even if they carry a large number of bombs.

Congressional skeptics and arms control critics, of course, have long worried that the Russians and Chinese might misread any US launch of a conventional ballistic missile as a nuclear strike and react with nuclear rocket strikes of their own. This fear, however, seems misplaced. First, it has to be more destabilizing to continue to threaten China and Russia with nuclear strikes from quick-reaction ballistic missiles based in relatively vulnerable fixed silos in the US Midwest than basing more of our nuclear weapons on slower-flying, recallable, nuclear-capable bombers.

Finally, Russian or Chinese apprehensions about whether proposed US conventional rockets are actually nuclear can be addressed directly: Simply allow Chinese and Russian observers access to US dedicated conventional ballistic-missile bases, give them a chance to send the coordinates of the bases to their militaries, and let them stay on base if they want.

The X-37b Option

In addition to this conventional ballistic-missile scheme, there is another non-nuclear, long-range, quick-strike option that the United States could pursue. On April 22, 2010, the US Air Force successfully launched an experimental unmanned robotic space plane known as the X-37B. Now orbiting earth, it can stay aloft for up to 9 months and land anywhere it is directed. The Air Force says it was designed to ensure that our war fighters will be provided the capabilities they need. The X-37B could conceivably serve as a quick-alert space surveillance system, an anti-satellite weapon, or a space bomber. Some aerospace experts speculate the United States might fly 10 or more of these systems in space at any one time to accomplish any or all of these missions.

Finally, the United States could augment its efforts to develop medium-range ballistic and cruise missiles that could be launched off ships and planes. It could even hint that it might take up Russia's recent dare to back out of the 1987 Intermediate Nuclear Forces (INF) agreement, which banned all US and Russian ground-launched missiles with ranges between 500 and 5,500 kilometers (km) by threatening to do likewise.

Of course, if the United States were to consolidate the conventional ground-launched strike systems described and the target-acquisition system they require as part of a long-term US conventional deterrence initiative, it would hardly sit well with Russian or Chinese officials. On the other hand, key US and allied military targets are themselves increasingly vulnerable to a first strike from Chinese and Iranian non-nuclear ground-launched missiles and from possible use of Russian and Chinese nuclear missiles. As such, the United States is obliged to do what it can to neutralize these threats.

None of this is at odds with taking a more cooperative approach. If the United States made it clear that it is going to deploy both enhanced non-nuclear offensive and defensive missile systems, it would be certain to get the attention of Moscow and Beijing. Washington might explain that the United States would prefer to place steep limits on the deployment of medium- and long-range ground-launched missiles—whether they are nuclear or non-nuclear. This would approximate the two-track diplomatic approach that proved successful in the 1980s, when the United States deployed intermediate nuclear missiles while negotiating for their elimination. The result was the eradication of an entire class of ground-launched nuclear missile systems under the INF Treaty.

The logical place to begin in this endeavor would be to propose updating and globalizing the INF understanding by making its limits more precise. One could do this by using the missile range-payload limits of the Missile Technology Control Regime (MTCR), which limits the export of missiles and related technology for systems capable of delivering 500 kilograms (kg) (the weight of a crude first-generation nuclear weapon) more than 300 km. The advantages of updating INF and other proposed missile caps using range-payload limits are several. First, Russia and the United States have already given up all ground-based missiles more than 500 km in range. Second, updating this agreement to factor in MTCR limits and extending it to other key nations, such as China, India, Pakistan, and beyond is an endeavor Moscow and Washington could readily cooperate on to their mutual advantage. Third, it would constructively integrate efforts to prevent the further spread of nuclear-capable missile technology to additional states with efforts to eliminate ground-launched versions where they are currently deployed.

Also, progress on expanding such missile limits could make cooperation on a number of fronts much easier. For starters, the major powers could focus on defending against much smaller ground-based missile fleets owned by much smaller states. Against these less-robust missile forces, the United States, Russia, China, India, and others could cooperate in deploying missile defenses that would give smaller states a clear disincentive to rely heavily on large, ground-based missiles to provide for their security. Finally, with deep ballistic missile cuts, space cooperation—which might otherwise be off limits for fear of indirectly lending assistance to Russian or Chinese military ballistic-missile programs—would be much easier to conduct.

This alternative world would approximate what President Ronald Reagan hoped for through realization of his other disarmament dream, which was to rid the world of what he called "nuclear missiles," i.e., reaction ready, ground-based, nuclear-capable missiles. It is a dream that is a natural for missile-defending Reagan Republicans and nuclear-disarming Obama Democrats. Certainly, if our government is serious about getting the United States and others to rely more on conventional deterrence and less on living with the hair-trigger prospect of mutual nuclear missile strikes, the surest way to start is to make America's long-range missiles less nuclear and its missile defenses more credible against the missile threats that remain.

Chapter 14

Missile Defense and Arms Control

Jeff Kueter

Many countries view ballistic and cruise missile systems as cost-effective weapons and symbols of national power. In addition, they present an asymmetric threat to US airpower. Many ballistic and cruise missiles are armed with weapons of mass destruction.[1]

National Air and Space
Intelligence Center, 2009

The National Air and Space Intelligence Center's matter-of-fact statement encapsulates the strategic challenges posed by ballistic missile proliferation and, at the same time, establishes the rationale for investments in missile defenses across the globe. Simply put, states are investing in missiles, and the underlying skills and technologies to improve them, because missiles are effective and efficient weapons capable of filling a range of national security missions. Over 25 nations have ballistic missile capabilities today. Even though the aggregate number of missiles may be down relative to the Cold War, that statistic reflects reductions by the superpowers and masks the growth observed elsewhere in the world. The expansion of missile arsenals and the diverse uses contemplated for these arsenals explains the growing interest in missile defense. Missile defenses are becoming commonplace and, with the notable exception of US-Russian arms control, noncontroversial. Stripped of the hangover of Cold War strategic thinking and seen from the views of nations other than the United States and Russia, the choice to erect defenses against ballistic missile threats is a logical and rational one.

Nowhere is this transformation better seen than in Asia. As ballistic missile arsenals grow in size and increase in sophistication, nations throughout Asia are investing in the development of defenses to counter those threats. Ballistic missile defense (BMD) programs run from Japan and South Korea in the north through Taiwan, south to Australia, then west to India into the Gulf States, including Israel; and ending in Turkey. Also included are Russia and China.

These developments are not speculative. They involve investment in real systems and deployment of real operational capability. As these systems are purchased or indigenously developed and subsequently deployed, they have challenged, and will continue to challenge, prevailing conceptions of the contributions of missile defense regional and international security. Cold War thinking concluded that missile defenses would destabilize the strategic nuclear balance. Such concerns seem less prevalent today. The United States and Russia still consider these issues in their bilateral discussions, but they do not appear as relevant in other contexts. The diversification of missions contemplated for ballistic missiles and their spread appears to have changed the logic for defense.

Perhaps the most intriguing question posed by these developments is why. Are these nations truly concerned about the threats posed by ballistic missiles? Are they being "encouraged" to purchase these capabilities by the United States? Does the United States see the extension of defensive capabilities as supporting its own interests? How will the extension of missile defenses affect and, in turn, effect changes in, the nuclear weapons landscape?

The available evidence suggests that all of these factors play a role in the growing investment in BMDs. Interest in defense is driven fundamentally by concerns about the dramatic increase in the size of regional missile arsenals and the proliferation of ballistic missile technology. States throughout Asia and around the world face neighbors, rivals, and adversaries with ever growing and ever more sophisticated missile arsenals. That trend shows no signs of abating. Further, the proliferation of missile technology is decoupling from the proliferation of weapons of mass destruction (WMDs). Traditionally, ballistic missiles were the preferred delivery systems for nuclear, chemical, or biological warheads and, consequently, nations pursuing WMDs would also pursue more advanced missile systems. This remains true, but the availability of increasingly powerful conventional munitions and more accurate missiles allows missile arsenals to serve the more traditional airpower roles of long-range, precision strikes. Shorter-range missiles with conventional munitions also play important battlefield roles in certain areas of the world.

The United States has clear interests in the expansion of missile defenses into Asia (and elsewhere). As the principal supplier of missile defense systems and components, it has apparent economic advantages from such expansion. More deeply, the expansion of US-built defenses enables integration of those systems with US capabilities, thereby expanding the coverage and capability of the US sensor and interceptor network. Finally, beyond that practical consideration, missile defenses offer vehicles for strengthening bilateral or alliance ties and may be the foundation for new defensive security guarantees by the United States.

This chapter explores how BMDs bolster defensive security guarantees and advance US regional and global security interests. At the same time, the motives, as well as plans, for investment in missile defense by leading nations will be discussed. A brief review of the ballistic missile threat precedes that discussion.

Evolution of Ballistic Missile Arsenals

Missile arsenals are expanding in size, in the number of countries possessing them, and technical sophistication. The Barack Obama administration's 2010 Ballistic Missile Defense Review (BMDR) adds authority to these observations, noting that:

> The ballistic missile threat is increasing both quantitatively and qualitatively, and is likely to continue to do so over the next decade. Current global trends indicate that ballistic missile systems are becoming more flexible, mobile, reliable, survivable, and accurate, while also increasing in range.[2]

Accentuated by the spread of technology, further maturation of indigenous capabilities, and the deepening of experiential knowledge that comes with the design, construction, and testing of ballistic missile systems, the ballistic missile is a fixture of modern arsenals and will remain so for years to come.

Driving this trend is the simple utility of the missile. Defense analysts have occasionally described ballistic missiles as the "poor man's air force."[3] This description implies that those unable or unwilling to invest the large and sustained amounts of funding necessary to field modern conventional forces can still attain military might with ballistic missiles at much less relative cost. A ballistic missile arsenal (particularly one composed of sophisticated missiles of varied range capabilities) offers the potential to coerce, threaten, or blackmail adversaries.[4] Of course, many states also acquire ballistic missiles for deterrence and dissuasion purposes. The National Air and Space Intelligence Center aptly describes the many uses of ballistic missiles today:

> Missiles are attractive to many nations because they can be used effectively with a formidable air defense system, where an attack with manned aircraft would be impractical or too costly. In addition, missiles can be used as a deterrent or an instrument of coercion. Missiles also have the advantage of fewer maintenance, training, and logistic requirements than manned aircraft. Even limited use of these weapons could be devastating, because missiles can be armed with chemical, biological or nuclear warheads.[5]

China offers an illustration of a highly diversified missile program. China invests in all classes of missiles. Its intercontinental ballistic missile (ICBM) program can reach targets in Asia, Europe, and parts of North America. China's medium-range and anti-ship missile programs serve modest nuclear and robust conventional missiles. China is known to be testing its ballistic missiles against "airfield targets" at the 2nd Artillery missile range in the Gobi Desert. Concrete pads, aircraft, and hangers seen from Google Earth show the impacts of being hit with conventionally armed submunitions. Estimates suggest an intermediate-range ballistic missile (IRBM) can be packed with 990 1-pound (lb) submunitions. Coordinated, multi-missile attacks could hold US airbases in Asia at risk and could inflict massive damage on them and their resident aircraft if an actual missile strike were to occur.

States with active development programs have conducted "several hundred launches of ballistic missiles over the past decade."[6] The BMDR notes that some states are increasingly acquiring and testing "advanced liquid-propellant systems and even solid-propellant systems," while also improving range and accuracy and incorporating "more aggressive denial and deception practices"[7] to ensure survivability against pre-launch attack. Modern ballistic missiles, like China's CSS-5, are accurate to 50 meters of the target and travel more than 1,100 nautical miles. North Korea's IRBM may have a range of more than 2,000 miles. Intercontinental threats are not as apparent today and reside mainly in Russia and China, but North Korea's Taepodong-2 may have a range in excess of 3,000 miles once deployed.

These advantages offer clear incentives for the acquisition of missiles and the investment in the infrastructure to manufacture them indigenously. Proliferation presents more than concerns about the number of countries acquiring weapons. The weapons being acquired are increasing in quality, sophistication, and range. Those qualitative features compound the deterrence and defensive challenge. The BMDR elaborates:

> Globally, the intelligence community continues to see a progression in development from short-to-medium- and in some cases intermediate-range missiles. Development programs reflect increasing ambition in improving payload, range, precision, and operational performance.[8]

No strategy for addressing the threats posed by ballistic missiles is complete if it does not anticipate the evolutionary improvement of missile arsenals in the years to come.

The states most actively pursuing ballistic missile systems also rank as the most likely proliferators of the technology and knowledge needed to develop and mature indigenous missile capabilities elsewhere. The Missile Defense Agency (MDA) cites China's sale of solid-propellant technologies to Pakistan as a critical enabler of Pakistan's Shaheen II medium-range and Abdali short-range missiles.[9] Iran and North Korea are known to regularly exchange technologies and personnel to further advance each others' missile, and perhaps WMD, programs.

Complicating efforts to control the spread of critical technologies is their dual-use nature.[10] Not only do some technologies have nondefense industrial uses; others also contribute to legitimate space exploration aspirations. Consequently, specialty metals or sophisticated manufacturing tools may be exported for perfectly reasonable ends, only to be repurposed or reverse-engineered for resale.

Expanding proliferation networks further heighten the attractiveness of such weapons. Leveraging these relationships allows states and nonstate actors to forgo the considerable expense of indigenous development and production—which once constituted a severe handicap for poor and technologically primitive countries—and acquire sophisticated capabilities quickly. Now, even WMDs and their associated technology increasingly are available for purchase.[11] As the AQ Khan network demonstrated, nonstate actors are engaging in illicit transfers. While transfers of WMD and missile capabilities to terrorist organizations do not appear to have happened yet, the Department of Defense (DoD) believes there is "potential for a substantial increase in the transfer of advanced capabilities" from states with mature missile and WMD programs to less capable entities.[12] Australia's Ministry of Defense echoes DoD's pessimism, arguing:

> The number of states with a "break out" capability to rapidly produce WMD will also probably increase [over the next 20 to 30 years] with the proliferation of dual use infrastructure.[13]

The spread of more advanced missiles does not threaten only the United States. Other nations are becoming more sensitive to the security challenges presented by missile programs. Japanese defense officials are speaking out about the risks posed by North Korea's pursuit of nuclear weapons and the missiles to deliver them. In the wake of a North Korean nuclear test in the spring of 2009, Japanese officials pressed the international community to adopt a more aggressive stand against North Korea. The nuclear test "constitutes a grave threat to the security not only of Northeast Asia but of the entire international community when taken together with the enhancement of its ballistic missile capability," the Japanese Defense Minister said.[14] Japan's representative to the United Nations (UN) called North Korea's actions "a grave threat to the national security of Japan. . . ."[15] Editorializing about a reported North Korean missile test, the Daily Yomiuri called for Japan's Self-Defense Forces "to try to intercept the missile to minimize possible damage," should it errantly come toward Japan.[16]

The ballistic missile threat extends beyond North Korea. States throughout the Middle East are acquiring short-range, SCUD or SCUD-derived missiles. Iran's aspirations run higher, and are reflected in their fielded capabilities and in their stated intentions for the continued development of those capabilities. In South Asia, missile proliferation is the latest installment of the Indian-Pakistan rivalry. In North Pacific Asia, North Korea's increasingly sophisticated missile programs, coupled with its role as profligate exporter of technology and know-how, make it both a source of regional instability and a breeder of instability elsewhere. The Australian Ministry of Defence notes that:

> Threats posed by ballistic missiles and their proliferation, particularly by states of concern such as North Korea, constitute a potential strategic challenge to Australia . . . and other threats to regional security and stability.[17]

Absent from Figure 14-1, used by the MDA to show the current state of foreign ballistic missile programs, are the arsenals of Russia and China, which remain among the world's largest and most sophisticated. Both figure prominently in regional security calculations.

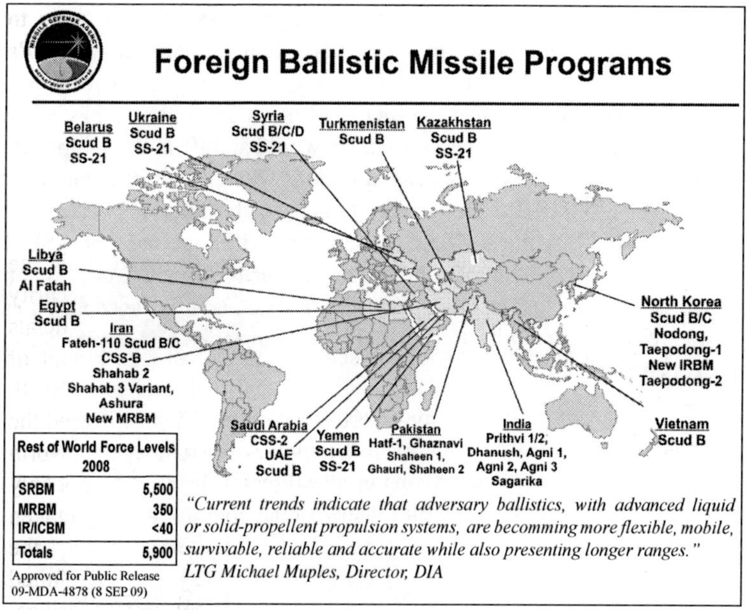

Figure 14-1. Foreign Ballistic Missile Programs.

A brief summation of leading missile arsenals follows. Several themes become clear in this abbreviated review. The upward trend in the investment of time and resources is obvious. The exchange of materials and knowledge among nations is evident. The pursuit of more capable and sophisticated missiles is a priority. The use of missiles to deliver nuclear or other WMD payloads and conventional missions provides new rationales for defenses.

China

China has the most active ballistic missile development system in the world.[18] The MDA says China is "qualitatively and quantitatively improving its strategic forces."[19] In terms of ICBMs and strategic submarine-launched ballistic missiles (SLBMs), the DoD's 2009 Military Power of China report notes that since 2000, "China has shifted from a largely vulnerable, strategic deterrent based on liquid-fueled ICBMs fired from fixed locations to a more flexible strategic force."[20] This change is manifested by two new classes of ICBMs—the DF-31 and DF-31A—both solid-fueled, road mobile, and deployed in 2006 and 2007, respectively.[21] With the eventual addition of the long-range JL-2 SLBM, China's ICBM potential "could more than double in the next 15 years especially if [multiple independently targetable reentry vehicles or MIRVs] are employed."[22] Of particular regional concern must be Beijing's development of medium-range ballistic missile (MRBM) capabilities, especially anti-ship ballistic missiles (ASBMs), which could possibly sink aircraft carriers or deny other warships access to desired areas during a conflict.[23] These ASBMs would significantly complicate US freedom of action on the seas in regions where they are deployed.[24] China's CSS-5 MRBM can strike "targets in the Pacific Theater and most of Asia,"[25] while a CSS-5 variant comprises the nascent ASBM capability. The US-China Economic and Security Review Commission supports that conclusion, noting that Chinese air and missile capabilities will give it the capability to strike US bases in Japan and elsewhere in East Asia.

Finally, China is also consistently expanding its short-range ballistic missile (SRBM) arsenal of CSS-7 and CSS-6s opposite Taiwan. Estimates have this arsenal growing by around 100 missiles per year, adding further tensions in the Straits and East Asia region.[26]

North Korea

North Korea maintains an extensive indigenous missile program and is the quintessential example of a "secondary proliferator." It has received extensive foreign support from China, Russia, and Pakistan on many of its programs, notably the Nodong MRBM and Taepodong-1 (TD-1) IRBM. The North Koreans now act as "the Third World's greatest supplier of missiles, missile components and related technologies."[27] North Korea has aided many countries, including Iran and Pakistan, with missile development—not to mention helping Syria construct a nuclear reactor, first exposed in 2007.[28] North Korea is an emerging nuclear power. It has withdrawn from the Nuclear Nonproliferation Treaty (NPT) and restarted its once shuttered nuclear facilities. North Korea followed that test with a 3-4 kiloton underground nuclear explosion in May 2009.[29]

The Taepodong-2 (TD-2) represents North Korea's hope for an ICBM capability. Based partly on the TD-1 IRBM design, the first test in July 2006 ended in failure, breaking apart only about 40 seconds into flight.[30] Pyongyang, however, demonstrated a much improved TD-2 during an April 2009 test.[31] If fully developed, a three-stage TD-2 could "deliver a several-hundred kilogram payload up to 15,000 km, which is sufficient to strike all of North America."[32] The TD-1 was first tested in August 1998, a move that caused much consternation in East Asian capitals, particularly Tokyo. The TD-1 is a liquid-fueled, road-mobile missile able to fly at least 2,500 km.

North Korea conducts missile tests on important US holidays such as Independence Day and Memorial Day. It tested six mobile theater missiles on July 4-5, 2006, before once again grabbing the world's attention with a spate of testing beginning on May 25, 2009. North Korea tested seven SRBMs on July 3-4, 2009.

Currently, North Korea deploys at least 200 road-mobile, liquid-fueled Nodong MRBMs and may be developing two new MRBM and IRBMs based on the old Soviet R-27 SLBM.[33] The Nodong has served as the model for Pakistan's Ghuari and Iran's Shahab-III MRBMs. In February 2009, South Korea reported that the Democratic People's Republic of Korea (DPRK) completed its new IRBM with a 3,200-km range potential.[34] The Nodong's potential 1,300-km range can strike most of East Asia, including Guam.[35] From an SRBM standpoint, North Korea deploys hundreds of road-mobile, liquid-fueled SCUD variants to threaten South Korea. It produces an extended-range version of the Russian SCUD B among its SRBM arsenal.[36]

Russia

Russia not only possesses an extensive arsenal of missiles but contributes to the proliferation problem by selling missiles, technology, and expertise, both openly and secretly. According to the National Air and Space Intelligence Center, Russia retains the largest strategic missile force in the world—comprising ICBMs and SLBMs—despite mandated arms control reductions and attrition due to aging.[37] Russia's prioritization on modernizing its long-range strategic missiles predated the New START negotiations and does not appear to be impeded by it. New START will impose top-end limits on the size of the Russian and US ICBM and SLBM arsenals, setting a cap of 800 ICBMs, SLBMs, and bombers. Russia's current ICBM arsenal includes a road-mobile version of its standard SS-27 Topol-M silo-based ICBM deployed in 2006, with a MIRVed Topol-M currently under development.[38] From an SLBM standpoint, Russia deploys the Sineva, but views the solid-fueled Bulava SLBM as its advanced replacement, due to its potential to carry 10 individually targeted nuclear warheads and travel 5,000 km.[39] The Bulava failed during a December 2009 test, but Moscow reiterated its commitment to the program, despite its poor record.[40] Finally, Russia still has a large SRBM arsenal of variants on the SCUD design, accounting for a significant portion of its proliferation activities, including to North Korea. The Russian SCUD-B "has been exported to more countries than any other type of guided ballistic missile."[41]

India

India is actively developing its missile capabilities, consistently seeking longer ranges to deal bolster deterrence against its two chief peer competitors, Pakistan and China. India's most ambitious project is the three-staged, solid-fueled, road-mobile Agni-V IRBM, with an expected maximum range just shy of ICBM status at 5,000 km.[42] India is developing its predecessor IRBM, the Agni-III. The rail-mobile, nuclear-capable Agni-III has been successfully tested and will probably serve as the nuclear deterrent vis-à-vis China until the Agni-V is deployed.[43],[44] The Agni-III will allow India to strike as far away as Beijing; the deployed Agni-II MRBM already allows New Delhi to strike all of Pakistan and most of China.[45] While planning to field updated or new SRBMs, India already deploys a variety of SRBMs, including the ship-launched Dhanush and air-launched Prithvi-II.[46]

Pakistan

Always trying to match India in military capabilities, Pakistan maintains an active missile development program and deploys a number of systems. Also like India, it will probably consider arming its MRBM/IRBM missiles with nonconventional warheads. Pakistan has tested the solid-fuel Shaheen-II MRBM six times since 2004, and the US intelligence community expects its deployment soon.[47] The Shaheen-II represents an improvement over the Ghauri-II MRBM, which is liquid-fueled and can fly only two-thirds as far.[48] Pakistan also currently deploys around 50 sophisticated, solid-fueled, road-mobile SRBMs, including the Hatf-1, Shaheen-I, and Ghaznavi launchers.[49]

Iran

Many believe that along with North Korea, Iran might combine nuclear warheads with long-range ballistic missiles in the coming years. Already possessing the largest ballistic missile inventory in the Middle East, Iran, many believe, would "choose missile delivery as its preferred method of delivering a nuclear weapon" because it is "inherently capable of carrying a nuclear payload."[50] Iran is another case demonstrating the perils of proliferation, as it has received past assistance and technology from North Korea, Russia, and China.[51]

Additionally, Iran's pursuit of space launch capabilities offers legitimate cover for its pursuit of long-range missiles. The linkages between the Safir-II Satellite Launch Vehicle (SLV) and ICBM development are widely acknowledged.[52] The Safir-II first delivered a satellite into orbit in February 2009 and did so again in February 2010.

Recent intelligence estimates suggest that a committed Iran, with access to foreign technology, could begin ICBM testing by as early as 2015.[53] In addition to its SLV program, Iran possesses other missiles, all under active development. One of its most advanced missiles, the Shahab-III MRBM, is based on the North Korean No Dong MRBM. The Shahab-III has a range up to 2,000 km, placing parts of southeastern Europe in danger, and Iran might have the ability to mass produce such missiles.[54] The two-stage, solid-fueled Sajjil-2 represents an even more advanced MRBM, with a potential 2,500-km range when fully developed. Iran is also developing its SRBM capabilities, with varying degrees of past or current cooperation with China, North Korea, and Russia. The arsenal includes road-mobile, liquid-fueled SCUD variants and the road-mobile, solid-fueled Fateh-110.[55]

Consideration of Iran's missile program also should take note of its advancing nuclear ambitions. The UN Security Council sanctioned Iran three times for its nuclear program, with the United States managing to push through a fourth set of sanctions in 2010 in response to continued Iranian intransigence. The US Intelligence Community judges that Iran is "technically capable of producing enough highly enriched uranium (HEU) for a weapon in the next few years."[56]

Missile Defense Characteristics

Two basic concepts underscore contemporary approaches to ballistic missile defense—hit-to-kill and layering. Hit-to-kill is a reference to the physical destruction of an attacking ballistic missile. Layering is both a physical and strategic construct in which the defense is organized to exploit the weaknesses of a missile as it travels through its flight phases and provides the defender with multiple opportunities to detect and destroy the attacking missile.

Hit-to-Kill

All currently operational ballistic missile defense systems are based on surface-launched interceptor missiles.[57] These interceptors use "hit-to-kill" capabilities to destroy their targets—attacking ballistic missiles. Hit-to-kill is descriptive—the interceptor literally "hits" the attacking missile to "kill" it. By aiming for and directly colliding with the attacking ballistic missile at extremely fast closing speeds, the interceptor uses kinetic energy to destroy the target.

The use of directed energy, or lasers, to apply heat to the missile is another way to destroy missiles. The laser destroys the boosting missile by burning through its metal skin until the skin cracks. Directed energy programs have had varying levels of support through the years. Most recently, the Airborne Laser (ABL) represented efforts to use directed energy for missile defense. Space-based lasers were briefly considered during the 1980s. The MDA's support for directed energy shifted from a push for an operational program, and instead relegating the ABL to a research test bed before it was moved to long-term storage in early 2012.

Layering a BMD

A ballistic missile's flight is comprised of three segments, or phases. The first phase is the initial, rocket-propelled boost segment, in which the missile expends its fuel in order to leave the Earth's surface and exit the atmosphere into space. The second phase is the unpowered, ballistic, midcourse phase, during which time the missile's payload travels outside the atmosphere in a ballistic flight in the direction of its target. The third and final, or terminal, phase is the one in which the missile's warheads re-enter the Earth's atmosphere and deliver their destructive payloads on their targets. (see Figure 14-2.)

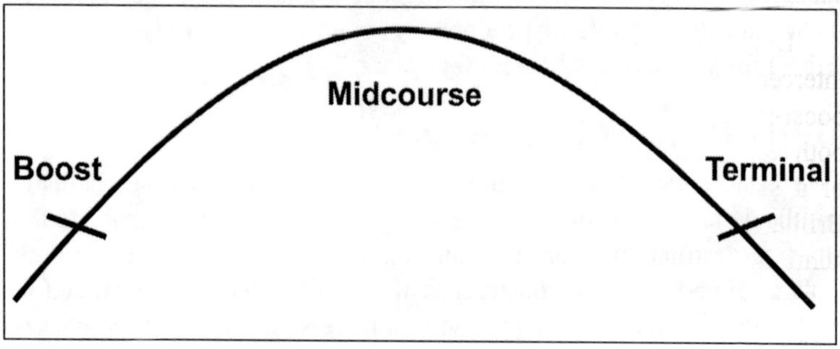

Figure 14-2. Diagram of the Three Phases of a Ballistic Missile's Flight.

In the missile's launch, or boost, phase, the missile is initially moving slowly, fighting inertia and atmospheric drag—all the while lofting all its fuel, as well as its payload—into the sky. Running only on internal fuel, the missile must escape the atmosphere and buildup speed to fly for most of its unpowered flight through space. It must do all of this within the few minutes that its fuel supply lasts.

While its motors are firing, a boosting missile burns immense quantities of highly flammable fuel, which generates immense amounts of thrust, and with it, immense amounts of heat. Infrared sensors can detect a boosting ballistic missile's heat plume from a great distance, especially from a space-based vantage point.

Another important aspect of a boosting ballistic missile is that in order to accelerate the missile's payload to the necessary velocity and loft it out of the atmosphere, all of the missile's contents must be retained inside the missile until the boosting is done. This is true regardless of the number of warheads inside the missile. This means that the boosting missile is a very "rich" target, in that all of a missile's destructive cargo—its warheads and decoys—can be destroyed simultaneously. Stopping the boosting missile requires shooting down only one target.

As a consequence, a missile is most conspicuous and most vulnerable in the boost phase. However, the actual interception of a boosting ballistic missile is also the toughest phase in which to actually reach it. A missile's boost phase lasts only some 300 seconds or less for ICBMs. Newer-generation solid-fuel rockets can take as little as 180 seconds to complete boosting, which offers precious little time in which to effect an interception. Any boost-phase missile-defense system must sense, decide, launch, and fly out to intercept a boosting ICBM, all the while constrained by the target's 180 to 300-second time frame, severely curtailing the effective range of a boost-phase defense weapon.

During the 1980s and early 1990s, kinetic or directed energy interceptions from space-based platforms were the preferred option for boost-phase defense. The Strategic Defense Initiative (SDI) invested in both techniques, and the US Government was ready to begin procurement of a space-based kinetic energy system more commonly known as Brilliant Pebbles when the program was cancelled by the Bill Clinton administration.

There are no boost programs currently under development by the United States. In recent years, the ABL and ground-based Kinetic Energy Interceptor (KEI) were designated boost-phase programs. The KEI was terminated altogether after a few years, and the ABL has moved to a pure research and development (R&D) platform before being mothballed in February 2012.

Midcourse Phase

By the midcourse phase of a ballistic missile's flight, the weapon has left the atmosphere, and all of its propellant has been expended. In the airlessness of space, any and all payloads are released from the confines of the missile's nose and are set adrift to follow ballistic trajectories. There are now multiple targets for the defenses to sort out. Worse, countermeasures, chaff, decoys, spent booster stages (especially if they are deliberately fragmented), and housing shrouds are deployed as clutter with which to deceive defending sensor systems and conceal the real weapons.

Once the fuel is spent, the weapons also have little or no capability to maneuver and are set on their trajectories until they re-enter the atmosphere. Ballistic missiles spend the majority of their time in this mid-course phase, which lasts for as long as 20 minutes in the case of ICBM payloads. This phase affords the longest time during which to engage these targets. That and their relative inability to maneuver or change direction beyond their ballistic trajectory affords some advantages to the defense.

But there are significant challenges to successful midcourse interception. The defenses must correctly discriminate between warheads and decoys, and see through countermeasures, over distances of thousands of miles. Because of the distances that need to be traveled from the interceptor launch site to the target in space, the number of available shot opportunities is limited. This conundrum is of particular concern— because a likely response by the offense is to launch several missiles at once, complicating the defender's tracking, discrimination, and interception options. While the midcourse phase is paradoxically the longest time window in which to attempt an interception, it is also the most complex.

Terminal Phase

The terminal phase is the third and final phase of a ballistic missile's flight. During this time, the warheads and decoys enter the atmosphere at extremely high speed. The warheads are designed to survive atmosphere re-entry heating in order to reach their ground targets and will continue on to their targets at speed, though decelerating due to atmospheric drag. Chaff and decoys will either lag behind the warheads or burn up altogether in the upper atmosphere. The terminal phase is thus inherently "self-discriminating," with only the warheads surviving re-entry to reach the lower atmosphere.

There are three very difficult challenges to be met in attempting interceptions during this phase. First and foremost, warheads entering the lower stratosphere take only 30 to 60 seconds to complete their transit and strike their ground targets. Second, defenses must successfully stop all of the warheads delivered by the missile—a challenging task, as well. Third, more technologically advanced states such as Russia possess Maneuvering Reentry Vehicles (MARVs), which can glide in the atmosphere (at very high speeds) in order to effect evasive maneuvers, making them much more difficult to intercept. In fact, Russia boasts that its MARV capabilities render missile defenses obsolete.[58]

In short, the terminal phase is the shortest time period in which to attempt to intercept a ballistic missile's warheads, requiring very-high-performance weapons to perform successfully in the short response time. Interception ranges and thus coverage zones are even more restricted for terminal-phase defenses.

Missile Defense Today and Tomorrow

The US missile defense program today consists of four classes of interceptors, numerous sensors and radars, battle management and command and control functions, and a globally integrated communications network. The defense is oriented to defeat missiles in the midcourse and terminal phases of flight. There are no active development programs focused on boost defense. Figure 14-3 summarizes the current and planned architecture as of fiscal year 2011.

Figure 14-3. Current US Missile Defense Systems

In fiscal year 2011, the MDA transitioned its funding for boost-phase developments to a program focused on Directed Energy. The agency intends to use the ABL Test Bed to push various high-power laser programs, while sustaining critical industrial capabilities. Critics of the ABL felt the chemical laser employed by the system was inefficient and costly, and pointed toward a rising class of laser technologies that appear to offer significant efficiency improvements. As yet, those laser systems are not capable of producing the amount of power needed to destroy a missile. Nevertheless, directed energy systems have great potential for missile defense missions as well as other defense needs. The MDA Directed Energy Program is structured to coordinate and cooperate with other DoD R&D efforts in this area to ensure that results and innovations are shared across the defense science and technology enterprise.

The Aegis and Ground-based Midcourse Defense (GMD) systems comprise the lion's share of the US missile defense effort. The Aegis system has assumed the central focus of the Obama administration's plans. By 2015, the administration plans to have 32 naval vessels outfitted to perform missile defense missions, up from 21 in 2011. Those ships will carry more than 430 Standard Missile-3 interceptors and 100 Standard Missile-2 (SM-2) Terminal interceptors, up from 60 and 40 in 2011, respectively. The Obama administration has embraced the potential of the system and is investing ever larger sums in new variants of the interceptor.

This emphasis is seen most clearly in the Obama administration's regional defense initiatives. The Phased Adaptive Approach (PAA) centered on Europe is focused on "addressing missile defense interoperability with NATO and our allies and partners as the threat from the Middle East is anticipated to increase over the next decade."[59] Designed to intercept short-, medium-, and intermediate-range missiles coming from Iran, the PAA replaced the Bush administration's proposed European "Third Site" GMD-based architecture with an Aegis-based system. The PAA will deploy ship-based Aegis SM-3 IA interceptors to the Mediterranean along with AN/TPY-2 and SPY-1 radars and a command, control, battle management, and a communications (C2BMC) system by the end of 2011.

The four-phase plan calls for additional ship-based assets, an improved interceptor (the SM-3 IB), and an Aegis Ashore battery in Romania to be deployed by 2015. In Phase 3, the SM-3 IIA interceptor that presently is under development in cooperation with Japan is scheduled for use at a site in Poland and at sea. Additional sensors and tracking capabilities also should be brought online by 2018. Finally, by 2020, Phase 4 calls for deployment of the SM-3 IIB interceptor to "provide an early intercept (pre-apogee) capability against MRBMs and IRBMs and provide an additional layer for a more enhanced homeland defense against ICBMs from today's regional threats."[60] With the exception of its radars and target discrimination capabilities, the GMD system is not expected to support the PAA.

Further development of the SM-3 family of interceptors is a work-in-progress. The SM-3 IB, which is planned for use in 2015, continues to encounter divert and attitude control issues and a slipping flight test schedule. The others, which are even more advanced, likely will encounter the delays expected of new and advanced technical systems. "Any new program is going to have issues to deal with," Lieutenant General Henry Obering (Ret.), former director of the Missile Defense Agency, said in a discussion of the current state of the missile defense program: "What's a little disturbing to me is there was a lot of painting the SM-3 Block 1B program as proven and reliable and just another flight test of the current version, and it's not."[61]

Current plans call for emplacement of 30 ground-based interceptors (GBIs), based principally in Alaska, with four more stationed in California. Review of a recent flight test failure has yet to reveal the cause, and the MDA believes more ground and non-intercept flight tests of the new kill vehicle are required before another intercept test is planned. Work on a two-stage GBI continues "as a potential hedge to allow for a longer intercept window of time if ICBMs were launched against the United States from Northeast Asia or the Middle East."[62] Limited financial resources, manpower, targets, and range availability will force a further delay in the 2-stage GBI test schedule, since the investigation of the 3-stage GBI failure takes precedence. The MDA does not envision a 2-stage flight test until FY 2014.

Both the Aegis and GMD systems are intended to intercept and destroy ballistic missiles during the midcourse phase of their flights. As previously noted, this puts enormous pressure on the radars and sensors to track and discriminate the warhead from countermeasures that may be used. Critics of the GMD system in particular question whether it has the capability to do that against even the most rudimentary of targets. They also contend that tests of the GMD, and to a lesser extent, the Aegis system, lack operational realism. The target discrimination capacities of the US missile defense are closely guarded for precisely these reasons. Little public information is available about these efforts. Tests of both systems in their operational configurations have occurred over the last half-decade. As of fiscal year 2011, Aegis performed successfully in 10 of 12 such tests[63] and the GMD in three of five, with the two failures being the most recent tests. Certainly, more testing is needed, but the tests require targets, which are very expensive and prone to their own failures. They also require range time, which is in demand for other military purposes, and are very expensive.

The final interceptor components of the US missile defense are terminal interceptors—the Terminal High Altitude Area Defense (THAAD), the Sea-based Terminal, and the Patriot Advanced Capability 3 (PAC 3). By 2015, 9 THAAD fire units and more than 430 interceptors are scheduled for deployment. Sixty PAC 3 fire units and nearly 800 interceptors will be in place, along with 100 sea-based terminal SM-2 missiles. Each of these systems represents the last line of defense and is capable of defending a very defined, limited area. Originally contemplated as point defenses, the terminal systems also are quite attractive internationally. PAC 3 is a relatively mature system and cheap compared with purchasing an Aegis vessel or GBI field. THAAD is relatively new, but has a proven record of test success—seven for seven in its present configuration—and is being pushed for export by the United States.

Declining budgets and political pressure to deploy capability and demonstrate test success places a large strain on the missile defense budget and detracts from its ability to invest in future concepts. R&D investment in the present program is oriented toward evolving the SM-3 toward longer ranges and will remain the focus of effort through 2020, according to current plans. Associated with that effort is the expansion of related sensor, radar, and command, control, and battle management capabilities. MDA envisions creation of a precision tracking and surveillance satellite constellation and is examining use of the Predator Unmanned Aerial Vehicle (UAV) as an airborne sensor to complement existing terrestrial assets.

In short, under current plans and budgets, the US missile defense of the 2020s will look much like the missile defense of today. The absence of clear and sustained investment in advanced concepts means any radical change of course will require some time before it would be ready for testing, and even longer before deployment.

For those nations that rely on US-developed technologies, their future missile defenses will look much the same. Sales of the PAC 3, THAAD, and eventually the Aegis system will populate the defensive arsenals of US friends and allies with capabilities that are easily integrated with the US command and control network. Indeed, because of the expense of the sensor, radar, and battle management systems, some nations may opt to integrate as a matter of priority.

Japanese interest in the missile defense mission predates the emergence of North Korea's missile capabilities. Japan was one of the first countries to express willingness to work with the United States following the announcement of the SDI in the 1980s. North Korean activities are largely credited with catalyzing Japanese public awareness of the heightened threat posed by ballistic missiles in the region. Following a Nodong test in 1993, Japan and the United States began jointly studying threats and approaches in a formal fashion. A joint technology study was launched in response to the 1998 North Korean test, which produced a joint research agenda and helped fashion the groundwork for the more formal partnership that has evolved.

By 2003, the Japanese government had announced its intention to purchase and deploy missile defense assets, including the PAC-3 and Aegis ballistic missile defense systems. Shortly thereafter, the United States and Japan signed a formal memorandum outlining joint research projects and a cooperative testing agenda designed to benefit both parties, with a particular emphasis on improvements to the SM-3 interceptor used by the Aegis BMD.

Japan signed a license to produce the PAC-3 system in 2005.[64] Today, PAC-3s are stationed at several bases in Japan.[65] In 2006, the US Army activated an X-band radar in northern Japan to track regional ballistic missiles.[66] The two nations began working on the radar in 1998. The powerful radar can identify objects from thousands of miles away and is designed to differentiate between decoys and real missile warheads.

The signature element of the Japanese missile defense architecture is its investment in the Aegis and SM-3 systems. The cooperative research program produced a lightweight nosecone for the SM-3 that was flight tested in 2006.[67] According to the MDA, the new nosecone eliminated the need for additional maneuvering, allowing for faster interception opportunities. Japan's significant investment of resources and technical know-how in the SM-3 IIA distinguishes its contributions from those of nearly every other US missile defense partner. No other country has invested so many of its own resources into developing a new missile defense system, with the notable exception of Israel.

In December 2007, the Japanese Aegis system performed its first successful interception. A second test in December of 2008 failed to intercept the target.[68]

Tests since that time have proven successful, including the one in October 2010.[69]

South Korea's commitment to the construction and deployment of the Korean air and missile defense (KAMD) network by 2012 has been in place for several years.[70] The KAMD consists of PAC-2 interceptors, Aegis destroyers equipped with surface-to-air missiles with some application to ballistic missile defense, and the installation of an early warning radar. South Korea is spending $1 billion to purchase 48 PAC-2 systems, including launchers, missiles, and radars, from Germany in response to the North Korean missile threat.[71] The PAC-2s reached initial operational deployment in 2010. The PAC-2, which was used by the United States during the first Gulf War against Iraqi SCUDs, uses blast fragmentation to destroy the attacking missile, rather than the more sophisticated hit-to-kill of the PAC-3. Independently, the US Army maintains more than 60 PAC-3s in South Korea.

The other element of this defense is the outfitting of its Aegis destroyers, with sea-to-air missiles purchased from the United States. The announced plan calls for Standard Missile 6s (SM-6s) to be placed aboard the South Korean vessel, Sejong the Great, with future commitments to arm two additional Aegis vessels once they are constructed.[72] The SM-6 was developed by the US Navy to address primarily cruise missile threats, but from the onset, the new missile was seen to have applications to the short-range or theater ballistic missile challenge. That characteristic fits well with the expressed intent of South Korea regarding its missile defense plans. South Korea has avoided integration with the long-range US missile defense architecture and instead has focused on acquiring capabilities applicable to the North Korean threat.

This is not without pressure from the United States. In the spring of 2008 and several times since, US Lieutenant General Walter Sharp, Commander of US forces in South Korea, publicly encouraged the South Korean government to build a layered missile defense system, including airborne lasers and the PAC-3.[73] Instead, South Korea continues to improve the theater defense it is assembling. In June 2008, the country's Defense Ministry announced the purchase of a new radar system to aid the detection of North Korean launches.[74]

South Korea reiterated its policy of independence, but then partnership again in 2010. In a restatement of the country's policies, the South Korean defense ministry said discussions about the sharing of information and use of resources would continue, but was careful to note that "this does not mean (South) Korea will participate in the US regional defense system."[75]

Taiwan's security environment presents a different context for evaluating Asian missile defense trends. Facing a substantially larger and increasingly more sophisticated Chinese missile threat, Taiwan has sought US assistance to bolster its defenses, but those requests quickly become enmeshed in the larger US-Taiwan-China relationship. Nevertheless, the United States did approve sales of the Patriot PAC-3 system to Taiwan in 2008 as part of a much larger sale of arms to the island nation.

In October 2008, the Bush administration agreed to sell Taiwan 330 PAC-3 missiles to address the growing SRBM arsenal of China, believed to number more than 1,400.[76] Earlier that year, the US Army provided Raytheon Corp. with a $79-million foreign military sales award to upgrade Patriot system radars and provide engineering and training services for Taiwan.[77] The upgrades will allow three existing Patriot launchers to be armed with newer PAC-3 missiles, enabling Taiwan's existing missile defenses to launch either PAC-2 or PAC-3 interceptors.[78] Prior to the sales, Taiwan possessed approximately 200 PAC-2 interceptors. A total of six PAC-3 batteries are planned to be online in 2011.[79]

Unsurprisingly, expanding Taiwan's defensive capabilities arouses Chinese criticism. Surprisingly, the capabilities also sparked debate over their defensive value to Taiwan. An article in the Naval War College Review, for instance, claims the defenses would still allow nearly 1,000 Chinese SRBMs to hit their targets, and the Patriot radars are attractive targets for a first strike.[80] Even proponents of growing Taiwanese missile defense acknowledge that more interceptors are needed before the defense can credibly deter China, but they see advantages for the United States and Taiwan from the forward progress.[81] US access to a new Taiwanese early warning radar bolsters the international, Internetted sensor capabilities underpinning the long-range US defensive shield, for example.

In 2004, the United States and Australia entered into a 25-year agreement that provides the framework for cooperative actions on missile defense.[82] The framework agreement, similar to that between the United States and Japan, loosely defines activities and technical areas in which the two countries might work together. Specifically mentioned are the development and testing of advanced radar technology and provision of missile defense capabilities on Australian naval vessels.

Australia is in the midst of constructing three new Aegis destroyers under its Air Warfare Destroyer program. Citing the North Korean long-range missile threat, the Australian government initiated planning for ballistic missile defense capabilities to become part of these vessels.[83]

The United States and Australia have studied the integration of Australia's radar networks into the missile defense architecture, notably the Jindalee over-the-horizon (OTH) radar. Long before the signing of the cooperative agreement in 2004, the United States and Australia jointly conducted Project DUNDEE (Down Under Early Warning Experiment) to test whether the Jindalee radar could detect theater ballistic missiles. The 1997 experiment saw the radar successfully detect and track representative theater ballistic missiles.[84] Australia's Pine Gap radar is an established element of the international early warning system and may have contributions to missile defense.[85]

Singapore's Aster-15 missile and Formidable-class frigates have the ability to network with other vessels in a manner analogous to the US Aegis system.

To varying degrees, Japan, South Korea, Taiwan, and Australia have each pursued missile defense options in response to the proliferation of ballistic missiles in their region. So long as North Korea and China continue to invest in the acquisition and improvement of their short- and long-range missile capabilities, these nations will likely continue their investment in defenses.

Israeli missile defense systems generally are interoperable with their US counterparts. Israeli-US technical cooperation is long established, and the United States has provided Israel with significant financial resources to support its missile defense program. In Fiscal Year (FY) 2012, for example, the MDA is requesting more than $100 million for Israeli Cooperative Programs, which include the Arrow system and a program known as David's Sling.

Elsewhere in the Middle East, interest in missiles abounds. Saudi Arabia, Kuwait, Bahrain, Qatar, and the United Arab Emirates (UAE) all are involved in missile defense discussions with the United States in one form or another. While one suspects Iran is the primary threat motivating this interest, the spread of SCUDs and other short-range missiles throughout the region makes the picture more complex. In terms of systems, the US military has stationed its own assets in the region, namely, a mix of Aegis, PAC-3, and THAAD batteries. None of the Arab states have acquired advanced capabilities, but that will change. The UAE are the long-rumored home for the THAAD system. Once sales like that are allowed to proceed, others will be sure to follow.

Turkey presents a complicated case. As both a Middle Eastern and European power, with ties to the Muslim world as well as NATO, Turkey has security positions that generally reflect careful balancing. As NATO's embrace of missile defense became firmer and eventually formal policy, Turkey's awkward position has become ever more acute. During negotiations within NATO and even during the Bush administration's push for a European missile defense site, the Turks were critical of defensive efforts.[86] The planned defense did not defend all of NATO, they argued; in particular, large parts of southern Europe and Turkey were left "undefended" by the then-notional system. Turkey also wanted to avoid naming Iran as the chief missile threat to NATO.[87] When the Obama administration unveiled its initiative for Europe, Turkey was suggested as a possible location for a radar system. Reports suggest the Turks were initially supportive of the idea and then cooled on it, at least publicly. Leaked diplomatic cables reveal the complexity of Turkey's position. On the one hand, Turkey's dependence on Iran for energy is well known and was judged a major factor in Turkey's public positions on the relationship of Iran to NATO's efforts. On the other hand, Turkish defense officials secretly agreed with US assessments of the implications of a nuclear Iran for regional stability and agreed with the need to construct a missile defense suitable to protect Turkey and the rest of Europe.[88]

In the weeks before the Lisbon agreements in late 2010, when NATO nations agreed to the goal of constructing a European missile defense, Turkish leaders pressed for numerous concessions to secure their approval, but most were dropped or pushed off for further discussion.[89]

China and Russia both have or are developing missile defenses of their own. Chinese missile defenses mimic the US hit-to-kill approach. In a highly public test in 2010, official Chinese reports touted the successful test of a ground-based midcourse defensive capability.[90] In 2007, China tested an anti-satellite system using much the same capability. Details remain murky, but if China is pursuing a midcourse interception capability, it will encounter the same difficulties confronting similar US systems—namely target discrimination and tracking.

The Chinese strategic position explains its interest in defensive options. Facing what it perceives is an increasingly hostile United States and suspicious of US encirclement via client-allied states, wary of Russian intentions, and guarded about India's aspirations, China has perceptions of its security environment that continue to reflect a longstanding sense of insecurity. At the same time, China recognizes its growing power and ability to influence regional and global affairs. The twin, seemingly exclusive, dynamics explain China's embrace of offensive missile development and proliferation of missile technologies and investment in its own defense.

The Chinese military announced in January that it has successfully intercepted a missile in mid-flight in a test that came in the midst of growing tensions with Taiwan. China called the system being tested "ground-based midcourse missile interception technology." Chinese missile defense systems are shrouded in secrecy, but US military analysts believe China has augmented its air defenses with "homemade technologies adapted from Russian and other foreign weaponry."[91] A 2009 Pentagon report says the Chinese air force has received eight battalions of upgraded Russian SA-20 PMU-2 surface-to-air missiles since 2006, with another eight on order.[92] The Chinese defense budget for 2009 reached $71 billion, with no disclosed amount for missile defense.

While it remains difficult to assess the types of missile defense systems China employs and where it will employ them, the Hongqui-9 is one known missile defense system deployed in China. It is a long-range, high-altitude surface-to-air missile system and is designed to track and destroy aircraft, cruise missiles, air-to-surface missiles, and tactical ballistic missiles.[93] According to a 2008 DoD report, the Chinese have also deployed 32 S-300PMU systems (SA-10 Grumble), 64 S-300PMU1 systems (SA-20A Gargoyle), and 32 new S-300PMU2 systems (SA-20B Gargoyle). These systems are the Russian equivalents of the US PAC-1 and PAC-2 systems.

Russia's involvement in missile defense debates is extensive. Not only is this involvement a complicating factor for US-NATO efforts vis-à-vis Europe, but Russia's continued investment in its own missile technologies presents enormous technical challenges of missile defense systems that look to check sophisticated strategic threats. Additionally, Russian investment in defensive capabilities, drawing on its Cold War systems, continues to present targeting challenges on the strategic level. More worrisome is the prospect that those systems may be sold on the international market and proliferated globally. Russia's objections to the expansion of the US missile defense into Europe is well known; it dominated headlines in the last years of the Bush administration and throughout the New START nuclear weapons reductions negotiations. US assurances that the planned defenses would not be capable of intercepting Russian missiles were unpersuasive or ignored, leaving many Western analysts to conclude that Russian objections were rooted elsewhere. Indeed, the planned emplacement of US military assets in Poland and the Czech Republic—two former client states of the Soviet Union—was known to irritate many in Russian leadership. The Obama administration's reversal of the Bush plan for Europe at first was interpreted as a capitulation to Russian objections. The administration's subsequent announcement of the PAA, which calls for interceptors and radars to be placed in Romania and Poland, did not initially produce the same level of reaction from Russia as the Bush plan did. With the start of the New START negotiations, Russian efforts to constrain missile defenses shifted to the treaty negotiation table. Ultimately, the

United States rejected many of those limitations, although some analysts question the outcome.

An outcome of those discussions, however, is the expressed desire to find a more formal role for Russia to play in US missile defense plans. Harkening back to President Ronald Reagan's promises to share SDI technology, the pursuit of US-Russian/Soviet cooperation in regional or global missile defenses is not new. Current discussions are serious, with the Russians claiming they seek "red-button" control over whether to fire an interceptor.[94]

Russian investments in the country's own missile defenses are notable. The central systems are the S-300 and S-400 surface-to-air systems. Basically terminal defense systems akin to the US PAC-3 or THAAD missile defenses, the S-300 and S-400 were originally designed as cruise missile or anti-aircraft defenses. They subsequently were modified for ballistic missile defense missions. Deployment is fairly limited. Public reports put 30 battalions of S-300s in the Russian arsenal. A gradual replacement of the S-300 with the more capable S-400 is planned. A limited number of S-400 battalions are known to exist.

Defensive Security Guarantees

The internationalization of missile defense offers new opportunities for the United States and other nations to forge defensive alliances. The limits of the current technology virtually demand such arrangements, particularly if a large area is to be defended from attacks originating from many sources. For the United States, with its global interests and requirement to defend globally dispersed targets, a distributed sensor and interceptor architecture is a necessity. The United States has welcomed international partnerships and sales of completed systems, both of which are intended to link with US capabilities. For nations developing their own missile defense systems, like India or China, bilateral or multilateral partnerships are less important, because the area to be defended is smaller, allowing their defenses to be more focused.

Beyond the practical considerations for the United States, its investments in missile defense offer the potential to give new life to old alliances and add value to newer relationships. In a manner similar to the offensive nuclear umbrella extended by the United States to its European and Asian allies throughout the Cold War, the rudimentary structure of a defensive security umbrella is now forming. Much of the debate during the Cold War concerning missile defense focused on whether the introduction of defenses would destabilize deterrence relationships between the United States and the Soviet Union.[95] As the bilateral superpower competition gave way to a multilateral environment with few enduring conflicts, the United States has begun to see missile defense as an important tool to strengthening its new and longstanding regional alliances. The 2010 BMDR speaks extensively to this new emphasis.

The BMDR establishes a strategy and policy framework that assigns international outreach and partnerships a role of high prominence. It states:

> . . . The United States will seek to lead expanded international efforts for missile defense. It will work more intensively with allies and partners to provide pragmatic and cost-effective capacity. The United States will also continue in its efforts to establish a cooperative [ballistic missile defense] relationship with Russia. The United States, with the support of allies and partners, seeks to create an environment in which the acquisition, deployment, and use of ballistic missiles by regional adversaries can be deterred, principally by eliminating their confidence in the effectiveness of such attacks, and thereby devaluing their ballistic missile arsenals. This will help undergird a broader strategic objective: to strengthen deterrence in key regions through the integrated and innovative use of military and nonmilitary means that adapt regional deterrence architectures to 21st-century requirements.[96]

Current US thinking sees several roles to be played by missile defenses. The first are the practical contributions already alluded to. The BMDR commits the United States to partnerships to "provide pragmatic and cost-effective capacity" and help maintain "military freedom of maneuver." Missile defense is a tool to broaden ties with Russia. But, most importantly, missile defense is a means to deter regional adversaries and "adapt regional deterrence architectures to 21st century requirements."[97] In this context, the term "regional deterrence architecture" is a euphemism for the function of alliances. The BMDR is even more explicit on the notion of the guarantee implied by the US missile defense umbrella. It states:

> Ballistic missile defenses help support US security commitments to allies and partners. They provide reassurance that the United States will stand by those commitments despite the growth in the military potential of regional adversaries.[98]

These defenses also are called "an essential element of the US commitment" to regional alliances.

When viewed in context of the broader Obama administration strategic defense policies, the significance of these statements comes into clearer focus. At roughly the same time that the Obama Department of Defense (DoD) was issuing the BMDR, it also was negotiating the first major reductions to the US nuclear weapons arsenal in many years and doing so in the context of the President's desire to seek a world with zero nuclear weapons. The prospect of nuclear disarmament raised worries in some quarters about the continued vitality of US security guarantees to its allies, particularly NATO and Japan.[99] The nuclear guarantee was characterized as the foundation of these nations' own security policies. Consequently, the credibility of the US nuclear program is a major security concern not only for the United States, but for many nations.

The expansion of missile defense may bolster the intangible aspects of the nuclear umbrella. At its core, the nuclear umbrella is a US commitment to stand by and come to the aid of the allied nation and to do so in a meaningful and substantive way. The deterrent function of the nuclear arsenal is judged to have a positive dissuasive effect on an adversary. Missile defenses, if they are sufficiently robust, can have the same effect.

Like the nuclear deterrent, missile defenses must be credible. By reducing the probability that a ballistic missile strike will successfully hit its target, the presence of a defense may dissuade an aggressor from a strike. For the current threat environment, in which the number of missiles used in a conflict should be low, a defense can credibly manage a likely threat scenario. If the number of missiles involved in an exchange grows, the technical limitations of current missile defense architectures may be overwhelmed, at worst, or put in a position in which the offensive has greatly improved its probability of a successful strike. In such a circumstance, the credibility of the defense is weakened. Nations under the umbrella would be expected to explore offensive and defensive steps unless the United States moved to strengthen the defense and restore its credibility.

Critics of missile defenses insist they can never achieve the reliability needed. Like a nuclear second-strike capability, reliability is in the eye of the beholder. If the United States and its allies can create enough doubt about the probability of a successful missile strike, the defense may succeed in deterring attacks beyond what it can actually do. The defense is not the only option available in times of crisis, but it is an important complement to those capabilities. The United States and its allies will retain other offensive military and nuclear capabilities with which to respond in the event a defense is overwhelmed. The purpose of defense is not necessarily to repel 100 percent of the attacker's force. A defense also can sufficiently weaken the attacking force to make a counterattack more successful. Third, a defense forces the attacker into a large-scale attack to overwhelm it, which in turn, raises the probability that the United States would respond to such an attack. As Paul Bracken argued, "Missile defense links active protection of an allied nation's population to the likelihood of triggering the American security guarantee. The larger the attack, the more probable is a US response."[100]

The use of the ballistic missile for offensive actions other than the delivery of nuclear weapons offers another opportunity for allied nations to work together. Collective defense of airfields, bases, and other militarily significant targets is noncontroversial. Investment in air defenses or port defenses is expected, and sharing of capabilities between allied nations commonplace. As the use of the ballistic missile shifts from a delivery device for weapons of mass destruction to a delivery device for conventional munitions in its role as the "poor man's air force," the role of defense shifts as well. Nations in regions where missiles are expected to play this role will invest in defenses to limit the impact of those strikes and to deter their adversaries from using them in the first—using the same logic that might drive the investment in a new air defense. The United States can apply the traditional methods of arms sales, training, and co-development to missile defenses. Such methods have served it well as alliance maintenance tools by providing allied or friendly nations with the systems, infrastructure, training, and knowledge needed to address their security needs. At the same time, such actions expand the global reach of weapons systems that are interoperable with those of the United States, increase opportunities for joint training exercises with those nations to improve the fighting effectiveness, and offer export markets for US industry, which is increasingly important as pressures mount on the US defense budget.

Conclusion

The strategic logic for missile defense has undoubtedly changed. The proliferation of technology and capability, coupled with what appears to be clearer intent to use missiles for offensive and deterrent purposes, is driving demand for defenses across the globe. During the Cold War, the United States and the Soviet Union wrestled with the concern that introducing defenses would upset their delicate balance of terror. In a world where many nations possess missiles, bilateral deterrent relationships resting exclusively on offensive retaliation appear to have less value. That is particularly the case when we consider that many nations plan to use their ballistic missile arsenal as delivery vehicles for conventional munitions and for battlefield applications. Just as a nation might respond to the introduction of a new class of aircraft with more sophisticated air defense systems, so today nations are responding to the introduction of missiles with missile defenses.

By moving to exploit this new interest, the United States will not only be able to improve the effectiveness of its own defense, but reap the ancillary benefits of strengthening its alliances and relationships. Current defensive architectures rely on an interconnected suite of sensors and radars to track attacking ballistic missiles. These systems, in turn, provide data to the interceptors that attempt to hit the attacking missile. Numerous limitations vex the defense. The sensor and tracking capabilities have to be refined enough to detect and follow small objects over thousands of missiles amidst clutter and debris designed to hide them. The interceptors face range limitations by virtue of how big they are and how fast they fly. As a consequence, the objective of the US missile defense system is to obtain as many opportunities to destroy the attacking missile as possible across its path of flight. This requires different kinds of defensive systems. The spread of missile defenses that are compatible or interoperable with those of the United States offers significant leveraging opportunities that should improve the effectiveness of the defense.

More importantly, the spread of defenses offers opportunities to revitalize old alliances and build new ones. As the proliferation of ballistic missiles creates new security concerns for US friends and allies, the operational nature of the current complement of defenses likely binds the nations together. More broadly, investing existing alliance relationships with the new mission gives them new purpose and currency. Defense also can come to complement the offense. As the United States pursues nuclear arms reductions, it can use the expansion of missile defense to allay the concerns of those nations that sit under its nuclear umbrella who may have begun to question the credibility of the US commitment to their security. Through the extension of a defense security guarantee, the United States reassures its allies of its commitment to employ its military forces in their defense, thereby helping to restore credibility to the guarantee formerly provided by offensive retaliation.

Missile defense is not a panacea, but it does offer new tools to address the new threats faced by the United States and many other nations. Continued technical improvements should result in improvements to the defense, but offenses also are expected to continue innovating to defeat the defense. A perfect defense is a fleeting goal. Instead, a more realistic assessment of the complementary role defense can play in addressing the tactical and strategic challenges posed by expanding missile arsenals would conclude that the defense decreases the probability of a successful attack, complicates offensive planning, and provides options other than preemption or retaliation in times of crisis.

Endnotes

1. *Ballistic and Cruise Missile Threat*, NASIC-1031-0985-09, Wright-Patterson Air Force Base, OH, National Air and Space Intelligence Center, 2009, p. 3.
2. *Ballistic Missile Defense Review,* Washington, DC: US Department of Defense, 2010, p. iii.
3. Ballistic missiles are powered during their initial phase of flight (usually called "boost phase") before leaving the atmosphere and following an unpowered, inverted-U shape trajectory toward a predetermined target. Ballistic missile ranges can vary from 100 or so kilometers (km) to more than 10,000 km.
4. Ballistic missiles are classified by range as follows: Short-Range Ballistic Missiles (SRBMs) = 150 - 799 km. Medium-Range Ballistic Missiles (MRBMs) = 800 - 2,399 km. Intermediate-Range Ballistic Missiles (IRBMs) = 2,400 - 5,499 km. Intercontinental-Range Ballistic Missiles (ICBMs) = 5,500 km and greater.
5. *Ballistic and Cruise Missile Threat,* p. 4.
6. US Missile Defense Agency, *Foreign Ballistic Missile Capabilities*, Washington, DC: Department of Defense, 2009, p. 6.
7. *Ballistic Missile Defense Review,* p. 3.
8. *Ibid.*, p. 7.
9. *Foreign Ballistic Missile Capabilities*, p. 5.
10. *Ibid.*, p. 5.
11. *Ballistic Missile Defense Review,* p. 7.
12. *Ibid.*, p. 8.
13. Government of Australia, Ministry of Defence, *Defending Australia in the Asia Pacific Century: Force 2030*, Canberra, Australia: Department of Defense, 2009, p. 39.
14. "Japan Seeks Understanding for New U.N. Resolution on N. Korea," *Japan Economic Newswire*, May 30, 2009.
15. Yukio Takasu, Statement by H. E. Ambassador Yukio Takasu, Permanent Representative of Japan to the United Nations at the Meeting of the Security Council on Non-Proliferation/DPRK, *States News Service,* June 12, 2009.
16. "SDF Must Protect Us Against N. Korean Missile," *The Daily Yomiuri,* March 28, 2009.

17. *Defending Australia in the Asia Pacific Century*, p. 85.
18. *Military Power of the People's Republic of China*, Washington, DC: Department of Defense, 2009, p. 46.
19. *Foreign Ballistic Missile Capabilities*, p. 7.
20. *Ballistic Missile Defense Review*, p. vii.
21. *Foreign Ballistic Missile Capabilities*, p. 8.
22. *Ibid*, p. 4.
23. *Ballistic Missile Defense Review, p.* vii.
24. "US Bases in Japan Are under Threat of Chinese Missiles: Report," *Japan Economic Newswire,* November 18, 2010.
25. *Foreign Ballistic Missile Capabilities*, p. 11.
26. *Ibid*, p. 17.
27. Daniel Pinkston, *The North Korean Ballistic Missile Program,* Carlisle, PA: Strategic Studies Institute, US Army War College, 2008, p. 57.
28. Dennis C. Blair, *Annual Threat Assessment of the US Intelligence Community for the Senate Select Committee on Intelligence*, Washington, DC: US Senate, 2010, p. 14.
29. *Ibid.*
30. Steven Hildreth, *North Korean Ballistic Missile Threat to the United States*, Washington, DC: US Congressional Research Service, 2009, pp. 2-3.
31. *Ballistic Missile Defense Review,* p. 4.
32. *Foreign Ballistic Missile Capabilities*, p. 7
33. Hildreth, *North Korean Ballistic Missile Threat*, p. 4.
34. *Ibid.*
35. *Ibid.*, p. 5.
36. *Ballistic and Cruise Missile Threat*, p. 11; and *Foreign Ballistic Missile Capabilities*, p. 16.
37. *Ballistic and Cruise Missile Threat*, p. 30.
38. *Ibid.*, p. 18.
39. *Ibid.*, p. 22.
40. "Another Test Failure for Russia's Bulava Missile," *Defense News,* December 10, 2009, available from *www.defensenews.com/story.php?i=4413711*; and "START Treaty won't keep Russia from developing Bulava missiles," *RIA Novosti,* February 7, 2011.

41. *Ballistic and Cruise Missile Threat*, p. 8.

42. "India to soon test N-capable Agni-III, missile defence system," *Times of India,* January 25, 2010, available from *timesofindia.indiatimes.com/india/India-to-soon-test-N-capable-Agni-III-missile-defence-system/articleshow/5499677.cms.*

43. *Ibid.*

44. "Agni-5, India's answer to China's lethal missile," *Deccan Herald,* February 10, 2010.

45. *Foreign Ballistic Missile Capabilities*, p. 12.

46. *Ibid.*, p. 17.

47. *Ballistic and Cruise Missile Threat*, p. 15.

48. *Ibid.*, p. 17.

49. *Ibid.*, p. 11. The actual SRBM inventory may be much larger, because launchers can be reused to fire additional missiles.

50. Blair, p. 13.

51. Steven Hildreth, *Iran's Ballistic Missile Programs: An Overview*, Washington, DC: US Congressional Research Service, 2009, p. 3.

52. Chip Cummins, "Iran Unveils New Satellite Capabilities on Eve of Revolution Anniversary," *The Wall Street Journal,* February 3, 2010.

53. Hildreth, *Iran's Ballistic Missile Programs*, p. 2.

54. *Ibid.*, p. 4.

55. *Foreign Ballistic Missile Capabilities*, p. 16.

56. Blair, p. 13.

57. Hit-to-kill capabilities can be deployed aboard aircraft, but there is no active program for an air-launched capability.

58. Jeff Kueter and Robert Jastrow, *What is the Meaning of the Russian Wonder Weapon?* Washington, DC: George C. Marshall Institute, 2004.

59. Lieutenant General Patrick O'Reilly, Statement before the House Armed Services Committee Subcommittee on Strategic Forces, March 31, 2011, p. 7.

60. *Ibid.*, p. 9.

61. Turner Brinton, "Former MDA Chief Prescribes Changes for Missile Defense Plans," *Space News,* April 11, 2011, p. 16.

62. O'Reilly, p. 5-6.

63. The Standard Missile-31A (SM-31A) successfully intercepted an IRBM on April 15, 2011.

64. "Japan Licensed to Produce Patriot PAC-3s," *Defense Industry Daily,* July 19, 2005.
65. "Japan Shoots Down Test Missile in Space: Defense Minister," *Agence France Presse,* December 17, 2007.
66. "US Army Activates X-Band Radar in Northern Japan," *Associated Press,* September 28, 2006.
67. "US-Japan SM-3 Interceptor Test Successful, Using Innovative Japanese Nosecone," US Missile Defense Agency, Press Release, , March 8, 2006.
68. "Despite failures, missile defense system OK'd," *Japan Times,* December 17, 2008.
69. Jim Wolf, "US and Japan stage successful missile-defense test," *Reuters,* October 29, 2010.
70. Sung-ki Jung, "Seoul Begins Deploying Patriot Missile Interceptors," *The Korea Times,* September 16, 2008.
71. "Patriot Missile Defense Systems to be Deployed in South Korea." *The Korea Times,* September 16, 2008.
72. Won-sup Yoon, "South Korea May Join US-led Missile Defense Network," *The Korea Times,* January 20, 2008.
73. Sung-ki Jung, "US Urges Seoul to Bolster Missile Defense," *The Korea Times,* April 4, 2008.
74. "South Korea to Buy Radar to Detect North Korean Missiles," *Agence France Presse,* June 26, 2008.
75. "S. Korea Rules Out Joining US Regional Missile Defense," *Yonhap,* October 25, 2010.
76. "A Complex Matter," *Defense News,* October 13, 2008; and John Tkacik, *Taiwan Arms Sales: Less Than Meets the Eye,* Washington, DC: Heritage Foundation, October 8, 2008.
77. "Raytheon Awarded $79 Million to Upgrade Taiwan's Patriot Air and Missile Defense Capabilities." *Raytheon,* Press Release, April 23, 2008.
78. "Proposed Missile Defense Upgrade for Taiwan Announced," *Agence France Presse,* November 13, 2007.
79. "Taiwan Missile Defence Shield Ready Next Year: Report," *Agence France Presse,* September 6, 2010.
80. William Murray, "Revisiting Taiwan's Defense Strategy," *Naval War College Review*, Summer 2008.
81. John Tkacik, "Pricing Taiwan's Missile Defense," *Taiwan Times,* December 6, 2008.

82. "United States and Australia Sign Missile Defense Agreement," US Department of Defense, Press Release, July 7, 2004.
83. "Ballistic missile system 'moving closer,'" *The Sydney Morning Herald,* November 22, 2006.
84. "Ballistic Simulation Tests Australian Radar System," *Jane's Defence Weekly,* September 17, 1997.
85. Patrick Gray, "Aussies to Bear Missile Shield," *Wired,* November 10, 2004.
86. Desmond Butler, "Analysis: Turkey hesitates on missile defense," *Associated Press,* October 21, 2010.
87. "Turkey reiterates NATO missile shield should not take any country as threat," *BBC Monitoring Europe,* December 4, 2010.
88. Sara Carter, "Turkey Talked of Iranian Threat, Secret Cables Said," *The Washington Examiner,* January 4, 2011.
89. Steven Fidler and Adam Entous, "NATO Agrees to Extend Missile Shield," *The Wall Street Journal,* November 19, 2010.
90. "China: Missile Defense System Test Successful," *USA Today,* January 11, 2010.
91. *Ibid.*
92. *Military Power of the People's Republic of China.*
93. "Hongqi-9 (HQ-9)," *Missilethreat.com*, start here Claremont Institute, available from *www.missilethreat.com/missiledefensesystems/id.27/system_detail.asp*.
94. Andrew Osborn, "Russia Wants Red Button Rights for US Missile Defense System," *The Telegraph,* April 8, 2011.
95. For a summary review of these debates, see Keith Payne, *The Great American Gamble: Deterrence Theory and Practice from the Cold War to the Twenty-First Century*, Fairfax, VA: National Institute Press, 2008.
96. *Ballistic Missile Defense Review,* p. 12.
97. *Ibid.*
98. *Ibid.*
99. For example, see John Bolton, "Folding Our Nuclear Umbrella," *Washington Times,* April 28, 2010.
100. Paul Bracken, "Thinking (Again) about Arms Control," *Orbis,* Winter 2004, available from *www.fpri.org/orbis/4801/bracken.armscontrol.html*.

Chapter 15

A Hardheaded Guide to Nuclear Controls

Henry D Sokolski

With truly nettlesome problems, like preventing the spread of nuclear weapons, it is tempting to celebrate any current success as a turning point for entirely vanquishing the problem. With the fall of the Berlin Wall, the end of history was foretold. With Saddam Hussein's toppling and Maummar Kaddafi's termination of Libya's strategic weapons programs, Washington pundits portrayed the remaining "Evil Axis" holdouts—Iran and North Korea—as the next dominoes to fall. Now, with the ratification of a follow-on New Strategic Arms Reductions Treaty (New START)—the first legally binding arms control agreement to be reached in nearly 20 years—the elimination of nuclear weapons is being portrayed as a practical possibility.

It is easy to dismiss such optimism. What is more challenging is harnessing such enthusiasm to make things better or, at least, to not make them worse. This requires sound insight into what is and is not possible, and, in Washington, sensitivity to an increasing number of contentious political views regarding nuclear controls.

Here, a significant stumbling block is how heavily the Barack Obama administration's nuclear agenda depends on the successful negotiation and ratification of legally binding bilateral and international control agreements. These formal agreements include arms reduction treaties to follow New START, the Comprehensive Test Ban Treaty (CTBT), a

Fissile Material Cutoff Treaty (FMCT) banning further military nuclear production, and a variety of multilateral and international nonproliferation and nuclear fuel-supply arrangements. These formal devices are, at best, an awkward way to secure the support of administration critics in Congress who are skeptical of traditional nuclear controls. Nor are any of these treaty-based agreements—some of which require ratification by North Korea, Iran, Pakistan, India, Egypt, and China—likely to come into force any time soon, if at all.

This suggests developing a more practical additional set of control measures that are not at odds with the current agenda, but are more likely to secure bipartisan support and can be implemented without necessarily securing the legal consent of so many other states. Before fleshing out this agenda, it is critical to first clarify the character of the long-term nuclear threats the United States and its friends face, and to identify which ones are most tractable.

Washington's Current Agenda

With the ratification of the New START follow-on agreement late in 2010, the Obama administration has argued that additional nuclear weapons-reductions agreements can occur not only between the United States and Russia, but the world's other nuclear weapons states. Beyond this, the administration and its supporters hope that such agreements will help persuade the world's non-nuclear weapons states to do more to steer clear of dangerous civilian nuclear fuel-making activities and to open their civilian nuclear facilities to more intrusive international inspections.

It is improbable, however, that all states will fall into line. Certainly, barring regime change in either North Korea or Iran, neither Pyongyang's renunciation of its nuclear arsenal nor Iran's cessation of nuclear weapons-related activities seems all that likely. Also, whichever reductions are achieved quickly or easily among existing nuclear weapons states are unlikely to capture Russia's large number of tactical nuclear weapons. The near-term odds, moreover, of China, India, Pakistan, or Israel reducing their nuclear weapons-related holdings seem slim.

Some nuclear trends, moreover, could easily make further reductions less likely. Before 2020, the United Kingdom (UK) is expected to find its nuclear forces eclipsed by those of Pakistan, Israel, and India. Soon thereafter, France could share the same fate.[1] China has enough separated plutonium and highly enriched uranium to increase its current presumed stockpile of roughly 200 nuclear warheads by a factor of 5 to 10.[2] Meanwhile, Japan, which already has over 2,000 bombs' worth[3] of weapons-usable plutonium on its soil, could soon begin operation of a reprocessing plant capable of separating out an additional 1,000 bombs' worth of weapons-usable plutonium annually.[4] US and Russian reserves of nuclear weapons-usable material stocks—still large enough to be converted back to many tens of thousands of weapons—will decline only marginally, while similar nuclear stores in Japan and other nuclear weapons states could easily double.[5] Compounding these developments, even more nuclear weapons-ready states are likely to emerge: As of early 2011, at least 35 states had announced their desire to build large reactors—all potential bomb-starter kits—before 2030.[6]

None of this is likely to bolster the cause of nuclear weapons abolition or nonproliferation. Certainly, ratification of major arms reductions treaties with Russia (New START and its follow-ons), CTBT, FMCT, international civilian nuclear fuel banks, and enhanced inspections of civilian nuclear programs are unlikely to be enough to head off the troubling trends described. What is worse, these arms control measures, if executed improperly, could actually make matters worse.

Thus, critics of strategic arms reductions with Moscow warn that if the current New START follow-on agreement is superseded with reductions down to 1,000 or fewer strategic nuclear warheads, it might undermine the credibility of US nuclear security alliances. In this case, these critics argue, states like Japan, Saudi Arabia, and Turkey might be tempted themselves to go nuclear.[7]

As for pushing ratification of a CTBT, this too might backfire: India, whose last nuclear test series was followed by Pakistani nuclear tests, conducted a loud, public debate in 2009 over whether or not to resume nuclear testing. One of the key Indian arguments made for resuming testing was to beat what many Indians feared was an approaching nuclear test ban deadline. Meanwhile, American test ban treaty opponents have recommended that the US Senate tie the treaty's test limits to which nuclear weapons activities other states, like Russia, will agree are permissible under a CTBT. In this regard, some Russians have voiced that very low-yield nuclear tests that release a lower nuclear yield than the explosive energy of the non-nuclear triggering mechanisms in a nuclear explosive are permissible. Yet, pegging the treaty to such clarifications would encourage low-level nuclear testing.[8]

As for securing a nondiscriminatory global ban against the military production of separated plutonium and enriched uranium for nuclear weapons, this also could inflict unintended harm. Here, a worry is that the FMCT only bans the production of fissile material for military purposes. Could its finalization encourage increased civilian production of fissile material that might be used to make weapons? The short answer is yes. Furthermore, there is little to fend off such an ostensibly "peaceful" activity. The odds of inspectors catching military diversions from civilian nuclear plants, in fact, can be quite low.[9]

Then there is the potential problem of setting a double inspections standard. While most nuclear weapons states might lack the incentives to cheat (since the fissile material cutoff would still allow them to keep their nuclear weapons holdings), non-nuclear weapons states would likely insist that their civilian nuclear fuel-making activities be inspected no more carefully than those of weapons states under a cutoff. It would be difficult to persuade states that do not have nuclear weapons not to make nuclear fuel or to do so under stricter conditions than those of nuclear weapons states, which are free to do so under relatively loose nuclear "safeguards." Affording non-nuclear states access to international civilian nuclear fuel services is also unlikely to deter them, since, unless they are breaking the nuclear rules, they already have access to such services from a variety of providers, and major nuclear supplier states have argued that they have a legal right to make their own fuel.

Finally, with the growing popularity of "peaceful" nuclear energy, nuclear supplier states are claiming that exporting new power reactors will not increase proliferation, since their export will come with the application of "enhanced" nuclear inspections. Yet, in many of the most worrisome cases—e.g., Syria, Iran, India, Pakistan, Saudi Arabia, and North Korea—even enhanced inspections may be too unreliable to deter or prevent significant military diversions effectively. As it is, most remote nuclear inspection monitoring systems are unable to guarantee the continuity of inspections over a majority of the world's spent or fresh fuel—materials that can be used as feed for nuclear enrichment and reprocessing plants to accelerate the production of weapons-usable materials. These nuclear fuel-making plants, moreover, can be hidden from nuclear inspectors and, even when declared, used to make weapons-usable fuel without those inspectors necessarily detecting such activity in a timely fashion. For all these reasons, then, one needs somehow to be sure that any recipient of a large reactor (even of a reputed "proliferation resistant" light-water reactor) is entirely out of the nuclear bomb-making business and will stay away from such activities in the future.[10]

Several of these points are beginning to receive attention in the United States. The debate over these issues, though, needs to be broadened. Even if Washington and the European Union's (EU) favorite nuclear control initiatives—START follow-ons, CTBT, FMCT, civilian nuclear fuel banks, and intrusive nuclear inspections—are all adopted and implemented in ways that avoid the risks already discussed, the United States and its allies would still face a series of additional, major nuclear weapons proliferation threats.

Nuclear Reductions and Arms Competitions

The first of these is that as the United States and Russia incrementally reduce their nuclear weapons deployments, China, India, Pakistan, and Israel may increase theirs. Currently, the United States is planning to reduce US and Russian strategic weapons deployments to as low as 1,000 warheads each.[11] As a result, it is conceivable that in 10 years' time, the nuclear numbers separating the United States and Russia from the other nuclear weapons states might be measured in hundreds rather than thousands of weapons. In such a world, relatively small changes in any state's nuclear weapons capabilities could have a disproportionate impact on the perceived balance of power.

Compounding the increased volatility that these trends could produce are the large and growing stockpiles of nuclear weapons-usable materials (i.e., of separated plutonium and highly enriched uranium) that are being held in several states. These stockpiles already exceed tens of thousands of crude bombs' worth of material in the United States and Russia and are projected to grow in Pakistan, India, China, Israel, and Japan. This growth will enable these states to increase their current nuclear deployments much more quickly and dramatically than any of the superpowers could during the worrying early years of the Cold War.

Finally, 20 years out, there could be more nuclear weapons-ready states—countries that could acquire nuclear weapons in a matter of months, like Japan and Iran. As already noted, more than 35 states have announced their desire to launch large civilian nuclear programs. If they all realize their dreams of bringing their first power reactors online by 2030, it would constitute more than a doubling of the 31 states that currently have such programs (most of which are now operating in the United States, Europe, Japan, and South Korea).

If this civilian nuclear expansion and the large reactors it promises to bring online are realized, it could have major military implications. Every current weapons state first brought a large reactor online prior to acquiring its first bomb. The UK, France, Russia, India, and the United States all made many of their initial bombs from reactors that also provided power to their electrical grids. The United States still uses a "proliferation resistant" light-water power reactor operated by the Tennessee Valley Authority to make all of its weapons-grade tritium for its nuclear arsenal.[12]

Other plants besides large power reactors, of course, would be needed to chemically separate out weapons-usable plutonium from the spent power reactor fuel or to enrich the uranium used to power such machines. Yet, as the recent cases of Iran and North Korea demonstrate, such fuel-making plants can be built in ways that can be difficult to detect and operated to make timely detection of illicit production improbable.[13] Certainly, if all of the announced civilian nuclear power programs are completed as planned, the world in 2030 would be far less stable. Instead of there being several confirmed nuclear weapons states—most of which the United States can claim are either allies or strategic partners—there could be an unmanageable number of additional nuclear weapons-capable states, armed or weapons ready (i.e., able to acquire weapons in 12 to 24 months), to contend with.[14]

In such a world, the United States, its allies, and the EU might know who their friends and potential adversaries might be, but they would have difficulty knowing what such states might do in a crisis—close ranks, go their own way in developing weapons options, or follow the lead of some other nuclear-capable nation. As for possible adversaries, the United States, its allies, and the EU would have difficulty determining just how lethal these adversaries' military forces might be.

Finally, these nuclear trends would surely aggravate the prospects for nuclear-charged terrorism and irredentism. Not only would there be more opportunities to seize nuclear weapons and nuclear weapons materials, there would be more military and civilian nuclear facilities to sabotage. In addition, the potential for miscalculation and nuclear war could rise to a point that even non-nuclear acts of terror could ignite larger conflicts that could turn nuclear.

This sort of international volatility could easily mimic that which preceded World Wars I and II—periods in which overly ambitious arms control agreements were sought while states raced to complete significant covert and overt military programs. Ultimately, the latter only helped heighten tensions and subsequently were employed in unrestricted warfare. If such wars should break out in the future, though, the key difference would be that the ammunition in such conflicts, increasingly, might not just be highly explosive, but nuclear.

What is to be Done?

Can the United States and like-minded nations avoid or mitigate these trends? The short answer is yes, but only if they attend more closely to several basic principles.

First, as nuclear weapons deployments decline, greater care must be taken to ensure military reductions or additions actually decrease the chances for war. If American nuclear security guarantees are to continue to neutralize the nuclear weapons yearnings of key US allies, it is critical that Washington avoid doing anything to undermine the correlation of forces it currently enjoys against America's key nuclear competitors. In addition to enhancing its conventional military capabilities and making roughly equal nuclear reductions with Russia, then, the United States and the North Atlantic Treaty Organization (NATO) in the near- to mid-term will have to keep other nuclear-armed states, such as China, either from trying to catch up with either the United States or Russia, or—as in the case of India and China, Pakistan and India, and Japan and China—with each other.

This means that additional nuclear restraints, either in the form of nuclear weapons reductions or further limits on the production or stockpiling of weapons-usable fuels, will need to be reached not only with Russia, but with China, India, and Pakistan. As a practical matter, this also means that other nuclear weapons-ready or virtual weapons states (e.g., Israel and Japan) will have to be asked to curtail or end their production of nuclear weapons-usable materials or to dispose of some portion of what they currently have.

Conventional Force Enhancements and the Demand for Nuclear Weapons

In any effort to maintain the relative parity of competing nuclear-armed states forces through non-nuclear military assistance or buildups, it may be necessary to enhance conventional forces in a manner that avoids increasing one or both sides' interest in acquiring more nuclear weapons. Unfortunately, this is not a simple matter.

Consider long-range precision strikes and advanced command, control, and intelligence systems in the case of India and Pakistan. Pakistan believes it must threaten to use its nuclear weapons first to deter India's superior conventional forces. Precision strike systems, however, could conceivably target Pakistan's nuclear weapons. As a result, one could imagine that arming India with such weapons would only put Pakistan even more on nuclear alert and encourage Islamabad to acquire even more nuclear weapons to ensure that their nuclear forces could not be knocked out by precise Indian conventional strikes. Exporting the wrong kinds of advanced non-nuclear weapons systems in India or helping it to build them in disproportionate numbers could adversely influence Pakistan's nuclear weapons plans.[15]

Ballistic missile defenses (BMD) could also be tricky. Under the right circumstances, having such defenses could afford a non-nuclear form of deterrence that might facilitate reducing the numbers of deployed nuclear weapons. Instead of "neutralizing" a possible opponent's missiles by targeting them with nuclear or non-nuclear offensive weapons, active missile defenses might be used to counter them after launch. Such defenses also could be useful as a form of insurance against cheating on any future nuclear-capable ballistic missile reduction agreements. As already noted, though, to secure these benefits, more than just their deployment may be necessary.

Again, consider the Indian and Pakistani case. While Pakistan insists it must use its nuclear weapons first in any major war against India, New Delhi is hoping to use its conventional forces to capture enough of Pakistan from a "Cold Start" to get Islamabad to sue for peace quickly. India has also begun to develop missile defense systems of its own to counter both Pakistani and Chinese offensive missile threats.

Under these circumstances, sharing equal amounts of missile defenses with India and Pakistan would only give India yet another non-nuclear military edge against Islamabad. This, in turn, risks encouraging Pakistan to beef up its offensive nuclear missile forces even more. The only way to counter this and help secure the benefits of missile defense for both countries would be to address the underlying conventional asymmetry between them.

Missile Limits

One idea regional security experts have long favored is creating low-, medium-, and high-density conventional deployment zones on both sides of the Indo-Pakistani border to equalize each side's ability to launch "quick" conventional attacks against one another. A key element of these proposals is that both sides eliminate their existing short-range ballistic missiles (SRBM), since their use could mistakenly prompt nuclear reactions. If such military confidence-building measures were implemented, they might be effective enough to attenuate the perceived stability risks of deploying more advanced, discriminate, non-nuclear military systems.[16]

Elsewhere other measures might be desirable. As China increases its medium- and long-range nuclear-capable missile superiority over Taiwan and its capability to target US carrier battle groups with advanced, long-range, conventional missiles, the United States and its Pacific allies must worry that Beijing may be able to overwhelm the missile defenses they are now deploying.[17] China, meanwhile, is developing missile defenses of its own to counter possible US nuclear and precise conventional intercontinental missile attacks. Countering offensive Russian long-range missiles may also be a Chinese objective. All of these missile threats and defensive efforts suggest that diplomatic efforts might be focused usefully on reaching offensive, long-range missile limits to ensure that whatever missile defenses are deployed there will not immediately be overwhelmed.

In this regard, several precedents exist. The Strategic Arms Reduction Treaty (START), which limits US and Russian strategic missile delivery systems, is one. The Intermediate Range Nuclear Forces (INF) Treaty, which covers Russian and NATO missiles with ranges between 500 and 5,500 km, is another. The Missile Technology Control Regime (MTCR), which limits commerce in large missiles capable of lifting at least 500-kilogram (kg) payloads 300 kilometers (km) or farther in range, as well as goods and technology that might contribute to such systems, is another still.

The trick in reaching new, additional missile limits is to make sure they are aggressive enough to capture the missiles that matter most—those optimized for use in massive, coordinated first strikes[18]—so as to reduce the need or desire for nations to deploy more nuclear warheads without creating new categories of permissible missiles. It certainly would make little sense to eliminate ballistic missiles above the 500-km range, only to end up legitimizing slightly lower-range missile systems that are above the limits restricted by the MTCR.

Yet another related concern in limiting offensive, long-range missiles, while making room for the deployment of missile defense systems that employ large ballistic missile interceptors themselves, is to make sure the proliferation of missile defenses does not itself result in the further spread of large ballistic missiles or related technologies. Here, one might start by prohibiting the export of ballistic missile-based defensive systems that employ rockets in excess of the MTCR's category one missile limits (i.e., missiles capable of lifting 500 kg more than 300 km). Alternatively, agreements might be reached to encourage states to move away from the employment of missile defense systems that rely on large ballistic missile systems toward alternatives (e.g., small boost-phase missile interceptors borne on drones, directed energy systems, etc.). In either case, the aim would be the same—to ensure efforts to reduce the spread of offensive, nuclear-capable missiles that do not end up increasing such proliferation. This brings us to the second general principle.

Reducing existing nuclear weapons and nuclear-capable delivery systems should be related more closely to preventing their further spread. Currently, the connection between reducing nuclear arms and preventing their spread is mostly symbolic. As the United States and Russia reduce their nuclear deployments, other nuclear-armed states, it is argued, ought to follow; this, in turn, should persuade non-nuclear weapons states to submit to much-more-intrusive inspections of their civilian nuclear activities.[19] Putting aside the hard cases of Iran and North Korea, this line of reasoning ignores several key technical developments and turns on several questionable political assumptions.

First, after the International Atomic Energy Agency (IAEA) failed to detect the covert nuclear programs in Iraq, Iran, Syria, and North Korea, it is an open question if even "enhanced" international nuclear inspections will be able to detect illicit nuclear activities reliably. This is especially so if, as some believe, large civilian nuclear programs do spread to regions like the Middle East.

Second, not only the United States but Israel, Japan, NATO, India, Russia, and China are planning to deploy BMD systems—each for very different reasons. Yet, the United States and the allied approach to controlling nuclear strategic threats is practically silent as to whether these defense programs should be promoted or restricted and, if so, how. Nor, outside of strategic reduction talks with Russia, is there much discussion as to whether or how other states' development of large, long-range missiles (both nuclear and non-nuclear) should be approached.

Then, there are political questions. How likely is it that Russia will agree to further nuclear cuts beyond the current START negotiations? Will there be yet another START agreement to reduce strategic nuclear weapons deployments to 1,000 warheads on each side? Will Russia agree to limit its nonstrategic nuclear weapons? Which demands will Moscow make for such reductions? Will Russia demand the United States and NATO cripple their conventional and missile defense plans? Finally, when, if ever, might such agreements be reached? The success of America and the EU's arms control and nonproliferation policies depend on the answers to these questions being favorable to the United States.

Finally, and related to the political issues noted above, are the questions related to enforcement. If there are no new penalties or risks for developing nuclear weapons-related capabilities, how likely is it that states without nuclear-capable missiles or atomic weapons will keep clear of trying to acquire them? Certainly, the Greater Middle East is watching what, if anything, the United States and its allies might do to penalize Iran's nuclear misbehavior. Most states in the region are already hedging their nuclear bets by acquiring "peaceful" nuclear programs of their own. Similar dynamics are at play in the Far East in relation to North Korea's nuclear weapons program. Beyond these two cases, there is the general worry that the enforcement of nuclear nonproliferation limits lacks any teeth. What, if anything, will be done to prevent further nonproliferation violations?

These questions all suggest the need for promoting an additional set of more immediate incremental arms control and nonproliferation measures to complement the set of arms control treaties and understandings (which may or may not succeed) that the United States and the EU are currently pushing. In this regard, there are a number of possibilities.

Fissile Material Controls

To date, the United States has given only very basic guidance on how it intends to reduce the production of nuclear weapons-usable materials—i.e., highly enriched uranium and separated plutonium. President Obama has called for the negotiation of a FMCT. But most versions of this agreement explicitly allow "civilian" nuclear fuel production, which is virtually identical to military production. Also, after decades of fruitless talks in Geneva, it is unclear if any such agreement could ever be negotiated, much less brought into force.

Some officials, including those currently advising Secretary Hilary Clinton, have suggested a complementary approach to negotiating a FMCT, known as the Fissile Material Control Initiative (FMCI). Instead of a binding treaty, both Nonproliferation Treaty (NPT) weapons states and nonweapons states would simply identify which portion of their separated plutonium and highly enriched uranium stocks were in excess of either their military or civilian requirements and secure or dispose of them.[20] One could also make it more difficult for states to access whatever surpluses they declare by requiring the prior consent of all parties participating in the initiative for any state to regain access to these materials.[21]

Yet another practical idea, which would have direct bearing on India's nuclear weapons activities, would be to ensure that implementation of the US civilian nuclear cooperative agreement with New Delhi does nothing to help India make more nuclear weapons-usable fuels than India was producing when the deal was finalized late in 2008. Under the NPT, the states that had nuclear weapons in 1967—the United States, Russia, France, the UK, and China—swore not to help any other state outside of these five ever to acquire nuclear weapons directly or indirectly. That would include India, which tested its first nuclear explosive in 1974. Meanwhile, under the Hyde Act, which authorized the civilian US-India nuclear deal, the White House is required to report to Congress on just how much uranium fuel India is importing, how much it is using to run its civilian reactors, how much uranium it is producing domestically, and the extent to which the operation of its unsafeguarded reactors is expanding India's stockpiles of unsafeguarded plutonium with either the direct or indirect help of NPT weapons states.[22]

If India's unsafeguarded plutonium stockpiles grow faster per year than was the case prior to the nuclear cooperative agreement's finalization in 2008 and this growth could be shown to be related to Indian uranium imports from one or more of the NPT weapons states, the latter would be implicated in violating Article I of the NPT. To prevent such a violation or, at least, limit the harm it might do, the United States should be prepared to alert all other nuclear-supplying states and ask that they suspend civilian nuclear assistance until India's unsafeguarded nuclear weapons-usable material production declines. The logical place to make this request would be the Nuclear Suppliers Group (NSG). Such vigilance could also be matched with efforts to keep Pakistan from expanding its nuclear weapons capabilities as well.

Finally, the United States, China, Japan, and South Korea could reconsider the merits of expanding civilian recycling of plutonium-based fuels. As has already been noted, prior to the nuclear accidents at Fukushima, Japan was planning to open a commercial plutonium-reprocessing plant in Rokkasho. Projected to cost over $100 billion over its lifetime, the plant is designed to produce roughly 1,000 Nagasaki-sized bombs' worth of weapons-usable plutonium annually. Although it originally was supposed to produce plutonium-based fuels for a large-breeder reactor program, the Japanese breeder effort has fallen many years behind schedule. Japan has also decided not to expand its current fleet of light-water reactors, which might burn mixed oxide fuels containing recycled plutonium. As a result, the many tons of plutonium that will be produced at Rokkasho are only likely to add to the 2,000 bombs' worth Japan already has stored on the site. Technical difficulties have already delayed the plant's opening several times. The Japanese government is currently reviewing if it should proceed with its fast reactor and plutonium-recycling program as a part of its post-Fukushima energy review.

South Korea, meanwhile, sees Japan's plutonium-recycling effort as something of a model. Seoul, which the United States had previously caught trying to use its civilian nuclear program to make plutonium weapons, now wants to revise the civilian nuclear cooperative agreement it has with the United States to allow it to recycle plutonium. Where is China on all of this? Not far behind. In 2009, Beijing announced that it had contracted with the French firm, AREVA, to build a plutonium-reprocessing plant nearly identical to the one the French built for Japan at Rokkasho. Whether China will keep this program on schedule after its own post-Fukushima nuclear pause is unclear. Finally, despite congressional interest in domestic commercial reprocessing, the US Department of Energy's own blue ribbon panel on the future of nuclear power has decided that such a program is not needed at this time.[23]

Nuclear experts have repeatedly determined that none of these plutonium-recycling programs are as economical as simply burning fresh uranium fuel and storing the waste above ground. All of the programs run proliferation and physical security risks. That is why the bipartisan, congressionally mandated Commission on the Prevention of Weapons of Mass Destruction, Proliferation, and Terrorism called on Congress and the Executive Branch to maintain the moratorium Presidents Gerald Ford and Jimmy Carter imposed on US commercial reprocessing in 1976.[24] Discussing the merits of expanding such a moratorium with China, Japan, and South Korea might make sense. In exchange for Japan, the United States, and South Korea holding off, it might be possible to persuade China to do so as well. It may even be possible to get Chinese officials to announce publicly what they have intimated to US experts privately—that China has not made highly enriched uranium or plutonium for weapons for many years. If China were to agree to hold off, it would be helpful in continuing efforts to get India and Pakistan also to agree to halt their own nuclear weapons fissile material production efforts.

Repressing Nuclear Testing and NPT Violations

As already noted, getting the US Senate to ratify the CTBT will not be easy. More important, it may be many years at best before this agreement is ever brought into force. Certainly, focusing solely on finalizing this treaty is likely to come at a cost. North Korea might test a third nuclear weapon. In 2009, India's nuclear scientists seriously debated whether and when India might have to resume nuclear testing to perfect a thermonuclear device. Yet, if India tests, Pakistan would almost certainly follow suit.[25] It may not be possible to hem Pyongyang in, but India, Pakistan, China, France, the UK, and the United States have all gone on record previously announcing their policy not to test. Rather than wait for yet another nuclear explosion, it would be useful to get all of these states to recommit themselves now to the moratorium they previously said they supported. Certainly, if the United States cannot get these states to recommit, the prospects for ever bringing the CTBT into force would seem even more remote.

Enforcing the moratorium, of course, is a separate matter. Here, it would make sense to exploit the implicit legal ban against non-nuclear weapons states testing that is contained in the NPT. For nearly as many years as the NPT has been in force, civilian nuclear supplier states have tried through the NSG to bolster the NPT by imposing commonsense restrictions on civilian nuclear exports. Why not secure agreement there to block further civilian nuclear trade with any NPT nonweapons state that tests? Given Tehran's dependence on Russian civilian nuclear assistance, this would be immediately relevant in Iran's case.[26]

One could build on this by also seeking agreement to cut off supplies of nuclear-capable missile technology under the MTCR as well. Currently, violators of the NPT and IAEA safeguards and states that withdraw from the NPT while still in violation are not prohibited from receiving nuclear-capable missile technology and assistance from missile technology supplying states. Why not eliminate this loophole with the adoption of an automatic cutoff to goods controlled by the MTCR to these nuclear violators?

Finally, as missile defense capabilities grow and spread internationally, one could consider linking the treatment of serious NPT control violations not just with access to NSG and MTCR goods but with the freedom of states to test nuclear-capable missiles with flight paths that go outside their borders. Currently, countries that flaunt the nuclear rules, such as North Korea, are free to fire nuclear-capable missiles over Japan toward the United States. Under current international law, this is legal. Yet, such missiles are indistinguishable from those designed to carry nuclear warheads, and their development and testing are inherently destabilizing. If a finding is made at the IAEA or the United Nations Security Council (UNSC) that a state is in violation of its NPT obligations, one might ask if there should be an international norm against such flights, just as there is with other illicit outlaw activities, such as piracy, drug running, and slave trading. If so, one could give states with the technical power authority to shoot such objects out of international air space (e.g., the United States, Russia, Israel, and soon Japan, NATO, and China) as "outlaw" objects. Similarly, if progress is made on creating additional limits on missile deployments (e.g., global INF, etc.), violators of these understandings could also be banned from receiving controlled missile and nuclear goods and be subject to similar missile testing restrictions until they were determined by the appropriate authorities to have come back into full compliance.

The presumption here, of course, is that organizations such as the IAEA are fully able to make such determinations. In fact, they are not, which brings us to the third principle that the United States and other states need to focus on.

International nuclear inspectors should be encouraged to distinguish between nuclear activities and materials that they can reliably safeguard against being diverted to make bombs and those that they cannot. The NPT is clear that all peaceful nuclear activities and materials must be safeguarded—that is, inspected in a manner that can reliably prevent them from being diverted to make nuclear weapons. Most NPT states have fallen into the habit of thinking that if they merely declare their nuclear holdings and allow international inspections, they have met this requirement.

This is dangerously mistaken. After the nuclear inspections gaffes in Iraq, Iran, Syria, and North Korea, we now know that the IAEA cannot necessarily detect covert nuclear activities early enough to allow others to intervene to prevent possible bomb making. We also now know that inspectors annually lose track of many bombs' worth of nuclear weapons-usable plutonium and uranium at declared nuclear fuel-making plants. Privately, IAEA officials admit that the agency cannot ensure continuity of inspections for spent and fresh fuel rods at more than half of the sites that the agency inspects. Finally, we know that declared plutonium and enriched uranium can be diverted from their related production plants and made into bombs so quickly (in some cases, within hours or days) that no inspection system can offer timely warning of a country's bomb-making efforts. Yet, any true safeguard against military nuclear diversions must reliably detect them early enough to allow outside powers to intervene to block a bomb from being built. Anything less is only monitoring that might, at best, detect military diversions after they occur.

In light of these points, it would be useful for the IAEA to concede that it cannot safeguard all that it inspects against possible military diversions. This would finally raise first-order questions about the advisability of producing or stockpiling plutonium, highly enriched uranium, and plutonium-based reactor fuels, and believing that these materials and activities can be safeguarded. At the very least, this concession would suggest that nonweapons states ought not to acquire these materials or facilities beyond what they already have.

In this regard, the United States and other like-minded nations might independently assess whether or not the IAEA can meet its own inspection goals; under what circumstances (if any) these goals can be met; and, finally, whether these goals are set high enough. The US House of Representatives approved legislation in 2009 to require the IAEA to make such assessments routinely and to report its findings. Similar legislation has been proposed in the Senate.[27]

Compare Costs

Finally, to ensure safe, economically competitive forms of clean energy, greater attention should be paid to comparing costs and discouraging the use of government financial incentives for energy commercialization projects, especially nuclear power. Supporters of nuclear power insist that its expansion is critical to prevent global warming. Yet, they generally downplay or ignore the nuclear weapons-proliferation risks associated with the further spread of this technology. That said, it may be impossible to prevent the spread of nuclear power if it turns out to be the cheapest, quickest way to provide low- or no-carbon energy. Given the security premium associated with the further spread of nuclear power technologies, though, no government should pay extra to promote it.

Certainly, creating new, additional government financial incentives specifically geared to build more commercial nuclear plants and their associated fuel-making facilities will only increase the difficulty of comparing these nuclear alternatives accurately with non-nuclear alternatives. Not only do such subsidies mask nuclear power's true costs; they tilt the market against less subsidized, potentially sounder alternatives.[28] This is troubling, since nuclear power continues to enjoy massive government support, and the most dangerous forms of civilian nuclear energy—nuclear fuel-making in most nonweapons states and large-power reactor projects in war-torn regions like the Middle East—are poor investments as compared with much safer alternatives.[29]

There are several ways to avoid this trend. The first would be to get as many governments as possible to open all large civilian energy projects in their countries up to international competitive bidding. This is already done in a number of countries. The problem is that when states want to build large civilian nuclear reactors, they limit the competition to nuclear bids only, rather than open the competition up to any energy option that can meet a given set of environmental and economic criteria.

This practice flies in the face of the Energy Charter Treaty, which has been ratified by the EU and is supported by Washington. This agreement calls on states to encourage open international bidding on any large energy project or transaction. Meanwhile, the Global Energy Charter for Sustainable Development, which the United States and many other states also support, calls on states to internalize many of the external costs (e.g., those associated with government subsidies and quantifiable environmental costs, such as the probable prices of carbon) in determining the costs of large energy projects.

Although these agreements have not yet played a significant role in reducing carbon emissions, they could. Certainly, the surest way to ensure that carbon reductions are accomplished in the quickest, cheapest fashion is to: a) include all the relevant government subsidies in the price of competing energy options; b) assign a range of probable prices to carbon for each option; c) use these figures to determine what the lowest cost energy source or technology might be in relation to a specific timeline; and, d) compete each option on the basis of both price and time.

Enforcing total adherence to these principles will be challenging. One can, however, do better or worse, and the downsides of not trying far exceed the risks of even partial failure. A good place to improve on a largely blank slate would be for Washington to suggest a modest carbon-abatement data-collection action plan for the Group of Twenty Finance Ministers and Central Bank Governors (G-20) that would include establishing common energy project cost accounting and international bidding rules. Beyond this, it would be useful to call on the G-20 to give the IAEA notice of any state decisions they believe might violate these principles by favoring nuclear power over cheaper alternatives. The aim here would be to encourage the IAEA to ascertain the true purpose of such nuclear projects.[30]

As a complementary effort, the world's advanced states could also work with developing countries to create non-nuclear alternatives to address their energy and environmental needs. In the case of the United States, this would entail implementing existing law. Title V of the Nuclear Nonproliferation Act of 1978 requires the Executive Branch to do analyses of key countries' energy needs and identify how these needs might be addressed with non-fossil, non-nuclear energy sources. Title V also calls on the Executive Branch to create an alternative energy cadre to help developing nations explore these alternative options. To date, no US President has chosen to implement this law. The US Congress has indicated that it would like to change this by requiring Title V country energy analyses (and outside, nongovernmental assessments of these analyses) to be done as a precondition for the US initialing of any new, additional US nuclear cooperative agreements.[31] The United Nations (UN), meanwhile, has an alternative, renewable (non-nuclear) energy initiative of its own—the International Renewable Energy Agency (IRENA) aimed at assisting developing states. As with most of the other suggestions already made, the United States and other states can emphasize these initiatives without waiting for any international treaty agreement.

What Is Possible

For those who have already settled in with our government's current catalogue of treaty-based fixes, the list of incremental control recommendations in this chapter might seem too far off the beaten path to be viewed as anything but too ambitious. This, however, gets things backwards. Our government's current arms control and nonproliferation agenda is more than slightly ambitious itself: After the New START follow-on agreement that has just been reached, there is little chance any of the other treaties President Obama highlighted in his April 5, 2009, Prague, Czech Republic, speech—additional nuclear reduction treaties with Russia or other states, the CTBT or the FMCT—can be brought into force before the end of Obama's first term or even before the 2016 presidential elections.

In sharp contrast, several of this chapter's suggestions involve implementing nothing more than existing law (e.g., the Hyde Act on India, the Nuclear Nonproliferation Act of 1978 on alternative energy cooperation, conducting energy assessments, and making sure US nuclear cooperation is safeguarded in a manner that affords timely warning of possible military diversions). Nor do any of these suggestions require negotiating or ratifying formal bilateral or international treaties. Most of the suggestions regarding sanctions involve modifying current NSG and MTCR guidelines, something that is done on a routine basis. The assessments of what the IAEA can and cannot safeguard, and how sound its own standards are to accomplish this, can be done with or without other states' cooperation.

Most of the other suggestions also can be implemented without waiting on international consensus or the consent of other countries. Yet, none of the ideas offered are at odds with our government's arms control objectives and ought, like the Fissile Material Control Initiative and recommittment to existing nuclear test moratoria, to make it easier to negotiate formal international treaties and bring them into force. Finally, more than a few of the suggestions—such as promoting a moratorium on the further expansion of commercial recycling of plutonium in the United States and Asia and encouraging the G-20 to compete large energy projects and adopt sound energy accounting rules—could save many billions in unnecessary spending.

Still, seasoned political experts in Washington would rightly be wary of either Democrats or Republicans seizing on these ideas. Certainly, until the presidential elections in November 2012, few, if any, in the majority party would have the time or the inclination to suggest that the head of their party do something different than what is already on the foreign affairs agenda. Meanwhile, Republicans running for office are unlikely to be drawn to anything other than criticizing the Obama administration. This hardly leaves much room even for incremental innovation.

November 2012, however, is not that far off. Certainly, by then, the glory of negotiating the START follow-on agreement will largely have worn off, and the prospect of not bringing any new treaty agreements into force for many years will begin to set in. In this environment, Democratic supporters of the President may actually look for new, additional ways to demonstrate their support of the President's nuclear control goals of reducing the amount of nuclear weapons and nuclear weapons-usable materials, ending nuclear weapons testing, preventing the spread of nuclear weapons-related capabilities, and lowering the risks of nuclear use and theft.

Republicans, on the other hand, are likely to be focused like a laser beam on the prospects of defeating President Obama in 2012. Assuming that President Obama does not defeat himself, though, this will place a premium on the Republican Party to explain not just what it is against, but what it is for. In the case of nuclear controls, Republicans may find fault with the formal treaties President Obama is trying to negotiate and bring into force. Yet, they will be hard pressed to take major exception to President Obama's general goals of reducing the chances of nuclear use or theft, blocking the further spread of nuclear weapons-related capabilities, keeping other states from testing nuclear weapons, reducing the production and amounts of weapons-usable materials, and securing verifiable nuclear weapons reductions—not just with Russia but with the world's other weapons states. The question will be not whether Republicans support these goals, but rather in what different ways they might try to achieve them. For very different reasons, then, Democrats and Republicans will both have an interest in developing an additional list of nuclear control measures to those currently in play. One could do much worse than starting to consider those listed here.

Endnotes

1. See "Pakistani Nuke Arsenal on Track to be World's Fifth Largest," *Global Security Newswire*, February 2, 2011, available from *gsn.nti.org/gsn/nw_20110201_5282.php*; Anthony H. Cordesman, "Study on a Possible Israeli Strike on Iran's Nuclear Development Facilities," Washington, DC: Center for Strategic and International Studies,

March 14, 2009, available from *csis.org/files/media/csis/pubs/090316_israelistrikeiran.pdf*; "Key Facts: Israel, Nuclear," *Jane's CBRN Assessments,* December 1, 2009; and Thomas Graham, "Nuclear Weapons Stability or Anarchy in the 21st Century: China, India, and Pakistan," Arlington, VA: The Nonproliferation Policy Education Center, Unpublished Analysis, June 9, 2011, available from, *www.npolicy.org/article.php?aid=621&rt=&key=thomas%20graham&sec=article*.

2. See International Panel on Fissile Materials, *Global Fissile Materials Report 2010*, available from *www.fissilematerials.org/ipfm/site_down/gfmr10.pdf*; Andrei Chang, "China's Nuclear Warhead Stockpile Rising," *UPIAsia.com,* April 5, 2008, available from *www.upiasia.com/Security/2008/04/05/chinas_nuclear_warhead_stockpile_rising/7074*; and "长城工程 (Great Works)," Baidu (China), January 13, 2011, available from *baike.baidu.com/view/981670.htm*, Google Chrome, trans.

3. A crude bomb's worth of plutonium (enough to make a bomb with a Hiroshima-sized yield) is conservatively defined by the Department of Energy as 4 kilograms (kg) of plutonium. Japan currently is storing 8.7 metric tons (i.e., 8,700 kg) of weapons-usable separated plutonium on its soil (see Endnote 2). For a more detailed analysis of how much material is required to produce Hiroshima-like yields, see Thomas B. Cochran, "The Amount of Plutonium and Highly Enriched Uranium Needed for Pure Fission Weapons," Washington, DC: The Natural Resource Defense Council, April 13, 1995, available from *www.nrdc.org/nuclear/fissionw/fissionweapons.pdf*.

4. See "Spent Fuel Causing Headaches for Nuclear Plants,"June 29, 2011, available from *www.asahi.com/English/TKY201106280424.html*, and Chester Dawson, "In Japan, Provocative Case for Staying Nuclear," *The Wall Street Journal*, October 28, 2011, available from *online.wsj.com/article/SB10001424052970203658804576638392537430156.html?KEYWORDS=nuclear+reprocessing*.

5. See *Global Fissile Materials Report 2010*.

6. World Nuclear Association, "Emerging Nuclear Energy Countries," November 2011, available from *www.world-nuclear.org/info/inf102.html*.

7. See Josh Rogin, "Exclusive: House Republicans Ding Obama on Nuke Treaty in Previously Unreported Letter," September 16, 2009, available from *thecable.foreignpolicy.com/posts/2009/09/16/exclusive_house_republicans_ding_obama_on_nuke_treaty_in_previously_unreported_lettter*.

8. On these points, see Jonathan Medalia, "Comprehensive Nuclear-test-ban Treaty: Issues and Arguments," *CRS Report for Congress,* RL

34494, Washington, DC: Congressional Research Service, March 12, 2008, pp. 20 ff., available from *www.fas.org/sgp/crs/nuke/RL34394.pdf*; and US Congressional Commission on the Strategic Posture of the United States, *America's Strategic Posture,* Washington, DC: United States Institute of Peace Press, 2009, p. 83, available from *media.usip.org/reports/strat_posture_report.pdf*.

9. On the inherent difficulty of effectively safeguarding declared nuclear fuel plants against incremental or abrupt military diversions, see Marvin M. Miller, "Are IAEA Safeguards on Plutonium Bulk-Handling Facilities Effective?" *Nuclear Control Institute*, 1990, reprinted in Paul Leventhal, *et al.*, eds., *Nuclear Power and the Spread of Nuclear Weapons,* Washington, DC: Brassey's, 2002; Brian G. Chow and Kenneth A. Solomon, *Limiting the Spread of Weapon-Usable Fissile Materials,* MR-346-USDP, Santa Monica, CA: The Rand Corporation, 1993, pp. 1-15; Andrew Leask, Russell Leslie, and John Carlson, "Safeguards as a Design Criteria: Guidance for Regulators," Canberra, Australia: Australian Safeguards and Non-proliferation Office, September 2004; and Edwin S. Lyman, "Can Nuclear Fuel Production in Iran and Elsewhere Be Safeguarded against Diversion?" in Henry Sokolski, ed., *Falling Behind: International Scrutiny of the Peaceful Atom,* Carlisle, PA: The Strategic Studies Institute, US Army War College, 2008, pp. 101-20.

10. On these points, see Henry S. Rowen, "This 'Nuclear-Free' Plan Would Effect the Opposite," *The Wall Street Journal*, January 17, 2008, available from *www.npolicy.org/article.php?aid=165&rt=&key=This%2%E2%80%98Nuclear-Free%E2%80%99%20Plan%20Would%20Effect%20the%20Opposite&sec=article&author=*; David Kay, "Denial and Deception Practices of WMD Proliferators: Iraq and Beyond," in Brad Roberts, ed., *Weapons Proliferation in the 1990s*, Cambridge, MA: Harvard, MIT Press, 1995; Victor Gilinsky *et al.,* "A Fresh Examination of the Proliferation Dangers of Light Water Reactors," Washington, DC: Nonproliferation Policy Education Center (NPEC), 2004, available from *www.npolicy.org/article.php?aid=172&rt=&key=A%20Fresh%20Examination%20of%20the%20Proliferation%20Dangers%20of%20Light%20Water%20Reactors&sec=article&author=*; and Andrew Leask, Russell Leslie, and John Carlson, "Safeguards As a Design Criteria—Guidance for Regulators," Barton, Australia: Australian Safeguards and Non-proliferation Office, September 2004, available from *www.asno.dfat.gov.au/publications/safeguards_design_criteria.pdf*.

11. See Elaine M. Grossman, "US Blueprint for New Nuclear Arms Cuts Expected by Year's End," *Global Security Newswire,* November 8, 2011, available from *www.nti.org/gsn/article/us-blueprint-for-new-nuclear-arms-cuts-expected-by-years-end/*.

12. Within the oldest and most significant nuclear states, government-run, dual-use reactors were long connected to electrical grids to produce nuclear weapons fuels and electricity. In the United States, these include the Hanford dual-purpose reactor in Washington State (which is no longer operating), and the Tennessee Valley Authority's tritium-producing light-water reactors (whose operations are about to be expanded). Also included are Russia's RBMK (Reaktor Bolshoy Moshchnosti Kanalniy) reactors, which made plutonium for Russia's arsenal until the 1990s; France's gas-cooled natural uranium and breeder reactors, which did the same for France through the 1980s; India's unsafeguarded heavy water reactors and planned breeder reactors, which currently provide tritium and plutonium for India's nuclear weapons program; and Britain's early Magnox power plants, which provided the bulk of the plutonium for the United Kingdom's nuclear arsenal. See *50 Years of Public Power,* Richland, WA: Energy Northwest, 2007, available from *www.energy-northwest.com/downloads/EN_Annual_Report_2007_small.pdf; Global Secuirty.org*, "RBMK Reactor," available from *www.globalsecurity.org/wmd/world/russia/rbmk.htm*; "The French Nuclear Reactor Fuel Reprocessing Program: An Intelligence Assessment," Washington, DC: US Central Intelligence Agency, September 1984, approved for release July 1992, available from *www.gwu.edu/~nsarchiv/NSAEBB/NSAEBB184/FR30.pdf*; Paul Brown, "First Nuclear Power Plant to Close," *The Guardian*, March 21, 2010; "British Nuclear Facilities," The Nuclear Weapon Archive, available from *nuclearweaponarchive.org/Uk/UKFacility.html*; Zia Mian, A. H. Nayyar, R. Rajaraman, and M.V. Ramana, "Fissile Materials in South Asia and the Implications of the US-India Nuclear Deal," International Panel on Fissile Materials Research Report, September 2006, available from *www.fissilematerials.org/ipfm/site_down/ipfmresearchreport01.pdf*; Christine Kucia, "Tritium Production Licenses Granted to Civilian Power Plants," *Arms Control Today,* November 2002; and Daniel Horner, "Obama Budget Seeks Rise in Tritium Capacity," *Arms Control Today*, June 2009.

13. See Endnotes 9 and 10; and Henry Sokolski, "Assessing the IAEA's Ability to Verify the NPT," in Sokolski, ed., *Falling Behind*, pp. 3-62.

14. See Victor Gilinsky, "Nuclear Power and Weapons: A New Look at an Old Problem," presentation made at a Non-proliferation Policy Education Center Workshop, "Reassessing Nuclear Proliferation's Key Premises," London, UK, November 3-4, 2011, available from *npolicy.org/article.php?aid=1114&tid=30*.

15. The threat of India implementing a Cold Start is mostly theory. For a practical critique of this strategy, see Muhammad Azam Khan, "Understanding India's 'Cold Start' Doctrine," *The Express Tribune*, October 19, 2011, available from *tribune.com.pk/story/276661/understanding-indias-cold-start-doctrine*.

16. On these points, see Peter Lavoy, "Islamabad's Nuclear Posture: Its Premises and Implementation," in Henry Sokolski, ed., *Pakistan's Nuclear Future: Worries beyond War,* Carlisle, PA: Strategic Studies Institute, US Army War College, 2008, pp. 129-166; and General Feroz Khan, "Reducing the Risk of Nuclear War in South Asia," September 15, 2008, available from *npolicy.org/article.php?aid=112&rt=&key=Reducing%20the%20Risk%20of%20Nuclear%20War%20in%20South%20Asia&sec=article*.

17. See Mark Stokes, "China's Evolving Conventional Strategic Strike Capability: The Anti-ship Ballistic Missile Challenge to US Maritime Operations in the Western Pacific and Beyond," Project 2049, September 14, 2009, available from *www.project2049.net/documents/chinese_anti_ship_ballistic_missile_asbm.pdf*.

18. First-strike missile systems that can be launched in large numbers with the greatest level of positive command and control, coordinated precision, and speed are generally viewed as being the most "destabilizing" by arms control experts and strategic planners. These systems, which Reagan loosely referred to as "nuclear missiles," most clearly include ground-launched ballistic missile systems with single or multiple warheads. Air- and sea-launched systems, in comparison, are lacking in each of these attributes.

19. See, e.g., Gareth Evans and Yoriko Kawaguchi, *Eliminating Nuclear Threats: A Practical Agenda for Global Policymakers*, Canberra, Australia: International Commission on Nuclear Non-proliferation and Disarmament, 2010, pp. 3-36.

20. See, e.g., Robert Einhorn, "Controlling Fissile Materials and Ending Nuclear Testing," presentation before the International Conference on Nuclear Disarmament, Oslo, Norway, February 26–27, 2008, available from *www.ctbto.org/fileadmin/user_upload/pdf/External_Reports/paper-einhorn.pdf*.

21. See Albert Wohlstetter, "Nuclear Triggers and Safety Catches," in Robert Zarate and Henry Sokolski, eds., *Nuclear Heuristics: Selected Writings of Albert and Roberta Wohlstetter,* Carlisle, PA: Strategic Studies Institute, US Army War College, 2009, pp. 374-377.

22. See the Henry J. Hyde United States-India Peaceful Atomic Energy Cooperation Act of 2006, "Implementation and Compliance Report," available from *www.bis.doc.gov/ap/documents/report_109-721.pdf*.

23. On these points, see "Rokkasho Reprocessing Plant Delayed Again," *World Nuclear News*, September 8, 2009, available from *www.resourceinvestor.com/News/2009/9/Pages/Rokkasho-reprocessing-plant-delayed-again.aspx*; Massafumi Takuba, "Wake Up. Stop

Dreaming: Reassessing Japan's Reprocessing Program," *The Nonproliferation Review*, March 2008; The World Nuclear Association, "Nuclear Power in China," October 2008, available from *www.world-nuclear.org/info/inf63.html*; Frank von Hippel, "South Korean Reprocessing: An Unnecessary Threat to the Nonproliferation Regime," *Arms Control Today*, March 2010, available from *www.armscontrol.org/act/2010_03/VonHippel*; and Rebecca Smith, "Panel to Weigh Nuclear Waste Options," *The Wall Street Journal*, March 26, 2010, available from *online.wsj.com/article/SB10001424052748703409804575144033667206698.html*.

24. See the Commission on the Prevention of Weapons of Mass Destruction Proliferation and Terrorism, *The World at Risk*, New York: Vintage Books, Random House, 2008, p. 51.

25. On these points, see Heejin Koo, "North Korea May Test Third Nuclear Bomb, Defector Agency Says," *Bloomberg News Service*, September 9, 2009, available from *www.bloomberg.com/apps/news?pid=newsarchive&sid=a.R3wxVSAX78;* and Daniel Horner, "Indian Scientist Triggers Debate on Testing," *Arms Control Today*, October 2009, available from *www.armscontrol.org/act/2009_10/India*.

26. Although the NPT does not legally prohibit nuclear weapons states from further testing, if there was sufficient support, an additional agreement might also be sought to expand such trade restrictions to nuclear weapons states as well.

27. See Section 416 of the House State Authorization Act of 2010 and 2011, "Implementation of Recommendations of the Commission on the Prevention of WMD Proliferation and Terrorism," available from *www.govtrack.us/congress/billtext.xpd?bill=h111-2410*.

28. On these points, see Doug Koplow, "Nuclear Power as Taxpayer Patronage: A Case Study of Subsidies to Calvert Cliffs Unit 3," available from *www.npolicy.org/article.php?aid=179&rt=&key=Nuclear%20Power%20as%20Taxpayer%20Patronage:%20A%20Case%20Study%20of%20Subsidies%20to%20Calvert%20Cliffs%20Unit%203&sec=article&author=*.

29. Some Middle Eastern states, such as Algeria, Libya, and states bordering the Persian Gulf, have significant proven reserves of relatively clean-burning natural gas, which can be used to produce power and industrial heat for a fraction of the costs of any nuclear system. New methods of drilling for gas are opening up new finds in the region (e.g., off Israel's coast). In addition, the few states in the region that lack their own natural gas resources are themselves still major pipeline transit points, and so have ready access to this resource at very low prices. In fact, the key

challenge to maintaining these cheaper energy supplies is ensuring that the natural gas is being given away through excessive state subsidies. Meanwhile, the growing availability of natural gas in the United States, Europe, and Asia has already reduced demand for liquefied natural gas and could conceivably reduce demand for this fuel from the Middle East. On these points, and on how uneconomical nuclear fuel-making can be for small numbers of nuclear power plants, see "An Unconventional Glut," *The Economist,* pp. 72-74, available from *www.economist.com/business-finance/displaystory.cfm?story_id=15661889*; Peter Tynan and John Stephenson, "Nuclear Power in Saudi Arabia, Egypt, and Turkey—How Cost Effective?" February 9, 2009, available from *www.npolicy.org/article.php?aid=352&rt=&key=Nuclear%20Power%20in%20Saudi%20Arabia,%20Egypt,%20and%20Turkey%20%E2%80%93%20how%20cost%20effective?&sec=article&author=;* and Frank von Hippel, "Why Reprocessing Persists in Some Countries and Not in Others: The Costs and Benefits of Reprocessing," April 9, 2009, available from *npolicy.org/article_file/Why_Reprocessing_Persists_in_Some_Countries_and_Not_in_Others-The_Costs_and_Benefits_of_Reprocessing.pdf.*

30. For more on these points, see Henry Sokolski, "Market Fortified Nonproliferation," in *Breaking the Nuclear Impasse*, New York: The Century Foundation, 2007, pp. 81-143. Current membership and investment and trade principles of the Energy Charter Treaty and the Global Energy Charter for Sustainable Development is available from *www.encharter.org* and *www.cmdc.net/echarter.html.*

31. See Letter from Congressmen Brad Sherman, Edward Markey, and Ileana Ros-Lehtinen to Secretary of State Hillary Clinton, April 6, 2009, available from *bradsherman.house.gov/pdf/Nuclear Cooperation PresObama040609.pdf.*

About the Contributors

DAN BLUMENTHAL is current commissioner and former vice chairman of the US-China Economic and Security Review Commission, and Resident Fellow at the American Enterprise Institute (AEI). Previously, he was Senior Country Director for China, Taiwan, and Mongolia in the Secretary of Defense's Office of International Security Affairs and practiced law in New York prior to his government service. He regularly contributes to AEI's Asian Outlook series and is published in numerous scholarly journals and periodicals, including Foreign Policy and The Wall Street Journal. Mr. Blumenthal holds a J.D. from Duke Law School and an M.A. from the School of Advanced International Studies (SAIS) at John Hopkins University.

IAN EASTON is an Asia analyst in the China Security Affairs Group at the Center for Naval Analyses (CNA). Prior to joining CNA, he was a Research Affiliate at the Project 2049 Institute. Before joining Project 2049, he provided research and analysis for the Asia Bureau of Defense News, as well as translation services for the Foundation on Asia Pacific Peace Studies (APS). He has written widely on the strategic effects of Chinese nuclear weapons and missile development, including "The Assassin under the Radar: China's DH-10 Cruise Missile Program." Mr. Easton received his formal Mandarin Chinese training at the National Taiwan University's Mandarin Training Center in Taipei, and at Fudan

University in Shanghai, China. He holds a master's degree in China Studies from National Chengchi University in Taipei.

RN GANESH is a Vice Admiral (Ret.) and currently serves as an adjunct faculty member in the International Strategic and Security Studies Programme at the National Institute of Advanced Studies (NIAS) in Bangalore. He is a veteran submariner with operational experience that includes command of both conventional and nuclear submarines and an aircraft carrier, in addition to service as a Flag Officer in Command of the Western Fleet as well as the Southern Naval Command. His last appointment was as the Director General of the Indian nuclear submarine program, which he continued to head after retiring from active service until 2004. Vice Admiral Ganesh is the author of numerous articles on maritime security and strategic affairs.

VICTOR GILINSKY is an independent energy consultant who works primarily on matters related to nuclear energy. He was a two-term Commissioner of the US Nuclear Regulatory Commission from 1975-84 under Presidents Ford, Carter and Reagan. Prior to his appointment as commissioner, he served as Assistant Director for Policy and Program Review in the Atomic Energy Commission as head of the RAND Physical Sciences Department. Dr. Gilinsky holds a Ph.D. in physics from the California Institute of Technology (Caltech).

THOMAS W. GRAHAM is an Analyst in the Nonproliferation and National Security Department at Brookhaven National Laboratory. Previously, Dr. Graham worked at General Lee Butler's Second Chance Foundation, oversaw the International Security Program at the Rockefeller Foundation, served as a Foreign Affairs Officer at the Arms Control and Disarmament Agency, and was a consultant to the Lawrence Livermore National Laboratory. He has been a scholar at Stanford, Harvard, and the Massachusetts Institute of Technology (MIT). Dr. Graham received his Ph.D. from MIT.

FEROZ HASSAN KHAN is a former Brigadier General in Pakistani Army and is currently a Lecturer in the Department of National Security Affairs and researcher in the Center for Contemporary Conflict at the US Naval Postgraduate School in Monterey, CA. He has held a series of visiting fellowships at Stanford University; the Brookings Institution; and Sandia National Laboratory. General Khan is the author of numerous publications on nuclear arms control and nonproliferation issues in Pakistan, including "Prospects for an Indian and Pakistani Arms Control and Confidence Building Measure in South Asia," in Naval War College Review, Summer 2010, Vol.63, No. 3. General Khan holds an M.A. from the School of Advanced International Studies (SAIS) at John Hopkins University,

JACOB W. KIPP is an Adjunct Professor at the University of Kansas and a weekly columnist on Eurasian Security for the Jamestown Foundation. He has held positions as a senior analyst in the Soviet Army Studies Office (SASO) at Ft. Leavenworth, Kansas; Director of the Foreign Military Studies Office (FMSO, the successor organization to the SASO); and Deputy Director of the School of Advanced Military Studies (SAMS). Dr. Kipp has published extensively on Soviet and Russian naval and military history. His most recent publications include "Russian Military Doctrine:

Past, Present, and Future," in Stephen J. Blank, Russian Military Politics and Russia's 2010 Defense Doctrine. Dr. Kipp has a Ph.D. in Russian history from Pennsylvania State University.

JEFF KUETER is President of the George C. Marshall Institute in Washington, DC. Previously, he served as Research Director of the National Coalition for Advanced Manufacturing at Washington Nichibei Consultants. Mr. Kueter's work is focused on national security and the environment, and his articles have appeared in the Boston Globe, The New York Times, and other major publications. He is the author of "Do We Need a Code of Conduct for Space?" and "Iranian Missiles and US Defenses," and is the coauthor of "Returning to Fundamentals: Deterrence and National Security in the 21st Century." Mr. Kueter has an M.A. in Political Science and an M.A. in security policy studies with an emphasis on science and technology studies both from George Washington University.

STEPHEN J. LUKASIK is a former Director of the Advanced Research Projects Agency in the US Department of Defense. He taught physics and engineering at Stevens Institute of Technology, and technology policy at the RAND Graduate Institute, and in the Technology Management program at the Pepperdine University Graduate School of Business and Management. Dr. Lukasik was a Visiting Scholar at the Stanford University Center for International Security and Cooperation and is currently Distinguished Senior Research Fellow in the Center for International Security, Technology and Policy, Georgia Institute of Technology. Dr. Lukasik has a Ph.D. in physics from the Massachusetts Institute of Technology and is a founder of The Information Society journal.

MICHAEL MAZZA is a research fellow at the American Enterprise Institute (AEI) and the program manager for AEI's annual Executive

Program on National Security Policy and Strategy. His focus is on defense policy in the Asia-Pacific, as well as Chinese military modernization, cross-Strait relations, and security on the Korean peninsula. Mr. Mazza also writes regularly for AEI's Center for Defense Studies blog. Previously, he served as a research assistant in AEI's Foreign and Defense Policy Studies department. His work has appeared in several publications, including The Diplomat and The Wall Street Journal. Mr. Mazza received an M.A. in international relations from the School of Advanced International Studies (SAIS) at Johns Hopkins University.

RICHARD L. RUSSELL is a Professor at the National Defense University's Near East South Asia Center for Strategic Studies. He is also an Adjunct in the Security Studies Program and a Research Associate in the Institute for the Study of Diplomacy, both of which are in the Edmund A. Walsh School of Foreign Service, Georgetown University. Dr. Russell served for 17 years as a political-military analyst at the Central Intelligence Agency, where he analyzed security issues relating to the Middle East and Europe. He is the author of numerous works, including Sharpening Strategic Intelligence: Why the CIA Gets It Wrong and What Needs to be Done to Get It Right (Cambridge University Press, 2007). Dr. Russell holds a Ph.D. from the University of Virginia.

HENRY D SOKOLSKI is the Executive Director of the Nonproliferation Policy Education Center (NPEC) in Arlington, VA, and an adjunct professor at the Institute of World Politics in Washington, DC. He previously served as a military legislative aide and Special Assistant for Nuclear Energy Affairs in the US Senate, as Deputy for Nonproliferation Policy in the Cheney Pentagon, and as a member of the CIA's Senior Advisory Group. Mr. Sokolski also was appointed by Congress to serve on the Deutch WMD Commission and the Commission on the Prevention of WMD Proliferation and Terrorism. He has authored and edited numerous books on proliferation, including Nuclear Power's Global Expansion: Weighing Its Costs and Risks (Strategic Studies Institute, 2010).

MARK STOKES is the Executive Director of the Project 2049 Institute. Previously, he was the founder and president of Quantum Pacific Enterprises, and vice president and Taiwan country manager for Raytheon International. He has served as executive vice president of Laifu Trading Company; a senior associate at the Center for Strategic and International Studies (CSIS); and member of the Board of Governors of the American Chamber of Commerce in Taiwan. Mr. Stokes was also team chief and senior country director for the People's Republic of China, Taiwan, and Mongolia in the Office of the Assistant Secretary of

Defense for International Security Affairs. He is a 20-year US Air Force veteran. Mr. Stokes holds graduate degrees in international relations and Asian studies from Boston University and the Naval Postgraduate School.

BRUNO TERTRAIS has been a Senior Research Fellow at the Fondation pour la Recherche Stratégique (FRS) since 2001. His past positions include Research Assistant, NATO Assembly (1989-90); Director, Civilian Affairs Committee, NATO Assembly (1990-92); Europe Desk Officer, Ministry of Defense (1993-94); Visiting Fellow, the Rand Corporation (1995-96); Head of Defense Policy Planning Unit, Ministry of Defense (1996-97); Special Assistant to the Director of Strategic Affairs, Ministry of Defense (1997-2001). He is also a member of the editorial board of The Washington Quarterly and Survival. Dr. Tertrais holds a Master's degree in Public Law and a Ph.D. in political science from the Institut d'études politiques de Paris.

FRANK VON HIPPEL is a Professor of Public and International Affairs at Princeton University and co-chair of the International Panel on Fissile Material. He is a former Assistant Director for National Security in the White House Office of Science and Technology. Dr. von Hippel has served on advisory panels to the Congressional Office of Technology Assessment, US Department of Energy, National Science Foundation, and US Nuclear Regulatory Commission, and has held research positions at the University of Chicago, Cornell University, and Argonne National Laboratory. He has written extensively on the technical aspects of nuclear energy and nonproliferation. Dr. von Hippel holds a Ph.D. in theoretical physics from Oxford University.

Index